W9-AUC-112

Nuclear Inertia

To Tinne, Kathy, Bram and their generation

When it comes to nuclear weapons, the world has changed faster than US policy...almost a decade after the end of the Cold War, our nuclear policy resides in that already distant part. The Clinton-Gore administration has had over seven years to bring the US force posture into the post-Cold War world. Instead, they remain locked in a Cold War mentality

Presidential candidate George W.Bush in 2000.

Unfortunately, the Department of Energy continues to ask Congress to fund a Cold War arsenal, and the nuclear weapons complex necessary to maintain that arsenal, even though we no longer face a Cold War adversary...The Cold War ended over a decade ago, but the stockpile has changed very little since then

David Hobson (Republican House representative and Chairman of the Energy and Water Development Appropriations subcommittee) in a hearing in the US Congress in July 2003.

CONTENTS

LIST OF TABLES

LIST OF FIGURES

ACRONYMS

ABM: anti-ballistic missile
ACDA: Arms Control and Disarmament Agency
AFP: Agence France Press
AP: Associated Press
BASIC: British American Security Information Council
BCSIA: Belfer Centre for Science and International Affairs
BMD: ballistic missile defence
CBW: chemical and biological weapons
CIA: Central Intelligence Agency
CINC: commander in chief
CINSAC: commander in chief of Strategic Air Command
CISAC: Committee on International Security and Arms Control
CSIA: Centre for Science and International Affairs
CSIS: Centre for Strategic and International Studies
CTBT: Comprehensive Test Ban Treaty
CWC: Chemical Weapons Convention
DEFCON: Defence Condition
DIA: Defence Intelligence Agency
DLC: Democratic Leadership Council
DOD: Department of Defence
DOE: Department of Energy
DPC: Defence Planning Committee
EU: European Union
FY: fiscal year
GAO: General Accounting Office
GNP: Gross National Product
HEU: highly enriched uranium
IAEA: International Atomic Energy Agency
ICBM: intercontinental ballistic missile
IISS: International Institute for Strategic Studies
INESAP: International Network of Engineers and Scientists Against Proliferation
INF: intermediate-range nuclear forces
JCS: Joint Chiefs of Staff
KT: kiloton
LOW: launch-on-warning
LUA: launch-under-attack
MAD: mutual assured destruction
MAO: massive attack options
MEADS: Medium Extended Air Defence System
MIRV: multiple independently targeted re-entry vehicle
MIT: Massachusetts Institute of Technology
MT: megaton

MTCR: Missile Technology Control Regime
NATO: North Atlantic Treaty Organization
NGO: non-governmental organization
NMD: National Missile Defence
NNWS: non-nuclear weapon states
NNSA: National Nuclear Security Administration
NPG: Nuclear Planning Group
NPR: Nuclear Posture Review
NPT: Nuclear Nonproliferation Treaty
NRDC: Natural Resources Defence Council
NSC: National Security Council
NSDD: National Security Decision Directive
NSG: Nuclear Suppliers Group
NUWEP: Nuclear Weapons Employment Policy guidance
NWFW: nuclear weapon free world
NWFZ: nuclear weapon free zone
NWS: nuclear weapon states
OSTP: Office of Science and Technology Policy
OTA: Office of Technology Assessment
PAL: permissive action link
PD: Presidential Directive
PDD: Presidential Decision Directive
PPNN: Program for Promoting Nonproliferation
SAC: Strategic Air Command
SACEUR: Supreme Allied Commander Europe
SALT: Strategic Arms Limitation Talks
SIOP: Single Integrated Operational Plan
SIPRI: Stockholm International Peace Research Institute
SLBM: sea-launched ballistic missiles
SLCM: sea-launched cruise missiles
SOD: Secretary of Defence
SORT: Strategic Offensive Reductions Treaty
SSBN: strategic submarine
SSP: Stockpile Stewardship Program
START: Strategic Arms Reduction Talks
STRATCOM: Strategic Command
THAAD: Theatre High Altitude Area Defence
TMD: Theatre Missile Defence
TNT: tri-nitro-toluene
UK: United Kingdom
UN: United Nations
UNIDIR: United Nations Institute for Disarmament Research
US: United States
USIA: United States Information Agency
USIS: United States Information Service
USSR: Union of Soviet Socialist Republics

ACKNOWLEDGEMENTS

Psychologists regard the age of ten as a marker. The decision made by NATO to deploy Euromissiles on 12 December 1979 – two weeks after my tenth birthday – was such an event. Trying to understand the rationale behind the nuclear logic became an intellectual challenge.

During my studies, Herman Vos (Sint-Jan Berchmanscollege Mol), Christian Franck (Facultés Universitaires Notre Dame de la Paix, Namur), Luc Reychler and Paul Van de Meerssche (Katholieke Universiteit Leuven), Nicholas Wheeler (Hull University) and Harald Müller (Bologna, SAIS, Johns Hopkins University) introduced and encouraged my interest in the fascinating and intricate relationship between international security and nuclear weapons. Independently of each other (in as far as I know), Michael Brown (Georgetown University) and Harald Müller recommended the topic for my Ph.D. and for this book that results from it.

Thanks to the material support of the local Rotary Club Tessenderlo and especially Michel Goelen, the Belgian Rotary District 1630 and more particularly Paul Gelders, the local Rotary Club Peabody (Mass., US) with Ralph and Teresa, the Rotary Foundation, and Frans Spaepen (Harvard University), I had the opportunity to stay for two years at one of the most intellectually stimulating institutes in the world in the field of international security and arms control: the Belfer Centre for Science and International Affairs (BCSIA) at the John F.Kennedy School of Government (Harvard University). This Pre-Doctoral Research Fellowship at the International Security Program at BCSIA, headed by Steven Miller, from September 1997 until August 1999 opened a lot of doors. Sean Lynn-Jones (Harvard University) helped me most in getting through the first difficult months, methodologically speaking.

Others who were particularly helpful are Matthew Bunn and John Holdren (both at Harvard), George Lewis (MIT), Steve Fetter (Maryland University), Janne Nolan and John Steinbruner (both at Brookings Institution at that time and now respectively at Georgetown and Maryland University) as well as Frank von Hippel (Princeton University) and Patrick Morgan (University of California, Irvine). The same applies to all the other governmental and non-governmental experts who were willing to be interviewed: Graham Allison, Steve Andreasen, William Arkin, Coit Blacker, George Bunn, Lee Butler, Ashton Carter, Marie Chevrier, Joseph Cirincione, Thomas Cochran, Owen Coté, Ivo Daalder, Lynn Davis, Jonathan Dean, John Deutch, Sidney Drell, Lynn Eden, Jason Ellis, Richard Falkenrath, Cathleen Fischer, Bob Frosch, John Galvin, Lisbeth Gronlund, Hugh Gusterson, Morton Halperin, Carl Kaysen, William Kaufman, Leo Mackay, Michael May, Jack Mendelsohn, Dutch Miller, Frank Miller, Ken Myers, Patrick Nopens, Stan Norris, Joseph Nye, Mitsuo Okamato, Wolfgang Panofsky, Christopher Payne, Barry Posen, George Rathjens, John Reppert, Jack Ruina, Scott Sagan, Harvey Sapolsky, Ivo Schalbroek, Thomas Schelling, Terry Scott, Stephen Schwartz, Larry Smith, Gary Stacey, Stephen Van Evera, Wilfried Van Hoeck, Paul Walker, Stephen Walt, Jennifer Weeks, Michael Wheeler, Dean Wilkening, and John White.

The basic criterion for succeeding in such an endeavour is motivation, which in its turn is basically determined by education, starting at home. It was my parents, Rina and Frank, who contributed most to who I am. Their love and affection for each other and for their children without isolating us from the rest of the world help explain my interest in politics and society.

Last but not least, my thanks goes to Astrid. Her empathic intelligence – she knows how to write a Ph.D. - and her patience and understanding meant I could keep focussed on the project without endangering 'our' project.

INTRODUCTION

Paradoxically the end of the Cold War raised both the expectations for the elimination of the gigantic nuclear weapons arsenals and the likelihood of the first atomic explosion since 1945. In the aftermath of the events of 11 September 2001 the bipolar world of the Cold War almost seems a period of stability. While nuclear weapons in the second half of the 20th century were instruments of deterrence, terrorist organizations like Al Qhaeda might actually use them if they succeed in acquiring them. The same logic may, according to some, even apply to the so-called rogue states.

As a result, the proliferation of weapons of mass destruction, and nuclear weapons in particular, became the principal threat to international peace and security. Because of the threat of asymmetrical warfare, this applies even more to the most powerful state in the world, as was recognized by both presidential candidates in the US in 2004.

It is logical to assume that the nuclear weapons policies of the former superpowers would have been adapted after the fall of the Berlin Wall to the radically changed circumstances. The Soviet Union and the Warsaw Pact no longer exist. Russia became a "Partner for Peace" in the Atlantic Alliance and is now represented at the NATO Headquarters. Yet despite the fact that the Cold War is over, the nuclear weapons policies of neither the US nor Russia differ fundamentally from say twenty, thirty or forty years ago: the nuclear doctrines of the Cold War are still in place. There are still 25,000 nuclear weapons on earth, more than 90 % in possession of Russia and the US. The George W.Bush administration also earmarked millions of dollars for research and development of new types of nuclear weapons, more particularly low-yield nuclear weapons, the so-called mini-nukes.

This book aims to clarify the nuclear weapons policy of the world's only remaining superpower, the US. How many nuclear weapons did it dismantle after the Cold War ? How many nuclear warheads does the US still possess today ? How many atomic bombs are planned to be kept in the US arsenal after 2010 ? What doctrine guides the policy ? Does the US explicitly renounce the first use of nuclear weapons ? And what about day-to-day operational policy ? Are the B-52 and B-2 bombers, the fourteen nuclear submarines and over 500 intercontinental ballistic missiles based in silo's still on alert ready to be launched ? What are the targets in the computerized nuclear war plans ?

To be able to judge the extent to which the policy has changed, an analytical framework is set up in the first chapter that elaborates the concepts of minimum and maximum deterrence. In Chapter 2, four reasons are described why we could have expected a move from maximum to minimum deterrence in the US after the Cold War. In the following four chapters, US nuclear weapons policy after the Cold War is described and evaluated: the nuclear force structure (Chapter 3), declaratory policy (Chapter 4), operational policy (Chapter 5) and the policy with regard to nuclear testing, nonproliferation, elimination, and missile defence (Chapter 6).

I could have skipped the first part by simply stating that US nuclear weapons policy had not changed very much since the end of the Cold War, something the US government denies. US Assistant Secretary of State for Arms Control Stephen Rademaker for instance stated at the Arms Control Association on 3 February 2005 that the charges that the US is not making enough progress toward the goal of nuclear disarmament and is not complying with their obligations under Article 6 of the NPT 'are utterly without foundation'[1]. It is up to the reader to judge whether the latter is true or not. Based on the theoretical framework including different parameters laid out in the first chapter, my analysis shows that the existing US nuclear weapons policy can only be categorized as maximum deterrence, just like during the Cold War. In an op-ed article in the *Washington Post* on 2 May 2005, John Hamre, former deputy Secretary of Defence and current president of the Center for Strategic and International Studies (CSIS) in Washington DC, seems to agree: 'America is sleepwalking through history, armed with nuclear weapons. The Cold War left us with a massive inventory of weapons we no longer need, an infrastructure we can no longer use or maintain, and no thought of where our future lies'[2].

The second and last part of the book deals with the reasons 'why'. Why did US nuclear weapons policy not change very much after 1989 ? While nobody really expected such changes during the George W.H.Bush (1989-1992) and George W.Bush (2001-2008) administrations because of the closeness to the geo-strategic revolution of the former and the ideological reasons of the latter, the same cannot be said of the Clinton administration (1993-2000). An opportunity was missed. Les Aspin, who was Clinton's first secretary of defence, had a clear intention to change US nuclear weapons policy drastically and announced this intention at the start of the Nuclear Posture Review in October 1993. But due to lower level bureaucratic resistance, both from the military and the civilian officials in the Defence Department and because of a lack of political leadership in the Clinton administration, the policy review resulted in maintaining the status quo. This part of the book tries to describe that period and the key players involved in more detail. It also tries to determine the more structural factors that can explain the end result: bureaucratic interests, grooved thinking, lack of strategic and tactical leadership, lack of civilian control of the military, in short domestic politics. In Chapter 7 a framework is developed that distinguishes strategic (or "objective") factors and purely domestic political factors. Political leadership can in theory transcend differences between them. The following Chapter considers the main players in US nuclear weapons policy on the basis of the Cold War experience.

How powerful is the nuclear bureaucracy ? The fascinating story of the Nuclear Posture Review inside the Clinton administration is discussed in Chapter 9. Chapter 10 broadens the analysis by looking into the different political appointees involved in the Nuclear Posture Review and the extent in which they behaved like political leaders. Lastly, Chapter 11 asks the question to what extent this analysis can be generalized to other nuclear weapons issues in the 1990s and beyond.

Future American presidents will probably be confronted with the spectre of more nuclear weapon states or nuclear terrorism, or even both. The question about the future of nuclear weapons and US nuclear weapons policy in particular may therefore be perceived as more urgent and may be answered in a more rigorous and consistent way as during the first fifteen years after the Cold War, when the crucial issues were swept under the carpet and the most marked policy characteristic was inertia.

PART I

US NUCLEAR WEAPONS POLICY AFTER THE COLD WAR

CHAPTER 1

MINIMUM AND MAXIMUM DETERRENCE

Because of their unique destructive characteristics, nuclear weapons are paradoxically not perceived as real weapons to be used, but as instruments of deterrence. No rational decision-maker, according to the theory of nuclear deterrence, will risk a nuclear counterattack. Even limited nuclear retaliation may destroy a major city with casualties running in the hundreds of thousands. A 250-kiloton weapon – a regular yield in today's nuclear arsenals – is, for instance, more than ten times more powerful than the Hiroshima bomb and corresponds roughly to 35,000 powerful conventional bombs. In October 1949, the General Advisory Committee to the US Atomic Energy Commission that was chaired by Robert Oppenheimer – chief scientist at the Manhattan project – recommended *not* producing the H-bomb, calling it a "weapon of genocide" and "beyond any military objectives"[1].

Nuclear deterrence can be defined as the threat of using nuclear weapons to prevent the enemy from attacking vital interests. The main consequence for international politics is – according to this logic – its stabilizing effect. The period of major interstate wars would be over. The theory of deterrence, however, became only gradually accepted over time. In the beginning, the US military, for instance, regarded nuclear weapons as the next generation of conventional weapons. Over time nuclear deterrence became the bedrock of the national security policies of the nuclear weapon states[2].

The dilemma of nuclear deterrence – like deterrence in general – is that it can also fail. Risk-takers may speculate that the announced nuclear counterattack for whatever reasons – for instance because of non-proportionality, because of the risk of escalation or because one believes that the enemy is simply bluffing – will not be carried out. The chance is small that democratically elected governments will take such risks. The world, however, does not only consist of democracies.

If nuclear weapons are not used after a deterrence failure and if this happens a couple of times, the effect of deterrence will automatically fade away. Nuclear deterrence is therefore a violent paradox: its purpose is to threaten to use nuclear weapons in order not to use them in the end.

Advocates of nuclear weapons claim that despite the fragile theory, the fear of a nuclear counterattack always prevails: nuclear deterrence will always work in practice. This is called "existential deterrence". Lawrence Freedman puts it more prosaically: 'The Emperor Deterrence may have no clothes, but he is still the Emperor'[3].

Opponents of nuclear weapons argue that a prudent security policy should not base the fate of millions of people on such a fragile concept for a prolonged period of time. The inherent nature of people and organizations does not guarantee that all conditions for stable nuclear deterrence will always be fulfilled.

The concepts of minimum and maximum deterrence[4]

When a state at a certain moment decides to acquire a nuclear arsenal, it still has to decide *how* the concept of nuclear deterrence will be implemented.

The key questions on which opinions may differ relate to force structure, declaratory and operational policy:

1) What is a credible second-strike capability ? In theory, a second-strike capability is an arsenal capable of launching a nuclear counterattack with sufficient destructive capacity after a first-strike by the opponent, which in its turn is a surprise attack by the opponent trying to eliminate all nuclear weapons in one single blow. What is a sufficient destructive force ? How probable is a first-strike ? Is having the same number of nuclear weapons as the opponent – so-called strategic parity – necessary ? How large should the nuclear arsenal be ?

2) What kinds of attack must be deterred and declared as such ? Attacks threatening the survival of the state or other "vital" national interests as well ? Will nuclear deterrence be limited to deterring nuclear weapons attacks or will it also include massive or smaller conventional, chemical and biological weapons attacks ? What about extended deterrence, i.e. providing a nuclear umbrella to other states ?

3) How can the ability to prevent accidental or unauthorized launches or both in times of peace, i.e. negative control, be balanced with the ability to use nuclear weapons effectively and rapidly in times of war, i.e. positive control ? What about the alert-levels ? What will the nuclear war plan look like in practice ? Which and how many targets and target categories are desirable ?

These three categories of questions are also intimately linked: for instance, targeting or "deterrence" requirements determine the quantity of nuclear weapons, which in turn might exclude some declaratory postures.

The following questions are even more fundamental: a) How much credit is given to nuclear deterrence ? How different are nuclear weapons from conventional weapons ?; b) To what extent is one willing to use nuclear weapons if deterrence fails, and what will nuclear retaliation look like ?; c) What about the importance of the disadvantages of nuclear weapons, namely the safety and proliferation risks ?

For heuristic purposes, two basic answers can be sketched out: minimum deterrence and maximum deterrence. These are two schools of thought on how the theoretical concept of nuclear deterrence can be implemented in a logical and consistent way. In reality, most postures fall between these two extremes.

Minimum deterrence

In the framework of minimum deterrence nuclear weapons are basically seen as fundamentally different from conventional weapons. The deterrence effect of nuclear weapons results more or less automatically from the inherent destructive characteristics of nuclear weapons. Minimum deterrence is closely linked to the concept of existential deterrence. It is the existence of nuclear weapons that deters and all the rest including the intricacies of force structure, declaratory and operational policy does not matter very much. A secure second-strike force, for instance based on stealth submarines, does not require a very large arsenal. First-strikes by the enemy are seen as unlikely because of the deterrent effect and not very effective because nuclear weapons may be rebuilt allowing retaliation later on, except in the event that the territory is occupied. Because of this trust in basic deterrence and because a first-strike is consequently not really feared and because retaliation can be limited, there is no need for high alerts in times of peace.

According to the theory of minimum deterrence, nuclear weapons should only be used as a very last resort, namely if the survival of the state is at stake. They should be used in a "limited" way because of their destructive power, although this should not be emphasized publicly in order not to undermine the deterrent effect.

The reason for minimizing the role of nuclear weapons relates to their disadvantages: the proliferation and safety risks and also the risk that nuclear deterrence might fail. Because safety risks are taken serious, pre-emptive strikes and prompt launch doctrines, which require high alert-levels, do not belong to the concept of minimum deterrence. Retaliation can easily be implemented in a delayed fashion. Because of the disadvantages of nuclear weapons, most (although not all) advocates of minimum deterrence are also in favour of elimination in the long term. Nuclear weapons are regarded as a temporary evil.

The nuclear *force structure* is limited under a system of minimum deterrence. Because of the nature of nuclear weapons, because large-scale use is not seen as a legitimate policy and because the overall goal is to minimize the emphasis on nuclear weapons, large numbers of nuclear weapons are not required. A few dozen nuclear warheads are sufficient if they are based on (quasi) invulnerable delivery vehicles like stealth submarines or mobile ICBMs. A missile defence system by the opponent will influence these deterrence requirements. But even with a shield that is capable of destroying a dozen ballistic missiles, the number of nuclear weapons must not exceed 100[5].

Because the role of nuclear weapons is limited to deter attacks threatening the survival of the state and because a small number of nuclear weapons is regarded as sufficient, strategic nuclear weapons can do the job. There is no need for sub-strategic nuclear weapons[6].

There is no need for strategic parity, in the sense of having approximately the same number of weapons as the opponent. A minimum deterrent is sufficient, regardless of the size of the opponent's arsenal.

In the case of "invulnerable" delivery vehicles (like stealth submarines or mobile ICBMs), one type of delivery vehicle is sufficient. If that is not the case, it is still possible to disperse and hide nuclear weapons using two types.

As there will always be the possibility of using nuclear weapons in a delayed fashion (except in the event that the territory is occupied), a prompt launch capability is not required. On the contrary, prompt launch capabilities enhance safety risks.

As nuclear deterrence is only used to defend the survival of the state, nuclear weapons need not to be deployed in other states.

The key force structure characteristics that can be used to distinguish minimum and maximum deterrence are the overall number of nuclear weapons and the principle of strategic parity. The other elements rely on them (like types of delivery vehicles and the need for sub-strategic weapons) or result from declaratory (extended deterrence) or operational policy (prompt launch capability).

Declaratory policy makes the circumstances in which nuclear retaliation can be expected clear to the enemy. Because of credibility and proliferation concerns, nuclear weapons are only legitimised as a deterrent against nuclear attacks. Only the latter endanger the survival of the state. The use of nuclear weapons against conventional, chemical and biological weapons attacks is explicitly denounced. Nuclear weapons will only be used as a very last resort and that should be announced as such.

Nuclear deterrence may only be extended to non-nuclear attacks that may threaten the survival of the state in the case of small states that may easily be overrun by non-nuclear means. This may for instance be the case for Israel.
States that cannot easily be overrun by non-nuclear means can announce that they would never be the first to use nuclear weapons.

Legally binding negative security guarantees – which are promises by the nuclear weapon states not to attack the non-nuclear weapon states – can also be offered by states that cannot easily be overrun by non-nuclear means.

Because of safety reasons, there is no room for a (declaratory) prompt launch doctrine in the form of a launch-on-warning (LOW)(= launching nuclear weapons in the event of tactical warning[7] that an enemy attack is underway) or a launch-under-attack (LUA) doctrine (= launching nuclear weapons after the first enemy missiles have exploded on the territory)[8]; instead, one explicitly declares that in the event of attack one will "ride out" (= waiting to retaliate until the attack is over) and use nuclear weapons in a delayed fashion.

Operational policy can be split up in safety measures and targeting policy. Safety concerns are taken very seriously by minimum deterrence advocates. Because the risk of accidents and unauthorized use is taken seriously and because retaliation has not to be prompt, alert-levels are kept to a very strict minimum. For the same reasons, permissive action links (PALs) and other safety devices are installed on all deployed nuclear weapons in order to minimize safety risks.

With respect to targeting policy, punishing the adversary in a retaliatory strike can be done with a few nuclear weapons with a strict minimum of preplanning; targets should in principle not be selected in advance[9].

Because large-scale use is not regarded as legitimate and because the force structure is limited, massive attack options (MAO) – a single attack with hundreds of nuclear weapons or more – are excluded.

Counterforce options – attacks against the nuclear forces of the enemy – make no sense because the purpose is not to eliminate the nuclear capabilities of the opponent, but to punish the opponent in case deterrence fails. Contrary to widespread beliefs, minimum deterrence does not automatically mean countervalue (read countercity) targeting[10]. If any criterion regarding targeting stands out it is the latter. Counterforce targeting requires pre-planned options and, depending on the numbers of the adversary, massive attack options.

Maximum deterrence

In the framework of maximum deterrence, nuclear weapons are regarded as different from conventional weapons; however, the difference should not be emphasized. Nuclear weapons are also weapons. Advocates of maximum deterrence have less confidence in the deterrent effect of nuclear weapons as such. The fear of a first-strike is always present. A small force structure is therefore regarded as a liability as this might trigger a first-strike by the opponent. Unlike minimum deterrence, the deterrence effect does not automatically result from the existence of nuclear weapons as such, but from the way a secure second-strike capability is constructed. The main thrust of maximum deterrence is that the nuclear posture – force structure, declaratory and operational policy – compensates for the so-called lack of credibility of minimum or 'existential' deterrence. Maximum deterrence strategists believe that they are able to add the necessary "touch of credibility" in order to make nuclear deterrence work.

Nuclear weapons should be used as a last resort; but, in contrast to minimum deterrence, this should not be emphasized. A more effective declaratory strategy is to create ambiguity about what the reaction will be. This allows other "vital interests" beyond the survival of the state – for example the security of allies – to play a role in the deterrence game.

In the event that nuclear weapons have to be used, it is best to give the impression that they will be used on a massive scale in order to bolster deterrence, especially if the survival of the state is at stake. On the other hand, limited nuclear options should also be available, either for other-than-survival-of-the-state interests, or for bolstering deterrence in general by creating ambiguity. The message to the opponent should be that one is prepared to fight and to be able to win at each level of violence. Beside punishment, damage limitation becomes a second goal. All this implies the need for a huge force structure that is able to eliminate the force structure of the enemy as soon as possible, or at least to limit damage.

The maximum deterrence theory claims that the better the perception of being prepared to use nuclear weapons, the more credible the deterrence effect. Positive control, which is the ability to use nuclear weapons if needed, is regarded as being more important than negative control, which is the ability to prevent accidents or unauthorized use. Because of the fear of a first-strike, the impression should at least be given and plans should accordingly be made to use nuclear weapons in a pre-emptive way, or at least to launch them promptly in the event of a tactical warning (LOW) or if under attack (LUA). As a result, high alerts are needed, both in crisis situations and in times of peace. The overall advantages of nuclear weapons are assessed as being larger than their disadvantages. In order not to undermine the credibility of the deterrent effect, it is best not to debate the disadvantages of nuclear weapons overly. A nuclear weapons free world is seen as both impractical and undesirable.

Under a system of maximum deterrence, the *force structure* is large. As the credibility of the deterrent effect depends partially on the nature and the quantity of targets, and even more on the size of the opponent's arsenal, which has to be eliminated as soon as possible in times of crisis, a large number of nuclear weapons are recommended. In addition, a large arsenal may impress potential risk-takers, at least more than a small arsenal.

Sub-strategic nuclear weapons are useful for executing limited nuclear strikes or for deterring other-than-survival-of-the-state interests.

Having the same number of nuclear weapons as the opponent is a minimum requirement because of the possibility of a first-strike; superiority is desirable.

Nuclear weapons should be deployed on as many categories of delivery vehicles as possible (bombers, ICBMs, SLBMs – the so-called triad) in order to be capable of responding in the way planned; a triad also bolsters flexibility.

Because of the risk of a first-strike, a prompt launch capability is required.

Nuclear weapons can be based on the territory of other states to extend the stabilizing deterrence effect to these states.

To keep the opponent guessing and to bolster the credibility of the nuclear deterrent, *declaratory policy* should be as vague and ambiguous as possible. The concept of vital interests should be kept vague as well. It should be declared that nuclear weapons may be used not only in retaliation to nuclear attacks but also in retaliation to conventional, chemical or biological weapons attacks. The impression should be given that a massive attack will follow if the survival of the state is at stake; at the same time, however, the possibility of launching limited nuclear strikes in the event of attacks against less vital interests should also be declared. A declaratory policy of extended deterrence is also possible.

Because of that mission, a no first use policy and legally binding negative security guarantees are by definition excluded.

In order to enhance the deterrent effect, at least the impression should be given that a nuclear attack will not be ridden out; pre-emptive strikes, LOW and LUA are the preferred options, or at least declared as such.

Declaratory policy plays a more significant role under maximum deterrence than under minimum deterrence.

The same applies to *operational policy*. To bolster deterrence, at least the impression should be given of being able to react as soon as there is a tactical warning of an upcoming attack. Therefore, the nuclear forces should be on hair-trigger alert, ready for launch as soon as an attack is prepared by the enemy (pre-emptive strike), or underway (launch-on-warning), or as the first enemy weapons reach their targets (launch-under-attack). The goal consists of wiping out as many of the opponent's nuclear weapons in order to limit the damage in a subsequent phase of the conflict and in preventing the opponent from reaching his objective, and forcing him to stop violence at a level beneath all-out nuclear war.

	Minimum deterrence	Maximum deterrence
I. Force structure		
Number of nuclear warheads	Very low levels (tens if based on invulnerable delivery vehicle). Max. 100 in the case of a limited NMD.	High levels (depending on the number of the opponent)
Sub-strategic nuclear weapons	No	Yes
Strategic parity	No	Yes, if possible superiority
Triad	No	Yes
Prompt launch capability	No	Yes
Nuclear weapons based in other states	No	Yes
II. Declaratory policy		
Nuclear deterrence versus conventional, CBW, nuclear attacks	Nuclear attacks (*)	Conventional, CBW, and nuclear attacks
No first use	Yes (*)	No
Legally binding negative security guarantees for non-nuclear weapon states (NNWS); NWFZ	Yes (*)	No
Ride out policy	Yes	No
III. Operational policy		
A. Safety policy		
Alert-levels	Low (at least for warheads; not for delivery vehicles in case of very low number of delivery vehicles)	High
Permissive Action Links (PAL) and other safety devices installed	Yes	No (or very limited)
B. Targeting policy		
Predetermined targets; war plan like SIOP	No	Yes
Massive attack options	No	Yes
Counter-force targets	No	Yes

(*): This applies especially to states that cannot easily be overrun by non-nuclear means (like the US or Russia for instance)

Table 1: Minimum and maximum deterrence

PALs and other safety devices make it more time-consuming to use nuclear weapons during a crisis, and are therefore not generally considered as a primary concern. Pre-delegation, which is the delegation of authority to use nuclear weapons to lower levels of personnel, is considered useful.

With respect to targeting policy, because the impression has to be created of being able to react promptly against the enemy forces in order to limit damage, nuclear war planning is extremely important. Targets should be carefully selected in advance. Because of the large numbers and high alert-levels, targeting also becomes a complicated business. Nuclear war plans have to be imagined for different scenarios: targets (and target categories) should be identified and prioritised; weapons should be linked to these different targets on the basis of damage expectancy criteria; and an integrated operational war plan has to be created in order to maximize the effect of the attack, for instance to prevent the same targets being attacked twice.

Different attack options should be considered: both limited and massive attack options. The main target category should be the opponent's nuclear force (counterforce) in order to wipe out most of these forces in a retaliatory strike and to limit the possible damage of a counterattack by the enemy. Other possible target categories are command and control facilities, conventional forces, and industrial/economic targets. In principle, cities can also be targeted. However, democracies do not find the last category a legitimate target. In practice, however, many industrial sites and conventional forces are located inside or near cities.

Assessment of minimum and maximum deterrence
While both approaches have advantages and disadvantages, minimum deterrence is preferable on a number of grounds. Due to the large numbers of nuclear weapons, the high alert-levels and the possible pre-delegation, both the risk of accidents and unauthorized use is much higher in times of peace in the case of maximum deterrence.

Proponents of maximum deterrence claim that minimum deterrence would be destabilizing during a crisis. They point to the alert-levels that have to be raised in these circumstances, which will be perceived as threatening and might trigger a pre-emptive attack. The counter-argument is that the disadvantages of a maximum deterrence posture during a crisis situation are even more substantial. A maximum deterrence policy may be perceived by the opponent as designed for implementing a first-strike, which in turn requires the opponent to put its nuclear weapons on high alert. Having nuclear weapons on high alert during a crisis may enhance crisis instability. This is especially true when one believes that bureaucratic-organizational processes – similar to those at the eve of the First World War – will precipitate the decision to strike first.

The main criticism against minimum deterrence is that it does not have much credibility. The counterargument is that the credibility issue is inherent to nuclear weapons because of their destructive capacity. Some risk-takers may, indeed, be more deterred by maximum deterrence. For others, the opposite will be true. To give the impression of using nuclear weapons early in a conflict can either enhance or diminish the deterrence effect. It is highly questionable whether most risk-takers believe more in a vague declaratory policy with more and smaller (and therefore more usable) nuclear weapons on high alert. Many of them may simply believe that maximum deterrence is big talk, and when push comes to the proverbial shove the deterrer - especially if democratically elected - will *not* use nuclear weapons. Risk-takers like playing on the edge of rationality and may just test how far they can go without being punished. Maximum deterrence can at most create the impression of escaping the paradox of nuclear deterrence.

Implementing the operational plans corresponding to maximum deterrence is simply not feasible in the case of first-use and in particular in the case of a first-strike by the enemy. Regardless of declaratory policy, decision-makers can in practice choose one of the four following postures in the event of an upcoming nuclear attack by the enemy: pre-emption, LOW, LUA or ride-out. Pre-emption – or a pre-emptive first-strike – aims at destroying all or most of the enemy's nuclear forces before the latter can be used. This strategy can only be considered when strategic warning indicates that the nuclear forces of the enemy are dispersed, as this can be interpreted as preparations for a nuclear attack. Pre-emption is extremely risky because the warning signals can be wrong. In addition, a pre-emptive first-strike may leave a substantial part of the enemy's forces intact for retaliation.

A second option is launching a nuclear retaliatory attack in the case of so-called tactical warning (= warning by radar and/or satellites) that an enemy attack is underway. This strategy corresponds to a so-called launch-on-warning (LOW). One of the problems related to LOW is that decision-makers have an extremely short period of time available for deciding to retaliate. For most neighbouring states, LOW is consequently excluded by definition, except if one considers automatic response as "decision-making". Even if there is a thirty minutes flight time before the missiles arrive, as between the territory of the US and Russia, it takes time to detect the launch, to verify it and to communicate what is happening to the decision-makers. At most, American and Russian political decision-makers have only fifteen minutes to decide (and less in the absence of well-functioning satellites). In most cases, there will only be a few minutes left. Like pre-emption, such a policy is in any event extremely dangerous because one has to make sure that the (tactical) warning is 100 % correct. Risk-takers might simply not believe that democratically elected leaders would take decisions with such devastating consequences in such a short period of time.

In the event that the decision-makers decide not to LOW but to launch-under-attack (LUA), which means that retaliation is postponed until the first explosion occurs in order to be sure that the tactical warning was not false, another problem arises for executing the nuclear war plans, namely the vulnerability of the command and control facilities. The command and control facilities can be disabled by electromagnetic pulse caused by a nuclear explosion, and/or they can be eliminated directly. And as Bruce Blair has made clear on different occasions: 'If command and control fails, nothing else matters'[11]. In theory, there are technological fixes to neutralize EMP effects. This is, however, not the case with respect to the direct elimination of the command and control system. John Steinbruner (Maryland University) concludes: 'The precariousness of command channels probably means that nuclear war be uncontrollable, as a practical matter, shortly after the first tens of weapons are launched'[12]. The counterargument by the advocates of maximum deterrence is that it is simply too risky to believe that there will be no retaliation.

Invulnerable delivery systems (like submarines) that are able to function without a centralized command and control system can never be excluded. A delayed nuclear counterattack can in principle always be executed. This argument however strengthens the concept of minimum instead of maximum deterrence. Also in the fourth case, ride-out, i.e. waiting to counter-attack until the initial attack is over, we are back to a minimum deterrence scenario.

If deterrence fails and if a maximum deterrence operational policy is successfully implemented (which is highly unlikely), destruction will be much higher than in a minimum deterrence scenario because of the higher number of nuclear weapons that are available and that will be used. Talking about damage limitation then, at most, becomes a theoretical exercise.

Furthermore, maximum deterrence corresponds to high numbers of nuclear weapons and a robust command and control system, which is much more costly than a minimum deterrent.

Lastly, minimum deterrence legitimises the existence of a nuclear deterrent only by referring to the existence of nuclear weapons in other nuclear weapon states. This makes negative security guarantees and a no first use declaratory policy possible (at least in the case that the nuclear weapon state cannot easily be overrun by non-nuclear means). Assuming that there is a link between the nuclear postures of the nuclear weapon states and proliferation, minimum deterrence consequently minimizes the risk of proliferation, at least in the short and medium term.

Advocates of maximum deterrence sometimes argue that extended deterrence may also prevent nuclear proliferation. Extended deterrence, however, is problematic. By extending a nuclear umbrella, one may provoke new fears in the region and therefore *stimulate* proliferation. More fundamentally, as Patrick Morgan contends: 'One of the perpetual problems of deterrence on behalf of third parties is that the costs a state is willing to bear are usually much less than if its own territory is at stake, and it is very difficult to pretend otherwise'[13].

To conclude, many experts agree that the cost-benefit analysis favours minimum deterrence[14]. But even minimum deterrence does not escape the weaknesses of nuclear deterrence in general.

CHAPTER 2

TOWARDS A MINIMUM DETERRENT ?

The Cold War nuclear postures of both the US and the former USSR are prime examples of maximum deterrence. While there was no consensus about the desirability and feasibility of elimination, most analysts in the immediate aftermath of the Cold War agreed that some sort of minimum deterrence posture for the US was preferable (see appendix).

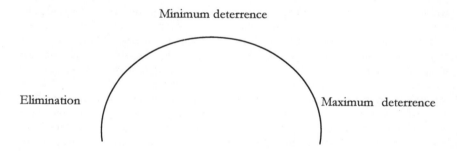

Minimum deterrence

Elimination

Maximum deterrence

Figure 1: The range of nuclear policy scenarios after the Cold War

Rationale behind a US minimum deterrent after the Cold War

The arguments in favour of a switch to minimum deterrence in the US in the post-Cold War period can be divided into four parts: 1) minimum deterrence for the sake of minimum deterrence; 2) minimum deterrence as a result of the changed threat assessment; 3) minimum deterrence in a bilateral context as a means to reduce the risks relating to the deteriorating Russian nuclear arsenal; and 4) minimum deterrence in a multilateral context as a step towards consolidation of the disarmament and nonproliferation regime.

Based on the above-mentioned evaluation of minimum and maximum deterrence (see chapter 1), a shift could have been expected towards minimum deterrence in US nuclear policy much earlier than 1989. The Chinese deterrent comes closest to the practice of minimum deterrence.

Another reason is the changed threat assessment. The threat of a Russian invasion into Western Europe, let alone a Soviet nuclear first-strike on US territory, disappeared after 1989. As a result, the only theoretical justification for a maximum deterrence doctrine disappeared. The time was ripe for a shift towards minimum deterrence. Even if the theoretical advantages of minimum deterrence were disbelieved and even if unconvinced by the changed threat assessment, a minimum deterrence posture after the Cold War was preferable because it would have diminished the danger of the deteriorating Russian nuclear arsenal. This logic only applies if Russia would also have switched to a minimum deterrence posture. The latter could have been facilitated by the US.

Four specific dangers in Russia have to be distinguished: 1) the risk of accidents; 2) the risk of unauthorized use; 3) the risk of authorized use after a false alarm; and 4) the risk of proliferation to "rogue states" or terrorists[1]. Firstly, the nuclear power accident in Chernobyl is an early indication that the quality of Russian nuclear technology was not equal to that of the West. Another example is the lack of funds that led to the decay of the famous space station "Mir". While there have not been major nuclear weapons accidents, the risk was and still is substantial. A local electricity company cut off power to an important strategic nuclear command building in September 1994 because of unpaid bills[2]. The best-known accident is that of the Kursk in August 2000, when 118 Russian soldiers died when the nuclear submarine – one of Russia's newest – sank in the Barents Sea.

Secondly, the risk of unauthorized use is enhanced because the Russian military, which is supposed to control and guard the weapons systems, are badly paid. The risk exists that some of them may abandon the weapons and delivery vehicles, which would make it easier to steal them or use them without authorization. The risk of unauthorized use is greatest with regard to the sub-strategic nuclear weapons because they lack PALs. Some experts claim that strategic forces do not have safety problems[3]. Bruce Blair, however, disagrees: 'Although Russian safeguards on nuclear forces of all types are generally technically impressive, they are really, in the final analysis, just gimmicks designed to buy time, and their effectiveness depends crucially on the overall cohesion of the Russian military'[4]. In September 1998, a 19-year old sailor based on a nuclear attack submarine killed seven of his colleagues and threatened to blow up the submarine[5]. Gen.Valynkin, in charge of Russian nuclear weapons security, stated in January 2003: 'the information we have obtained indicates that international terrorists have been looking for opportunities to gain unauthorized access to [Russian] nuclear facilities and to provoke acts of terrorism and sabotage using nuclear devices'[6].

Unauthorized use is also a possibility at the highest levels of command. During the coup against Gorbachev in August 1991, the authority to launch the strategic nuclear weapons lay for three days in the hands of Defence Minister Yazov and the chief of the General Staff Moiseyev[7].

The fact that Russian missiles are officially no longer targeted does not make any difference, as the missiles automatically switch back to their original targets once launched[8].

Thirdly, there is a possibility that nuclear weapons use is authorized following a false alarm. This scenario has become more likely due to the disintegrating early-warning system in Russia. Seven out of ten Soviet radars are stationed outside Russia and in the second half of the 1990s only three out of nine of the more modern Russian radars worked[9]. The Russian satellite system is also falling apart. The overall result was, and still is, that Russia is not capable of detecting a missile attack on a permanent basis. As a result, the Russian president will have even less time available than during the Cold War to decide on a possible retaliatory strike. Paradoxically, this requires the Russian system to be even more ready to launch-on-warning, with all the corresponding dangers. Russian experts have confirmed that launch-on-warning (LOW) was the main Soviet posture in the 1980s[10]. Bruce Blair believes it is still the case after the Cold War[11].

The most serious incident took place in January 1995, when a false alarm triggered a strategic alert of the Russian nuclear forces. It was the first time that such an alert reached the desk of President Yeltsin[12]. A Norwegian civilian rocket that was meant to study the Northern Lights caused the alarm. Incidentally, it was the biggest rocket Norway ever launched and could indeed have resembled a US Trident SLBM launch on Russian radar screens. During that episode, President Yeltsin had to decide in a very short timeframe whether to launch the Russian nuclear arsenal. Later on, it was discovered that Russia was informed about the launch, but that either administrative inefficiency or organizational mistakes or both had resulted in the information not reaching the guards at the radar stations. The incident not only made it clear that there was a lack of bureaucratic efficiency, but more fundamentally that the Russian satellite system was not capable of detecting US SLBM launches. Senior officials in Russia later admitted that 70 % of Russia's early-warning satellites were past their operational life or in serious disrepair[13]. A RAND study in 2003 noted that Russia was only capable of monitoring the American ICBM fields seven hours a day[14]. That the Russian president has to take far-reaching decisions based on a lack of information is not very reassuring.

Fourthly, the global risks of proliferation and nuclear terrorism are considerably aggravated by the perilous situation in Russia. Although the Russian economy started to recover in recent years, the living standards of the average Russian only improved slightly. Those who are supposed to guard the nuclear weapons may try to steal and sell the weapons and/or the fissile material in order to gain a decent living. As Matthew Bunn (Harvard University) pointed out: 'A nuclear-security system designed for a single state with a closed society, closed borders, and well-paid nuclear workers has been splintered among multiple states with open societies, open borders, unpaid workers, and rampant corruption'[15]. States or terrorist organizations may try to buy or steal fissile material or complete weapons systems. In September 1998, a US team was shown a completely unguarded building in Moscow that contained 100 kg of highly enriched uranium[16]. During the same month, a sergeant killed two of his colleagues, injured a third and stole ammunition from the Mayak facility, where more than 30 tons of plutonium is stored. In the same year, employees of a Russian nuclear facility in Chelyabinsk were caught

attempting to steal fissile material of a quantity just short of the few kilograms that
are needed for one nuclear device. Around the same time, an employee in Arzamas
was charged with attempting to sell documents on nuclear weapons designs to
agents of Iraq and Afghanistan for $3 million[17]. In August 2003, the deputy
director of Atomflot, the organization that repairs the Russian nuclear icebreakers
and nuclear submarines, was arrested in Murmansk because he tried to steal nuclear
fissile material. According to former Assistant Secretary of Defence Graham
Allison, 'almost every month, someone somewhere is apprehended trying to
smuggle or steal nuclear materials or weapons'[18].

Furthermore, those who are supposed to develop and produce nuclear weapons
in Russia have no prospects. This considerably enhances the risk of brain drain.
States or non-state actors interested in acquiring nuclear weapons may be very
willing to give Russian scientists more than a decent salary, especially in
comparison with the Russian standard of living.

The best solution to the deteriorating Russian nuclear arsenal after the Cold War
would have been to help Russia to secure its nuclear materials and to make both
Russian and US nuclear systems safer against accidents, unauthorized use and
proliferation. Taking the nuclear weapons off alert would have made the Russian
systems much less prone to accidents and unauthorized use[19]. In the case of low
alert-levels, political decision-makers have much more time – measured in days or
weeks instead of minutes – to decide about a possible retaliatory strike.

Lastly, a move towards minimum deterrence could have been expected in order
to consolidate the existing international disarmament and nonproliferation regime.
The latter consists of different arms control and disarmament treaties (like the
NPT, START, CTBT), informal export-control regimes (like the NSG, MTCR),
international organizations (like the International Atomic Energy Agency, CTBTO)
and unilateral promises by the nuclear weapon states (like security guarantees)[20].
The cornerstone of the regime is the Nuclear Non-Proliferation Treaty
(NPT)(1968) with 188 signatory states in 2005. Only Israel, India and Pakistan have
not signed the treaty. North Korea left the treaty in January 2003. The treaty is a
deal between the so-called nuclear weapon states (NWS) – those having exploded a
nuclear device before 1967 – and the non-nuclear weapon states (NNWS). The
NNWS promised not to acquire nuclear weapons. The NWS also promised to
disarm their nuclear weapons.

The goal of nuclear elimination is enshrined in the NPT that was signed by the
US in 1968. Article 6 is worth quoting in length: 'Each of the Parties to the Treaty
undertakes to pursue negotiations in good faith on effective measures relating to
cessation of the nuclear arms race at an early date and to nuclear disarmament, and
on a Treaty on general and complete disarmament under strict and effective
international control'. Clinton's Deputy Secretary of State Strobe Talbott made the
significance of article 6 clear in an article in *Foreign Affairs* in March/April 1999:
'The NPT was explicitly *not* intended to legitimise those arsenals *indefinitely*'. He
continues: 'Rather, it represented a bargain: states that had not tested at the time of
signature would promise never to develop or acquire nuclear weapons; in
exchange, the parties agreed to share the benefits of peaceful nuclear technology
with one another and to work toward the eventual *elimination of all nuclear weapons*[21].
The 2000 NPT Review Conference made it clear in unambiguous terms that article

6 meant "elimination", regardless of conventional disarmament. One of the thirteen steps that was agreed upon at the Conference was the following: 'An unequivocal undertaking by the Nuclear Weapon States to accomplish the total *elimination* of their nuclear arsenals leading to nuclear disarmament to which all States parties are committed under Article VI'[22].

It can be argued that the political climate during the Cold War prevented the NWS, and the US in particular, from fulfilling the obligation of elimination. But following this logic, it could have been expected that the NWS, including the US, took concrete and radical steps towards the goal of elimination – read adoption of a minimum deterrence posture – *after* the Cold War.

In 1995, the NNWS and NWS agreed to extend the NPT indefinitely, 25 years after the treaty came into force. The NNWS only did so because a package deal was concluded. One of the documents that was called *Principles and Objectives for Nuclear Nonproliferation and Disarmament* included an action programme for nuclear disarmament that is worth repeating: 'the determined pursuit by the NWS of *systematic and progressive efforts* to reduce nuclear weapons globally, with the ultimate goal of *eliminating* those weapons, and by all states of general and complete disarmament under strict and effective international control'[23].

The UN General Assembly asked the opinion of the International Court of Justice with regard to the legality of nuclear weapons. The main conclusion of the – not legally binding – opinion of the Court in July 1996 was ambiguous. It said that 'the threat or use of nuclear weapons would generally be contrary to the rules of international law applicable in armed conflict, and in particular the principles and rules of humanitarian law. However, in view of the current state of international law, and of the elements of fact at its disposal, the Court cannot conclude definitively whether the threat or use 'of nuclear weapons would be lawful or unlawful in an extreme circumstance of self-defence, in which the very survival of a state would be at stake'. Both the advocates and opponents of nuclear weapons cried victory.

More significantly, the Court was unanimous concerning the following paragraph: 'There exists an obligation to pursue in good faith *and bring to a conclusion* negotiations leading to *nuclear* disarmament *in all its aspects* under strict and effective international control'[24]. To be clear, the text does not only speak about starting up negotiations – like article 6 – but also about bringing them to a conclusion. It also specified the concept of nuclear disarmament and it did not link nuclear to conventional disarmament. If nuclear elimination does not happen, the Court warned: 'In the long run, international law, and with it the stability of the international order which it is intended to govern, are bound to suffer from the continuing difference of views with regard to the legal status of weapons as deadly as nuclear weapons. It is consequently important to put an end to this debate of affairs: the long-promised complete nuclear disarmament appears to be the most appropriate means of achieving that result'[25].

Indications of the growing expectations and the rising tide of anger of the NNWS with regard to elimination can for instance be traced back in the voting behaviour on UN resolutions. What follows is a non-exhaustive list of complaints by the NNWS since 1996:

Malaysia introduced a UN General Assembly resolution in November 1996 based upon the advice of the International Court of Justice calling 'upon all states to fulfil [this] obligation immediately by commencing multilateral negotiations in 1997 leading to an early conclusion of a Nuclear Weapons Convention prohibiting the development, production, testing, deployment, stockpiling, transfer, threat or use of nuclear weapons and providing for their elimination'. In the UN First Committee, the US and 21 other states voted against; 94 including Sweden, Ireland and China voted in favour; 29 states including the EU states Austria, Finland, and Denmark, together with Japan and Australia abstained. In the General Assembly, 115 states voted in favour, 22 voted against and 32 abstained.

In June 1998, paragraph 4 of the Joint Declaration by the Ministers of Foreign Affairs of Brazil, Egypt, Ireland, Mexico, New Zealand, Slovenia, South Africa and Sweden – the so-called New Agenda Coalition – stated: 'We can no longer remain complacent at the reluctance of the NWS and the three nuclear weapons-capable states to take that fundamental and requisite step, namely a clear commitment to the speedy, final and total elimination of their nuclear weapons and nuclear weapons capability and we urge them to take that step now'. The text also referred to the conclusions of the Canberra Commission (see appendix) and the International Court of Justice.

A UN resolution introduced by the New Agenda Coalition (that had lost Slovenia as a result of pressure by the US) led for the first time ever to a split vote between the nuclear and non-nuclear NATO member states in November 1998 despite huge pressure from the US[26]. In the UN First Committee, 97 states including Sweden, Ireland and Austria voted in favour, 19 against and 32 including all the NATO NNWS (except Turkey) abstained.

In November 1998, Germany asked for a no first use policy within NATO.

One month later, the Canadian Parliament published its report *Canada and the nuclear challenge: reducing the political value of nuclear weapons for the twenty first century*. The Canadian government wholeheartedly supported the report.

At the opening of the 2001 UN First Committee meeting UN Under Secretary-General Jayantha Dhanapala said: 'When it comes to weapons of mass destruction, there is no question that the world would be better off pursuing the total and verifiable elimination of such weapons than in perpetuating the fantasy that their possession can be permanently linked to an assortment of exclusive, but by no means leak-proof clubs'[27]. During the conference, the US was the only country that voted against a resolution that asked to put the Comprehensive Test Ban Treaty on the General Assembly's agenda for 2002.

Different writings by the Director-General of the International Atomic Energy Agency (IAEA) Mohamed ElBaradei since 2002 are in favour of 'a timetable'[28] towards nuclear elimination: 'A clear road map for nuclear disarmament should be established, starting with a major reduction in the 30,000 existing nuclear warheads and bringing into force the Comprehensive Nuclear Test Ban Treaty'[29]. In another interview, he reminds us: 'We need to bite the bullet and see how we can move *beyond* nuclear weapons deterrence, and I think that we have not done that yet'[30].

In January 2003, Roberto Amaral, the newly appointed Brazilian minister of science and technology, said in a radio interview that Brazil had nuclear (weapons) ambitions. The year before, presidential candidate Lula da Silva (who later on became president), had made similar comments, referring to the non-compliance of article 6 of the Nuclear Nonproliferation Treaty by the nuclear weapon states[31]. In October 2003, Amaral announced that Brazil would start enriching uranium in 2004[32].

At the NPT Prepcom in April-May 2003, three NATO member states – Belgium, the Netherlands and Norway – repeated their demand in the form of a Working Paper to establish 'without further delay an ad hoc committee in the Conference on Disarmament to deal with nuclear disarmament'[33].

The New Agenda Coalition resolution in October 2003 was for the first time also supported by Finland. Six states voted against (the US, the UK, France, India, Israel and Pakistan), 38 abstained, and 121 voted in favour (including Sweden, Ireland, Austria and Canada). Even Germany apparently hesitated to vote in favour, but finally abstained[34].

In an op-ed article of 27 January 2004, the foreign ministers of Sweden, Greece and Finland criticized the nuclear weapon states: 'Nuclear disarmament is an integral part of the NPT regime…The perception of a lukewarm attitude by the NWS to their NPT commitments…nourish security concerns and resentment. This, in turn, makes our appeal to the aspiring NWS less credible'[35].

In April 2004, the German ambassador to the UN criticized the draft Security Council resolution introduced by the US for combating the proliferation of weapons of mass destruction because the resolution proposed additional obligations for the Non-Nuclear Weapon States and kept quiet about nuclear disarmament[36].

A couple of weeks later, Roberto Abdenur, the Brazilian Ambassador in the US, criticized the American demand for more stringent inspections of the Brazilian nuclear facilities: 'We believe firmly it is not enough to have an increasingly stricter and narrow non-proliferation (agreement) without balanced movement, parallel movement, in the area of disarmament'[37].

Around the same time, the last preparatory meeting for the NPT 2005 Review Conference ended in disarray because of a similar clash between the nuclear weapon states and the non-nuclear weapon states[38].

The nuanced New Agenda Coalition resolution at the UN First Committee got the support of 135 states in October 2004, including seven NATO member states (Canada, Belgium, Germany, Luxemburg, the Netherlands, Norway and Turkey), Japan, Pakistan and China. Twenty-five states abstained and only five voted against (the US, the UK, France, Israel and Latvia).

Like three of its predecessors, also the Seventh NPT Review Conference in May 2005 failed to adopt a final document, basically because of the rivalry between the non-nuclear weapon states and the nuclear weapon states. The level of frustration of the non-nuclear weapon states and especially those of the Non Aligned Movement, represented by Egypt, was high. They felt that they had to fulfill additional obligations (like signing and ratifying the Additional Protocol of the IAEA), while the nuclear weapon state did not take their disarmament obligations seriously. That impression was triggered by the refusal of the US at the 2005 Conference to refer to the '13 disarmament steps' that had been agreed in the 2000 NPT Review Conference. When the US position became clear in the beginning of 2005, the Brazilian ambassador in the US Roberto Abdenur was upset: 'If a nuclear power says the 13 steps belong in the past, what confidence do we non-nuclear developing states have in the NPT ?'[39].

The longer the nuclear weapon states - including the US - wait to eliminate their arsenals, the higher the likelihood that nuclear weapons will spread further to other countries. States situated in a region with a high propensity for conflicts may decide to build nuclear weapons in the future. The latter will be more difficult to prevent in a nuclear weapons world than in a nuclear weapons free world. Some NNWS may also believe that the NWS have no legitimacy anymore to oppose them to go nuclear because they themselves do not fulfil their obligations. NPT signatories situated in regions like the Middle East or East Asia for instance may decide to follow the example of India and Pakistan. Iraq, Iran, Libya and North Korea have already given a glimpse of possible future scenarios. While the Iraqi threat has been "eliminated" by war in March-April 2003 and Libya halted its programme after diplomatic pressure at the end of 2003, the cases of Iran and North Korea seem harder to resolve (see Chapter 6). States like Saudi-Arabia[40], Algeria, Turkey, Egypt and Brazil have also shown an interest in going nuclear. The secret network with the Pakistani Dr. Khan as a key figure that has been discovered after the disclosure of Libya's programme is telling. If the ship indictments of vessels exporting missile components from North Korea to Pakistan in 1999, Scuds from North Korea to Yemen in December 2002, aluminium tubes from Germany to Egypt in April 2003, and centrifuges to Libya in October 2003, as well as terrorism, are added to that the proliferation threat becomes clear.

All this puts enormous strains on the NPT and the overall nonproliferation regime. Although elimination of nuclear weapons would not take away the underlying causes of conflicts, it will complicate the efforts to acquire nuclear weapons considerably. Proliferation can best be prevented in a world with an intrusive verification system. The latter is only possible if all states have the same non-nuclear weapons status. Such a world has the smallest potential for proliferation in the first place because of the absence of nuclear neighbours and the absence of the corresponding security dilemma.

The US still admits that the NPT is crucial with regard to nonproliferation. President Clinton was quite blunt when he noted in March 1995: 'The NPT is the principal reason why scores of nations do not now possess nuclear weapons'[41]. Secretary of State Madeline Albright repeated this three years later: 'A generation ago it was predicted the world would have 20 to 30 nuclear states. No measure has done more than the NPT to prevent that'[42]. After the defeat of the ratification of the Comprehensive Test Ban Treaty in the US Senate, she warned: 'The answer is that global standards do matter. Over the years, nations have increasingly embraced the view that it is unnecessary and dangerous to develop nuclear weapons'[43].

Cliton's Secretary of Defence William Perry apparently even accepted a link between horizontal (more and more countries) and vertical proliferation (more and more nuclear weapons inside one country): 'By reducing our [nuclear] arsenals, we reduce the risk that nuclear weapons or nuclear material will fall into the wrong hands'[44]. Arms Control and Disarmament Agency Director John Holum made the link between proliferation and disarmament clear in 1998 by warning: 'Think about the potential proliferation consequences of an extended delay in US ratification [of the CTBT], accompanied, as would probably be the case, by such a delay in ratification by Russia and China...It could send the message that the weapon states are unwilling to ever break with their cold war reliance on nuclear arms – exactly the wrong signal to send !'[45]. Holum did not only admit a link between US arms control policy and proliferation. He also implicitly admitted in 1998 that the US still relied on a Cold War doctrine.

Lastly, after the Cold War the US found itself in a position that was never more suitable to take the lead in eliminating nuclear weapons. The US was *by far* the only superpower left. The political relations among the five formal nuclear weapon states had never been more favourable since the beginning of the Cold War. The US was the only state in the world with a reliable conventional power projection capability. It possessed the most advanced conventional weapons, which many experts regarded as having sufficient deterrence capability[46]. Some saw a leading role for the US in moving the world towards a NWFW[47]. A shift from a maximum to a minimum deterrence was the least the non-nuclear weapon states expected as a concrete step towards elimination.

A growing consensus on a US minimum deterrence posture after the Cold War

These expectations were shared by a growing number of non-governmental experts after the Cold War both inside and outside the US. The *Strategic Survey* (IISS) observed in 1997-1998: 'In the last few years, there has been a dramatic change and remarkable upsurge of interest in, and support for, abolishing nuclear weapons… The view must now be taken seriously'[48].

There were of course experts who did, and still do, not agree with the above-mentioned expectations, or who do not believe in a minimum deterrence posture. But as far as can be judged on the basis of an overview of the literature, they were in a minority by far. There were only two collective reports or studies criticizing minimum deterrence. There was not a single international report that advocated maximum deterrence. Most strikingly is that most, if not, all of the maximum deterrence advocates were to a certain extent personally linked to the US government (especially the Defence Department and the Department of Energy) and/or the Republican Party.

The two comprehensive studies after the Cold War in favour of maximum deterrence are one led by Robert Joseph and Ronald Lehman *US Nuclear policy in the 21st Century* of August 1998 sponsored by the National Defence University; and the other is *Rationale and Requirements for US Nuclear Forces and Arms Control*, edited by Keith Payne of the National Institute for Public Policy in January 2001.

The overall majority of (non-governmental) experts was in favour of minimum deterrence (see appendix). In principle, all of them regarded elimination as desirable, although there was a difference in perception concerning its feasibility and concerning the extent a new commitment toward that goal was needed. Nearly all of them accepted that this required a step-by-step process spread over a couple of decades. All of them advocated a minimum deterrence posture for the US or at least an amalgam of concrete steps in that direction. Some were of course more radical than others. A few had already advocated steps towards minimum deterrence before 1989; for most of them, the end of the Cold War changed their thinking. Many of them had experience in the US government, some of them at the highest levels.

CHAPTER 3

NUCLEAR FORCE STRUCTURE POLICY

Number of strategic nuclear weapons

The end of the Cold War led to two successful bilateral arms control agreements: the Strategic Arms Reduction Talks Treaty (START) I in 1991 and the Strategic Offensive Reductions Treaty (SORT) in 2002. START II (1993) never entered into force.

START I, the successor of the Strategic Arms Limitation Talks (SALT) II (1979) that on its turn was never ratified, was signed on 31 July 1991. It reduced the number of delivery vehicles to 1,600 and the "accountable" deployed strategic nuclear warheads for each party from 13,000 to 6,000 warheads, of which at most 4,900 warheads on ballistic missiles.

Less than two months after signing START I, President Bush unilaterally announced to take another 10 Poseidon submarines out of the arsenal, each carrying 160 warheads. In his 1992 State of the Union, Bush unilaterally signalled the end of the development of the small "Midgetman" intercontinental ballistic missile (ICBM), a reduction in the acquisition of cruise missiles from 1,461 to 640 and B-2 bombers from 132 to 20, and announced the halt of the W88 warhead production for the Trident II SLBM. He also proposed to eliminate all ICBMs with multiple warheads, to reduce the number of nuclear weapons at sea by a third, and to switch a part of the bombers to a non-nuclear mission. Yeltsin did not agree with disarming the multiple warheads. But a few weeks later Yeltsin on his turn proposed a zero alert and a new arms control treaty with strategic levels of 2,000-2,500. He also proposed putting all sea-launched ballistic missiles (SLBMs) in ports. The US in its turn did not agree with those proposals.

START I was ratified by the US Senate in October 1992 and by Russia one month later. It went into effect in December 1994 and had to be executed before December 2001. However the pace of implementation of START I in the US and Russia differed in the first half of the 1990s. The US started to de-activate all or most of its weapons, while Russia destroyed ICBM complex per ICBM complex.

Already in June 1992, President Yeltsin and President Bush agreed on a "joint understanding" for a follow-up on START (I). The numbers of the deployed strategic nuclear warheads under START II would reduce further from 6,000 to 3,000-3,500 in 2003. The START I levels were further adapted downwards as a result of a different counting method. The most significant element of START II was that the most destabilizing nuclear weapons – the ICBMs with multiple warheads and *in casu* the US MX and the Russian SS-18 as well as their silos – had to be eliminated. The US Minuteman III ICBMs also had to be downloaded from three to one warhead each. The US decided to transfer the MX warheads to the Minuteman III missiles, to store the remainder of the warheads as a hedge, and to denuclearise the B-1 bomber.

START II was signed by outgoing President Bush on 3 January 1993. It reduced the number of deployed strategic nuclear warheads by 50 % to 3,000-3,500, of which at most 1,750 on SLBMs. The US Senate ratified START II in January 1996. The Russian Duma failed to do so until April 2000.

At the Helsinki Summit in March 1997, talks were held on a follow-up START (III) Treaty. But President Clinton insisted that the start of formal negotiations had to wait until the Duma ratified START II. It was agreed in Helsinki that the goal of a future START III Treaty would be to reduce the levels of deployed strategic nuclear weapons to 2,000-2,500 on each side by the end of 2007. In addition, for the first time there was a proposal to add a protocol on the destruction of dismantled missiles and warheads. In Helsinki, the US and Russia also agreed to postpone the implementation date for START II from 1 January 2003 to 31 December 2007. However, the agreement of September 1994 that said that the delivery vehicles had to be de-activated at the end of 2003 was kept.

In 1999, the US unilaterally decided to remove nuclear weapons from four submarines, irrespective of the ratification of START II by the Duma.

In April 2000, the Duma finally ratified START II. But the exchange of instruments and its implementation was linked to the approval by the US Senate of the 1997 Helsinki agreements that included the demarcation agreements with regard to missile defence. US Congress did not agree with these conditions and START II therefore stalled. START II would finally never enter into force.

During the presidential campaign in 2000, George W.Bush had promised to reduce the US nuclear weapons arsenal considerably. In a written answer to questions posed by the *Arms Control Association* in September 2000, candidate Bush criticized the Clinton administration as follows: 'When it comes to nuclear weapons, the world has changed faster than US policy...almost a decade after the end of the Cold War, our nuclear policy resides in that already distant past. The Clinton-Gore administration has had over seven years to bring the US force posture into the post-Cold War world. Instead, they remain locked in a Cold War mentality'. Bush promised: 'America should rethink the requirements for nuclear deterrence in a new security environment. The premises of Cold War nuclear targeting should no longer dictate the size of our arsenal...I will pursue the lowest possible number consistent with our national security. It should be possible to reduce the number of American nuclear weapons *significantly further than* what has already been agreed to under *START II*'[1].

Presidential candidate Bush's biggest defence priority however seemed to be National Missile Defence. In his first major foreign policy speech, candidate Bush proclaimed at the Citadel on 23 September 1999: 'At the earliest date possible, my administration will *deploy* anti-ballistic missiles, both theatre and *national*'. In the eyes of the Republicans, the Anti-Ballistic Missile (ABM) treaty (1972) had to be abolished. He continued: 'If Russia refuses the changes [to the ABM treaty] we propose, we will give prompt notice, under the provisions of the treaty, that we can no longer be a party to it'[2].

In office, the George W.Bush administration first tried to convince the Russians to agree with the burial of the ABM treaty. When this approach failed, it proposed reductions in the field of offensive strategic nuclear weapons as a kind of bargaining tool, or at least as a softener, vis-à-vis Russia. At the Bush-Putin summit in Crawford (Texas) in November 2001, President Bush announced a *unilateral* reduction of the American deployed strategic weapons to 1,700-2,200 in 2013. Three weeks later, on 13 December 2001, President Bush finally did what the arms control community had hoped that would never occur, namely the announcement of the unilateral withdrawal from the ABM treaty.

Contrary to what could have been expected, Russia's reaction was muted. Although President Putin criticized the American decision, he did not announce retaliatory measures. Instead Putin announced similar strategic weapons reductions, although he also asked to codify the unilateral statements in a formal treaty. Reluctantly, the Bush administration agreed. Reportedly, President Bush personally had to convince Secretary of Defence Rumsfeld, who did not like the idea of a legally binding treaty. On 13 March 2002, President Bush said 'that there needs to be a document that outlives [both of us]'[3]. The Strategic Offensive Reductions Treaty (SORT) was signed in Moscow on 24 May 2002. The treaty, which in contrast to former treaties is only a few paragraphs long, pointed out that the US and Russia would reduce their arsenals to the level of 1,700-2,200 deployed strategic nuclear weapons in 2013. The US unilaterally agreed to reach the level of 3,800 deployed strategic warheads in 2007. To reach the levels outlined in SORT, the US is planning to remove four submarines from strategic service (as was already agreed in the Clinton administration) and to retire the 50 MX missiles. However, in contrast to START II, the Bush Nuclear Posture Review prescribes to retain the MX silos.
On 20 June 2002, SORT was submitted for ratification to the Senate. SORT was ratified by the US Senate in March 2003 and by the Russian Duma two months later. The first meeting of the Bilateral Implementation Commission established under SORT took place in April 2004.

How should we evaluate these reductions ? At first sight, the apparent massive reductions in the US nuclear arsenal seem quite an achievement. A more detailed look yields a more balanced view. The number of deployed strategic nuclear warheads in 2003 – 6,500 – was *more* than the corresponding numbers in 1960, 1965 or 1970, the year when the Nuclear Nonproliferation Treaty entered into force. The US arsenal, for instance, still contained 600 B-83 bombs – of which 480 deployed – each with a maximum yield of 1.2 megaton, which is 85 times more powerful than the Hiroshima bomb.

What is the relative weight of building down a substantial number after first having built up an irrational overkill-capacity, especially if the build-down does not really affect this overkill-capacity ? Former Secretary of Defence Robert

McNamara explains: 'it is doubtful that survivors – if there were any – of an exchange of 3,200 warheads (the US and Russian numbers projected for 2012), with a destructive power approximately 65,000 times that of the Hiroshima bomb, could detect a difference between the effects of such an exchange and one that would result from the launch of the current US and Russian forces totalling about 12,000 warheads'[4]. The reaction of the *Financial Times* to the signing of SORT is therefore not surprising: 'It is hard to see why either Washington or Moscow needs to preserve arsenals of 2,000 nuclear warheads. A figure of 200 would have given a much more positive signal'[5]. Former CINCSAC General Lee Butler, when retired, claimed: 'Arsenals in the hundreds, much less in the thousands, can serve no meaningful objective…they owe more to bureaucratic politics and political demagoguery than to any defensible strategic rationale'[6].

Beside operational and deployed nuclear weapons, hundreds of weapons and warheads are being stored. They can be used to build up the operational levels quickly. The INF, START and SORT agreements, for instance, called only for reductions in *deployed* strategic nuclear weapons. On the other hand, the US did dismantle nuclear weapons after the Cold War, 13,000 in total. The rate of destruction diminished in the second half of the 1990s and beyond.

The US government will probably defend itself by declaring that it too regards the existing arsenal as excessive and that it foresees further reductions in the future. This, however, also has to be put in perspective. Firstly, the number of deployed strategic nuclear weapons is supposed to fall to 3,800 in 2007. The latter are still the same numbers as during the Cuban missile crisis. Under SORT, that must only be implemented in 2013, there will still be more strategic warheads on missiles than in 1970 when the Nuclear Nonproliferation Treaty entered into force.

Secondly, as Russia withdrew from START II one day after the US left the ABM Treaty in June 2002, Russia will for instance keep its destabilizing SS-18 ICBMs (with multiple warheads).

Sub-strategic nuclear weapons

Most US sub-strategic nuclear weapons were no longer deployed after the Cold War. President Bush also scrapped the modernization of the nuclear artillery shells and the follow-on of the Lance short-range missile in May 1990. In September 1991, after the coup against Gorbachev, he unilaterally decided to destroy all nuclear artillery shells, nuclear depth bombs and ground-launched tactical nuclear missiles, and to remove sub-strategic nuclear weapons from surface ships and attack submarines. This was already accomplished in June 1992. Bush also decided to end the MX rail programme and the programme for short-range attack missiles for bombers. The development of two other tactical air-to-surface missiles was also cancelled. Gorbachev responded with similar plans in October 1991.

Through the Spratt-Furse Amendment, Congress prohibited research and development of low-yield nuclear weapons, the so-called 'mini-nukes', in 1993. One year later, President Clinton decided not to re-deploy naval tactical nuclear weapons. Also 320 SLCMs to be stationed on attack submarines were stored on land. However the dual aircraft capability of the Navy carriers had to be maintained. The 650 B61 bombs of which 480 are based in Europe also remained. In 1997, a new (tactical) nuclear weapon was introduced into the US arsenal, namely the B-61-11 earth-penetrating bomb (see chapter 11).

Clinton's Assistant Secretary of Defence Ed Warner defended the existence of sub-strategic nuclear weapons in the US arsenal in a hearing on 31 March 1998 as follows: 'The Nuclear Posture Review reaffirmed that we not only need a strategic nuclear deterrent, but also flexible, responsive, *non-strategic* nuclear forces. Maintaining the capability to deploy nuclear forces to meet various regional contingencies continues to be an important means for deterring aggression, protecting and promoting US interests, and reassuring Allies and friends'[7].

The George W.Bush administration kept the same policy, but in addition favoured the development of new low-yield nuclear weapons – the mini-nukes – and a more capable nuclear earth-penetrator – the so-called 'bunker-buster' – that could be used against hardened targets like underground facilities in "rogue states" that are suspected of producing weapons of mass destruction (see chapter 11). In 2002, already $10 million was spent on a study to modify an existing warhead. One year later, in November 2003, Congress lifted the 10-year old ban on research and development of low-yield nuclear weapons. This allowed the Bush administration to carry out research and development on mini-nukes. For the advanced development phase a new approval is needed from Congress[8]. In addition, $15 million was approved for the development of a high-yield Robust Nuclear Earth Penetrator, the so-called "bunker-buster"[9]. In March 2004, the head of the National Nuclear Security Administration Linton Brooks stated that the whole program could cost $485 million over the next five years[10].

The main criticism against mini-nukes and bunker-busters is that they further legitimise nuclear weapons and may therefore stimulate nuclear proliferation. From a military perspective, bunker-busters may not work. The enemy can simply dig a bit deeper. As Stanford physicist Sidney Drell writes: 'Taking into account realistic limits on material strengths, about 50 feet is the maximum depth to which a warhead dropped from the air into dry rock soil could maintain its integrity until detonated…For the shock to reach down to 1,000 feet with enough strength to destroy a hard target in dry rock, the warhead would require a yield significantly larger than 100 kilotons'[11]. The latter cannot be called 'mini-nukes'. Scientists also maintain that even mini-nukes would create dangerous plumes of radioactive dust. A one-kiloton nuclear weapon detonated 10 metres underground would dig a crater bigger than a football field and would eject one million cubic feet of radioactive debris into the air. In addition, mini-nukes would be more likely to disseminate chemical or biological agents in bunkers than incinerate them. Presidential candidate John Kerry followed this criticism in his 1 June 2004 speech: 'As President, I will stop this Administration's programme to develop a whole new generation of bunker-busting nuclear bombs. This is a weapon we don't need. And it undermines our credibility in persuading other nations. What kind of message does it send when we're asking other countries not to develop nuclear weapons, but developing new ones ourselves ?'[12].

Strategic parity
Strategic parity between the US and Russia, which corresponds to the goal of possessing more or less the same number of nuclear weapons as the opponent, remained the dominant paradigm after the Cold War. The START I, START II and SORT agreements – like the SALT I and INF Treaties during the Cold War – are examples of balanced reductions. Even the so-called unilateral reductions

announced by Bush in September 1991 were part of a *de facto* reciprocal agreement with Gorbachev.

When the US Senate ratified START II in 1996, it added the explicit requirement always to retain at least roughly the same number of strategic nuclear weapons as Russia. For instance, the National Defence Authorization Act fiscal year 1998 signed by President Clinton in November 1997 stated that START I levels had to be maintained as long as Russia had not ratified START II.

The George W.Bush administration declared on different occasions that the period of strategic parity as well as MAD was over. However, there are no indications that this is the case. In a congressional hearing on SORT in July 2002, Secretary of Defence Rumsfeld made it abundantly clear 'that it would not be in [the interest of other states] to think they could sprint to parity or superiority'. US nuclear weapons levels would still be sufficiently high that countering them 'would require a substantial investment' over a long period of time[13].

With arsenals numbering thousands, the logic behind strategic parity can easily be questioned. The underlying military reason for strategic parity – the fear of a first-strike – was already subject to a lot of criticism during the Cold War. However, the underlying fear of a first strike still dominated thinking in February 2002, at least in the mind of Under Secretary of State for Arms Control and International Security John Bolton, who stated: 'The overall question is whether we think we've got a deterrent capability that's robust enough to prevent a first use against us and also that we've got an adequately sized force in the event there's a need to use it'[14]. To proclaim that Russia had the capabilities and the intention to disarm the US nuclear arsenal after the Cold War in such a way that the US could have not retaliated without causing a lot of havoc however makes no sense. As Bruce Blair maintained: 'Such a pre-meditated genocidal attack by either the US or Russia against each other is implausible and unthinkable, almost as absurd as a British or French attack on the US'[15].

"Hedging"

Opponents of minimum deterrence have pointed to the possibility of a possible deterioration in the US-Russian relationship in the medium or long-term. Economic and social instability could lead to political chaos and a new autocratic regime. This line of thinking led the US to adopt a "hedge" policy during the Nuclear Posture Review in 1993-1994: to retain a capability to upload the existing nuclear force structure (and future force levels) to Cold War levels. The US decided for instance to keep sufficient delivery vehicles with multiple warheads, especially Trident II SLBMs and Minuteman III ICBMs, which could be uploaded with reserve warheads if needed. It is worth quoting Clinton's Special Assistant for National Security Affairs Bob Bell in length who explained this policy in January 1999 as follows: 'Our strategy says that while [a Russian nuclear strike] is unthinkable today, and while we are going to do everything in our power to help Russia to keep them on the road to democratisation and free market economy reform, that we have to *hedge* against the remote but not non-zero [sic] prospect of a reversal in which intentions change much faster than capabilities could be restored'…'Now if you were to conclude not only that it's "implausible, unthinkable and almost absurd" to imagine a strategic exchange with Russia, not only today, next week, but, into the next decades of the 21st century, if it really is "over, over there", and that is forever and with very, very high certainty then, of course, much more would be possible in terms of reducing the central strategic numbers'[16].

There are, however, some problems with the logic behind hedging. The US hedge capability is superior than that of Russia. The Russian reconstitution capability would only have been 35-50 % of the US under START II and 40-60 % under START III[17].

In addition, the principle of hedging does not make sense with the current number of weapons. Hedging against potential political surprises may be part of a prudent security policy in case of very low numbers. This was (and still is) not yet the case. The following conversation between senator Dale Bumpers and Secretary of Defence William Perry in March 1995 is highly indicative: 'I am told that Russia has about 500 cities with 50,000 or more people. START II then will leave us with six or seven operational nuclear warheads for each of those cities. Is that not enough to deter even a resurgent Russia, regardless of how many strategic nuclear weapons it has ?' Perry answered: 'The US START II force is based on the tenet of "rough equivalency". Therefore, a START II force would be *insufficient* for deterring a resurgent Russia that is non-compliant with its treaty obligations'[18]. In other words, Perry was saying that more than 3,000 deployed strategic nuclear weapons, of which most on alert, were *not* sufficient as a deterrent against a resurgent Russia...

US superiority

Russia has neither the financial means nor the economic infrastructure to maintain high nuclear force levels after the Cold War. In the 1990s, it was expected that the Russian nuclear infrastructure, including its strategic nuclear weapons arsenal, was deteriorating to such an extent that Russia would have reached the START II or even START III or SORT levels much earlier than the US because most of its weapons systems were at the end of their lifetime. In 1998, General Yakovlev stated that 62 % of Russian ICBMs were already beyond their guaranteed lifetime. Only 19-28 nuclear submarines remained operational, of which only two were at sea at any given time[19]. Only 70 Russian strategic bombers were left in 1997[20]. In 2004, 700 Russian ICBMs with 3,100 warheads remained.

Some new systems have been built or were in the process of being built be able to maintain at least START III or SORT levels in the future. The silo-based single-warhead SS-27 Topol-M – the first ten were deployed in December 1997 – was planned as the backbone of the future Russian ICBM force. However the programme ran into financial difficulties. At the end of 2003, only 40 missiles had been built. Other systems, like a mobile ICBM with multiple warheads and a new nuclear submarine, are in the process of being built[21]. A new bomber is planned for 2014-2016. But even Clinton's Assistant Secretary of Defence Ed Warner admitted: 'fiscal realities suggest that, even with these replacement programmes, significant declines in Russia's strategic forces are still to come'[22]. The large nuclear weapons exercise in February 2004, right before the Russian presidential elections, turned out to be a nightmare. Many missiles experienced launch failures.

As a result, the US probably never enjoyed a better first-strike capability against Russia than in the second half of the 1990s, especially taking into account the accuracy of the D-5 Trident SLBMs. According to Blair and von Hippel, 'at any given time Russia has perhaps 200 survivable warheads, while the US has approximate 2,000'[23]. This is another reason why Russia was and still is concerned about a US national missile defence system.

Furthermore, the *quality* of the US nuclear weapons arsenal is much better. This applies especially to the hard-target capability that is supposed to be used against hardened ICBM silos. Under SORT, the US number of hard-target capability weapons is 684 while the Russian number would only be 60-80 % of that amount[24]. In any event these high levels of hard-target capability make no sense because there will not be many hard targets left. There are only 500 hardened Soviet targets, including 200 "less" hardened targets like support command and storage facilities[25].

Triad

The famous triad made up of ICBMs, SLBMs and bombers was, and still is, in place after the Cold War. Fewer numbers of delivery vehicles have been ordered than planned during the Cold War. President George W.H.Bush for instance reduced the number of B-2s ordered from 132 to 20. The Clinton administration, in contrast, ordered one additional B-2.

New delivery vehicles – like a small ICBM – have been cancelled. Ed Warner stated in 1998: 'We have no development or procurement programmes for a next-generation bomber, ICBM, SLBM, or strategic submarine. The programmes we do have are designed to sustain the safety, reliability, and effectiveness of our remaining forces, and to ensure the continued high quality of our strategic forces'[26]. This statement must be put in perspective. Firstly, it is said in a *Nuclear Weapons Systems Sustainment* document released by the Defence Department, that 'a follow-on Submarine Launched Ballistic Missile (SLBM) is intended'[27]. In the Annual Report of the Secretary of Defence of January 2000, it was noted that 'the Air Force has begun exploratory tasks to plan for a replacement to the Minuteman III [ICBM] around 2020'[28]. A Defence Science Board report of October 1998 also pointed to the need for the development of new strategic submarines to be deployed in 2025, a long-range plan for strategic bombers, and the development of some nuclear capable Joint Strike Fighter aircraft[29].

Secondly, old weapons are being replaced by new ones. The longer-range and more accurate Trident II (D-5) SLBMs will replace the remaining Trident I (C-4) SLBMs on four nuclear submarines. As a result, all nuclear submarines will have the more accurate D-5 missiles installed by 2006. These missiles were and are still being built *after* the Cold War for the total cost of $37.5 billion or $66 million per missile. Production has been extended through 2013 and the total number to be produced is 540 instead of the 390 initially planned. For instance, the *Alaska* test-launched its first D-5 missile in March 2002 and was fully operational three months later[30]. The Navy plans to spend another $5 billion in the next decade on modernizing Trident II to extend its service life until 2040[31].

Thirdly, some parts of the delivery vehicles continue to be modernized. For instance, SLBMs received a new re-targeting system in 2003 to support the principle of adaptive targeting and to make it possible to attack mobile targets. For $6 billion, the Minuteman III ICBMs are also having new guidance systems installed, which will improve their accuracy, and they will be re-motored. This will extend their service life at least until the year 2020. A Rapid Execution and Combat

Targeting system has also been installed in ICBM alert facilities in the second half of the 1990s[32].

Fourthly, not all ordered systems were cancelled after the Cold War. For instance, a new nuclear submarine was commissioned in September 1997. The twentieth B-2 had its maiden flight in 1998.

These modernization programmes are not only intended to keep the existing quality, but to improve it. When Senator Warner asked DOD J-5 Director Wesley Clark in 1995 whether the reduction from 18 to 14 submarines did not signify a bargaining low, Clark answered: 'What we have done, senator, is when we went through the nuclear posture review we looked at all of the modernization requirements for the forces. We tried to pick the best balance *within the triad*, and then picking the modernization that was required to keep each of the systems up to *peak* operating capability or take advantage of *new* technology'[33].

The George W.Bush administration introduced the concept of the "New Triad": offensive nuclear and non-nuclear weapons, (missile) defence, and a reliable basic nuclear infrastructure. The old triad, however, remains in place and will probably remain so until at least 2013. The head of the US Strategic Command Gen.Mies repeated the advantages of each leg of the triad in July 2001 as follows: '*ICBMs* continue to provide a reliable, low cost, prompt response capability with a high readiness rate. They also promote stability by ensuring that a potential adversary takes their geographically dispersed capabilities into account if contemplating a disarming first-strike...The *strategic submarine* force is the most survivable leg of the triad, providing the US with a powerful, assured response capability against any adversary...The US must preserve a sufficiently large strategic nuclear submarine force to enable two-ocean operations with sufficient assets to ensure an at-sea response force capable of deterring any adversary in a crisis...*Strategic bombers*...allow force dispersal to improve survivability and aircraft recall during mission execution. The low-observable technology of the B-2 bomber enables it to penetrate heavily defended areas and hold high-value targets at risk deep inside an adversary's territory...the B-52 bomber can be employed in a stand-off role using long-range cruise missile to attack from outside enemy air defences'[34]. The George W.Bush's NPR called for a new ICBM to be operational in 2020, a new SLBM by 2030 and a new bomber by 2040.

The argument in favour of a triad fails if we consider that submarines have become more or less invulnerable and possess a hard-target capability since the introduction of the D-5 Tridents. SLBMs could therefore easily do the deterrent job alone. To argue, as the Clinton NPR did, that Russia – in economic disarray – might find a breakthrough in antisubmarine warfare is not very convincing. The authors of the 1993 GAO report *The US Nuclear Triad*, who had access to classified data, concluded that 'submerged SSBNs are even less detectable than is generally understood, and that there appear to be no current or long-term technologies that would change this. Moreover, even if such technologies did exist, test and operational data show that the survivability of the SSBN fleet would not be in question'[35]. Even in the unlikely event of non-survivability of submarines, relying on the combination of submarines and bombers might do the job. If one leg of the triad should be removed, most experts agree that it should be ICBMs[36].

Maintaining a triad is another indication of the maximum deterrent nature of US nuclear policy after the Cold War. Despite the fact that even CINCSAC Habiger agreed in 1996 that 'it may become more difficult in time to sustain each leg of the triad as forces are drawn down further'[37] and that one of his successors, Gen. Lance Lord launched the idea to seek alternative uses for the ICBMs (such as conventional precision strikes or missile defence)[38], it seems unlikely that there will be any change before 2012.

Total number of warheads and delivery vehicles
Immediately after the Cold War in 1990, the US possessed 21,000 nuclear warheads, 1,000 ICBMs, 608 SLBMs and 324 long-range bombers[39]. In 1993, the US arsenal contained 16,750 warheads in total, 550 ICBMs, 440 SLBMs and 192 bombers. Five years later, the US had 12,070 warheads, 550 ICBMs, 432 SLBMs and 92 bombers. For 2003, the numbers are 10,642 warheads, 540 ICBMs, 384 SLBMs and 72 bombers.

A more detailed description of the levels of US strategic nuclear delivery vehicles and warheads in 2004 is as follows[40]:
-    72 long-range bombers (carrying 1,660 warheads): 56 B-52s (with advanced cruise missiles or air-launched cruise missiles) and 16 B-2s (each carrying at most 16 B83, B61-7 or B61-11 bombs);
-    529 ICBMs (carrying in total 1,490 warheads): 29 MX each carrying ten W87 warheads; and 500 Minuteman III missiles (three wings) each carrying W78 or W62 warheads, either one or three warheads per missile;
-    360 Trident I (C-4) and Trident II (D-5) SLBMs on 15 Ohio-class submarines[41] (in two bases[42]) carrying 2,736 W88 or W76 warheads in total.

The total number of deployed strategic nuclear warheads in 2004 was 5,886. The corresponding figure for Russia was 5,000. The number of deployed sub-strategic nuclear weapons at the beginning of 2004 was 1,120. Russia in contrast was estimated at having deployed at least 3,380 in 2002[43]. The total number of operational nuclear warheads in 2004 therefore was 7,006 for the US and 8,400 for Russia.

To get the total of actual warheads, three other categories must be added:
1. Spare warheads for operational forces: 382 in 2004. The subtotal operational warheads and spares corresponded to 7,388 in 2004.
2. Active reserves for strategic warheads as a "hedge" or augmentation force for possible redeployment on bombers and missiles; and inactive reserves of strategic and sub-strategic warheads in case of reliability and safety problems: 3,000.
3. Warheads waiting to be dismantled: a few hundred in 2004.
As a result, the total number of actual US warheads (operational + spares + "hedge" + inactive reserve + waiting to be dismantled) was more or less 11,000 in 2004[44]. The corresponding destructive capacity in 2004 was still more than 2,000 megatons of TNT[45].

On 1 June 2004, the Bush administration announced that the US would reduce the total stockpile of warheads by almost one-half before 2013. It is estimated that the total stockpile would then amount to 6,000 warheads and bombs, of which 2,000 strategic operational nuclear weapons, as agreed upon under SORT in 2000[46].

	US	USSR/Russia
1989	22,174	35,805
1990	21,211	33,417
1991	18,306	28,595
1992	13,731	25,155
1993	11,536	22,101
1994	11,012	18,399
1995	10,953	14,978
1996	10,886	12,085
1997	10,829	11,264
1998	10,763	10,764
1999	10,698	10,451
2000	10,615	10,201
2001	10,491	9,126
2002	10,600	8,600
2003	10,650	?
2004	10,388	?

Table 2: Total number of US and Russian strategic and sub-strategic nuclear warheads after the Cold War[47]

Beside the total number of warheads, there are still two other categories relevant for a possible future build-up:
1) the so-called 'pits' from dismantled warheads, i.e. a hollow shell of plutonium clad in a corrosion-resistant metal[48], which can be re-used: 5,000 in 2003, which corresponds to 15 tons of plutonium. The total number of actual US warheads and the pits and secondaries from dismantled weapons added up to 17,000 in 2003. These numbers correspond to Cold War levels.

The Clinton administration decided to build a new facility in Los Alamos to rebuild pits – the core of nuclear warheads – for the W88 with a planned production later on of up to 80 warheads per year, despite the fact that President George W.H.Bush had announced in 1992 that the production of W88 would halt[49]. In April 2003, Los Alamos produced its first "certifiable" pit since for 14 years and it set itself a goal of producing 20 pits per year. The George W.Bush administration plans a "modern" pit facility that would be able to produce 125-450 pits per year in 2020.

2) Stocks of fissile material: there is enough fissile material in the US after the Cold War for making thousands of additional nuclear warheads: 50 tons of plutonium (beside 35 in the 10,000 stockpile and the 15 tons already mentioned) and 420 tons of highly-enriched uranium (beside 225 tons in the 10,000 stockpile)[50].

In January 1992, President Yeltsin declared a halt to the production of fissile material for military purposes in the year 2000 and advocated a bilateral agreement. President Bush announced a stop of production of "military" plutonium in July 1992 formalizing the existing situation since 1988.

In his speech at the UN General Assembly in September 1993, President Clinton promised that the US would place some of its excess military plutonium under the control of the International Atomic Energy Agency and proposed a multilateral and verifiable convention prohibiting the production of highly enriched uranium and plutonium for nuclear explosive purposes (a so-called "cut-off treaty").

In June 1994, the US and Russia signed an agreement to halt production of weapons-grade plutonium. Five months later, the US purchased and successfully removed 600 kg of highly enriched uranium from Kazakhstan with the consent of Russia, code-named "Project Sapphire".

The Clinton administration also decided to withdraw 200 tons of fissile material, of which 38 tons of weapons grade plutonium, from the nuclear stockpile in March 1995. Two months later, the Clinton-Yeltsin summit resulted in a joint statement pledging never again to build nuclear weapons from excess uranium or plutonium from dismantled weapons, newly produced fissile material, or civil material. In 1996, the US announced that it would eliminate its excess highly enriched uranium by blending it to lowly enriched uranium. The US also offered a $100 million research and aid package to Russia in February 2000 on the condition that Russia halted its reprocessing and "civilian" plutonium programmes.

The Bush administration continued most of these programs, but reversed US policy with respect to the so-called cut-off treaty in July 2004 by stating that the US was no longer interested in adding a verification mechanism. The latter contradicts the conclusions of the 2000 NPT Review Conference. In addition, different US-Russian cooperation agreements came to a halt because of liability problems.

Prompt launch capability

In September 1991 President Bush decided to take the bombers off alert. The prompt launch capability of the missile force, however, remained in place after the Cold War.

To maintain a prompt launch missile capability in the post-Cold War period is not only another indication of a maximum deterrence posture, but is also at odds with the overall US foreign policy goal of co-operating with Russia. A prompt launch policy can only be legitimised out of fear for a first-strike. The only state that has a first-strike capability (although only in theory) and that at the same time is regarded as a partner is Russia.

Nuclear weapons stationed abroad

The ministers of defence at the informal NATO summit in Taormina in October 1991 agreed with President Bush's proposal to remove 80 % of the American sub-strategic nuclear weapons out of Europe: 3,000 artillery shells and short-range missile warheads and 2,000 additional warheads, something which was already accomplished in October 1992. All US nuclear weapons were removed from South Korea in 1992. On safety and financial grounds, there are advocates inside the Pentagon for withdrawing all from Europe as well[51]. At the NATO's meeting in December 2003, the idea of withdrawing all American nuclear weapons from Europe was discussed (also in the framework of restructuring the American bases in Europe), but apparently nothing was decided.

In total, 480 B61 nuclear free-fall bombs for dual-capable aircraft remained in Germany, Belgium, the Netherlands, Italy, Greece, Turkey and the UK. The weapons from Greece were removed in 2001. Each of the warheads has four yield options: 0.3 KT; 1.5 KT; 10 or 60 KT (depending on the version of the B61); and 45, 80 or 170 KT (depending on the version of the B61). The George W.Bush administration first called for modernizing these facilities in Europe to maintain the system through 2018[52]. NATO's Nuclear Planning Group confirmed on 9 June 2005 that: 'The nuclear forces based in Europe and committed to NATO continue to provide an essential political and military link between the European and North American members of the Alliance'[53].

At the end of 2003, there were rumours that most, if not all, of the American nuclear weapons would be withdrawn from Europe as a result of the restructuring of American military bases in Western Europe, and especially Germany. The NATO Supreme Allied Commander Europe (SACEUR) Gen.Jones confirmed in a hearing at the Belgian Senate on 9 March 2004 that there would be another round of 'significant reductions' of American nuclear weapons in Europe[54]. In October 2004, Hans Kristensen, researcher at the NRDC, denied that any changes had taken place (yet)[55]. According to *The New York Times* of 13 February 2005, Gen.Jones even stated informally 'that he favours eliminating the American nuclear stockpile in Europe'. But he added that that idea had met resistance from some NATO political leaders[56].

It is difficult to find a military or strategic rationale for these weapons. The main justification for the presence of American sub-strategic nuclear weapons in Europe during the Cold War was that a Russian conventional attack against Europe could have been answered without fearing immediate escalation to the intercontinental nuclear level. This policy of extended deterrence was never perceived as very credible by either side. It completely lost its remaining legitimacy after the Cold War. Russia had neither the intention nor the conventional capabilities for attacking Europe. As a result, there was no longer any military rationale to keep them in Europe. The Italian Minister Edo Ronchi, for instance, proclaimed in October 1999: 'The [American] warheads should absolutely be eliminated in all of Europe. There is no reason to keep them after the end of the cold war'[57].

US government officials disagreed. 'Nuclear forces based in Europe and committed to NATO provide an *essential* political *and military* link between the European and North American members of the Alliance. The presence of North American conventional and nuclear forces in Europe remains *vital* to the security of Europe', declared Under Secretary of Defence for Policy Walter Slocombe in 1997[58]. The 2001 NPR also stated: 'Dual capable aircraft and deployed weapons are important to the continued viability of NATO's nuclear deterrent strategy and any changes need to be discussed within the alliance'[59].

Another reason for keeping American nuclear weapons in Europe during the Cold War was to prevent Germany from building its own nuclear weapons. As late as 1991, Secretary of Defence Dick Cheney warned: 'If the United States cuts back so much that all we can do and all we can talk about is defending the continental US, we'll create an incentive for other nations that do not now feel the need to develop their own nuclear arsenals to do so'[60]. Implicitly he referred to Germany. Keith Payne, who was closely involved in the 2001 NPR, repeated this argument in 2005 vis-à-vis Japan[61].

This logic, however, does not sound very credible, as both Germany and Japan are non-nuclear weapon states that seem to take nuclear disarmament seriously. Germany's proposals for a nuclear weapons register[62] and a "no first use" are just two examples. According to Harald Müller, Americans regularly underestimate how deeply Germany's non-nuclear status is rooted in German political culture: 'Any German government that sought to effect a change in the country's nuclear status would risk public protest ranging all the way up to civil-war-style conditions compared to which the events surrounding the shifting of Castor containers would probably appear trivial'[63]. Right before the 2005 NPT Review Conference, the SPD, the FDP and the Greens in Germany said to be in favour of withdrawing the American nuclear weapons from Germany. German Defence Minister Peter Struck was willing to start a debate inside NATO. Also the Belgian parliament adopted a resolution in April 2005 demanding 'the gradual withdrawal' of the American nuclear weapons from Belgium.

The benefits of keeping American nuclear weapons in Europe for other – read political and bureaucratic – reasons has to be balanced against costs like possible negative perceptions in Russia and the non-nuclear weapon states. Russian Gen.Yuri Baluyevsky stated in 2003: '[US] tactical nuclear weapons deployed in Europe are for Russia acquiring a strategic nature since theoretically they could be used on our command centres and strategic nuclear centres'[64].

	US nuclear weapons policy during the Cold War	US nuclear weapons policy after the Cold War	Categorization of US nuclear weapons after the Cold War
Number of nuclear warheads	25,000-35,000 (of which 15,000 strategic)	11,500 (of which more than 8,000 strategic) in 2004	Maximum
Sub-strategic nuclear weapons	Yes	Yes	Maximum
Strategic parity	Yes	Yes	Maximum
Triad	Yes (since 1960)	Yes	Maximum
Prompt launch capability	Yes (since the end of the 1950s)	Yes	Maximum
Nuclear weapons based in other states	Yes, since 1950s in Europe and South Korea	Yes, but only in Europe	Maximum

Table 3: US nuclear force structure policy

CHAPTER 4

NUCLEAR DECLARATORY POLICY

Nuclear deterrence in general

As the Soviet threat disappeared, the overall emphasis on nuclear deterrence decreased. The NATO summit in London in 1990 regarded nuclear weapons as "weapons of last resort". Under pressure from France and the UK, however, this concept disappeared in NATO's Strategic Concept of November 1991, which stated that: 'Nuclear weapons make a unique contribution in rendering the risks of any aggression incalculable and unacceptable...The fundamental purpose of the nuclear forces of the Allies is political: to preserve peace and prevent coercion and any kind of war. They will continue to fulfil an *essential* role by ensuring uncertainty in the mind of any aggressor about the nature of the Allies' response to military aggression. They demonstrate that aggression of any kind is not a rational option'[1]. These sentences were repeated word for word in NATO's New Strategic Concept of April 1999.

Further, President Clinton's Presidential Decision Directive-60 of November 1997 formally put an end to the so-called prevailing strategy. This doctrine, established by President Reagan in 1981, stated that a nuclear war was winnable[2]. PDD-60 meant a substantial change in declaratory policy in the direction of minimum deterrence. The Reagan doctrine required the US to be able to fight and win a so-called protracted nuclear war, lasting weeks or more. It corresponded to an extreme form of maximum deterrence. Government officials in the Clinton administration admitted that the prevailing doctrine had never been taken seriously. 'What is different,..., is that we have not carried over what we think was an *unrealistic* – from the beginning – directive from President Reagan that we have a force capable of fighting and winning a protracted nuclear war', explained Clinton's National Security Council Special Assistant Bob Bell[3]. It was President Reagan himself who, together with Gorbachev in 1985, declared that a nuclear war could *not* be won. Lastly, operational policy was such that the US was probably never able to fight and win a nuclear war.

What is not trivial, however, is that this prevailing doctrine constituted formal presidential guidance for US nuclear policy for over 15 years, with major implications for force structure and operational policy. By signing PDD-60, President Clinton changed this doctrine in November 1997.

The reduced emphasis on nuclear deterrence, however, must be put in perspective. The US did *not* declare that it would never be the first to use nuclear weapons. It did not exclude any scenario. The major goal after the Cold War was still to create uncertainty in the "enemy's" mind. According to the Defence Department, the mission of US strategic forces was 'to deter aggression against the United States or its allies and to convince potential adversaries that initiating an attack would be futile'[4]. On his visit to Los Alamos Laboratory on 3 February 1998, President Clinton declared: 'our national security requires that we maintain a nuclear arsenal strong enough to deter *any* adversary'[5].

The 2001 NPR also repeated classic Cold War language: 'Nuclear weapons play a *critical role* in the defence capabilities of the United States, its allies and friends…These nuclear capabilities possess *unique properties* that give the United States options to hold at risk classes of targets [that are] important to achieve strategic and political objectives'[6].

One major argument for keeping nuclear weapons is to deter a *nuclear* weapons attack. President Clinton noted in his National Security Strategy of July 1994: 'We will retain strategic nuclear forces sufficient to deter any future hostile foreign leadership with access to strategic nuclear forces from acting against our vital interests and to convince it that seeking a nuclear advantage would be futile. Therefore we will continue to maintain nuclear forces of sufficient size and capability to hold at risk a broad range of assets valued by such political and military leaders'[7].

Sometimes the US explicitly talked about a possible nuclear attack of *Russia*. Assistant Secretary of Defence Ed Warner pointed out in March 1998: 'We cannot be so certain of future Russian politics as to ignore the possibility that we may once again need to deter the nuclear forces of a hostile Russia should the current policy of democratic reform be replaced by a return to aggressive authoritarianism. We do not believe that such a reversal is likely and we are working hard to avoid it. Nevertheless, it is prudent to maintain a secure and capable nuclear force as a hedge against it happening'. Warner also legitimised the US nuclear arsenal vis-à-vis *China*: 'China has a significant nuclear capability, and its future political orientation is far from certain'[8]. Lastly, the US mentioned *future "rogue states"* with nuclear weapons as a reason to keep nuclear weapons.

Nuclear deterrence vis-à-vis chemical and biological weapons attacks
Another major argument to keep American nuclear weapons was, and still is, to deter chemical and biological weapons attacks. That is new since the end of the Cold War. A scenario that would legitimise the use of nuclear weapons in the eyes of its advocates, is the following: the US is attacked by biological weapons, that 100,000 Americans are killed, that the attacking state is known, that there is reliable intelligence that the attacker will attack again, and that nuclear weapons are much better than conventional weapons in destroying the remaining biological weapons arsenal[9].

In 1990, Secretary of Defence Dick Cheney was the first senior political appointee emphasizing the possible use of nuclear weapons in case of a chemical or biological weapons attack, using the term "weapons of mass destruction". 'We are going to have to maintain our strategic deterrent, not only because the Soviets give every indication of wanting to maintain theirs – that is the only thing that qualifies them as a superpower – but also, obviously, because there is a growing proliferation of weapons of mass destruction and sophisticated weapons technology in the Third World', said Dick Cheney in the Senate Appropriations Committee already on the 12th of June 1990[10].

In the Clinton administration, Deputy Secretary of Defence John Deutch spelled the policy out in the Nuclear Posture Review briefing on 22 September 1994: 'a country who is considering using [chemical weapons] would have to take into account the existence of US nuclear weapons if they are planning to attack the US in a regional context'[11]. Secretary of Defence Perry already made that clear before. In March 1996, Perry stated: 'Despite our best efforts to reduce the danger of weapons of mass destruction, it is still possible that America – and our forces and allies – could again be threatened by these terrible weapons. That is why it is important for the United States to maintain a small but effective nuclear force'[12]. A few weeks later, Perry explained that the US distinguished three instruments against the spread of weapons of mass destruction: 1) prevention; 2) deterrence; 3) and protection if deterrence fails. 'The second line of defence is to deter the use of these weapons by maintaining strong conventional military forces and a residual nuclear force, *which is still quite powerful*'[13]. In a Congressional hearing in the context of the ratification of the Chemical Weapons Convention in May 1996, and more in particular with regard to possible retaliatory capabilities against a chemical weapons attack, Perry indicated: 'the whole range should be considered – precision-guided munitions, Tomahawk land-attack missiles – *and then we have nuclear weapons*'[14].

Presidential Decision Directive-60 in November 1997 formalized this policy at the presidential level by emphasizing for the first time the possible use of nuclear weapons in the case of a chemical or biological weapons attack.

The need for nuclear deterrence vis-à-vis chemical and biological weapons attacks is also emphasized by the George W.Bush administration. As State Department spokesman Boucher said in February 2002: 'If a weapon of mass destruction is used against the United States or its allies, we will not rule out any specific type of military response'[15]. That was also the message of September 2002 National Security Presidential Directive-17. The Bush administration also succeeded in convincing its allies to adopt a similar doctrine within NATO.

While nuclear weapons may have a deterrent effect against the use of chemical and biological weapons, there are major costs as well.

1) It is intellectually not honest to talk in terms of "weapons of mass destruction". There is a huge difference between the destructive capacity of chemical, biological and nuclear weapons. Chemical weapons can cause massive destruction but their destructive capacity per unit is much smaller than nuclear weapons, and their effectiveness depends a lot on external factors like weather circumstances. In addition, soldiers can to a large extent protect themselves against chemical weapons.

Biological weapons are the only category of weapons that potentially come close to nuclear weapons in terms of capacity to reek havoc and incite fear. However, there are several disadvantages to the use of biological weapons: the speed of destruction is much lower; the danger exists that the user will be affected as well; in many circumstances biological weapons are not very effective; like chemical weapons, biological weapons are less predictable, and more subject to countermeasures[16].

2) To categorize states that behave "wrongly" and call them "rogue states" is not very convincing. States like Iraq, Iran, North Korea, but also Syria, Sudan, Cuba, Algeria and Libya were suddenly categorized as "rogue", "revisionist", "renegade" or "backlash" states. The Pentagon started to use these categorizations at the beginning of 1990. The Clinton administration finally got rid of the term "rogue states" in the summer of 2000. From then on, they were labelled "states of concern". However, the George W.Bush administration was eager to re-introduce the concept of rogue states.

3) There are apparently different standards in play. Why did the concepts of "weapons of mass destruction" and "rogue states" became so prominent in the security discourse after the Cold War, while chemical and biological weapons already existed at least since the beginning of the 20th century and rogue states probably always existed ? Note that during the Cold War the US did *not* regard chemical and biological weapons or states like Iraq or Iran as posing a major threat to the US. On the contrary, during the Cold War the US saw states like Iran and Iraq as allies against the former USSR. The US provided them with conventional weapons. The US maintained an active chemical weapons arsenal itself until President Bush decided to eliminate chemical weapons in 1991. Depending on the definition of chemical weapons, the US has even used them on a massive scale in Vietnam. When a "rogue state" like Iraq used chemical weapons in the 1980s, there was no clear signal from the US.

It is true that Iraq as a non-nuclear weapon state signatory of the Nuclear Nonproliferation Treaty set a very negative precedent by trying to acquire nuclear weapons secretly. The same applies to North Korea. However, these programmes already existed in the 1980s (and even before) and the US intelligence community was aware of that. But again, the US only made a point out of it *after* the Cold War. It seems that the US was looking for new enemies after the Cold War.

And what about the reaction of the US vis-à-vis proliferating states like Israel that acquired dozens, if not hundreds, of *nuclear* weapons in the past ?

Finally, how legitimate is criticizing the acquisition of weapons of mass destruction by "rogue states" when – fifteen years after the Cold War – the US itself still maintains over 10,000 nuclear warheads of which hundreds on alert ? By relying on nuclear deterrence against chemical and biological weapons attack, the US sends very strong signals to the rest of the world that nuclear weapons are militarily useful and a legitimate defence instrument.

4) The threat of using nuclear weapons in retaliation to a chemical or biological weapons attack lacks credibility because of the difference in destructive capacity and the lack of proportionality. Advocates of the new policy always refer to the Gulf War in 1991. Saddam Hussein was apparently deterred from the use of chemical weapons against the Allied troops. The US nuclear threat was delivered by Secretary of State James Baker at the end of December 1990 in the form of a

letter of President Bush to Saddam Hussein, and probably through other ways as well. Different remarks have to be made with regard to this rather explicit threat. It is not at all clear whether this threat has effectively worked. Some claim that Saddam Hussein *did* use chemical weapons during the Gulf War in 1991[17]. The so-called "Gulf syndrome" – symptoms of sickness a lot of American soldiers experienced afterwards – is sometimes linked to the possible use of chemical weapons by Iraq.

In case the former hypothesis is not correct and Saddam Hussein did not use chemical weapons, there may have been other reasons why he had not used chemical weapons in 1991. For instance, Iraq may have lacked the technology for launching chemical weapons effectively[18]. Or it may have been unable to use them because the arsenal was destroyed by Allied bombings[19]. The weather circumstances may not have been ideal either. Even Secretary of Defence William Perry hesitated: 'It is an interesting consideration as to why they did not use [chemical weapons] during the war, whether our counterproliferation worked, namely the very great conventional force we had simply overwhelmed them, or whether they feared a response from nuclear weapons'[20].

Mostly forgotten, the US threatened to use nuclear weapons not only in response to a chemical weapons attack, but also if Iraq burned the Kuwaiti oilfields[21]. Iraq *did* burn the Kuwaiti oilfields in 1991. As a result, nuclear deterrence did not "work".

Senior participants in the 1991 Gulf War, like Secretary of State James Baker, later on declared that the US would have renounced the use of nuclear weapons in any event[22]. Some, like CIA Director William Webster and French President Mitterrand, had made similar statements before the start of the war[23]. Top of the bill, and despite the official declaratory ambiguity, Vice-President Dan Quayle told the press on 1 February 1991 – *during* the war – that 'I just can't imagine President Bush making the decision to use chemical or nuclear weapons under any circumstances'. He then quickly corrected himself by saying that no option would be ruled out[24].

In addition[24], Iraq *did* attack Israel – a *de facto* nuclear weapon state – with ballistic missiles during the Gulf War. Nuclear deterrence failed again.

To conclude, it is difficult to come up with a clearer example of the failure of nuclear deterrence than the Gulf War in 1991. Risk-takers certainly have noticed that the US and Israel did *not* retaliate with nuclear weapons and may speculate that the US will also be extremely hesitant next time. If such non-use by the US happens a few times after having threatened to use nuclear weapons, it will further erode the credibility of its nuclear deterrent. The latter is already low due to the gradually evolving nuclear taboo. In short, to deter chemical and biological weapons attacks with nuclear weapons is not credible and therefore not in the interests of the US. The same conclusion was drawn from politico-military simulation games organized by RAND[25]. Former UK MOD official Michael Quinlan therefore recommends: 'America's massive non-nuclear military power could amply punish the perpetrators of a biological or chemical attack without resorting to nuclear weapons'[26].

Finally, it should be noted that the US government itself doubts whether nuclear deterrence against chemical, biological, or even nuclear weapons attacks from rogue states will work. The leaders of such "rogue states" do not always behave "rationally". As Gregory Schulte, head of NATO's Nuclear Planning, pointed out: 'It may be difficult to assess the personality and intentions of the leaders of proliferating states. We might even consider these leaders to be "irrational", at least by our standards'[27]. In 1996, Secretary of Defence William Perry seemed to agree: 'Nuclear weapons in the hands of rogue nations or terrorists are especially dangerous because, unlike the nuclear powers during the Cold War, *they might not be deterred by the threat of retaliation*'[28]. A few months later, he asserted: 'The threat of retaliation may not matter much to a terrorist group or a rogue nation – *deterrence may not work with them*. This new class of "undeterrables" may be madder than MAD'[29]. MAD was even considered dead by the George W.Bush administration. That is also the reason for Bush looking for alternative defence instruments, such as mini-nukes and missile defence.

Of course, this does not mean that nuclear deterrence against rogue states will never work. The question, however, is whether the benefits of nuclear deterrence against attacks by rogue states weigh up against the costs mentioned above. Many non-governmental analysts after the Cold War believed that this was not the case.
In the case of terrorism, nuclear deterrence makes no sense at all as the attacker does not reveal its identity. It is perfectly possible to use biological weapons without leaving any "signature". By definition, nuclear deterrence cannot work in such circumstances.

5) The emphasis on nuclear deterrence against chemical and biological weapons attacks also contradicts another basic aspect of US declaratory policy, namely the negative security guarantees and the Nuclear Weapon Free Zones[30]. Michael Quinlan agrees: 'Although the negative security guarantees, first given in 1978, have never been withdrawn, the US has given a strong impression of diluting them through its reluctance to biological or chemical attack'[31].

On the one hand, the US promised not to use nuclear weapons against non-nuclear weapon states on the condition that they did not attack the US and were not allied with a nuclear weapon state. These are the so-called negative security guarantees, which the US promised for the first time in 1978 and repeated in 1995, as well as in the context of Nuclear Weapon Free Zones.

On the other hand, different statements by high-level officials in the US government left no doubt that the negative security guarantees do not apply in the event that non-nuclear weapon states should use chemical or biological weapons against the US. For instance, by signing the African Nuclear Weapon Free Zone treaty – the Pelindaba Treaty – without reservations in April 1996, the US promised not to use nuclear weapons in Africa. National Security Council Special Assistant Bob Bell, however, immediately made it clear that this 'will *not* limit options available to the US in response to an attack by an African Nuclear Weapon Free Zone party using weapons of mass destruction'[32]. President Clinton endorsed this ambiguous and contradictory policy by signing PDD-60 in November 1997. Bob Bell referred in this context to the principle of "belligerent reprisals". This legal principle states that the victim of an attack is allowed to violate international law if the attacker did so first. According to George Bunn, three conditions have to be fulfilled before one can speak about belligerent reprisals: 1) the reprisal must be necessary to stop the illegal attack or to prevent further violation; 2) the reprisal must be proportional; 3) and it must be for reasons of individual or collective self-defence[33]. It is extremely doubtful whether these conditions can be fulfilled in the case of nuclear weapons use.

Other US officials stressed that negative security guarantees were never meant to be legally binding. Robert Joseph, who became Under Secretary of State for Nonproliferation in June 2005, even recommended cancelling the negative security guarantees before he entered into office[34]. Michael May, a former director of Lawrence Livermore Laboratory, and Roger Speed disagree: 'Renunciation of US guarantees not to threaten non-nuclear states with nuclear weapons,..., would likely lead to the collapse of the NPT. It would certainly undermine the legitimacy and political acceptance of any US criticism of, or actions against, the spread of nuclear weapons and more generally could undermine US leadership in a post Cold War coalition for world order and stability'[35]. It also goes completely against the wishes of the non-nuclear weapon states. The *Principles and Objectives* document of the 1995 NPT Conference stated that 'further steps should be considered to assure NNWS party to the [NPT] against the use of nuclear weapons. These steps could take the form of an internationally *legally* binding instrument'[36].

No first use

In October 1991, Gorbachev proposed a no first use, but the US was not interested. Here, too, a window of opportunity may have been missed. As a result of the new emphasis on the possible use of nuclear weapons in the case of a chemical or biological weapons attack, and apparently also under pressure from its allies, the US did not declare a no first use policy after the Cold War. As Under Secretary of State Lynn Davis remarked in November 1996: 'for purposes of providing security and the alliance relationships that we have around the world, that we are not prepared to forgo the potential use under extraordinary circumstances of nuclear weapons'. She continued: 'And so we have not been prepared to join China in the call for a convention on the no first use of nuclear weapons'[37].

Russia abandoned its no first use policy - introduced in 1982 – in November 1993 as a result of its new military doctrine that relied more on nuclear deterrence because of its deteriorating conventional capability. China, by contrast, kept its no first use policy after the Cold War.

A no first use policy would have been legitimate after the Cold War for the following reasons:
1) The classic Cold War argument against no first use – to compensate for NATO's conventional inferiority – no longer made sense as NATO was and still is by far the strongest alliance in the world after 1989.
2) A no first use would have enhanced the overall deterrence effect by taking away the existing ambiguity with regard to deterrence against chemical and biological weapons attacks.
3) It would have reinforced the existing policy concerning negative security guarantees and Nuclear Weapon Free Zones.
4) A no first use would also have reinforced the overall nonproliferation and disarmament regime by de-legitimising nuclear weapons. As Harald Müller concluded: 'In simple words, it is absolutely impossible to explain to non-nuclear weapon states in much more precarious security situations than NATO members why the most powerful body the world has ever seen – and precisely this is the

Western alliance today – an alliance that is not facing any serious military challenge, must stick to the option to use nuclear weapons first in unspecified contingencies, including conventional ones, while they themselves are requested to renounce those weapons all together'[38].

5) A no first use would have met the demands of more and more NATO Allies, who were asking the US to change the NATO doctrine in favour of no first use. The German government platform of the SPD and the Greens in October 1998 explicitly called for a no first use. One month later, Canadian Foreign Minister Lloyd Axworthy – a former academic, long time opponent of nuclear weapons and one of the initiators of the landmine treaty – publicly stated he was also in favour of a no first use. Axworthy referred the issue to a parliamentary committee whose report was released on 10 December 1998[39]. A couple of weeks earlier, German Foreign Minister Joschka Fischer told Der Spiegel that he favoured a NATO no first use policy and that he would propose at the NATO Summit a few weeks later to adapt NATO's strategy in the context of the new Strategic Concept of April 1999[40]. Axworthy emphasized during the NATO meeting in December 1998: 'any discussion of using Alliance nuclear capabilities – even in retaliation – raises very difficult questions of means, proportionality and effectiveness that cause us significant concerns'[41]. In a report released only a few days before the opening of the NATO Summit in April 1999, the Canadian government asked NATO to use nuclear weapons only to deter nuclear weapon attacks, without however explicitly calling for a no first use[42]. The US, however, refused to adopt a no first use policy[43]. It even refused to discuss it inside NATO. Secretary of Defence Cohen anticipated at the Munich Conference on 6 February 1998: 'Any question about this policy undermines our deterrent capability'[44].

Negative security guarantees and Nuclear Weapon Free Zones

The US repeated its negative security guarantees right before the opening of the 1995 NPT Review and Extension Conference, when Secretary of State Warren Christopher emphasized: 'The US reaffirms that it will not use nuclear weapons against Non Nuclear Weapon States (NPT parties) except in the case of an invasion or any other attack on the US, its territories, its armed forces or other troops, its allies, or on a state towards which it has a security commitment, carried out or sustained by such a Non Nuclear Weapon State (NNWS) in association or alliance with a NWS'[45]. An accompanying fact sheet stressed that these guarantees went further than the assurances given in 1978: 'It is the administration's view that the national statements issued by all five NWS, their co-sponsorship of a Security Council resolution on security assurances which is under consideration in New York, and the common negative security assurances achieved by four of the five – together compromise a substantial response to the desire of many Nuclear Non-Proliferation Treaty NNWS for strengthened security assurances'[46].

The US also offered negative security guarantees to the Ukraine in December 1994 when the latter promised to give up the nuclear weapons on its soil. The US also signed the protocols of the Raratonga Treaty (Pacific) in March 1996, and those of the Pelindaba Treaty (Africa) one month later.

Declaratory operational policy

US declaratory operational policy was and still is – for deterrence purposes – very ambiguous. The annual report of the Secretary of Defence in 1998 mentions in one and the same sentence that: 'The US will *not* rely on a launch-on-warning nuclear retaliation strategy (*although an adversary could never be sure the US would not launch a counterattack before the adversary's nuclear weapons arrived*)'[47]. National Security Council Special Assistant Bell also contradicted himself. *The Washington Post*, revealing the story of PDD-60 on 7 December 1997, wrote: '[Bell who apparently was reading from notes] noted that the directive still allows the US to launch its weapons after receiving warning of attack – but before incoming warheads detonate'[48]. One month later, on 6 January 1998, Bob Bell declared that the press had misunderstood him and clarified: 'You still need *a robust force that can absorb a first strike, rather than have to launch on warning of an incoming missile*, and have that force spread across enough types of weapons systems, what we call triad'. He also maintained: 'I do not think we're in a hair-trigger posture'[49], and added that this was nothing new[50].

	US nuclear weapons policy during the Cold War	US nuclear weapons policy after the Cold War	Categorization of US nuclear weapons policy after the Cold War
Nuclear deterrence versus conventional, CBW, nuclear attacks	Nuclear attack by USSR or massive conventional attack by USSR on Western Europe	Conventional, CBW, and nuclear attacks; but no prevailing doctrine anymore	Maximum
No first use	No	No	Maximum
Legally binding negative security guarantees for non-nuclear Weapon States (NNWS); NWFZ	No, but negative security guarantees since 1978 + Tlatelolco Treaty	No, but negative security guarantees repeated in 1995 + Pelindaba, Raratonga	Maximum (although non-legally guarantees)
Ride out policy	No	No	Maximum

Table 4: US declaratory nuclear weapons policy

After the Cold War, US operational policy seemed still to rely on "prompt launch" – LOW or LUA – in the case of a nuclear attack. It did not say that the US would ride out. Such a prompt launch policy ridicules the idea that the US relies much less on nuclear weapons than during the Cold War. It is also at odds with the overall foreign policy goal of co-operating with Russia.

Even with a declaratory and operational ride-out policy, the US can still launch a devastating response, which is much more than a minimum deterrence posture would require. In the event that a Russian first-strike destroyed all US bombers and all ICBMs, which is very unlikely, the US SLBM force could still cause massive destruction. Assuming normal alert rates for nuclear submarines (70 % at sea), and a reliability of 80 %, the 1,613 SLBM warheads could have destroyed 65 % of the 2,500 remaining countervalue and counterforce targets in Russia in a ride-out attack. If the submarines would have been on alert (for instance during a crisis), and 90 % of them would have been at sea, the US would have been able to destroy 83 % of the 2,500 existing targets in a ride-out attack[51].

CHAPTER 5

NUCLEAR OPERATIONAL POLICY

A distinction should be made between safety and targeting policy.

Safety policy

Alert-levels

Safety, at least rhetorically, came more to the forefront after the Cold War. In 1994, Secretary of Defence William Perry, paraphrasing McNamara's Mutual Assured Destruction (MAD), spoke about "Mutual Assured Safety" (MAS).

Safety was substantially strengthened by President Bush in September 1991 when he put the bombers off alert. It now takes 12 to 24 hours to put them back on alert[1]. However a decision to put them back on alert may be seen as a provocation. The George W.H.Bush administration also put the airborne command and control on a lower level of alert[2]. Lastly, Bush decided to take 450 Minuteman II missiles off alert, the retirement of which was foreseen under START I, as well as 160 SLBMs each carrying 10 warheads on 10 Poseidon strategic submarines (SSBNs).

However the patrol rate of the nuclear submarines, still having two crews per submarine, remains equal to Cold War levels. Two thirds of all submarines – between 8 and 11 – are on patrol at any given time[3]. Half of them are on modified alert, requiring 18 hours to launch their SLBMs[4]. The others are still on high alert, which means that they are able to launch in 15 minutes time. The Annual Report of the Secretary of Defence of January 2000 pointed out that the ICBMs and SLBMs are in 'the highest state of readiness'[5]. Regardless of US declaratory policy, most ICBMs are still geared for launch in a time-span of two minutes. To conclude, there are still over 2,500 nuclear warheads ready to be launched in a very short timeframe. According to Sam Nunn, both the US and Russia kept 4,000 nuclear weapons on alert in 2003[6].

It is unclear whether the Clinton administration kept the option of launch-on-warning open. Some believe that LOW still dominated military planning in the 1990s[7]. According to Bruce Blair, only 47 % of the Russian target base could have been destroyed if US forces did not launch on warning[8].

Although the US government admits that a substantial part of its forces are still on (high) alert and that the US can still retaliate promptly, some officials explicitly deny that the nuclear forces are on "hair-trigger alert". This contradiction might be explained by confusion about the concepts. It can also be explained by a technical fix that was introduced in the 1990s. US ICBMs had two operational modes installed: "dormant" and "semi-dormant". This made it possible to stand down the ICBM force electronically and still be able to retaliate instantly[9].

Other analysts believe that the actual operational policy of the US corresponds to LUA[10]. American strategists recommended Russia to shift its policy from LOW to LUA[11].

Before he was elected George W.Bush stated in 2000 that: 'the US should remove as many weapons as possible from high-alert, hair-trigger status – another unnecessary vestige of Cold War confrontation'[12]. However, according to a leaked version of the 2001 NPR, 'a sufficient number of forces must be available on short notice'[13]. After the 11 September attacks, the American nuclear forces were put on DEFCON 3 alert, something which had not happened since the 1973 Middle East crisis, without triggering a similar action in Russia[14].

How should we interpret this data ? The high alert-rates and the declaratory operational policy of prompt launch indicate that US safety policy still belongs to maximum deterrence. Most of the related risks still apply, more particularly the risk of accidents and unauthorized use. To give just one example, a US and Russian submarine collided north of the Kola peninsula on 20 March 1993[15].

Keeping high alert-rates contradicts the overall foreign policy goal of co-operating with Russia. How can the US build up trust with Russia if the US continues to keep the bulk of its operational strategic nuclear arsenal on high alert ready to be launched within minutes against hundreds of targets in Russia ? As a result of the high alert-levels in the US, Russia also had to keep its nuclear weapons on high alert. The combination of high alert-rates and the deteriorating shape of the Russian nuclear force did not stimulate new thinking in the US. If there was new thinking, it went in the opposite direction. At the beginning of 2000 the US recommended the Russians to keep their LOW strategies because of the possible American deployment of a National Missile Defence system[16]. This is another example of a major inconsistency in US nuclear policy: trying to do something about the deteriorating Russian nuclear arsenal on the one hand and recommending Russia to keep a LOW posture on the other.

A more intrusive solution to the Russian safety risks would have been to take all nuclear forces off alert. This was proposed by Soviet Minister of Foreign Affairs Andrei Kozyrev in February 1992. However the US rejected it.

To conclude with Bruce Blair: 'The attention the Pentagon gives to addressing the safety of nuclear weapons operations, particularly Russian operations, pales by comparison to its commitment to classical deterrence…The standards of safety that have evolved through repetitive, experiential learning during thirty-five years of aggressive alert operations have not been extended to the circumstances of advanced crisis or to the actual initiation of combat operations. There is scant reason to believe that past experience would enable organizations to cope well with the stress and unpredictability of an intense nuclear crisis'[17].

Safety mechanisms

The Nunn-Lugar programme initiated in November 1991 was aimed to address both proliferation and safety concerns within Russia. The amount of money of this programme, however, remained limited: $3.1 billion from 1991 to 1999 and another $4.2 billion foreseen for fiscal year 2000-2005.

In September 1991 President Bush decided to remove the launch keys from ICBMs and to install safety pins in order to prevent ignition of the rocket motors[18]. Since 1994, the US and Russian missiles are no longer pointed to specific targets. The US missiles will not switch back to their original target destination in the case of accident or unauthorized use (unlike the Russian missiles), but are targeted to the oceans[19]. As a result of the Nuclear Posture Review in 1993-1994, PALs were installed on submarines. Consequently, all weapons systems were equipped with PALs from July 1997 onwards. Under Secretary of Defence Walter Slocombe claimed in 1997: 'Our nuclear weapons meet the highest standards of safety, security and responsible custodianship developed for our nuclear arsenal...Although accidents involving nuclear weapons occur, the last one was almost 20 years ago. Nor has any accident ever resulted in a nuclear detonation'[20].

In September 1998, Russia and the US signed an early warning agreement to prevent launches after a false alarm and to create a common early-warning centre. The US also proposed delivering lacking early-warning information to Russia[21]. In June 2000, Clinton and Putin signed a memorandum on the establishment of a Joint Data Exchange Centre in Moscow to share early-warning data on missile launches. The centre is not yet established.

In Europe, vaults have been built to better protect the stored American nuclear bombs[22].

Targeting policy

Predetermined targets

All nuclear war plans – the so-called Single Integrated Operational Plans (SIOPs) – in the Reagan and Bush era were based on NSDD-13 (1981). President Clinton only changed presidential guidance in November 1997 by approving PDD-60. Most, if not all, of the former SIOP targets, in Russia, were kept. The number of targets had already been reduced before during the second Reagan administration from 16,000 in 1985 to 14,000 in 1987 and to 12,500 in 1989. All targets in Central Europe were deleted as a result of the fall of the Berlin Wall. In 1991, the head of the US Strategic Command Gen.Lee Butler reduced the number further to 2,500 by targeting linked communication capabilities and other networks. According to Bruce Blair, the target list grew again from 2,500 to 3,000 targets after 1995[23].

Formally, the US (and Russian) nuclear weapons no longer point at any targets since May 1994. However the latter is easily reversible. It is mainly a symbolic gesture because all targets are kept in a computer database. US nuclear weapons could be re-targeted at the turn of a switch. In formal language, they 'could be returned to their previous targeting status on short notice'[24]. Some even explicitly admit that otherwise de-targeting would never have taken place[25].

STRATCOM also elaborated the concept of "adaptive planning". Under this concept, US military planners retain and update lists of targets in potentially hostile nations with access to nuclear weapons. They would do so, however, under the presumption that nuclear weapons, if they were ever to be used, would be employed against targets that would be designated in response to immediate circumstances – and in the smallest numbers possible', according to CISAC[26]. Nuclear weapons can, for instance, be used against rogue states, although in a generic and therefore not specified manner[27].

Massive attack options

There are still massive attack options (MAO) in the Single Integrated Operational Plan. The smallest Massive Attack Option (MAO 1) consists of attacking 200 Russian silos, bombers and submarine bases plus 100 other key targets with 680 US ICBM and SLBM warheads. MAO 2 adds nuclear related targets that have to be attacked by US SLBM warheads. MAO 3 also includes leadership targets for which bombers are used. The largest attack option (MAO 4) includes economic targets and requires the use of nearly all nuclear weapons on alert: almost 3,000 nuclear warheads on 600 missiles[28].

Finally it seems that very small limited options are included in the Single Integrated Operational Plan. Bruce Blair talks of 65 limited nuclear options – ranging from 2 to 120 nuclear weapons – for Russia alone[29]. Others disagree[30]. Military exercises organized by STRATCOM still show that the military prefer MAO[31]. The odds therefore are that only a very small number of weapons are allocated for limited nuclear options[32]. Beside the limited and selected attack options inside the Single Integrated Operational Plan, the so-called Strategic Reserve Force and also sub-strategic nuclear weapons can be used against "rogue states" and China[33].

George W.Bush's NPR admits that 'the current nuclear planning system,…, is optimised to support *large*, deliberately planned nuclear strikes'[34]. Also Vice-president Cheney repeated in March 2002: 'We do have and we maintain and continually update something called the Single Integrated Operating Plan (SIOP) that is classified, that is what actually deals with the selection of targets and how nuclear weapons might be applied'[35]. Sokolsky maintains that 'the [2001] NPR represents a continuation of Cold War targeting philosophy'[36]. The goal remains to introduce more adaptive planning.

Types of targets

As already mentioned above, PDD-60 of November 1997 put an end to the prevailing doctrine established in 1981. This led to the withdrawal of many industrial targets as well as many targets against conventional forces[37]. The Russian nuclear forces and the nuclear command and leadership infrastructure on the other hand were kept as targets of the Single Integrated Operational Plan[38]. These 1,500-2,000 targets are part of what is named the "stable nucleus" which is 'a core set of targets and special attacks that do not change substantially over time, thereby eliminating the need, and the time involved, in making major changes [to the nuclear war plans]'[39]. A further reduction in the force structure may take away all industrial and economic targets.

This counterforce policy also supports the thesis that the US still relies on a prompt launch policy, as counterforce targets are time-urgent targets.

Beside 2,000-2,500 targets in Russia, some 300-400 targets are related with China and at least 100-200 targets with other nations like Iran, North Korea, and Syria[40]. CINCSAC Lee Butler announced this shift in 1993: 'Our focus now is not just the former Soviet Union, but any potentially hostile country that has or is seeking weapons of mass destruction'[41]. Targeting third world nations was organized by STRATCOM instead of the regional commands[42]. According to Kristensen, the specific targets in "rogue states" were not the production or storage facilities of weapons of mass destruction, but the missiles carrying them[43].

The 2001 NPR also makes a distinction between immediate, potential and unexpected contingencies. North Korea, [Iraq], Iran, [Libya], Syria and China are considered as potential targets for immediate contingencies. As Kristensen pointed out: 'planners could "go global" in pursuit of enemies and targets. From the planner's perspective the world changed from a weapons rich to a target rich environment'[44].

	US nuclear weapons policy during the Cold War	US nuclear weapons policy after the Cold War	Categorization of US nuclear weapons policy after the Cold War
A. Safety policy			
Alert-levels	High since the end of the 1950s	High for ICBMs and SLBMs; low for bombers since 1991	Maximum
Permissive Action Links (PAL) and other safety devices installed	Yes, since 1960s except on SLBMs	Yes, also on SLBMs since 1997	Minimum
B. Targeting policy			
Predetermined targets; war plan like SIOP	Yes, thousands	Yes, hundreds, although officially not pointed to targets	Maximum
Massive attack options	Yes	Yes	Maximum
Counter-force targets	Yes	Yes	Maximum

Table 5: US operational nuclear weapons policy

The question is to what extent the US is technologically capable, for instance of hitting mobile missiles. Theoretically, only bombers are able to carry out this job, and according to some experts that is even a too demanding task. In a debate with respect to the future of the B-2, Chief of Staff of the Air Force General Larry Welch admitted in 1988 that 'the whole business of locating mobile targets…is a very complex task and we're a long way from having decided that we know how to handle this task'[45]. The 1991 Gulf War points to the same conclusions[46].

To conclude, at first glance, US targeting policy changed in the direction of minimum deterrence: officially missiles without targets; *de facto* much less targets; more limited options; adaptive targeting. But although there were more limited options, the basic targeting plans remained more or less the same after the Cold War[47]. The Single Integrated Operational Plan – the pre-planned nuclear war plan – is still in place and still includes massive attack options targeted against a mix of countervalue and counterforce targets. A RAND report in 1994 recommended substantial change: 'The Single Integrated Operational Plan (SIOP) should be history. The plans discussed publicly for refining the SIOP to make it more flexible do not go nearly far enough and leave some serious institutional problems uncorrected. Instead, a fully adaptive planning process similar to that being adopted by conventional forces should be implemented'[48].

CHAPTER 6

NUCLEAR TESTING, BALLISTIC MISSILE DEFENCE, NONPROLIFERATION, AND ELIMINATION POLICY

Some nuclear weapons issues are more difficult to square into the minimum/maximum deterrence dichotomy and therefore need to be dealt with separately.

Nuclear Testing

After having conducted over 1,000 tests during the Cold War, more than all the other nuclear weapon states combined, President Bush halted nuclear testing and announced a unilateral test moratorium in October 1992, due to strong pressure from the Democrats in Congress. President Clinton, extending the moratorium in July 1993, went further by proposing a Comprehensive Test Ban Treaty (CTBT) that would ban nuclear tests. At the same time, a Stockpile Stewardship Programme (SSP) was established to keep the remaining American nuclear weapons reliable and safe.

Multilateral negotiations for a CTBT started in the UN Conference on Disarmament in January 1994 and were successfully completed in September 1996, the year set forth in the Final Document of the 1995 NPT Extension Conference. The US was the first country to sign the CTBT.

At first glance, this may be regarded as one of the biggest arms control accomplishments of the Clinton administration. However this observation should immediately be put in perspective. The treaty requires that all 44 countries possessing nuclear reactors ratify the treaty. In October 1999, the US Senate voted against the CTBT ratification. This was one of the biggest blows to the nonproliferation regime in decades, as well as arguably the biggest foreign policy defeat of the Clinton administration.

In 1996, India had also made clear that it would not sign the CTBT because of the discriminatory nonproliferation regime between the nuclear weapon states and the non-nuclear weapon states and because of the lack of progress towards nuclear elimination. The Indian Minister of Foreign Affairs Kumar Gujral put it thus: 'The treaty in its current form only allows the five nuclear powers to sustain their nuclear hegemony. From a national perspective, the treaty will result in closing our option to have nuclear weapons. Whichever way you looked at it, we were left with no option but to resist the treaty'[1]. A posteriori, these remarks should have been taken seriously. In May 1998, India tested nuclear weapons.

Furthermore, it took a lot of time and political compromising to get the CTBT signed[2]. The labs for instance now receive $6.4 billion per year for the SSP programme, which is twice as much as they have got during the Cold War.

Lastly, thanks to computer simulations, sub-critical and hydrodynamic tests, the US retains the capability to maintain the safety and reliability of the existing nuclear arsenal. The CTBT therefore does not hinder the continued reliance on a US maximum deterrence posture.

In contrast to the Clinton administration, the George W.Bush administration did not favour the CTBT and did not want to submit it to the Senate. During his presidential campaign, Bush already said: '[The CTBT] does not stop proliferation, especially to renegade regimes. It is not verifiable. It is not enforceable. And it would stop us from ensuring the safety and reliability of our nation's deterrent, should the need arise'[3]. Once in office, it was even decided to leave the option to resume testing open. The 2001 NPR stated: 'While the US is making every effort to maintain the stockpile without additional testing, this may not be possible for the indefinite future'. The Bush administration also refused to participate in CTBT conferences in November 2001 and again in September 2003. During the 2002 Nuclear Nonproliferation Treaty Prepcom, US Ambassador Eric Javits stated that the CTBT 'is another example of a treaty we no longer support'[4]. Bush also funded studies (like the Foster panel) that asked for a shortening of the time needed to be able to re-start nuclear testing from two to three years to at most one year. In May 2003, Congress agreed to reduce the period from 36 to 18 months.

There remained a lot of pressure from the nuclear weapons establishment, especially the labs, as well as some high-level Republicans on the Hill to restart testing. The biggest indication was a memorandum from Edward Aldridge, the Under Secretary of Defence, to the Nuclear Weapons Council on 21 October 2002 asking for low-yield nuclear weapons testing[5].

From an arms control perspective, Bush's policy could have been worse. The administration could have withdrawn from the treaty as it did with the ABM treaty, something it has not (yet) done. It also retained the US test moratorium and it kept funding the CTBT Organization. On the whole, however, the US plays a very obstructive role. Together with India and North Korea, the US is the main party responsible for the fact that the CTBT cannot enter into force.

Ballistic Missile Defence
Because of the inherent problems of credibility of nuclear deterrence – both maximum and minimum deterrence – there have always been advocates for an alternative or at least for a complement to nuclear deterrence, namely missile defence.

A distinction should be made between ballistic missile systems that protect only a small region, for instance US troops during an intervention abroad (*theatre* missile defence), and a *strategic* missile defence system that is able to protect continental US territory against accidental launches or a deliberate attack of (a few) intercontinental missiles. The ABM Treaty (1972) banned large-scale missile defence. In practice, a very limited missile defence system has only existed for one year in the mid-1970s. The US abandoned the system because it was not regarded as efficient.

President George W.H.Bush scaled back Reagan's ambitious Strategic Defence Initiative (SDI) programme to the Global Protection against Limited Strikes system. The latter still planned to include space-based "brilliant pebbles" and hundreds of ground-based interceptors against a strategic missile attack. In 1991, Congress passed the Missile Defence Act, which asked for research and development for a Theatre Missile Defence (TMD) system.

President Clinton announced in March 1993 to limit the strategic missile defence programme to a ground-based system. Research on space-based interceptors was halted. One of the problems left was to agree with Russia on what exactly was allowed under the ABM Treaty. Demarcation negotiations in the Standing Consultative Commission started in 1993. The so-called US-Russian Demarcation Agreement of 1996 stipulated that BMD systems with a low interceptor velocity (not exceeding 3 km/s) could only be tested against missiles with a range smaller than 3,500 km or a velocity smaller than 5 km/s. Examples of these lower-tier systems are the Army Patriot Advanced Capability, and the Medium Extended Air Defence System (MEADS). The Army's Theatre High Altitude Area Defence (THAAD) and the Navy Theatre Wide (NTW) system in contrast are upper-tier theatre systems that are able to protect areas like an army division or a metropolitan area[6]. In 1995, the Clinton administration unilaterally decided – contrary to what it had said before – that THAAD and NTW were Anti-Ballistic Missile treaty compliant. Despite a so-called bilateral "agreement" of September 1997, Russia did *not* agree with the categorization of high-speed theatre missile defence systems[7]. Russia's criticism was that a strategic missile defence system can be built out of upper-tier theatre systems[8]. In principle three or four Navy Theatre Wide ships could cover the entire continental US[9].

The missile defence policy of the Clinton administration evolved over time. In the beginning, the Clinton administration only emphasized the development of *theatre* missile defence systems. It put $2 billion aside annually for that purpose. However, under pressure from the Republicans, the Department of Defence changed the missile defence research efforts from technology demonstration status to deployment readiness status in 1996. In that year, the US also developed the so-called "3+3" plan. During the next three years, components of National Missile Defence would be developed and after that period – at the earliest in the year 2000 – a decision would be made to deploy such a system three years later, if the threat at that time warranted such a decision.

When the conclusions of the Rumsfeld Committee were made public in 1998 and after the North Korean ballistic missile launch over Japan a couple of months later, President Clinton agreed in July 1999 to deploy a limited national missile defence system, in principle as soon as it would be technologically feasible, taking three other criteria into account as well: 1) the extent of the emerging missile threat; 2) the costs; and 3) arms control considerations. This decision was the result of the Congressional National Missile Defence Act of March 1999 supported by both Republicans and Democrats. At the same time, $6.6 billion were added to the development of NMD. The Clinton administration still hoped to find an agreement with Russia on NMD, but stated at the same time that it would go ahead even if the Russians would not agree.

The Clinton administration planned eventually to deploy 100 interceptor missiles in Alaska, especially focusing on the threat from North Korea. That system could then be extended to 250 interceptors, spread over two launch sites.

The first NMD integrated flight test in October 1999 was a success. Those in January and July 2000 failed. As the technology was still far from mature, as Russia remained adamantly opposed to amending the ABM Treaty, as China was even more critical, as the Allies were concerned, and as the North Korean threat seemed to become less acute, President Clinton decided on 1 September 2000 that it was too early to authorize the deployment of a limited NMD system. However research and development programmes continued.

George W.Bush made NMD his priority both before and after his election. He made it absolutely clear that the US would go ahead with the deployment, even if Russia remained opposed. On 13 December 2001, President Bush finally announced the unilateral withdrawal from the ABM Treaty. Russia did not make a big fuss about the withdrawal. Six months later, the ABM Treaty no longer existed. Research and development went full-speed ahead. In September 2004, six ground-based strategic missile interceptors at Fort Greeley in Alaska and two at Vandenberg Air Force Base in California were deployed at the end of 2004.

If missile defence takes away the need for nuclear weapons or is regarded as a prerequisite for nuclear elimination, then missile defence can in theory be valued positively. Bruno Tertrais, a French expert close to the government, for instance states: 'Missile defences could...remain one of the surest ways for states to rely less on the threat of nuclear retaliation'[10]. Different problems however arise with this proposition. The technology is still far from ready and many believe it will never be ready. For this reason STRATCOM will be very cautious to change from one paradigm (nuclear deterrence) to another (missile defence). In addition, nobody in the George W.Bush administration speaks in terms of replacing nuclear weapons by missile defence. Most advocates of missile defence – like Keith Payne, Robert Joseph, Baker Spring, Donald Rumsfeld, and Dick Cheney – are in favour of keeping the current maximum deterrence posture. Lastly, in a nuclear weapons free world, missile defence technology should be shared with all countries, which doesn't seem very realistic either[11].

Nonproliferation
Proliferation of "weapons of mass destruction" became the number one threat for the US after the Cold War until the events of September 11th. As Michael Klare contends: 'By the spring of 1990 senior Pentagon officials and many members of Congress had begun using a common analysis and terminology to describe the threat'[12]. The Bush administration made its new strategy (including nonproliferation) public on 2 August 1990, coincidentally the day that Iraq invaded Kuwait.

In the words of Clinton's first Secretary of State Warren Christopher the threat of weapons of mass destruction became 'the principal direct threat to the survival of the US and our key allies'[13]. CIA Director James Woolsey stated it very prosaically: 'We have slain the [Soviet] dragon. But we now live in a jungle filled with a bewildering variety of poisonous snakes'[14].

According to Clinton's Secretary of Defence William Cohen, proliferation was partly a reaction to US conventional superiority: 'a paradox of the new strategic environment is that American military superiority actually *increases* the threat of nuclear, biological, and chemical attack against us by creating incentives for adversaries to challenge us asymmetrically'[15].

As these weapons are not that difficult to produce and as they may be perceived as militarily and politically useful, proliferation was perceived as being likely. Detailed plans for the development of a first generation atomic bomb are available in real and virtual libraries. The difficulty for acquiring nuclear weapons consists in the acquisition of the necessary quantity of fissile material: plutonium or highly enriched uranium. Twenty kilograms of highly enriched uranium or six kilograms of plutonium are sufficient for a rudimentary atomic bomb. Most analysts agree with James Clapper, head of the Defence Intelligence Agency who declared in 1995: 'While it is possible to slow the proliferation of these weapons, a country that is intent on gaining such a capability will eventually do so'[16]. Iraq and North Korea were eye-openers in the first half of the 1990s; Iran and Libya followed in the period 2002-2004.

There is more or less a consensus that proliferation is not desirable. As John Holum, the Arms Control and Disarmament Agency Director, reported in the context of the 1995 NPT Conference: 'If these [nuclear] weapons get out of hand and they are spread as a preventive, the world becomes a much more dangerous place for everybody. The more weapons there are, the more likely...they will be used'[17]. Another consequence of nuclear proliferation is that '[rogue states] with nuclear weapons are likely to be harder to deter and more likely to coerce their neighbours or start a war in the first place', as Secretary of Defence William Perry claimed[18]. While the threat of a massive nuclear attack had more or less disappeared, the likelihood of a nuclear explosion – through accidents and/or proliferation – increased.

In addition, some of the "rogue states" – like North Korea but also Iran and Saudi-Arabia – are also known for sponsoring terrorism. The combination of weapons of mass destruction and terrorism became real for the first time when the Japanese sect Aum Shinrikyo used chemical weapons in the Tokyo underground system killing twelve and injuring more than 5,000 people in March 1995. The leader of the sect was sentenced to death at the beginning of 2004. After 11 September 2001, the US experienced a small-scale biological weapons attack with anthrax, killing four people. *Nuclear* terrorism is one of the scary dangers left. Nuclear weapons do not have to be launched by sophisticated ballistic missiles. A rudimentary atomic bomb – like the one used in Hiroshima – thrown down from a plane or hidden in a truck, can have the same devastating effects as a nuclear missile.

As a result of this threat, the US never placed more emphasis on nonproliferation than after the Cold War, at least rhetorically. According to one interpretation, the main reason for going to war with Saddam Hussein in 1991 was to destroy the country's capacity to build weapons of mass destruction[19]. The Gulf War in 1991 can therefore be regarded as a preventive war.

The Bush administration initiated the Nunn-Lugar initiative in November 1991, which aimed at improving the safety and proliferation risks in the USSR. For the same reasons, it bought 500 metric tons of highly enriched uranium from Russia in August 1992.

President Clinton was probably even more determined to reduce the risks of proliferation. In a speech at Los Alamos Laboratory at the beginning of his first term, he declared: 'There are still too many nations who seem determined to define the quality of their lives based on whether they develop a nuclear weapon…that can have no other purpose but to destroy other human beings. It is a mistake and we should try to contain and to stop it'[20]. A few months later at the UN General Assembly, he announced a series of concrete measures to contain the spread of fissile material.

The Clinton administration was aware that the likelihood that nuclear weapons could spread because of "loose nukes" in Russia was high. The number one priority therefore was to move all Soviet nuclear weapons to Russia. Clinton was successful in persuading Ukraine, Kazakhstan and Belarus to give up their nuclear weapons and to sign the Nuclear Nonproliferation Treaty. The Nunn-Lugar programme – later called the Cooperative Threat Reduction Programme – was extended as well. An International Science and Technology Centre became operational in Moscow in March 1994 to prevent Russian brain drain.

In February 1993, North Korea refused a special inspection of the International Atomic Energy Agency. One month later, it threatened to withdraw from the Nuclear Nonproliferation Treaty, which it had signed in 1985. In May 1994, North Korea moved its fuel rods out of the nuclear reactor. After a condemnation by the UN Security Council, the US started preparations for war. But finally it settled the issue thanks to an intervention of former President Jimmy Carter. In October 1994, an agreement with North Korea was signed.

Partly as a result of this crisis, Secretary of Defence Les Aspin launched the Counterproliferation Initiative on 7 December 1993. It was originally meant to be a non-nuclear instrument in the event nonproliferation would fail. It included better intelligence means, better safety measures for the military to operate in an environment in which weapons of mass destruction were used, the development of theatre anti-ballistic missile defence systems, and preventive military attacks[21].

In 1995, the Clinton administration was successful in extending the Nuclear Nonproliferation Treaty indefinitely.

After the Indian and Pakistani tests in May 1998, President Clinton remarked: 'I cannot believe that we are about to start the 21st Century by having the Indian subcontinent repeat the same mistakes of the 20th century, when we know it is not necessary to peace, to security, to prosperity, to national greatness or personal fulfilment'[22]. When Clinton was preparing his visit to India and Pakistan in the spring of 2000, he repeated: 'I will make clear our view that a nuclear future is a dangerous future for them and for the world'[23]. The US imposed economic sanctions, which were already relieved one year later and which were further relaxed by Bush after 11 September 2001, when the struggle against Al Qhaeda and the "war on terrorism" became the number one priority.

In August 1998, the US carried out a pre-emptive counterproliferation attack with cruise missiles against Sudan and Afghanistan. In Sudan, a chemical plant that supposedly produced chemical and/or biological weapons was hit. With operation Desert Fox against Iraq in December 1998, the US and the UK even fought a short air war in the name of nonproliferation.

At least until 11 September 2001, the Bush administration regarded the proliferation of weapons of mass destruction as the primary security threat. It is therefore not by chance that missile defence was Bush's priority. Even after the terrorist attacks, nonproliferation remained a key objective, as the combination of terrorism and weapons of mass destruction was regarded as "the sum of all fears". Where would terrorists get weapons of mass destruction from ? The answer, according to the Bush administration, was clear: from rogue states. The sharp focus on rogue states was further strengthened when Bush called Iran, Iraq and North Korea 'the axis of evil' in his January 2002 State of the Union. In 2002 Iraq dominated US foreign policy, leading to the resumption of UNMOVIC and International Atomic Energy Agency inspections in November 2002 and the war against Iraq a few months later.

In the midst of the preparations for the war against Iraq, two serious cases of non-compliance in the field of nonproliferation were uncovered. Already in March 2002, the US government refused to declare that North Korea was complying with the 1994 Agreement. In October 2002, North Korea admitted in bilateral talks with the US of having a secret highly enriched uranium programme, although it later denied it. The resulting escalation process after October 2002 led to the North Korean announcement of the withdrawal from the Nuclear Nonproliferation Treaty in January 2003. North Korea also started up its nuclear reactor again and started to reprocess 8,000 nuclear fuel rods. If the latter is true, it will have provided North Korea with four to five (additional) nuclear weapons. The Bush administration only used limited diplomatic means to counter the crisis. It refused for instance to hold bilateral negotiations. Negotiations between the US, Russia, China, North Korea, South Korea, and Japan were set up in the second half of 2003.

In February 2003, it became known that the third member of the "Axis of Evil", Iran, had a much larger nuclear weapons programme than had hitherto been known. Information from an Iranian opposition movement was confirmed by the International Atomic Energy Agency. At the May 2003 NPT Prepcom meeting – in preparation of the next NPT Review Conference in 2005 – Iran was accused by the US. US Ambassador Wolf asked: 'How many other NPT non-nuclear weapon states built an enrichment plant before their first power reactor was finished ? None. What responsible country would or could commit to building a production scale plant without extensive research and development ? None. How many other NPT non-nuclear weapon states with nuclear programmes based solely on light water reactors have also built large-scale heavy water plants ? None. Why has Iran sought clandestinely to acquire laser enrichment technology ?' [24]. The next day, the Iranian representative, Deputy Foreign Minister for Legal and International Affairs Ali Khoshroo, replied: 'How many nuclear weapon states other than the US have prescribed the use of nuclear weapons in conventional conflicts and developed new types of nuclear weapons compatible with its combat scenarios ? None. Which other nuclear weapon states have sought to utilize outer space for nuclear purposes more than the US ? None. How many nuclear weapon states other than the US have legislatively rejected the Comprehensive Test Ban Treaty and practically doomed its failure ? Why did the US through its unilateral withdrawal from the ABM and its abrogation of step 7 of the 13 steps threaten the strategic stability of the world ?'[25].

The ministers of foreign affairs of France, the UK and Germany succeeded in getting an agreement with Iran in October 2003. Iran promised to suspend its enrichment programme and to sign the Additional Protocol of the International Atomic Energy Agency. It also promised to release all the relevant information with regard to its enrichment and reprocessing programmes. However it became clear at the beginning of 2004 that Iran had not revealed everything. In November 2004, the EU finalized a new deal with respect to the nuclear programme of Iran, including the promise of an overall agreement between the EU and Iran that had still to be negotiated.

After the Iraq war in 2003, two other proliferators beyond the "axis of evil" came into the spotlight: Libya and Pakistan. Colonel Gadaffi surprised the rest of the world by announcing a complete halt of its weapons of mass destruction programmes in December 2003. This was a big success for the Bush administration after having negotiated in secret with Libya and the UK for at least nine months. Libya's decision to halt its nuclear weapons programmes was largely due to economic reasons. The dire state of the Libyan economy needed to be remedied in order to prolong the survival of its government. Thanks to information that became available from the Libyan nuclear weapons programme, the Pakistani metallurgist Dr.Khan was forced to admit that he had helped countries like Libya, Iran and North Korea obtain nuclear weapons.

George W.Bush's approach towards nonproliferation certainly differed from the Clinton policy, at least rhetorically. While the Clinton administration tried to strengthen the international nonproliferation regime in order to contain the proliferation puzzle, the Bush administration started from the assumption that the nonproliferation regime is not sacrosanct. It can only slow down and not prevent proliferation. The US National Security Strategy released in September 2002 stated: 'our enemies have openly declared that they are seeking weapons of mass destruction, and evidence indicates that they are doing so with determination. We cannot defend America and our friends by hoping for the best'[26]. Pre-emptive strikes – in fact preventive strikes – were regarded as the most effective instrument in countering proliferation. Iraq was the first test case. Missile defence was also emphasized. Parts of the nonproliferation regime – like the Nuclear Non-Proliferation Treaty (NPT), the International Atomic Energy Agency (IAEA) and the export control regimes – can be retained as they are regarded to be part of the narrowly defined US interest. However, there was no support in the Bush administration for a Comprehensive Test Ban Treaty (CTBT), an outer space treaty, the ABM treaty, the landmine treaty, and a Biological Weapons Protocol. Bush's nonproliferation policy is further summed up in the US National Strategy to Combat Weapons of Mass Destruction of December 2002. Interestingly, the chapter on counterproliferation in that document precedes the one about nonproliferation.

In a speech at the National Defence University in February 2004, President Bush announced a new major initiative vis-à-vis the proliferation of weapons of mass destruction[27]. More particularly, he asked to expand both the Proliferation Security Initiative (PSI) and the Cooperative Threat Reduction programme. The Proliferation Security Initiative was announced by President Bush in May 2003 and focuses on preventing the export of sensitive nuclear materials by interdicting shipments at sea, mainly limited to territorial waters, and by denying suspicious aircraft over-flight rights. Dozens of states joined the US, among them Germany, the UK and France. An early success of PSI is the seizure of a Libyan-bound ship carrying nuclear centrifuge equipment in October 2003, which made it easier for the US to pressure Colonel Gadaffi to change his policy. Russia joined PSI on 31 May 2004.

The Cooperation Threat Reduction Programme aiming at securing Russia's nuclear weapons legacy became only fully funded in the Bush administration after the terrorist attacks. In June 2002, the G-8 promised Russia $20 billion for the next 10 years, of which 50 percent provided by the US. The Bush administration also succeeded in removing fissile materials from the former Yugoslavia in the summer of 2002.

In his speech on 11 February 2004, President Bush also called for a Security Council resolution requiring states to criminalise proliferation. His most far-reaching and controversial proposal, however, was to forbid states to acquire enrichment and reprocessing equipment, unless they already possess such a full-scale functioning system, which is for instance not the case for Iran. That would set a ceiling on the number of states that would be able to produce nuclear weapons indigenously. In addition, Bush proposed that states that would like to get help for their civilian nuclear programmes in general, should first ratify the Additional Protocol of the International Atomic Energy Agency (IAEA)[28]. In exchange, Bush asked the nuclear suppliers to guarantee the rest of the world reasonably priced nuclear fuel. It is however doubtful that the non-nuclear weapon states will accept these plans, as it would undermine at least the spirit of article 4 of the Nuclear Nonproliferation Treaty[29].

To conclude, nonproliferation became one of the highest priorities in US foreign and defence policy after the Cold War, at least rhetorically. However, in practice this was not always the case. Even Clinton's Under Secretary of State for Arms Control and International Security Affairs Lynn Davis stated out of office that: 'No consensus exists within the United States as to the priority to be given to nonproliferation when this goal conflicts with other political or economic goals'[30]. She referred for instance to the relaxing of economic sanctions against India and Pakistan in October 1999.

More fundamentally, instead of taking concrete steps to eliminate nuclear weapons to diminish the risks of proliferation, the US explicitly re-legitimised its nuclear arsenal after the Cold War. It refused, for instance, to declare a no first use *because* of the future risk of proliferation. This is turning logic upside down. In addition, it kept a maximum deterrence posture. By stating that nuclear weapons remained politically and militarily useful or even "essential" to secure the vital interests of the US, other states situated in more unstable regions were indirectly stimulated to acquire nuclear weapons as well. Although the link between US nuclear policy and proliferation is debatable and ultimately not provable, many agree that it exists. The Nuclear Nonproliferation Treaty itself provides such a link.

With what legitimacy did the US condemn the Indian and Pakistani nuclear tests in May 1998, which – by the way – did not violate international law ? In the words of a spokesman of the Indian government after the US condemnation: 'The American position is hypocritical. They are sitting on a mountain of nuclear arms, and they are pontificating to India and the world'[31]. In the same vein, with what legitimacy did the US press Iraq, Iran and North Korea to give up their nuclear weapons programmes, when it can be argued that the US was (and still is) not fulfilling its obligations under the Nuclear Nonproliferation Treaty either ?

Elimination

The US did agree with stronger wording on nuclear disarmament in the context of the NPT Extension conference in 1995. Arms Control and Disarmament Agency Director John Holum stated in testimony before the Senate Foreign Relations Committee on 31 January 1995 that under article 6 'the NWS promise measures to reduce *and eliminate* their nuclear arsenals'[32]. A few months later Ralph Earle, his deputy director, was even clearer: 'It is in our complete self-interest, as it is in the self-interest of the Russians and others, to reduce and eventually eliminate (all) nuclear weapons'[33]. Secretary of State Madeline Albright also talked about 'our NPT commitment to move toward the elimination of nuclear weapons. That is a worthy goal, embraced by Presidents of both parties, including President Clinton'[34]. President Clinton wrote at the beginning of 1996 that a test ban 'will help fulfil our mutual pledges to renounce the nuclear arms race and move toward our ultimate goal of a world free of nuclear arms'[35]. When he signed the Comprehensive Test Ban Treaty in September 1996, he stated that the treaty 'points us toward a century in which the roles and risks of nuclear weapons can be further reduced and ultimately eliminated'[36]. In a radio address on 16 May 1998, Clinton concluded: 'We have an opportunity to leave behind the darkest moments of the 20th century and embrace the most brilliant possibilities of the 21st. To do it, we must walk away from nuclear weapons, not toward them'[37].

At the same time, there were many statements that ridiculed the idea of elimination, even in the Clinton administration. Walter Slocombe, Under Secretary of Defence for Policy in the Clinton administration, noted: 'the US is committed to Article VI of the NPT which calls for the complete elimination of nuclear weapons *in the context of general and complete disarmament'*. He continued: 'Until these conditions are realized, however, nuclear weapons will continue to fulfil an essential role in meeting our deterrence requirements and assuring our nonproliferation objectives'[38]. The head of the US Strategic Command Gen.Habiger told the press: 'Article 6 [of the NPT] says the ultimate goal of this treaty is the total elimination of nuclear weapons...But you need to read the small print: given the proper conditions and that's the hang-up. I doubt if we'll ever see the proper preconditions where you have zero nuclear weapons on earth'[39]. Arms Control and Disarmament Agency Director John Holum contended in 1997: 'Recall that Article VI of the NPT specifically places nuclear disarmament in a larger disarmament context – imposing this broader obligation on all states parties. It thus embodies the essential truth that nuclear disarmament cannot occur on demand or in a vacuum, but must be approached in tandem with broader improvements in the international security environment'[40].

Probably the clearest statement against elimination was a comment by Nicholas Burns, spokesman of the State Department, in the context of the Generals Statement in favour of elimination in December 1996. Burns repeated that 'the US continues to believe that nuclear deterrence plays a key role in defending the vital national security interests of the US'. When a journalist asked: 'Therefore the administration plans to keep some of its nuclear weapons *indefinitely* ?', Burns answered with a simple "yes". When another journalist then pointed to the goal of elimination, Burns answered: 'That is of course a goal that the US – successive administrations have committed themselves to. But, of course, *we must live in the real world. We must live practically.* We must prepare practically for the security of the American people and our allies around the world who are relying upon the US to provide for their security'[41]. This sounds very much like the conclusions of the Harvard Study Group from the beginning of the 1980s proclaiming that our only hope is to live with nuclear weapons[42]. In 1994, Chairman of the JCS General Shalikashvili had already remarked: 'It is the ultimate insurance policy for the US, what SAC did and now what Strategic Command is doing. It will *always* remain our ultimate insurance policy'[43]. The same message came across in the Secretary of Defence Annual Report of 1994[44]. PDD-60 of November 1997 also stated that nuclear weapons would remain the cornerstone of US national security for the "indefinite future"[45].

These statements led to considerable concerns on behalf of the non-nuclear weapon states. Does the US take its goal of elimination seriously ? These concerns were further increased by the emphasis on nuclear deterrence against chemical and biological weapons attacks, its nuclear force structure and operational policy.

The 2000 NPT Review Conference put an end to some of the ambiguity. The non-nuclear weapon states pushed the US and the other nuclear weapon states to agree with the 'unequivocal undertaking...to accomplish the total elimination' of its nuclear arsenal. The world "ultimate" disappeared, as well as the direct linkage with conventional disarmament. Although this wording may be seen as a breakthrough, it was not much more than what was understood by most non-governmental experts to be the correct interpretation of article 6 of the NPT.

Elimination became a taboo again under President George W.Bush. In a 2001 publication by the National Institute for Public Policy that is generally regarded as being the bible for Bush's nuclear weapons policy, it was stated that: 'Recent public proposals for nuclear "abolition" or deep force reductions...are likely to be flawed'[46].

In contrast, some analysts regard the Bush's Nuclear Posture Review as a substantial step forward because it acknowledges for the first time that conventional weapons combined with missile defence could replace nuclear weapons in the future[47]. The fact that the numbers may fall further before 2013, as they will be reviewed every two years can be seen through the same rosy glasses.

It is, however, prudent to be sceptical about this interpretation of Bush's NPR. The logic can also be turned upside down. If nuclear weapons are becoming more integrated with conventional weapons, the former may also become more usable, especially if low-yield nuclear weapons are being developed. And the build-up of the nuclear infrastructure may also prevent the reduction to much lower levels, if only because of increased bureaucratic resistance.

Conclusion Part I

Announcing the results of the Nuclear Posture Review (NPR) in September 1994, Secretary of Defence William Perry predicted that 'nuclear weapons will play *a greatly changed role* in our national security strategy'[1]. Two days later, he stated that 'there have been *fundamental* changes' with regard to US nuclear policy[2]. Under Secretary of Defence for Policy Walter Slocombe noted that spending on strategic forces as part of the Defence Department's budget diminished from 24 % in the mid-1960s to 7 % in 1991, and to 3 % in 1997. He concluded: 'But the Cold War is now over and it is important to recognise *the great degree* to which our nuclear deterrent has evolved from that period'[3]. A few months earlier, he mentioned in a congressional hearing: 'The US had made *remarkable progress* in fulfilling our NPT article VI commitment'[4]. One year later, Assistant Secretary of Defence Ed Warner claimed that US nuclear policy had '*dramatically* changed'[5].

Whether the changes in US nuclear policy after the Cold War are categorised as "minor" or "major" depends on the criteria that are used. The US government will always tend to defend its policy against outside critics and will always claim that "major" changes did occur. Abolitionists, in contrast, will always categorise these changes as "minor".

The Cold War levels have indeed come down to a considerable degree (depending on the category of weapons). On the other hand, the reductions say as much about the overkill-capacity of the former levels than about a change in the basic posture. The force numbers are still not in proportion to the existing threat or potential future threats. Maximum deterrence still reigns with regard to force structure, declaratory and operational policy. Even Deputy Secretary of Defence John Deutch – while in office – agreed that there had been no fundamental change as a result of the Clinton NPR. Explaining the outcome at a press conference on 22 September 1994, Deutch reported: 'It is one area where one wants to have continuity of policies and programmes. It's the nuclear programmes of this country…We are not looking for abrupt changes; we are looking for adaptation to change'[6]. A few weeks later, Senator Hamilton asked him the question: 'So the changes you've made from the previous administration are certainly not dramatic. They'd be evolutionary more than anything else ?' Deutch confirmed: 'That's correct'[7].

The Final report of the Henry Stimson Centre concluded in March 1997 that 'the basic principle guiding official US nuclear policy remains little changed from the time of the Cold War'[8]. Former head of US Strategic (Air) Command Gen.Lee Butler contended a year later: 'We have been unable so far to do better than just sort of go on intellectual autopilot'[9]. Keith Payne – a proponent of nuclear weapons and a harsh critic of nuclear disarmament – agreed in 1998 that 'the [Clinton] administration expresses the same basic approach to the declaratory and operational dimensions of deterrence as the US did during most of the Cold War'[10]. In 2005, the assessment is similar. Robert McNamara, former Secretary of Defence under Kennedy and Johnson, states: 'What is shocking is that today, more than a decade after the end of the Cold War, the basic US nuclear policy is unchanged'[11].

In Part II, the question is asked why US nuclear policy was not adapted more to the changed international political circumstances.

PART II

EXPLAINING INERTIA IN US NUCLEAR WEAPONS POLICY AFTER THE COLD WAR

CHAPTER 7

EXPLAINING POLICY INERTIA

In Part I, it became clear that the transformation of US nuclear weapons policy after the Cold War was much slower than one could have expected from a realistic or even Realist point of view. One of the basic assumptions behind Realism is that foreign policy is determined by national interests. Following the strategic rationale of most experts outside the government, fundamental change – a shift from a maximum to a minimum deterrence posture – should have been pushed through right after the Cold War due to the simple fact that it would have been in the interest of the US. The overall strategic costs of a "laissez faire, laissez passer" approach were much too high.

Why did US nuclear policy change so little in contrast to what could have been expected from a strategic or "national interest" point of view ? This is considered in Part II. To answer this question appropriately, we first have to answer the more general question: when do fundamental policy changes happen ? Which factors inhibit or facilitate radical policy change ?

Politics

The reasons for the relative status quo in US nuclear policy after the Cold War have little to do with the nature or characteristics of the international political system, but mainly with the domestic political situation in the US.

Politics – at least in a democracy – can be defined as the outcome of the policy-making process as well as the process itself by which societal issues are dealt with in such a way that the outcome of the process is meant to be in the interest of the society and the personal interest – broadly defined – of the political decision-maker. This definition starts from the assumption that policymakers care about their personal interests and more in particular their own political survival. In practice, this usually means being re-elected at the next elections.

The costs of changing policy should be perceived by the policy-maker as smaller than the overall benefits. A political decision-maker will always ask himself the question: what will be the impact of a particular decision on the likelihood that I (or my party) will be re-elected ?

Most of the time, there are proponents and opponents of policy change. Most political decisions are therefore compromises between different individuals and/or different groups (like political parties) in society, and will therefore lead at most to minor changes. Incrementalism is what can and will generally be expected[1]. Policy changes will be spread over a relatively long period and will consist of a series of minor changes. Fundamental changes are rare.

Changing policy fundamentally is most often not regarded as beneficial for the decision-maker. The reasons are twofold: firstly, fundamental changes create more psychological uncertainty; and secondly, there is an imbalance between the public reaction of the opponents and the advocates of fundamental change. Most of the time, fundamental changes will hurt at least some people. The latter will speak out in order to prevent the proposed changes. Their public statements in turn might damage the political reputation of the decision-makers, which by definition is not in their personal interest. Opponents will probably also remember the issue at the ballot box. On the other hand, the beneficiaries of change – who in the case of fundamental policy change will usually outnumber the opponents – will not feel the necessity to speak out as much because they expect decision-makers to make them better off. In addition, there is a lot of free-riding. Furthermore, that particular issue will probably not determine their voting behaviour.

As a result, the general political rule is that damaging a few and making all the rest better can sometimes do more harm to the personal interest of the decision-maker than doing nothing at all. In other words, political decision-makers generally care more about the potential negative reactions of some politically active and powerful interest groups than about the general positive appreciation of public opinion. The latter may be regarded as an example of a broader theory – called prospect theory – that says that individuals (including decision-makers) care more about potential losses than potential gains[2]. In short, political decision-makers are generally prepared to take more risks to maintain the status quo (and not to lose) than to change policy fundamentally (and to win).

Cost-benefit analysis: strategic and political factors

Two different kinds of costs and benefits must be distinguished with regard to political decision-making: strategic or "national interest" costs and benefits on the one hand, and (purely) political costs and benefits on the other[3]. The importance of each calculation differs from decision-maker to decision-maker.

The *strategic* costs and benefits refer to the "national interests", which the political decision-makers on the national level are in theory supposed to defend, also according to our definition of politics. If the chance is high that a status quo policy will result in considerable strategic costs for the nation in the short-term, political decision-makers may try to change policy in order to prevent these costs.

I also assume that one cannot expect political decision-makers to know each aspect of each political issue in detail. As a result, political decision-makers have to rely on experts for their strategic cost-benefit calculation. As Peter Haas argues: 'How states identify their interests and recognize the latitude of actions deemed appropriate in specific issue-areas of policy-making are functions of the matter in which the problems are understood by the policy-makers or are represented by those whom they turn for advice under conditions of uncertainty'[4]. In principle political decision-makers can rely on two kinds of experts: governmental and non-governmental experts. For the strategic calculus, political decision-makers can and should give more weight to non-governmental advice than that coming out of their administration. In the US political system, the political appointees may to a certain extent fulfil this role.

I further assume that the decision-maker gets representative advice. He should understand what the dominant paradigm inside the (non-governmental) expert-community is and to what extent this dominant paradigm is challenged. The more he perceives the advice as unanimous, the more he can rely on it without having to fear *ex post* criticism from other experts. I am mostly interested in cases where there is a clear majority or even quasi-unanimity within the non-governmental expert community.

I further assume that the knowledge and information is communicated in a clear and unambiguous way by the experts to the decision-makers.

As a result, the strategic calculation of the decision-maker, according to my definition, corresponds basically to the judgment of the community of non-governmental experts, who look both to the desirability and feasibility of policy change from the point of view of the national interest, without taking into account domestic politics. Consequently, the strategic calculation in contrast to the political calculation should, in principle, be the same for every decision-maker, regardless of his or her position or personal beliefs.

The *political* costs and benefits refer to the domestic political situation, and more particularly the possible reactions of different domestic political actors and constituencies – including the bureaucracy – with regard to a certain policy proposal. In the case of "national" strategic benefits, there will usually be a "silent majority" in favour, and sometimes a relatively small but agitated group against. As stated earlier, political decision-makers tend to care more about the reaction of the latter.

Political factors

1. Power distribution between domestic opponents and proponents of change
   a. Interests
   b. Beliefs
2. Tangibility of potential strategic benefits
3. Availability of justifications for not having to change policy
4. Time-scale of potential strategic costs: short, medium, long term
5. Dependence on other states with regard to potential strategic benefits

---

Table 6: Political factors determining the cost-benefit calculation of the decision-maker

The individual political calculation – in contrast to the strategic one – is different from decision-maker to decision-maker. But everybody can in principle make the political calculation for the person who finally has to decide.

Decision-makers have to take at least five key factors that determine his political cost-benefit calculation into account: 1) first and foremost, the political power distribution of the major domestic actors involved, i.e. the advocates and opponents of change; 2) the degree of tangibility of the results; 3) the availability of justifications for not having to change policy; 4) the period in which the strategic costs are likely to occur; 5) the degree of dependence on other states to obtain the strategic benefits. The last four variables are more structural by nature.

The more and greater the constraining political factors, the more negative the political cost-benefit calculation, and the less chance that a fundamental policy change will occur.

The power distribution of the major domestic actors involved

Power is the level of influence of the actors involved both before and after the decision, as perceived by the decision-maker. Influence can be operationalised by looking at: 1) the interests and beliefs involved, and more in particular their intensity, and 2) the political reputation of the players, i.e. the fact that these players were able to influence policy in the past. Strong beliefs are for instance only important if they are held by players having a relatively strong political reputation.

This calculation has to be made about the opponents and advocates of change. If the overall balance of the political calculation is negative, then there will be a tendency to a status quo, even if the strategic calculation is positive.

The intensity of the reactions of powerful political *opponents* – probably the main factor in the political calculation – depends mainly on the extent that interests and beliefs of opponents are hurt by the proposed changes[5].

When there are major domestic *interests* involved and the representatives of those interests are expected to speak out, the chance is high that no policy changes will be pushed through as public criticism can be extremely harmful for one's political image, which can endanger re-election.

As it is not very common that one single individual can halt changes, we are mainly talking about *interest groups*. The importance of interest groups is not measured quantitatively – in terms of percentage of the population – but qualitatively, in terms of being organized and capable of defending their interests in the political arena. The perceived power of those interest groups – their political reputation – is also a crucial variable.

Interest groups can make life difficult for policy-makers who plan to act against their interests. The instruments that interest groups use for making their demands to the political decision-makers range from speaking out publicly to cutting financial gifts to the policy-maker or his or her party. In extreme cases, policy-makers can be personally threatened or physically attacked. A more frequently used way for interest-groups to stop a policy-maker acting against their interests is hurting the political image of the policy-maker by asking and helping (e.g. financing) the opposition party (or parties) to speak out.

One particular interest group with a strong reputation is the bureaucracy. Bureaucracies are organizations that firstly care about their survival. Positively defined, their power and corresponding interests are measured in terms of money and personnel as well as their level of autonomy and prestige. As a result, "where you stand (on a specific issue) depends on where you sit (in the bureaucracy)". Bureaucratic interests may therefore contradict national interests.

Beside interests, individuals, but also expert communities, bureaucracies, and the society as a whole, form *beliefs* to give meaning to reality. Beliefs, according to Alexander George, provide people 'with a relative coherent way of organizing and making sense of what would otherwise be a confusing and overwhelming array of signals and cues picked up from the environment by [their] senses'[6]. Beliefs or images are necessary to interact successfully with the external world. Belief systems determine what kind of information is selected from the outside world, and how it is interpreted[7].

Beliefs can be strongly or weakly developed. Strong political beliefs might, for instance, exist because an issue was controversial in the past. They are gradually built up and are difficult to change. When there are strong domestic beliefs against change, policy change is not likely to be pushed through. Most of the time, however, people are "rationally ignorant" and have weak ideas about political issues.

Beliefs of non-informed decision-makers are most difficult to analyse. Most of the time, they do not have strong beliefs on complex (foreign policy) issues. Neither do they have strong personal interests (in the narrow sense) to defend. The only bias that may exist is that these decision-makers may "use" certain beliefs vis-à-vis the uninformed public to discredit their political opponents. The less public opinion is informed, the easier it is. The more some beliefs can be linked to other beliefs that are more known and sensitive for public opinion, the more these beliefs can be manipulated for purely political reasons.

To shift radically – or even more gradually – from one (genuine) belief to another is never easy and takes time. People tend not to change their beliefs because changes make life more uncertain, less predictable and therefore more stressful. Tolstoi once eloquently said: 'I know that most men – not only those considered clever, but even those who really are clever and capable of understanding the most difficult scientific, mathematical or philosophical problems – can seldom discern even the simplest and most obvious truth if it be such as obliges them to admit the falsity of conclusions they have formed, perhaps with much difficulty – conclusions of which they are proud, which they have thoughts to others and on which they have built their lives'[8].

Cognitive mechanisms help people hold to their beliefs, when objectively speaking they should change their mind. According to Holsti, there is a natural 'tendency of the individual to assimilate new perceptions to familiar ones and to distort what is seen in such a way as to minimize the clash with previous expectations'[9]. This is called cognitive consistency. Another cognitive mechanism is denial that David Barash defines as 'the mental process of refusing to confront facts that would cause us pain or otherwise disrupt our daily lives'[10]. Wishful thinking is still another. Wishful thinking according to John Steinbruner makes it possible 'to maintain consistency without changing the beliefs by casting them in a long-range time and adopting the inference of transformation; namely, that the immediate situation will succumb to a favourable trend over time'[11].

To change the beliefs of an *organization* is even more difficult. Most of the individuals that make up an organization prefer not to change their beliefs on a regular basis. In turn the resulting inertia creates a kind of self-fulfilling prophecy. Nobody expects big changes within an organization. As a result, most people within an organization will behave conservatively. In addition, each organization has a formal mission. From a practical point of view, it is impossible to change this mission very often. Besides, there exists what Morton Halperin calls "shared images" or common beliefs. Generally proposed changes within an organization also run counter to the interests of a sub-group within the organization, which further complicates the matter. To conclude, making substantial changes in an organization takes time.

Changes within *bureaucracies* are even more difficult to push through than changes within private organizations. Firstly, there are fewer incentives for (positive) change in the public sector, as the "quality of work" that is produced is not directly linked to job certainty, or at least less than in private companies. If private firms, in contrast, do not constantly adapt themselves to the new circumstances, they will not survive. Secondly, because of the latter, there is more room for strong "shared images" in bureaucratic organizations than in private organizations. Thirdly, government officials must defend the policy publicly, even when internal debates about policy change are going on. This tension causes stress and is therefore not liked.

The overall result is that bureaucracies are 'basically inert'... 'Time and resources of any person in the bureaucracy are limited and when a participant does desire change, he must choose carefully the issues on which to battle'[12].

The same logic applies even more to the society as a whole. If the majority of public opinion perceives a certain kind of policy that already exists for decades as still being in the national interest despite contrary claims of the expert-community, the chance is high that policy changes are not pushed through. If society as such is not ripe for a proposed policy change, the risk exists that policy-makers in favour of a policy change will be regarded as too progressive or even arrogant[13]. Changing policy, however, does not always mean that the former policy and the corresponding beliefs were wrong. The circumstances, for instance, may also have changed in the meantime. But the perception can linger in large parts of public opinion that the existing policy is still right, especially if the proposed change is perceived as fundamental and if there was a quasi-consensus on the existing policy before.

Societal inertia, however, does not automatically mean political inertia. In some instances, it is the responsibility of those who are in power and who have access to more information to *lead* public opinion (see leadership). On the other hand, this cannot be stretched too far because it can end up in authoritarianism. This tension is inherent to democratic policy-making.

Last but not least, interests and beliefs are also linked. Sometimes, those having interests consciously or unconsciously build up beliefs sustaining their interests. Vice versa, people with strong beliefs may after a while become so identified with a particular belief that interests are formed.

To conclude, the stronger the advocates for change, the greater the chance that political decision-makers will push through changes. But decision-makers are much more sensitive to what opponents declare. As a result, even if the advocates – let alone the silent majority – outnumber the opponents, it may be that decision-makers chose to follow the line of a few powerful political opponents.

Four more structural factors

Firstly, if the results of policy change are tangible, it would improve the chances that changes will be pushed through. Successful preventive actions in contrast are not very rewarding from a political point of view. For instance, preventing an environmental catastrophe is by definition not visible. It cannot easily be exploited for electoral reasons.

Secondly, the more political decision-makers have seemingly credible justifications for not having to change policy, the higher the likelihood that changes will not be pushed through. Most of the time, political decision-makers are able to justify the lack of change using different arguments for different audiences. The more complex an issue, the easier to find justifications and the easier the uninformed public will accept these justifications.

Thirdly, the more decision-makers expect that the strategic costs of a status quo policy will occur in the short-term, the more they will be interested in preventing these costs by changing policy. Neustadt explains: 'Trying to stop fires is what Presidents do first. It takes most of their time'[14]. The corollary is that decision-makers will be much less interested in preventing long-term costs, except if they expect to be in power for a long time. The latter is mostly not the case in democracies. Predictions about when the strategic costs may become real are, however, always uncertain. A major incident or catastrophe can of course remove the tendency towards procrastination substantially.

Lastly, the more the effect of a policy change depends on similar or other actions in other states, the more difficult it becomes to prevent the strategic costs of a status quo policy in the first place, and the greater the chance that decision-makers will not try to change policy, as they can always blame other states. This is of course an argument that cuts both ways. The behaviour of other states also depends on one's own behaviour.

Politicians have to take into account both their own (and other's) perceptions of the *political* factors, and the advice of the experts with regard to the *strategic* calculation. Four scenarios are imaginable (see table 7).

Some decisions are easier to take than others: if the political decision-maker is convinced of a positive effect of a certain policy change from a "national interest" point of view *and* if he estimates that the political cost-benefit calculation will be positive as well, he has no reason not to agree with the proposed changes (case 1); or if he perceives the strategic cost-benefit calculation as negative *and* if he is afraid of the political costs, he will not take the decision to change policy fundamentally (case 4).

Most of the time, the choice is not that easy. The strategic calculation may be negative and the political calculation may be positive. Or the strategic analysis may point in the direction of change while the political factors point to a status quo. In both cases, the final outcome is unclear.

I am especially interested in the scenario where the decision-maker faces a choice between (high) strategic benefits and (high) political costs (case 2).

According to my definition of politics, the tendency would be that the political factors will prevail and a status quo will result. The definitive outcome of the decision-making process, however, depends on a third factor, namely the level of leadership.

		Political cost-benefit analysis	
		In favour of fundamental change	Against fundamental change
Strategic cost-benefit analysis	In favour of fundamental change	FUNDAMENTAL CHANGE	*Unclear but tendency to no fundamental change (except leadership)*
	Against fundamental change	Unclear	NO FUNDAMENTAL CHANGE

Table 7: Four scenarios with regard to fundamental policy change

Leadership

Whatever the strategic and political cost-benefit calculation are, the final outcome lies solely in the hands of the decision-maker. Therefore, one more factor has to be integrated in the model: leadership. The presence of leadership may stretch the possible outcomes. More in particular, decision-makers have to determine the relative weight of the political and strategic calculation. Leadership can neutralize the political costs in case the decision-maker is very much convinced that change is in the national interest, even if the results will not likely be visible in the short-term. He or she should "only" convince public opinion.

Fundamental change can happen if *a sufficient number* of the highest political decision-makers show leadership qualities. As Booth and Wheeler stated, radical change in policy can happen 'if enough people, in the right place, change their minds'[15]. The bigger the impact of a decision, the higher the position of the decision-makers has to be.

Political leadership consists of two elements: 1) having the willingness to change policy fundamentally and believing in the rightfulness of the decision, despite the existence of restraining factors (strategic leadership); *and* 2) having the capacity to push changes through (tactical leadership)[16]. The less strategic leadership is present, the more tactical leadership is required (and vice versa).

Leadership = Strategic leadership + Tactical leadership

Table 8: Leadership

Strategic leadership

Strategic leadership consists in turn of three consecutive stages: 1) knowledge, 2) judgment, and 3) decision.

1) To understand thoroughly a political issue one must be able to situate it in the larger context without having to know every single detail. This demands *knowledge* and therefore sufficient objective information. For this, political decision-makers rely on non-governmental experts and on their administration. At the same time, this means getting rid of uncommitted thinking and cognitive processes like cognitive dissonance, negative or worst-case thinking, wishful-thinking, deep conservatism or ideological thinking, habit formation or grooved thinking, misperceptions, simplicity, bolstering, black-white thinking and denial. Knowledge supposes a rational and open mind on behalf of the decision-maker.

2) Knowledge however is not sufficient. Leaders should personally *judge* and believe that the proposed changes are in the interest of the nation as a whole. The decision-maker should understand the rationale of the expert-community and should agree that the strategic benefits of a policy change outweigh the strategic costs. The decision-maker should understand the low short-term strategic (and therefore also low political) benefits of the policy change and the dependence on the decisions of other states. However, he should be convinced that the short-term costs do not outweigh the long-term strategic benefits, that a policy change might influence the decision of other states in a positive sense and that the risks of creating high strategic costs do not weigh up against the risks going together with a status quo policy.

3) Finally, decision-makers have to take a personal *decision* to push through fundamental change, knowing that it will require a lot of time and energy. Convincing superiors, colleagues, the administration and public opinion requires overcoming potential political costs like rebutting arguments and criticism by opposition parties before and after the decision has been taken. 'A participant's determination of whether to get involved in one issue depends on his calculation of the risks to his own personal interests and position, as well as his perception of national security interests. He is concerned about the time and energy involved in getting caught up in an issue, as well as the consequences to his reputation for effectiveness if he loses', Halperin and Kanter comment[17].

A strategic leader acts in the interest of the nation, if necessary against parochial interests. He looks both to the long and short term. Only when he really believes that a policy change will be the right policy for the nation, he will take that decision. Alexander George puts it this way: 'It is, of course, one of the major role tasks of a leader that he accepts the responsibility to make difficult trade-off choices of this kind...Identifications with the role may bring with it an understanding and acceptance of the fact that one cannot be an executive without facing up to the fact that there will be occasions on which one simply cannot make a good decision without sacrifice of some of one's own interests or those of others'[18].

Most of the time, basic values determine whether he or she will take such a decision. However, prestige can also be a driving factor behind a decision-maker to take radical decisions. Values and prestige can also be complementary. In addition, the decision-maker may hope to get electoral success by behaving like a statesman. Strategic leadership therefore does not require altruism. Whether the expectations about political benefits will be finally realized, depends not only on the outcome, but also on how the decision and the outcome are later on framed, not the least by the media.

A decision to change policy not only requires vision, but also courage. A necessary condition for taking such a decision is risk-prone behaviour, as it always remains a (calculated) risk to fight against the opposition both inside the government (colleagues, superiors, bureaucracy) and outside the government (opposition party, think-tanks, interest-groups, media). In addition, there is also the (small) risk that despite the recommendation of the experts in the field, the strategic advantages in fact do not outweigh the disadvantages in the end.

A decision taken by such a leader neutralizes the restraining political factors described in the first part of the model. More particularly, a leader can and will "rock the boat" with those having interests and beliefs against the proposed policy change; he will "take the heat" by implicitly admitting that the existing policy is wrong, despite the fact that the policy is still generally perceived as beneficial; he will obtain only marginal political benefits in the short-term in case the advocates of change are weak and the results are not tangible; he will ignore a much easier path, namely doing nothing or using false justifications.

Strategic leadership = knowledge + judgment + personal decision

Table 9: Strategic leadership

Tactical leadership

Strategic leadership does not automatically lead to success in the short-term, especially if it is not accompanied by tactical leadership: knowing how to push a decision through. 'Generating creative ideas in the judgment process is not enough, however, to guarantee their acceptance. Decision-makers must also be capable of withstanding ridicule, fear of failure, and social pressure to conform so that creative ideas stand a chance of being seriously considered and accepted by others rather than rejected out of hand when they represent a divergence from common wisdom', according to Vertzberger[19].

Tactical leadership consists in being capable of pushing policy change through, both inside and outside the government. First of all, colleagues and superiors must be persuaded. If they agree, there is still the bureaucracy. Lastly, public opinion has to be convinced. Bruce Russett contends that 'leaders may try to expand their freedom of action by persuading much of the public to shift its mixture of acceptable policy in one direction or the other. A great leader will actually do that'[20].

Opponents inside and outside the government have to be moulded by different arguments, by different means, and by different tactics. Halperin and Kanter explain in detail how decision-makers should plan their efforts. 'They need to determine what decisions they hope to get made, by whom, and in what sequence. Next they must classify the other participants according to who has power with the President, who is likely to be neutral, who is an ally, and who is an opponent. It is then necessary to consider the kinds of arguments, the kinds of bargaining, and the kinds of coercive efforts that are required to achieve the desired decision. The resulting plans usually involve a series of *manoeuvres* and *arguments* designed to influence the outcome'[21].

Factors that will determine the final outcome of this struggle are: 1) whether the decision-maker possesses the necessary *political leverage*, which in turn depends on his formal position, his informal or earned authority, his communication skills, his capability of logrolling, and his ability to persuade others; 2) the political (for instance presidential) style; and 3) the bureaucratic culture of openness to new ideas.

Conclusion

Chapter 2 has explained in length the *strategic* reasons for a policy change. It concluded that fundamental policy change - a shift from maximum to minimum deterrence after the Cold War – was and still is desirable and feasible. In chapter 8, the *political* calculation will be made from the perspective of US decision-makers right after the Cold War.

CHAPTER 8

EXPLAINING NUCLEAR INERTIA: THE NUCLEAR ESTABLISHMENT AND CONSERVATIVES VERSUS THE ARMS CONTROL COMMUNITY

Which nuclear posture would have fitted US national interests best in the post-Cold War period ? The conclusion reached in Part I was that it would have been in the interest of the US to have changed nuclear policy fundamentally, and more particularly to have switched from a maximum to a minimum deterrence posture. There was quasi-unanimous support in the non-governmental expert-community for this.

But, as made clear in the previous chapter, strategic considerations are only one side of the coin. Ultimately, the decision for policy change must be taken by politicians, who by definition also have to look to the political context. The key question then becomes: which US nuclear policy could have been expected in 1989 or two or four years later, taking the *domestic* political situation in the US into account ? Which interests were still involved ? What kind of beliefs and belief systems played a role ? What was the power of the advocates of nuclear change ? Were the possible positive results of a policy change tangible ? Were there any justifications for not changing policy fundamentally ? Would the strategic costs have occurred in the short or in the long term ? Were other states involved ?

The political power of the arms control community is extremely small in comparison for instance with that of the nuclear establishment. The same applies even more to the American peace movement. The only player that could in theory have made a difference would have been public opinion. Many American citizens after the Cold War, if asked, would have been in favour of nuclear elimination, and therefore in favour of a shift from maximum to minimum deterrence.

On the other hand, many people – especially in nuclear weapon states – still regard nuclear weapons as a legitimate defence instrument. American political decision-makers therefore were not keen on having a societal debate about the future of nuclear weapons. 'Some elements of the US national security establishment, both inside the government and outside, seem to consider the whole subject of disarmament as a taboo, as if merely raising the issue will trigger a flood of domestic and international pressure to disarm immediately and without sufficient guarantees', as Michael Mazarr comments[1]. This tactic worked. Partially due to government rhetoric and silence, most people in the US believe that nuclear weapons have all (or mostly) gone after the Cold War.

Because of the political weakness of the proponents of change, American political decision-makers would not have gained a lot by advocating change in the short-term.

For estimating the power of the opponents of change of US nuclear policy right after the Cold War, it is useful to look to the power of the advocates of maximum deterrence *during* the Cold War. As the Cold War ended rather abruptly, one can assume that both the opponents of minimum deterrence right after the Cold War were more or less the same as those at the end of the Cold War.

The magnitude of interests and beliefs of the nuclear weapons establishment explain the "irrational" build-up of the nuclear arsenals during the Cold War for a large part. If US political decision-makers made their political calculation right after the Cold War, they certainly had to take the political power of the nuclear establishment into account.

The nuclear weapons establishment: a strong political player with parochial interests

The build-up of the nuclear weapons arsenals during the Cold War can be explained by the perceived intensity of tension in the late 1940s and 1950s and by the parochial interest groups created during this period. Gigantic bureaucratic organizations were gradually created, also in the domain of nuclear weapons. The major explanation for the further build-up of nuclear arsenals after having reached a nuclear overkill-capacity is indeed the power and influence of the nuclear weapons establishment.

Four specific determinants of bureaucratic interests can be distinguished: budget, personnel, autonomy and prestige. As James Fallows once pointed out: 'The Pentagon is in business to devise war plans and understand the enemy and protect the nation; but before any of those things, it is in business to spend *money*[2]. Although it is sometimes claimed that nuclear weapons are cheap, they are not. President Clinton tried to convince India not to produce nuclear weapons with the following argument: '[The US and the USSR] spent billions of dollars on elaborate command and control systems for *nuclear weapons which are not cheap*'[3].

The US alone spent more than $5.5 trillion on nuclear weapons during the Cold War[4]. This corresponds to more or less 30% of all US defence spending during that period. Only social security and non-nuclear defence received more public money in the US during the Cold War than nuclear weapons. The US produced over 70,000 nuclear warheads, 67,500 nuclear missiles (including more than 6,000 ballistic missiles) and 4,000 nuclear bombers[5].

After the Cold War, the nuclear weapons budget diminished in relative terms[6]. What matters, however, in the context of parochial interests are absolute numbers. In 1998, still $34.8 billion was spent on nuclear weapons in the US. The latter was

14 % of the defence budget that cannot, in its turn, be categorized as small. The total cost of the Trident II D-5 missiles, that were built after the Cold War, is $37.5 billion. To operate a Trident submarine (including two crews) for instance costs $92.5 million per year[7]. The operations and maintenance budget of SAC alone corresponded to $2 billion per year in 1992[8]. The cost of a Stealth B-2 bomber is $2.7 billion *per plane*. The modernization of the Minuteman ICBMs that aims at extending the service life beyond 2020 costs $6 billion.

Operational nuclear forces	24.7
- strategic nuclear forces	7.5
- tactical nuclear and dual-capable forces	1
- command, control, communications and intelligence	6
- operations and maintenance	4
- research and development (Defence Department)	0.4
- Defence Special Weapons Agency	0.3
- Stockpile Stewardship Programme (Department of Energy)	4.3
- other nuclear related defence programmes in the Department of Energy	0.9
- naval nuclear propulsion (Department of Energy)	0.33
Cold War legacies (e.g. environmental restoration)	5.8
National and theatre missile defence	3.7
Cooperative Threat Reduction	0.4
On-Site Inspection Agency	0.04
Arms Control and Disarmament Agency	0.035
Total	34.8

Table 10: Estimated spending on US nuclear weapons in 1998 (in billions of $)[9]

Minimum deterrence would have meant having much less strategic and sub-strategic nuclear weapons to maintain, and much less costly operations. A shift towards minimum deterrence would have corresponded to a 50 % reduction of the post-Cold War nuclear budget. For instance, a GAO report of 1998 stated that going to START II levels in 1999 would have saved $800 million a year for the US. Reaching these levels in 2003 would have yielded $700 million a year. Reaching START III levels would have saved $1.5 billion a year. Reaching the level of 1,000 nuclear weapons could have saved $2 billion per year[10].

Michael Brown posits: 'If ICBMs were eliminated from the force structure, for example, a whole series of organizations devoted to the development, operation, and maintenance of these systems would fall by the wayside, and both the Air Force and contractor budgets would be adversely affected'[11].

The number of people working for the US nuclear weapons establishment during the Cold War ran to hundreds of thousands. During the Manhattan project alone, over 150,000 people worked on a full-time basis on the development of the first generation of nuclear weapons for over three years. The nuclear arms race with the Soviet-Union created mammoth organizations: the Strategic Air

Command (SAC), for instance, had 240,000 people on its pay roll. In 1961, SAC possessed 68 military airbases. In the first half of the 1980s, the number of personnel in the Defence Department dealing directly with nuclear weapons and delivery vehicles was still 120,000[12]. Livermore and Los Alamos, where nuclear weapons were developed, each had a staff of 8,000 people and a budget of $1 billion in the second half of the 1980s[13].

After the Cold War, the number of people working in the nuclear arms establishment shrank. Comparable with the budget, governmental sources talk about a reduction of 70 % from the *height* of the Cold War[14]. Nevertheless, the number of people working for SAC in the Defence Department in 1992 was still more than 100,000. The number of people in the Department of Energy dealing with nuclear weapons was still between 90,000 and 100,000 in 1990[15].

A shift towards minimum deterrence would have had serious consequences for the number of personnel. As Harald Müller pointed out in 1998: 'There are strong vested interests inherent in the nuclear weapon complexes. Thousands of jobs and careers depend on the production, or at least the maintenance, of these weapons'[16]. In particular, scientists developing and maintaining the safety of nuclear weapons at the national labs (DOE), the companies producing nuclear weapons and Pentagon officials responsible for nuclear policy might have lost their jobs as a result of a shift towards a minimum deterrence posture.

From a bureaucratic point of view, to make trouble inside the government by proposing policy changes is not the best tactic for being promoted later on. There is an inherent tendency in bureaucracies toward conflict evasion. James Fallows quotes one defence bureaucrat saying: 'The only requirements [for bureaucrats] are to stay busy, generate paper, and make no mistakes. The reader tempted to criticize this behaviour is invited first to imagine himself in this situation, complete with a large mortgage and children in college...All pressures are to maximize mediocrity'[17].

Civilians in the Defence Department dealing with nuclear weapons had no reason to go against the interests of the military either. The job satisfaction of those civilian officials depends for a large part on their day-to-day relations with the military. Therefore, they had an interest in supporting the military's demands.

A third element of the bureaucratic identity is the degree of freedom and autonomy. The military are used to deciding *how* to use military force once the decision is made to use military force. Maybe contrary to what can be expected, this also applies to nuclear policy. In theory, nuclear weapons are one of the few military aspects in which civilians have always had a special interest, which in turn might have diminished the autonomy of the military. In practice, however, the military remained the guardians of the nuclear arsenal. The military have written the nuclear war plans since 1948. They determined how many weapons were needed and how they were targeted[18]. This also applies to the post-Cold War period.

The military that dealt with nuclear weapons regarded the demand for a shift from maximum to minimum deterrence as an interference in – if not distrust of – their professional capabilities. In addition, such a shift would have diminished their job satisfaction, as their role would have become more limited. They would probably no longer have had the authority to decide on the use of nuclear weapons in particular circumstances. The number of targeting options would also have been very much constrained, if not totally abolished. The alert-levels would have been much lower. As a result, the political decision-makers would have time to decide about a possible counter-attack. All this would have gone against the military adage "keep all options open" and against their demand for autonomy.

Lastly, nuclear weapons were seen – at least during the Cold War – as "the" most prestigious military instrument. SAC was by far the most prestigious department in the Air Force and probably in the Defence Department as a whole. Such feelings do not change overnight. A good example of this was Admiral Mitchell's testimony before the Senate in May 1993: 'Our programme has been blessed over the years since we have been in existence, almost 38 years now as a dedicated programme office. Most of us have grown up inside this programme. I personally participated in the development of the Polaris A3, Poseidon C3, Trident C4, and Trident D5...Our success is certainly not a matter of individual success for me...It is a government commitment that has been made...to stick to some very fundamental principles of how to do the job and do it well...I do not know of anybody that works in our programme that does not have just a little bit of that feel to them that says they are doing some things extraordinarily worthwhile'[19].

Changing from maximum to minimum deterrence – let alone from a nuclear job to a non-nuclear job – would have meant an enormous loss of prestige and a corresponding loss of job satisfaction. As numbers of nuclear capabilities, budget, and personnel go down, prestige would diminish even more. As Michael Brown points out: 'Changing nuclear doctrines and operational plans is especially difficult if particular doctrines and plans become closely identified with the "essence" of specific military organizations'[20].

These four elements – budget, personnel, autonomy and prestige – also overlap. Scott Sagan (Stanford University) describes the process of building new nuclear weapons during the Cold War as follows: 'The initial ideas for individual weapons innovations are often developed inside state laboratories, where scientists favour military innovation simply because it is technically exciting and keeps money and prestige flowing to their laboratories. Such scientists are then able to find, or even create, sponsors in the professional military whose bureaucratic interests and specific military responsibilities lead them also to favour the particular weapons system. Finally, such a coalition builds broader political support within the executive or legislative branches by shaping perceptions about the costs and benefits of weapons programmes'[21].

The fact that nuclear arms control stalled during the Cold War is therefore not only related to obstructive steps by the Soviets. Domestic politics and more particularly the parochial interests of the different services – and especially the Air Force – also played a significant role. Blacker and Duffy drew already in the 1980s attention to the fact that 'arms control policy in the US, and apparently in the Soviet Union, is immersed in a context of people and organizations all at odds with one another over the most effective means of promoting security, and, incidentally, all promoting their personal or institutional interests'[22]. Steve Miller (Harvard University) is not surprised by the fact that arms control stalled: '[arms control] engages the interests of a large, powerful complex, a not well understood process of defence decision-making and weapons acquisition, a process that generally seeks security not by constraining or eliminating weapons and military options but by providing them; this, it should not be forgotten, is the job that the Pentagon is hired to do, and it should come as no surprise that it seeks to fulfil that responsibility'[23]. Senator Alan Cranston applied this logic in the 1990s: 'I think one of the major obstacles to advancing the cause of nuclear abolition lies in what Lee Butler calls the "nuclear priesthood", people who have built their lives and their careers upon nuclear weapons or nuclear doctrine. They are spreading the gospel – and some of them are in very high and influential places – that we need nuclear weapons, and we need them forever'[24].

The end of Cold War and the diminished interest in nuclear weapons in the military.
When the extent of the geo-strategic revolution of 1989 became clear, slashes in the American defence complex became inevitable. Also the budget for nuclear weapons and the number of people dealing with nuclear weapons had to decline. In addition, because of the nuclear taboo, there was little prospect for a surge of the nuclear weapons business in the long-term. Together with the call for a general peace-dividend after the Cold War, one could have predicted pressure on the nuclear bureaucracy to downsize considerably.

To a certain extent that is also what happened. Even more, most of the military – even the JCS – were no longer enthusiastic about nuclear weapons. They would not have been unhappy with their elimination. In principle, it would have freed money for useable conventional weapons[25].

There is, however, a bureaucratic process that explains why the military did *not* advocate minimum deterrence let alone elimination after the Cold War: interservice and intraservice co-operation. 'Since the early 1960s, interservice disputes have been resolved in private, behind the closed doors of the meeting room of the JCS in the Pentagon. This process has been described by close observers as an elaborate, drawn out negotiation where log rolling replaces confrontation, and outcomes resemble lowest common denominator compromise rather than victory or defeat', according to Owen Coté (MIT)[26].

With regard to nuclear weapons policy after the Cold War, one can argue that about 99 % of the military were not in favour of nuclear weapons. But the remaining one percent – the nuclear bureaucracy – had a veto[27]. Co-operation between services and especially co-operation between departments within services prevented change.

The fear of a slippery slope
Changing one element of the nuclear policy could have had major consequences for the posture as a whole as force structure, declaratory, and operational policy are intimately linked. The military therefore feared that in case they would agree to change a minor element, they would open Pandora's box.

The defence establishment was afraid that giving away (parts of) the nuclear business would stimulate demands for reductions in other domains as well. It was extremely afraid that it had to reduce its size considerably as had been the case after the First World War and Second World War. The major premise of the US defence establishment after the Cold War became to give away as little as possible. Richard Kohn, chief historian of the Air Force in the 1980s, wrote in 1994: 'By Bill Clinton's inauguration a year ago, the military had accepted "downsizing" and reorganization, but not changes that invaded too dramatically the traditional functions of each of the individual armed services, or that changed too radically the social composition of the forces, or cut too deeply into combat readiness, or otherwise undermined the quality and ability of the military to fulfil its functions…Powell's larger motives were to establish a floor for the defence cuts he knew to be inevitable, and to work out a coherent strategy and force structure which would prevent the kind of helter-skelter debilitating reductions common to previous demobilizations after American wars'[28]. A shift from maximum to minimum deterrence had to be blocked in order to prevent the further unravelling of the defence department as a whole.

Bureaucratic opposition during the Cold War
Because presidents and political appointees are only in government for a relatively short period of time, career officials can always try to hold up proposed changes by bureaucratic manoeuvres in the hope that they just "sit out" the problem. 'People like Robert McNamara and James Schlesinger have come and gone; the Strategic Air Command and the Navy, with their outlooks unchanged, remained', Daniel Ford confirms[29].

The nuclear establishment, the Air Force and the Pentagon as a whole can make their opposition to a proposed policy change clear in more direct ways as well. First, the military can publicly speak out against the administration, which would be very embarrassing for the latter. Secondly, another major road for the bureaucracy to oppose the administration goes through Congress. Thirty-four senators can block any treaty ratification. As Steve Miller pointed out: 'This can involve a significant amount of cajolery and appeasement of key Senators in policy formulation, permitting senators to observe the negotiations first-hand, and political logrolling on military programmes (or on other unrelated issues) to secure or assure the support of important votes, as well as an effort to mobilize public opinion'[30]. Financial contributions to members of Congress with regard to missile defence are one example. In the period 1995-1999 alone, John Warner – Republican and chairman of the Armed Services Committee – received over $380,000 in the form of campaign contributions from the defence industry, according to William Hartung. Second on the list was John Murta – Democrat, ranking member of the Defence Subcommittee for Appropriations – with $366,000[31].

The Senate also depends a lot on the advice of the Joint Chiefs of Staff, which historically have been entrusted to be the guardians of national security. Although the advice of the military is in principle not binding, only in extremely rare occasions did Congress vote against the advice of the Chiefs.

In case the military do support treaty ratification, they have to be compensated. Paradoxically, there exists an implicit rule that says that arms control treaties have to be compensated by force modernizations[32]. As Paul Stockton argues: 'That leverage over ratification gives the services a powerful voice in the drafting of US treaty proposals, which the services – and their civilian allies in the executive branch – use to ensure that prospective treaties will accommodate the new weapons they deem necessary…arms development and arms control go forward in tandem, through an intra-governmental logrolling mechanism in which support for one is traded for the other'[33]. The Limited Test Ban Treaty (LTBT), for instance, led to an expanded underground testing programme[34]. SALT I led to accelerated defence spending for Trident and the B-1, and SALT II led to the development of the MX[35]. There was also a link between START I and the B-2. In 1990, CINCSAC Gen.Chain warned: 'There are several bills on the Hill to cancel the B-2. If those bills are passed, I will go and testify strongly against support of the START agreement'[36].

Beside treaty ratifications, all decisions with budgetary implications – for instance with regard to the force structure – have to be approved by Congress. But here again, Congress depends to a large extent on the military. Congress is not very knowledgeable about technological-military intricacies. As a result, 'Congress never has the chance to understand, let alone influence, the calculations that result in appropriations requests. By the time a weapons development or procurement programme reaches Congress for budgetary approval, it has developed such powerful constituencies – from the military-technical community, military officials, and even legislators who have a stake in the development – that it is considered on grounds often wholly unrelated to strategy, ranging from pure economic interests to a general perception that modernization is almost always a good idea', Janne Nolan explains[37].

In addition, due to the enormous defence budget, the military are crucial in bringing jobs and welfare to a particular city, region or district. Over the years, members of Congress became more and more dependent on the military in this regard.

Military-industrial-complex

The Pentagon has an enormous – one could even say disproportional – influence on American foreign and defence policy and on American society in general. The defence department and the defence industry form the so-called "military-industrial-complex", a concept that was coined by President Eisenhower in his farewell speech. In 1950, political scientist Harold Lasswell in his book *National security and individual freedom* had already warned against building a "garrison state"[38].

In the 1990s, many analysts perceived a crisis of civilian control over the military, of which the origins had to be found during the Cold War (see chapter 10). Military historian Richard Kohn explains that: 'the roots of the crisis [of civilian control] go back to the beginning of the Cold War, when the creation of a large, "peacetime" standing military establishment overloaded the traditional process by which civilian control was exercised…to require a network of arms producers and business suppliers that touched every community in the nation…The institutions were simply too large, their activities too diverse, and their influence too pervasive for effective oversight by the normal legislative or bureaucratic procedures traditionally used by civilians on Capitol Hill and in the executive branch'[39]. Bacevich agrees: 'This Cold War legacy invests the military with a capacity to tilt the debate in ways that advance its interests but do not necessarily serve the common good'. He even went on – in 1994 – to warn that this could 'pose a threat to the established order' in the future[40].

The nuclear targeting community: the core of the nuclear military-industrial complex

The nuclear targeting community defines the so-called nuclear deterrence requirements and nuclear damage expectancy levels. Deterrence requirements are the formal requirements to be met by the military in case deterrence fails and in case nuclear weapons have to be used. In theory, the deterrence requirements are defined by political decision-makers based on the existing threat. In practice, it happens the other way around. The requirements are proposed by the military to the decision-makers, and the latter more or less automatically accept them. In addition, the deterrence requirements are so vague that they have to be interpreted later on, again by the military. During the Cold War, the targeting or deterrence requirements, damage expectancy levels and corresponding alert-levels were used by the military to get the nuclear force structure they wanted. Military worst-case assumptions and "political guidance" justified the chosen probabilities. This process started already in 1952 when decisions had to be taken with regard to the number of bombers[41]. It is therefore not surprising that President Eisenhower already criticized SAC in 1959: 'They are trying to get themselves into an incredible position of having enough to destroy every conceivable target all over the world, plus a three-fold reserve'[42].

But what happened when there were more weapons than targets ? Nolan explains: 'If more weapons were there, we would have more targets. The guidance, which is supposed to determine the mix of targets and weapons, was useless. When the "economy recovery" targets were dropped from being SIOP-eligible (after PD-59), fewer targets should have meant fewer weapons, but we changed the mission to "war-supporting industry" and there was no change in the weapons-to-targets mix'[43].

Furthermore, Bruce Blair contends that 'the SIOP did not provide for the complete satisfaction of targeting requirements even under optimal conditions, a fact that implicitly promoted vigorous force modernization to close the gap'[44].

This interactive process between operational policy and force structure policy explains much of the irrational build-up and (lack of) build-down of the US nuclear arsenal. It also explains the absurdity of US targeting policy. For instance, one of the main command posts in the neighbourhood of Moscow was supposed to be hit by 69 nuclear warheads, while probably one would have been sufficient. Why 69 ? It is relatively easy to re-do the calculation. Assuming – as Bruce Blair does – that the highest kill probability against a hardened command post is 4 %. To attain a 50 % confidence in destroying the target requires 17 warheads. With 69 weapons, you attain a 94 % confidence rate, exactly what is known to be the "requirement" for such installations…[45].

In the same vein, the deterrence requirements and damage expectancy levels were used by the military to define the arms control levels. Starting from their desired force structure and the principle of strategic parity, the military derived what the requirements had to be in order to retain a desired percentage of the force structure. It is ironic that the Defence Department always stated that it could assure the deterrence requirements, even when the force structure was going down against their wishes. Apparently, the deterrence requirements were not 100 % determined by the external threat.

The only "logical" framework that legitimised this irrational acquisition process was maximum deterrence. This is another indication that maximum deterrence was not a concept in which one genuinely believed, but a concept constructed to justify existing policy. 'There is no element in US nuclear policy more corrosive to rational decision-making than our adherence to the dictum that the objective in nuclear war must be to destroy the opponent's nuclear forces', former CIA Director Stansfield Turner stressed[46]. Nolan adds: 'This was the crux of the civilian-military dispute:

civilians thought the SIOP should reflect policy objectives, but the military knew it should reflect only current capabilities…A document that connected political objectives to forces meant a budget blueprint that was bound to bring ceilings, if not outright cuts'[47]. The latter had to be prevented by all means in the eyes of the nuclear establishment.

A RAND report of 1994 formulated the following alternative: 'Practical operational considerations and budgetary constraints rather than "requirements" should be the main determining factor in sizing the force. The former are real, the latter are not'[48].

A similar role for military doctrines

Not only operational policy, i.e. the deterrence requirements, were used for getting the desired force structure. The same process applied to the military doctrines. The latter were adapted in function of bureaucratic interests. Different examples can be given of changes in nuclear doctrines during the Cold War that have their origins in parochial interests.

A first example is the *Navy* doctrine that changed from a counter-shore to a countercity targeting strategy. This evolution did not evolve from a change in genuine beliefs, but was caused by organizational interests. The Navy switched to SLBMs because it knew that otherwise it would be out of the nuclear business. 'Polaris…resulted [instead] from a fear felt at the highest level of the service that existing budget shares might change and budget dollars flow from general purpose Navy programmes to missile and bomber programmes in the other services, especially the Air Force'[49]. The Polaris missiles had the advantage of being solid-fuelled contrary to the liquid-fuelled missiles of the Air Force, which were older and more difficult to handle. Despite the fact that most Navy departments were against Polaris because they would lose 10 % of their budget, they nevertheless agreed because the alternative would have been worse. The size of the new nuclear force of the Navy would be determined, as Admiral Burke stated, by 'an objective of generous adequacy for deterrence alone (i.e., for an ability to destroy major urban areas), not by the false goal of adequacy for "winning"'[50]. This can be regarded as minimum deterrence thinking, placing a ceiling on the number of submarines.

Secondly, the first nuclear strategy of the *Air Force* consisted of massive bombing. It contained mostly countervalue (countercities) and no (or few) limited targeting options. Before 1950, the deterrence requirements of the Air Force started from the assumption that 70 Soviet *cities* had to be destroyed with 133 low-yield nuclear bombs in total[51]. This doctrine was only the continuation of the existing air force doctrines in the non-nuclear field that were successfully implemented during the Second World War. It can be argued that the doctrine also had organizational advantages. As Jack Snyder specified: 'The military is most likely to be allowed operational autonomy when the operational goal is to disarm the adversary quickly and decisively by offensive means. For this reason, the military will seek to force doctrine and planning into this mould'[52].

It was only when the Navy built nuclear submarines and created its corresponding minimum deterrence strategy, that the Air Force was more or less forced to switch to another strategy: more emphasis on counterforce than countervalue, and more emphasis on limited options. The reason for doing so had not much to do with a change of genuine beliefs, but with plain organizational interests. Air Force Chief of Staff Gen.Thomas White wrote on 11 May 1959 to the head of the US Strategic Air Command Gen.Thomas Power: 'This would lead to the conclusion...that attacking "cities" constitutes the most important segment of the strategic effort. This conclusion would not only be used as further justification of Polaris but...would be used as a strong position (which is already emerging) to eliminate virtually any strategic requirement other than Polaris, i.e. SAC'[53]. If the Air Force had not changed its strategy at the beginning of the 1960s, it might have been out of the nuclear business, as submarines had more strategic advantages. This might in turn have significantly hurt the Air Force as a whole, as SAC was the Air Force's most prestigious command.

The third example shows a more recent shift in the nuclear doctrine of the *Navy*, exactly in the opposite direction. Due to technological advances in the 1970s and 1980s and due to pressure from Secretary of Defence Schlesinger for more accurate SLBMs for his new targeting policy, the SLBMs of the second (and current) Trident generation (D-5) became as accurate as ICBMs. As a result, the Navy switched to a counterforce strategy in order to be able to bet on both options in the hope of surviving as the only "nuclear" service in the end: countervalue (minimum deterrence) and counterforce (maximum deterrence). The Air Force of course did not like this evolution. Daniel Ford already emphasized in 1985: 'SAC and the Pentagon bureaucracy, which have a great deal at stake in trying to justify continued reliance on land-based missiles and manned bombers, are not inclined to call attention to the potency of the nuclear submarine fleet'[54].

All these examples suggest that organizational interests to a very large extent influenced doctrines and in its turn the force structure.

Whose responsibility ?
The military, and more particularly the nuclear establishment, however, are not the only ones to be blamed. In fact, it is their job to prepare for the worst. The key problem was that there was more or less no civilian control with regard to the interpretation and implementation of the deterrence requirements. As political scientist Robert Dahl warned in his book *Controlling nuclear weapons*: 'We have in fact turned over to a small group of people decisions of incalculable importance to ourselves and mankind, and it is very far from clear how, if at all, we could recapture a control that in fact we have never had'[55]. Few civilians were willing to invest a lot of energy in it. Henry Kissinger wrote about the failure of its predecessors: 'When I entered office, former Defence Secretary Robert McNamara told me that he had tried for seven years to give the President more options. He had finally given up, he said, in the face of bureaucratic opposition and decided to improvise'[56]. Kissinger himself tried in the beginning of the 1970s, and failed as well[57]. It is therefore not surprising to find out that the power of the military over the nuclear planning process did not end in the 1980s.

Conservatives and strong beliefs against fundamental change
Minimum and maximum deterrence are two consistent but opposite beliefs. Beliefs are hard to change. Despite the changed political circumstances, it could have been expected that it would be hard to change minds from maximum to minimum deterrence.

Origins of maximum deterrence

The concept of maximum deterrence was not invented in 1945, but was only gradually established over time. After the Soviets acquired nuclear weapons in 1949, an arms race emerged as if nuclear weapons were conventional weapons. The quantity and quality of nuclear warheads and delivery vehicles rose tremendously. Parochial interests are only part of the overall explanation. The strategy that tried to clip together force structure and declaratory policy was maximum deterrence, which after a while became so entrenched in thinking about nuclear weapons, that minimum deterrence was never again regarded as a viable alternative, at least in government circles.

Seven years after Hiroshima, maximum deterrence still did not yet exist: the massive retaliation doctrine was still not born, ICBMs and SLBMs still had to be built, LOW was a concept still to be invented, and nuclear weapons were not yet geared on high alert.

The concept of maximum deterrence was only "constructed" later on, partially due to genuine beliefs and also to justify the high expenditures for nuclear weapons. After he retired, the head of the US Strategic Air Command Gen.Lee Butler formulated it as follows: 'For us, nuclear weapons were the saviour that brought an implacable foe to his knees in 1945 and held another at bay for nearly a half-century...These are powerful, deeply rooted beliefs...[These beliefs] gave rise to mammoth bureaucracies with gargantuan appetites and global agendas. They incited primal emotions, spurred zealotry and demagoguery, and set in motion forces of ungovernable scope and power'[58].

Paul Bracken (Yale University) calls into question the degree of honesty of the aforementioned beliefs: 'What passes for a strategic debate is little more than the construction of a façade of nuclear logic to permit getting on with the day-to-day job of deterrence. The most that can be said for this practice is that creating a veneer of rationality in the discussion of nuclear strategy is a ritual used to convince opponents that we are serious about deterrence'[59]. The more consistent a concept that was worked out, the more that the bureaucratic organizations could refer to it as the Holy Bible. Over time, new thinking disappeared and nuclear policy became a gigantic and inflexible process. It is therefore not surprising that the nuclear arms race reached absurdly high levels and that serious policy inconsistencies arose. The more the nuclear complex grew, the more interests were involved.

To conclude, it may have been that the origins of the concept of maximum deterrence had ideational grounds. At the end of the Cold War, however, the concept of maximum deterrence was an anachronism. It had survived because of parochial interests. The credo of maximum deterrence therefore became a false – not genuine – belief, although there were many (especially in the military) who still genuinely believed in the concept of maximum deterrence.

Could one have expected a change in beliefs from maximum to minimum deterrence after the Cold War ?

Glenn Buchan (RAND) proscribed in 1994: 'The new shape of the world should signal a sea change *in the way we think* about nuclear force structure issues...Unfortunately, this sort of change is hard to deal with, either intellectually or emotionally, for many of the long-time players'[60]. E.L.Doctorow once remarked:

'The bomb first was our weapon. Then it became our diplomacy. Next it became our economy. Now it's become our culture. We've become the people of the bomb'[61].

On the other hand, beliefs do adapt to changed circumstances, but slowly. The speed of adaptation depends on the individual or organization. A distinction will be made between experts and non-experts.

Although many *non-governmental experts* already dissociated themselves from the concept of maximum deterrence during the Cold War, the breakthrough in the advancement of the idea of minimum deterrence could have been expected after the Cold War. That is exactly what happened. After the Cold War, there existed more or less a consensus in the non-governmental arms control community that minimum deterrence was by far the most viable strategy (see chapter 2).

More interesting are the beliefs of the *governmental experts*, and in particular those of the military. With regard to the question of the future of nuclear weapons policy right after the Cold War, there were two camps within the US military: abolitionists and advocates of maximum deterrence.

As already said before, the majority of the US military was not interested in nuclear weapons and wanted to get rid of them after the Cold War. Most of the military did not believe in the usefulness of nuclear weapons and regarded them as irrelevant, preferring usable conventional weapons instead. As Colin Powell stated when Secretary of Defence Cheney asked him right before the Gulf War in 1991 to consider nuclear options: 'Let's not even think about nukes...You know we're not going to let that genie loose'[62]. Former CIA Director Stansfield Turner agrees: 'There is no foreign policy objective today that is so threatened that we would employ nuclear weapons and accept the risk of receiving just one nuclear detonation in retaliation'[63].

While still in office US Space Command Chief Gen.Charles Horner publicly defended the idea of elimination. In an interview in *Aviation Week and Space Technology* in the spring of 1993, he said: 'I want to get rid of nuclear weapons'. In a written statement for a Congressional hearing a few weeks later – on 22 April 1993 – he confirmed what he had said before: 'Nuclear weapons are expensive and lack utility other than for strategic deterrence. Strategic deterrence works only against rational actors. Nuclear weapons are unlikely to deter potential adversaries driven by ethnic, religious, or economic imperatives. Also, as weapons for theatre warfare, they are difficult to employ effectively and can be justified only as weapons of terror. A strategy of terror does not fit well in the successful conduct of modern warfare which puts an emphasis on low casualties, especially non-military casualties...[Elimination] should also reduce other nations' aspirations to acquire weapons of mass destruction...As a nuclear free nation, we could seize the moral high grounds. In concert with other non-nuclear nations, we could demand suspected nuclear weapons sites be opened for inspection with conventional military forces to back up our demands'[64].

In contrast to this very critical attitude towards nuclear weapons, a small group within the US military – the nuclear establishment or the so-called targeting community – survived and still survives because of the existence of nuclear weapons and more particularly because of a maximum deterrence posture. They were of course heavily opposed to radical changes after the Cold War.

Three levels of ideational constraints against change can be distinguished: from the point of view of working for an organization, a military organization, and an armed service.

From an *organizational* point of view, many of the lower level nuclear officials focused on their job. They were not asked to look to the overall geo-strategic picture. They shared an organizational mission, namely preparing for nuclear war. They were trained to believe in procedures and operations that belonged to maximum deterrence. This was their strategic culture. Most of them therefore did not question the basic assumptions of maximum deterrence, even after the Cold War.

This applies especially to those who had to execute nuclear policy. They had to believe in maximum deterrence. As civilian DOD official Frank Miller asserted in 1988: 'You can't expect a commander to tell his guys that the missiles they're in charge of would ride out an attack, that they're essentially useless. You'd have a morale problem'[65]. Gen.Horner added: 'I guess the most negative reaction [against change] comes from the military people who are in the business of maintaining deterrence by being ready to launch war. Of course, they're very close to the subject, so they're very myopic....many of them – and I'm talking about the senior officers... – came up the ranks, commanding nuclear submarines, missile boats or missile fields. They have to swallow hard because, of necessity, they've clung very close to these doctrines, I mean, they have to believe'[66]. With the help of cognitive processes such as denial and bolstering, they constructed their beliefs in such a way that they still could believe in maximum deterrence after the fall of the Berlin Wall.

There were also constraints that are typical for *military* bureaucracies. First of all, it is useful to refer to Barry Posen's theory of military innovation that states that innovative thinking occurs in time of threat and not in times of peace. As long as the existing military strategy is perceived as useful and as long as there are no new threats, this theory expects little change with regard to military strategy[67]. There are some clarifying examples of Posen's theory in the field of US nuclear weapons policy during the Cold War. In the beginning, the Air Force was not very interested in ICBMs because it preferred the existing situation, namely the predominance of bombers[68]. The same applies to the Navy and the introduction of SLBMs[69]. As Owen Coté concludes: 'radical doctrinal innovation is to a military organization what a revolution is to a political community'[70]. 'Certain types of weapon systems become the technological centerpiece of a military organization's doctrine...Large military organizations prefer to modify and improve an existing set of technologies, and postpone the day when these need to be replaced in toto', he adds[71].

More generally, Robert Levine and Thomas Schelling claim that not much "learning" about nuclear arms control took place during the Cold War[72]. The former head of the US Strategic Air Command Gen.Lee Butler agrees: 'From the earliest days of the nuclear era the risks, costs and consequences have never been properly understood nor calculated by the theorists, the planners and the poised practitioners of nuclear war'[73]. To conclude, applied to the end of the Cold War when the major threat had disappeared, no (or only minor) changes could have been expected.

Secondly, shifting to minimum deterrence would have contradicted a key principle of the military: keep all options open. Minimum deterrence would have excluded different nuclear options. The US would no longer have been allowed to use nuclear weapons first. Operational policy would have consisted of riding out a nuclear attack. As Leon Sloss put it: 'the Air Force really believes that the only way to survive is to launch weapons quickly'[74]. Bruce Blair also notes that 'the defence bureaucracy and nuclear combat commands will undoubtedly perpetuate the view that deterrence hinges on a posture of rapid reaction'[75]. That is also the reason the military never liked limited targeting options. A RAND report of 1994 prescribed: 'flexible planning is so culturally anathema to US strategic nuclear planning that the current institutional structure may have to be radically altered or scrapped entirely'[76].

Behind the belief of keeping all the options open lies the fear of being accused by the political decision-makers and/or society in the case of military defeat. This fear is not completely imagined: those who were blamed after Pearl Harbour in the Second World War were the military, while the main culprits were probably the political decision-makers. Also in Vietnam, the military were at least indirectly blamed for the defeat, while the military options during the war were kept limited by political appointees and their staff in the Office of the Secretary of Defence.

From the point of view of the *armed services*, the Navy – the only service that embraced minimum deterrence during the Cold War – shifted in the 1980s to maximum deterrence because of organizational interests (see before). As a result of the removal of many tactical nuclear weapons, the Army completely got rid of nuclear weapons in 1991. There was no service left that favoured minimum deterrence.

The overall result was that after the Cold War more or less nobody in the US military was in favour of a minimum deterrence posture. Steve Fetter (Maryland University) concludes that 'it was hard to find any middle view' in the military. It was either war-fighting and maximum deterrence, or nothing at all[77].

The relevance of beliefs of *non-experts* – public opinion and most of the political decision-makers – with regard to complex issues is debatable. Public opinion is not very much interested in foreign and defence policy, let alone nuclear policy. That does not mean that they do not share less refined beliefs about nuclear weapons.

The fact that public opinion is not well-informed means their beliefs are easier malleable and can be manipulated. Experts or credible political decision-makers who speak out clearly and convincingly therefore have the possibility substantially to influence public opinion and non-informed decision-makers. In principle, those inside the government have the advantage of having more information available. They also enjoy the prestige that goes with being part of the government. The best example is the case in which the Bush administration convinced Congress and public opinion in the US to go to war against Iraq in 2003.

If opponents of policy change state that the arguments of the advocates of change are not correct and that for instance "maximum deterrence remains more credible than minimum deterrence", public opinion and most political decision-makers will accept this statement, if it is claimed by a government expert in the domain of US security. Cognitive processes make people conflate the message with the messenger. This works extremely well with arguments that are specialized, technical and/or abstract.

Another factor making it even more difficult for public opinion and political decision-makers to obtain an informed opinion about what was going on with regard to nuclear weapons is the level of secrecy. While it is probably even worse in other nuclear weapon states, the level of nuclear secrecy in the US is such that it raises questions about the legitimacy of the democratic nature of the American political system. It originated in the super-secret Manhattan project, but the system of secrecy was extended during and after the Cold War. Documents are "born secret". Government officials have "clearances" and the obligation not to talk about certain aspects of nuclear policy. In the 1980s, four million Americans had some level of security clearance[78]. The US government also never released the exact number of nuclear weapons in its arsenal. In the same vein, the US has a "neither confirm nor deny" policy with regard to the presence of American nuclear weapons in Europe.

Even senior decision-makers were denied crucial information with regard to operational policy, more particularly targeting policy. Peter Feaver points out that: 'Top policymakers need to understand the intricacies of target planning to interpret correctly the targeting options that might be presented to them'. He warns: 'This requirement can be frustrated by the secrecy surrounding the generation of target plans and the powerful bureaucratic autonomy enjoyed by the Strategic Air Command'[79]. The former head of the Strategic (Air) Command Gen. Lee Butler made a similar comment in one of his speeches after he had retired: 'The narrow concerns of a multitude of powerful interests intruded on the rightful role of key policymakers, constraining their latitude for decision. Many were simply denied access to critical information essential to the proper exercise of their office'[80].

At least two additional processes made it more difficult for non-experts to believe in the feasibility of elimination, an idea that is closest to the idea of minimum deterrence. First of all, there exists a societal myth that nuclear deterrence had kept peace since the Second World War. Such myths do not wither away easily. People are quick to extrapolate these ideas into the future without thinking the issue through, without for instance taking into account the changed international circumstances. As Michael MccGwire argued: 'For some 40 years, the American people were told that nuclear deterrence kept the peace, that as long as enough money was invested in such weapons, deterrence couldn't fail, and that there was no danger of accidental or inadvertent nuclear war....it would be difficult to wean the US electorate from that version of the past'[81].

Secondly, beliefs are not always tested on their own merits. Sometimes other beliefs are consciously or unconsciously associated, which might make changes even more complicated. The debate between nuclear deterrence and nuclear elimination is sometimes presented as a debate between Realists and Idealists. Those who regard a nuclear weapons free world as desirable and feasible are categorized as "idealists" while those who are sceptical are labelled "realists". Some go even further and define those in favour of elimination as "unrealistic", "utopian", "soft" or as the British Air Marshal Sir Robert Saundby once said 'people who feel rather than think'[82].

Because the connotations of this idealist/realist bipolarity, it is very difficult to argue for "idealistic" changes even when the external circumstances have completely changed. Roles and beliefs are taken and they tend to change only very slowly.

In addition, so-called realists can easily refer to biological needs (for instance survival) in order to justify their beliefs. Consequently, it is generally more difficult for political decision-makers to justify a change in the direction of "softness" than the other way around. Or as a famous arms control study in 1993 pointed out: '[both the US and Russia] will be tempted to revert to the competitive habits of thought that developed so strongly in the years in which this or that marginal advantage seemed worth defending, not only against the other side but sometimes still more intensely against *those who seemed soft in one's own governmen'*...Such habits can obstruct the ways of thinking that are now appropriate'[83]. Later on, one of the authors of this study repeated the same message in even less ambiguous words: 'no political leader would willingly open himself to the charge that he had increased American vulnerability or conceded nuclear superiority to the Soviet Union. That would be tantamount to political suicide'[84]. Luckily, there are examples of politicians who showed leadership and who tried to go against these prejudices also on this account. President Kennedy in his speech before the UN General Assembly in September 1961 made clear: 'Men may no longer pretend that the quest for disarmament is a sign of weakness – for in the spiralling arms race, a nation's security may well be shrinking even as its arms increase'[85].

The advocates of maximum nuclear deterrence – the nuclear bureaucracy and the Republicans – are trained in exploiting these processes. Both groups also reinforce each other. In the case of a Democratic administration, the bureaucracy can always play it hard and "use" the conservative opposition in Congress. The other way around, Republicans can also "use" Republican-minded bureaucrats to write documents that are then leaked to the press.

Republicans
During the Cold War, American political decision-makers, especially Democrats, felt that they could not politically survive if the former USSR obtained more nuclear weapons than the USA. 'Regardless of the nature of beliefs about the potential utility of nuclear weapons or about the manner of their use, avoiding the *perception* of a future Soviet nuclear advantage has been the driving imperative behind decisions to expand nuclear weapons, from the time of Harry Truman to that of Ronald Reagan. Any time the US has failed to act in this manner, the political costs have been enormous', according to Janne Nolan[86]. Republicans would simply exploit soft policies. At least that was the fear in the Democratic camp.

Republicans not only criticize Democrats out of political opportunism or out of the political need to distinguish themselves from Democrats. Republicans are in general more conservative. For instance, Republicans are keener on defence spending. Harald Müller defined the attitudes of the conservatives in Congress ('with some followers in the Pentagon and the labs') already in 1998 as 'the moral equivalent of rogue state views: contempt for multilateralism and international organizations, an opportunistic attitude to international law that is (ab)used when it is convenient, and refused if it demands compromise, a complete reliance on unilateral military strength, and the relentless pursuit of the national interest – egocentrically defined – without regard to the claims and interests of others. For these people, arms control is but an impediment in the way of national strength'[87].

Because of the "soft" image of the Democrats and the "hard" image of the Republicans, Republicans can exploit these differences as soon as there is an external threat. Paradoxically, thanks to this "hard" image, the Republicans have the credibility to push through arms reductions without getting much criticism from the public. It can for instance be argued that the Bush administrations accomplished more in the field of nuclear arms control than the Clinton administration.

However there is no realistic ground whatsoever to argue that abolitionists are "idealists". Those who regard a NWFW as desirable base their arguments on realist assumptions. Mutatis mutandis, one can argue that those who believe that nuclear deterrence will always work, should be called "idealists". As Andrew Mack said: 'Nuclear disarmament should be taken seriously because only the most naïve optimist could believe that thousands of nuclear weapons can be deployed indefinitely without being used, by accident or design'[88]. But again, it is the perception that counts. After the Cold War, the perception that dominated in the US was that nuclear deterrence worked, that the "few" remaining nuclear weapons were stabilizing and that, as a result, there was no reason to change nuclear policy fundamentally.

To conclude, taking into account the existing beliefs and corresponding interests in Congress and in the bureaucracy, one could have expected that US nuclear policy would not have changed fundamentally after the Cold War. Some really believed in maximum deterrence. Most used the concept of maximum deterrence as a justification for keeping the existing policy in order to maximize parochial interests. Less nuclear weapons would have meant less money, less personnel, less prestige and less autonomy for the bureaucracies dealing with nuclear weapons. As it was politically impossible to say so openly, political decision-makers justified their opposition against minimum deterrence by using arguments that public opinion could understand and believe. Halperin concludes: 'The desire to avoid a major domestic row or to keep the good will of a significant domestic group leads presidents to alter their stands on national security issues in an effort to build a wide consensus or to maintain an appearance of consistency'[89].

Four additional factors
There are four addition factors that help explain nuclear inertia.

No visible results if policy change succeeds
In the optimal case, a shift from maximum to minimum deterrence enhances safety in peace-time, prevents accidents, unauthorized use and authorized use after false alarms; it adds credibility to the nuclear posture; it constrains nuclear proliferation; and it saves lives in the event of a nuclear war. It will, however, be extremely difficult to show that safety and stability have actually improved after a shift to minimum deterrence. It is by definition impossible to make acts visible that have been prevented in the first place. As a result, from a purely political point of view, political decision-makers did not have a lot of stimuli for changing nuclear policy after the Cold War.

Available justifications for not having to change policy fundamentally
A couple of justifications for not changing US nuclear policy after the Cold War may have been based on genuine beliefs. As most experts outside the government did not buy these arguments, the odds are that most of these beliefs were not genuine, but plain justifications.

For instance, many US government officials do not categorize US nuclear weapons policy after the Cold War as a status quo. They point to the "many" policy changes: the force reductions; the test moratorium and the signing of the Comprehensive Test Ban Treaty; the low alert-rates of the bombers; the abolition of SAC; George W.H.Bush's targeting review. They also claim that as long as the changes are going in the direction of elimination, everything is fine.

Others in the government – like Clinton's Under Secretary of Defence John Deutch – agree with the thesis that the changes in nuclear policy were not dramatic. Deutch argues that there has to be continuity of policy. This argument would have been correct if the choice was between incremental change and elimination, as the debate is sometimes framed[90]. However, the choice is more subtle: it is between incremental change on the one hand and fundamental change in the direction of elimination (like a shift from maximum to minimum deterrence) on the other. Deutch's argument sounds therefore more as another justification.

Deutch also justifies the relative slow speed of change by pointing to 'the whole set of complicated considerations that have to be taken into account'[91]. By framing it as a complex issue, he implicitly sends the message that those who do not know a lot about it, better keep quiet.

Opponents of change also stress the classic advantages of deterrence and of maximum deterrence in particular; they also point to the "success" of this posture in the past. US Ambassador Grey reacted after the vote of the New Agenda Coalition resolution in the UN First Committee in November 1998 as follows: 'Let me be perfectly clear. You will not make nuclear disarmament occur faster by suggesting that a fundamental basis of our national security for more than fifty years is illegitimate'[92]. He apparently forgot to mention that the Cold War had ended in the meantime.

For avoiding a public debate, it was sufficient that public opinion was convinced by just one of these justifications, and that was what happened.

Will the strategic costs of inertia occur in the short, medium or long term ?
It is impossible to predict when a state will "go nuclear" or when a nuclear accident (or war) may occur. However, it is fair to say that although such incidents may happen in the short term, the chances are by definition higher in the medium or long term. This gives political decision-makers the perfect alibi not to change nuclear policy fundamentally in the short term.

There are also cognitive processes like denial that unconsciously prevent action. A fundamental debate about the future of nuclear weapons is not held, partially because nuclear war seems so remote and because it has such an apocalyptic undertone. Charles Osgood once wrote: 'The more people can avoid thinking about negatives (like there being no more fuel for cars or a nuclear holocaust) – particularly when they seem remote in time and are highly symbolic in nature – the less likely they are to try to do anything about them until it's too late. Seated in the backyard on a nice spring day, watching the kids at play, and sipping a beer, the Neanderthal within us simply cannot conceive of the trees suddenly blackened and the voices of the children stilled – or there being no more beer'[93].

Are there other states involved in reaching the desired outcome ?

By definition, other states are involved when we are talking about preventing the spread and use of nuclear weapons. For "realists" or political opponents of a change in US nuclear weapons policy, it is easy to argue that in US policy a change will not prevent proliferation because there are much more factors and actors in the game. As Terry Deibel states: 'deterrence and defence seemed to depend on American decisions, whereas nonproliferation depended on the decisions of other governments'[94].

CHAPTER 9

THE NUCLEAR POSTURE REVIEW
IN 1993-1994

Despite the opposition to change as explained in the previous chapter, the model used in chapter 7 pointed out that policy change would still have been possible if there had been strong political leadership. That is why the politics behind the policy will now be analysed. It will tell us more both about the intentions and the qualities of the American political decision-makers after the end of the Cold War.

There are different reasons why a policy change could have been expected from the Clinton administration: a) Democrats are known to be more liberal, also in the field of foreign and defence policy; b) although Bill Clinton had emphasized domestic policy issues during his campaign, he had also announced that he was in favour of a comprehensive nuclear test ban (contrary to George W.H.Bush), and he put nuclear nonproliferation at the top of his foreign policy priority list during and right after his election campaign; c) Les Aspin who became Clinton's first Secretary of Defence had written an extensive paper on nuclear weapons in 1992, in which he had argued for major changes along the lines of minimum deterrence, or at least going substantially in that direction; d) Assistant Secretary of Defence for International Security Policy Ashton Carter, who was in charge of nuclear strategy in the first Clinton administration, had similar ideas as Aspin; e) the Clinton administration did initiate a major nuclear policy review that was publicly announced as such by Aspin and Carter in October 1993, the so-called Nuclear Posture Review (NPR) that aimed at looking at 'where... you go *after* START II'[1]; f) Clinton stayed in the White House for eight years, and had therefore a lot of time to push through radical reforms. The question why the US did not change nuclear policy fundamentally after the Cold War is therefore much more challenging from the point of view of the Clinton administration(s) than the George W.H.Bush administration.

The reason that we do not focus in detail on the politics behind the policy in the George W.Bush administration is that nobody expected big changes in US nuclear weapons policy from Bush, at least not in the direction of nuclear elimination.

The outcome of the 1993-1994 NPR is extremely relevant as it forms the basis of US nuclear weapons policy for the years thereafter. For instance, the famous "hedge" policy to keep 10,000 warheads in order to be able to rebuild the force quickly, had its origins in the 1993-1994 NPR.

In this chapter, the NPR will be described chronologically. A detailed political analysis will follow in the next chapter.

Goals

Secretary of Defence Les Aspin formally heralded the start of the NPR at a Defence Department press briefing on Friday afternoon 29 October 1993[2]. Also attending were Assistant Secretary of Defence for Nuclear Security and Counterproliferation (later re-named Assistant Secretary of Defence of International Security Policy) Ashton Carter, and the Director for Strategic Plans and Policy for the JCS (J-5) Barry McCaffrey.

The NPR had already been announced one month earlier as a follow-up of the Bottom-Up-Review that in turn was formally set up by Secretary of Defence Les Aspin in March 1993, two months after Clinton's inauguration. The Bottom-Up-Review dealt mainly with conventional weapons, although it also contained some – rather conservative – paragraphs with regard to nuclear weapons. Referring to counterproliferation, the Bottom-Up-Review stated for instance that 'to address the new nuclear dangers, the Department of Defence must emphasize…the maintenance of flexible and robust *nuclear* and conventional *forces to deter weapons of mass destruction attacks* through the credible threat of devastating retaliation'[3]. Originally, the Bottom-Up-Review aimed to be a comprehensive review for both conventional *and* nuclear forces. As the head of the US Strategic Command Gen.Lee Butler stated in a hearing on 22 April 1993, 'budget and force structure options regarding compliance with START II accords are being addressed in Secretary Aspin's Bottom-up-Review…which, amongst other things, is closely examining policy and strategy guidance for strategic forces and budget and force structure options for START II compliance'[4]. But the nuclear weapons part was apparently too difficult to resolve during the Bottom-Up-Review. Also because of Aspin's aspiration to make his mark in the nuclear field, it was taken up in the NPR.

The reason for a nuclear policy review being initiated at the beginning of the Clinton administration not only related to the fact that new administrations always start reviewing major policy aspects. This time, the world looked fundamentally different in comparison with four years earlier. As a result, as Aspin explains at the press conference in October 1993: 'early in his administration, the President asked us to review and redefine our strategy, tactics, doctrine, size and the shape of our forces *to meet the demands of the new international security environment*…The Bottom-up-Review undertook this task for our conventional forces. But, as we have seen, the world has changed *even more fundamentally* for our *nuclear* forces'[5].

The Cold War was gone and "new threats" had seen the daylight. In government, Aspin pushed through his own threat-based thinking that he had elaborated in 1992 as chairman of the House Committee on Armed Services. The Bottom-Up-Review spelled out four major threats: nuclear weapons and other weapons of mass destruction; regional threats, especially ethnic conflicts; failure of democratisation; and economic threats.

Aspin was more optimistic than the George W.H.Bush administration about Russia's future, although the situation in Russia of course remained uncertain. With the concept of co-operative security in mind, Aspin was convinced that it was in the national interest of the US to play a constructive role to keep Russia on the reform track. The danger of loose nukes made this objective even more urgent.

As Aspin had proposed changes in Russian nuclear weapons policy, he was aware that US policy had to be transformed as well. In Aspin's opinion US nuclear policy was outdated. For instance, formal presidential guidance introduced by President Reagan in 1981 – winning a protracted nuclear war – was still in place. The guidance became completely anachronistic when the Soviet threat disappeared. Nevertheless, US nuclear operational and force structure policy continued to refer to that document. Already in 1992, Aspin had proposed 'reconsidering deterrence-era policies'[6].

The goal of the NPR was clearly defined from the outset. As Secretary of Defence Les Aspin pointed out at the press briefing: 'One era has ended, and a new one begun. The world has fundamentally changed. We are responding with the first nuclear policy review in fifteen years. In fact, it is the first Defence Department revision ever to incorporate revisions of policy, doctrine, force structure, operations, safety and security, and arms control in one look'[7]. 'This kind of comprehensive approach is demanded by new circumstances', Aspin continued[8]. In other words, the objective was to do a bottom-up-review of US nuclear weapons policy. *The Washington Post* wrote two years later: 'For the first time in decades, everything about US nuclear policy was up for grabs'[9].

Aspin clarified that the study first of all had to make clear what the role of US nuclear weapons should be and '*then* determine the number of nuclear weapons [the US should have], rather than having the thing driven by some abstract number', referring implicitly to the deterrence requirements[10]. At the press conference, General McCaffrey contended that the purpose of the review was to 'get a much broader look at our nuclear posture than one that would be dictated by the next budget'. He also suggested that $10 billion per year – i.e. one third of the nuclear weapons budget – could be saved[11]. The NPR would also have a look to the remaining relevance of the triad and to the existing alert-levels. Lastly, it aimed at resolving the debate about the legitimacy of nuclear deterrence against chemical and biological weapons attacks and the question of no first use. '"We really are rethinking the basic purpose of nuclear weapons", an[other] official said, including the rationale for keeping them and whether they should be targeted in advance at any particular sites'[12]. In short, the NPR would review US nuclear force structure, declaratory and operational policy[13].

Aspin claimed: 'During the Cold War we counted on nuclear weapons to counter the conventional numerical superiority of the Warsaw Pact. For the United States, nuclear weapons were the equalizer. In this new world, our conventional military strength is unmatched. But if a potential adversary had nuclear weapons, we could turn out to be the equalize'[14]. In 1992, Aspin had used the same metaphor, adding that a world without nuclear weapons would be desirable. When Assistant Secretary of Defence Ash Carter was asked at the press briefing about the option of eliminating *all* US nuclear weapons, he said 'that is a conceivable option to look at and think about and consider. We are going to put all the alternatives on the table and study them'[15].

Whether the press briefing was a 'highly publicized call', as Janne Nolan claims[16], is unclear, but on the basis of the briefing one could have expected that US policy finally would be adapted to the new circumstances[17]. As Steve Fetter, who participated in the NPR, pointed out: 'You don't do a review like this, unless you are going to get different answers'[18].

Origins

Informally, the NPR had started earlier. Nuclear policy was one of Aspin's priorities, as one official involved in the exercise described it[19]. Aspin had closely followed nuclear policy in Congress for years. He had written a so-called White Paper on the subject in 1992 that was sent to more than a hundred experts around the country for feedback[20]. Once in government, Aspin was determined to make his mark. He had hired Ashton Carter – a professor at the John F.Kennedy School of Government at Harvard University, somebody who had dealt intensively with nuclear weapons issues before – to push through the necessary changes. The Aspin team started right from the beginning to look at new nuclear options[21].

At the same time, as already mentioned above, each new administration is supposed to hold reviews on all major policy issues. In the field of international security and especially with regard to arms control, these interagency reviews are led by the White House and more particularly the National Security Council. The Clinton administration for instance set up reviews for nuclear testing and the future of fissile materials.

Presidential Review Directive 34 initiated an interagency review about 'arms control *beyond* START I and START II'[22]. The Defence Department, however, apparently succeeded in convincing the National Security Council to halt the interagency review until the NPR would be over and to delegate the nuclear policy review to the Defence Department. One of the conditions for the Joint Chiefs of Staff (JCS) to discuss changes in nuclear weapons policy might have been to study it inside the Defence Department before opening it up to the other departments and agencies. The latter is what happened at the beginning of the 1970s with a similar review[23].

The other departments and agencies reluctantly agreed with this process. The outcome of the NPR was in any event expected to be discussed later on in an interagency review. In fact, the other departments had no choice: the White House had delegated the NPR to Aspin[24]. Some of the outsiders – like National Security Council Special Assistant to the President Bob Bell and Under Secretary of State Lynn Davis – would occasionally be briefed on the interim-results of the NPR.

Once the hurdle from shifting it from the interagency level to the Defence Department was taken, Secretary of Defence Aspin and Assistant Secretary of Defence Carter needed to overcome the bureaucratic obstacles inside the Department. More particularly, all the relevant players inside the Pentagon had to agree on the terms of reference, something which was far from evident. The latter is a classified text of thirty pages that spells out the goals of the study and the way to achieve these goals.

The logic behind the decision to delegate a comprehensive nuclear policy review to the Department of Defence is questionable[25]. One of the consequences was that the nuclear review became restricted to matters of force structure and alert-levels, constituting the *posture*, and that it left all the rest – including declaratory *policy* –

out. Some observers claim that this limited scope was clearly mentioned in the so-called terms of reference of the NPR[26]. As the scope of the NPR as announced at the press briefing was much broader than the terms of reference, Carter and certainly Aspin might have thought to push through other policy aspects as well, first in the Defence Department and later on in the interagency process.

Structure

The NPR was structured as follows: Assistant Secretary of Defence for Nuclear Security and Counterproliferation Ashton Carter was in charge on a daily basis together with his military counterpart Lt.Gen. Barry McCaffrey. Not much later McCaffrey was replaced as Director for Strategic Plans and Policy for the JCS (J-5) by Lt.Gen.Wesley Clark, who later on became known as the NATO Supreme Allied Commander in Europe during the Kosovo war and as presidential candidate in 2004.

Six working groups were set up, dealing with all major aspects of nuclear policy: 1) the role of nuclear weapons in US defence and national security; 2) the US nuclear force structure needed to carry out the required missions; 3) nuclear force operations and alert-levels (command and control); 4) security and safety of nuclear weapons; 5) the relationship between US nuclear force structure and counterproliferation policy; 6) the US nuclear posture and its relationship to the threat reduction policy with the former Soviet Union[27].

These working groups consisted of rather low level civilian and mostly military career officials from the Office of the Secretary of Defence, the Joint Staff, the Services, the different commands and other Pentagon agencies. The first and major working group was led by Frank Miller, who became Principal Deputy Assistant under Ashton Carter in 1993 and Acting Assistant Secretary of Defence for International Security Policy when Carter left office in September 1996. Frank Miller was generally regarded as "the nuclear tsar" in the Pentagon bureaucracy, as he had been dealing with these issues since 1981. He had also helped develop PD-59 in the late 1970s[28].

The working groups were encouraged to get input from outside – read non-governmental experts – and '[Ash Carter] urged them to free themselves from Cold War thinking and consider the issues creatively'[29]. The working groups had to report to Carter's office. In his turn, Carter had to report to a steering group led by Deputy Secretary of Defence William Perry (later replaced by John Deutch) and Vice-Chairman of the Joint Chiefs of Staff Admiral William Owens. Ultimately, Les Aspin was of course responsible: both because of his formal position as Secretary of Defence and because the NPR was mainly his idea.

Brainstorming

The Nuclear Posture Review Memorandum – the terms of reference – was signed on 5 November 1993, a week after the press briefing[30]. Drastic changes were advocated by outside experts like Bruce Blair and John Steinbruner from the Brookings Institution and Michael Mazarr from CSIS, who were invited to present papers at one or more of the working group meetings. However it became clear from the beginning that the participants of the working groups favoured no fundamental reforms. According to Janne Nolan, 'working group members tended to treat experts' articles and papers as obscure academic treatises, remote from the realities of operational planning...Officials "gave a polite reception" to the outsiders, according to one account, or "looked puzzled beyond redemption", according to another'[31].

In one of the first briefings held by Ashton Carter, Les Aspin was present together with all the other major players involved. When most participants, including Deputy Secretary of Defence William Perry, had already left the room, Les Aspin stayed on to discuss some tenets with Ashton Carter and a few others for over twenty minutes after the briefing[32]. This anecdote not only supports the thesis that Aspin was very much personally interested in the topic, but may also say something about how he was managing his time.

On 7 December, Secretary of Defence Les Aspin announced the Counterproliferation Initiative in a speech to the National Academy of Sciences, signed by President Clinton as PDD/NSC 18. The same image was used as during the press conference in October. 'For us, nuclear weapons were the equalizer...But today it is the US that has unmatched conventional military power, and it is our potential adversaries who may attain nuclear weapons. We're the ones who could wind up being the equalize'[33].

Another indication of the new wind blowing inside the Pentagon may have been that the NATO Defence Planning Committee and Nuclear Planning Group (DPC/NPG), traditionally dominated by the US, on 9 December 1993 did *not* mention that nuclear weapons, including the sub-strategic nuclear weapons deployed in Europe, were "essential" for the alliance. While this sentence had always been included, for instance in the communiqué of May 1993 and again in May 1994, the December 1993 document only referred to the Alliance Strategic Concept[34]. This may have been an indication of change in US nuclear thinking[35].

Les Aspin gone

On 15 December 1993 – only one month and a half after the NPR was announced – Secretary of Defence Les Aspin was the first of Clinton's principals who had to resign. Aspin agreed to "retire", but everybody understood that President Clinton had asked him to resign. Although the reasons for his resignation are related to other issues (like Somalia)(see chapter 10), it virtually meant the end of the NPR.

The first signals of a status quo policy immediately became visible. Although the Annual Report of the Secretary of Defence to the President and the Congress of January 1994 was formally signed by Aspin, Aspin's influence on the final text was weak. In congruence with the way the NPR was announced, the 1994 Annual Report indicated that the NPR was 'examining in integrated fashion the entire range of issues associated with US nuclear posture...that it will act as the foundation that shapes US nuclear force posture in the post-Cold War world'[36]. It went on to say that 'these force structure changes are not the complete answer. The Presidential guidance that governs nuclear planning is over 10 years old. The United States has not reviewed its basic nuclear policy in more than 15 years and has never undertaken a comprehensive review of all facets of its nuclear posture. Now it is clearly the time for a comprehensive, basic, wide-ranging, integrated review of the entire US nuclear posture'[37].

But some options like a no first use or the complete withdrawal of American nuclear weapons from Europe – let alone elimination – already seemed to have been totally discarded. The 1994 Annual Report clearly said that 'nuclear weapons are *an enduring reality* and are *not likely to disappear in the foreseeable future*'. In other words, after already two months (and probably much earlier) it became clear that elimination was not an option, contrary to what Ashton Carter had declared at the press briefing in October. The following sentence in the report was even clearer: '[The numbers of the nuclear weapons] may decrease and the nature of the threat faced from them may change, *but they simply cannot be eliminated from American defence policy* and security strategy'[38]. In contrast to the NATO summit communiqué of December 1993, the report also stated that the US 'continues to maintain air-delivered nuclear weapons in Europe'[39].

The Annual Report provided two basic justifications for US nuclear weapons: Russia and rogue states. The Report also foreshadowed the idea of hedging against Russia. 'The old Cold War tools of deterrence – strength, balance, and arms control – can still help the US respond to the threat that these nuclear weapons would pose in the hands of, for instance, a government in Russia that revived an adversarial relationship'[40]. The document mentioned that one of the requirements to guide US planning for strategic forces was 'the need to allow for additional forces to be reconstituted in the event of a reversal of the currently positive trend'[41].

Despite the negative security guarantees and the Nuclear Weapon Free Zones protocols, 'the role of US nuclear forces in deterring or responding to [chemical and biological weapons] threats must be considered'. Although the Bottom-Up-Review of September 1993 contained a similar statement, the January 1994 statement was much more significant because the NPR was supposed to deal with this question. This part of the report led to serious criticism from both inside and outside the government. This issue finally appeared too difficult to resolve in the NPR. It was finally agreed that no change in declaratory policy would be announced before the Nuclear Nonproliferation Treaty 1995 Extension Conference.

Lastly, the Annual Report – in contrast to what Aspin had said during the press conference in October – excluded force reductions beyond START II. Beside hedging, the other basic requirement for US nuclear guidance was 'the need to provide an effective deterrent while remaining *within START I/II limits*'[42]. According to William Arkin, it was basically Frank Miller who had written the chapters on nuclear weapons in the Annual Report[43].

In the meantime, Frank Miller's working group had briefed its interim-report to Assistant Secretary of Defence Ash Carter. This interim-report not only failed to come up with changes with regard to declaratory policy, it also advocated a status quo with regard to operational and force structure policy. According to one participant, Ashton Carter called the briefing "a disaster"[44].

To get around the bureaucratic opposition, Ash Carter asked two members of his own staff – Steve Fetter, an academic from the University of Maryland and a former fellow at Ash Carter's CSIA at the Kennedy School of Government (Harvard University), and Leo Mackay, a military advisor of Ash Carter since June 1993 who had just completed his Ph.D. about US nuclear policy after the Cold War at the Kennedy School of Government (with Ash Carter as one of his tutors) – to do their own analysis and to come up with new nuclear options. Carter provided Fetter and Mackay with the necessary clearances.

On 3 February 1994, William Perry – Aspin's Deputy and successor – was formally sworn in as Secretary of Defence. Under Secretary of Defence John Deutch became Perry's Deputy and Walter Slocombe replaced Frank Wisner as Under Secretary for Policy. William Perry had other priorities than Aspin. One month in office, Perry gave a keynote speech at the George Washington University, where he made clear that both US nuclear declaratory and force structure policy would *not* change fundamentally. Perry's underlying assumption was that the future of Russia was still unclear and that, consequently, US nuclear weapons policy was still a useful instrument for "hedging" against worst-case scenarios. He apparently did not see a contradiction between categorizing Russia both as a partner and a rival. For the same reasons, the US would not start with the implementation of START II until 'we see comparable reductions being made in Russia'[45]. Perry also indicated that nuclear weapons could be used to deter chemical and biological weapons attacks. By stating openly that he was in favour of a shift in that direction, he further narrowed down the options of the NPR.

Clash about operational policy

While probably most of the decisions with regard to declaratory and force structure policy had already been taken at the beginning of 1994, there was still room for changing operational policy, at least in the mind of Assistant Secretary of Defence Ashton Carter. Operational nuclear weapons policy had always been his major interest before he had joined the office. But also in government, 'Carter was most preoccupied with promoting safety over hair-trigger alert policies – away from what he saw as a de facto doctrine of launch on warning to a policy of "reassurance"', as Nolan describes[46]. According to him the end of the Cold War, the resulting disintegration of the USSR and the corresponding threat of "loose nukes" made a shift in operational policy highly desirable. As a RAND report, especially written for the NPR, recommended: 'Rapid response should be de-emphasized. In particular, the US should eliminate any options to launch ICBMs on attack if it has not done so already'[47].

During the first months of 1994, two teams were working in parallel with each other: the formal working groups on the one hand, and the Fetter-Mackay tandem on the other. Ashton Carter asked Steve Fetter to brief the Steering Committee, then chaired by Deutch and Owens, on 21 and 22 April 1994. According to drafts that circulated, Fetter would present six options: beside the status quo option (as preferred by the working groups), there were options containing limited or more radical ways of changing operational policy. The basic strategy behind the more radical options was to change US operational policy from a high-alert and LOW policy towards a low-alert and ride-out policy. According to Fetter's analysis, the latter would also have consequences for US force structure and targeting policy. A ride-out policy, for instance, would make ICBMs redundant. Some of the options therefore recommended the end of the triad. It would also have meant the end of counterforce targeting.

When the members of the working groups heard about the upcoming briefings by Ash Carter's office, there was strong opposition. They tried to prevent the briefings taking place as they regarded them as incompatible with the terms of reference of the NPR. The latter gave a mandate to the working groups for organizing the briefings and not to self-appointed personal assistants of the

Assistant Secretary of Defence. In addition, the terms of reference apparently stated that the outcome of the NPR had to be presented in the form of recommendations based on consensus and not in the form of options[48].

Because Carter was not willing to change Fetter's options and the corresponding briefing charts, the members of the working groups complained to their superiors, who took action. The whole story was leaked to like-minded members of Congress. Republican Senator Thurmond, who was the most influential Republican member of the Armed Service Committee, said in a Congressional hearing on 20 April 1994: 'For fifty years now we have had a bipartisan national security policy where the very survival of the US was at issue. Ten administrations agreed...we would enforce a policy of deterrence with a surely survivable Triad of nuclear forces...Now, I am afraid...that unanimity of policy [will] begin to slip away... The Nuclear Posture Review recommended a force roughly like we have now, a strong triad. But the Chairman of the group, Assistant Secretary Carter, is reported going to recommend...we abandon ICBMs !' Thurmond continued 'that the rationale for abandoning ICBMs is that they would not be able to ride out an attack...It appears like this administration is committed to a nuclear policy...based on guilt and shame'. He concluded that 'the US appears determined to go out of the nuclear weapons business'. Questioned by Senator Thurmond at the hearing, the head of the US Strategic Command Adm.Henry Chiles stated that he had 'not seen a working group report that would indicate that the working groups advocated such a step' and strongly maintained that 'ICBMs are necessary in our force of the future'[49]. He added: 'Draw down of our forces too rapidly, for whatever reason, may foreclose desirable options if events do not unfold as anticipated'[50].

Four Republican senators – Conrad Burns, Dirk Kempthorne, Alan Simpson, and Malcolm Wallop – wrote a letter to President Clinton and Secretary of Defence Perry on the same day, 20 April 1994, asking them to reject the NPR recommendation attributed to Ashton Carter to eliminate ICBMs because it was 'extremely ill-advised'. Their arguments were based on the classic logic of maximum deterrence: 'First and foremost, this move would put the US in a very vulnerable position regarding pre-emptive attacks. Using only a handful of weapons, any nation with ICBM capability could mortally wound the US's ability to defend itself'. They also referred to Perry's speech of March 1994 and concluded: 'we should not even consider the elimination of any leg of the triad. Such an act of unilateral disarmament would not save amounts of money, but would, in fact, be highly destabilizing and imprudent'[51].

When the members of the working groups realized that the steps they had taken had no effect and that the first semi-official briefing by Fetter on behalf of Carter on 21 April 1994 had taken place, they tried to prevent the second briefing. The Deputy Chiefs of Operation of the four services wrote an angry letter to both Director of the JCS Vice-Adm. Richard Macke and Vice-Chairman of the JCS William Owens on 22 April 1994. This classified letter was signed by Air Force Acting Deputy Chief of Staff for Plans and Operations Maj.Gen.Larry Henry, Army Operations Deputy Lt.Gen.John Tilelli, Navy Assistant Deputy Chief of Naval Operations for Plans and Operations Rear Adm. John Redd and Marine Corps Acting Operations Deputy to the JCS Brig.Gen. Thomas Wilkerson[52].

Nevertheless, the second briefing by Fetter to Deutch and Owens went ahead on 22 April 1994. Fetter apparently presented three options based on the working group recommendations and three options that the Carter's team favoured, including the option of a monad of 1,440 nuclear weapons based solely on 10 submarines, each carrying 24 missiles with six warheads. The last three options all assumed a ride-out posture. Fetter presented the costs and benefits of all six options[53]. But 'the core of the analysis tried to demonstrate empirically how a policy of prompt launch under alert conditions distorted the level of requirements well beyond what was needed for post-Cold War deterrence', Nolan points out[54].

It is unclear how Deutch and Owens reacted to these proposals. According to some, Deutch wanted to keep at least as much nuclear weapons as all the other nuclear weapon states combined[55]. Others claim that they were willing to consider the option of eliminating ICBMs. Nolan, for instance, writes: 'Concerns about operational doctrine aside, Deutch was reportedly attracted by the savings that would result from not having to rebuild the Minuteman III force, which otherwise would need investment for new motors and guidance packages over the next ten to fifteen years'.

But Nolan immediately adds: 'Any moves in this direction, however, were apparently distracted by further opposition to Carter'[56]. The military and civilian career officials were furious about the briefings. The regional military commanders summoned Ashton Carter in a meeting in the "tank" – the meeting place of the military in the Pentagon – on 25 April 1994[57]. It is unclear what exactly was said in this meeting and whether the military for instance threatened with countermeasures. But the commanders made very clear to Carter that he did not have the authority according to the terms of reference to present the briefings and that he had to stop pushing options that were not agreed upon by the working groups. Carter, according to Nolan, 'was visibly shaken and tried to reason with the officers, arguing that it is not appropriate for colonels and lower-level Pentagon personnel to craft US national policy'[58].

But Carter apparently felt intimidated and gave up pushing for major changes. The underlying reason for halting his efforts, however, was that none of his superiors – Walter Slocombe, John Deutch, William Perry, let alone Bill Clinton – supported him explicitly in his endeavour. The first indication that the advocates of change had lost the game was a NATO meeting in May 1994 that again confirmed 'the essential role of nuclear forces including sub-strategic forces'[59]. In the beginning of June, it became clear that the NPR would not change very much. It was Frank Miller himself who mentioned in a speech to the Centre for Security Policy on 8 June 1994 that the triad would remain in place. The services, which had to hand in their budget plans for the next five years at the beginning of June, had won the battle with Carter[60]. In July 1994, President Clinton presented his first National Security Strategy in which he set forth the following goals with respect to nuclear weapons: 'We will retain strategic nuclear forces sufficient to deter any future hostile foreign leadership with access to strategic nuclear forces from acting against our vital interests and to convince it that seeking a nuclear advantage would be futile. Therefore we will continue to maintain nuclear forces of sufficient size and capability to hold at risk a broad range of assets valued by such political and military leaders'[61]. When the outcome of the NPR was finally presented in September 1994, these words were quoted right at the beginning.

Endgame

After the clash in the tank, the NPR languished for weeks, if not months. Ultimately, Ash Carter had to be convinced by his aides to finalize it. After an off-site conference at the Wye Plantation near Washington DC in the summer of 1994, Leo Mackay and one of his colleagues drove Carter back in their car and convinced him to end the NPR by setting up a set of final briefings[62].

This exercise created a last bureaucratic battle. The military – both J-5 Director Wesley Clark and senior Air Force officials – strongly opposed options that were worked out by Carter's office to de-activate ICBMs and reduce their number from three wings (500) to one wing (150)[63]. Due to the game of leakages and a public statement by the head of the US Strategic Command Adm.Chiles, nothing would change in the end. Ride-out and de-activating would not happen.

The debate about the exact number of ICBMs to be retained, however, was an issue until the very last moment. On 12 September 1994, Chiles wrote a letter to Secretary of Defence Perry arguing strongly against *any* reduction of ICBMs. He also argued that de-activation costs would prevent savings in the near term. He also made clear that he preferred to keep more bombers. Chiles ended his letter that was immediately leaked to Congress with the following words: 'I believe vital national interests are at stake in the Nuclear Posture Review…If we dismantle strategic forces prematurely, it would take a long time at great expense to recover these national assets should they be needed again. The stability of our relationships requires we proceed cautiously'[64].

On Friday 16 September 1994, President Clinton was briefed on the NPR, although the briefing was initially scheduled to be held the day before. The question of the numbers of ICBMs was probably personally resolved by Clinton, as Deutch made clear the day after that all ICBMs would be kept[65]. On 22 September 1994, the day the NPR was briefed to the press, the *Washington Post* wrongly stated that the number of ICBMs would be reduced by 150, probably in an effort to silence the arms control advocates[66]. The number of ICBMs would not go down at all.

Final outcome

Not insignificantly, the results of the NPR were not published as a public report. On 22 September 1994, Secretary of Defence William Perry, Deputy Secretary of Defence John Deutch and Chairman of the JCS Gen. John Shalikashvili presented the final outcome of the NPR in the form of slides to the Senate Armed Services Committee in closed testimony[67] and another one at a press briefing. At the press briefing, Perry explained the outcome as finding a balance between "leading" – providing leadership for further and continuing reductions – and "hedging" against a possible worsening of the situation in Russia. He also stressed the need for safety for the remaining nuclear weapons.

Deputy Secretary of Defence John Deutch presented the slides that were prepared by Carter's office. With regard to the strategic force structure, the "primary concern" to keep strategic nuclear weapons was still Russia[68]. The US would keep the same number of nuclear warheads as before, but with a relatively small reduction in launch platforms: a reduction of nuclear submarines from 18 to 14; four of those remaining 14 would be retrofitted with the more modern D-5 Trident II SLBMs (instead of the existing C-4 Trident I SLBMs); a reduction of 28

B-52s while keeping 66 B-52 and 20 B-2s both for dual-capable missions; the B-1 would no longer have a nuclear role (although in secret the B-1 was apparently still given a nuclear role[69]); all 500 Minuteman III ICBMs would be kept and modernized by re-motoring them and by replacing their guidance systems. Deutch explained that 'the way we arrive at requirements for US nuclear force structures for this period of time through START II is to assess the capabilities of the former Soviet Union, *the targets that are there*, and we look at the kind of targeting and the kind of attack plans we might have and also are prepared to deal with hostile governments' not only in Russia but in other countries'[70]. The overall goal consisted in retaining a "roughly equivalent" number of forces as Russia.

With respect to the sub-strategic nuclear forces, the US would maintain dual-capable aircraft in Europe. It would remove the nuclear capability on surface ships, while maintaining dual-capable aircraft and the capability to launch SLCMs from attack submarines.

Concerning operational policy, 'the nuclear posture review did consider eliminating launch on warning from the repertoire of current options and adopting a strategy of delayed retaliation, but this proposal was decisively rejected'[71], according to Blair. PALs, however, had to be installed on SLBMs.

With regard to declaratory policy and more in particular the debate about nuclear deterrence against chemical and biological weapons: while one of the slides mentioned that conventional capabilities had to be developed in order to counter nuclear proliferation, Deutch kept the nuclear option open during the question and answer period by saying: 'No one is suggesting that if chemical or biological weapons were used that you would deter with nuclear weapons, but certainly a country who is considering using them would have to take that into account. That's how you contribute to deterrence'[72].

With respect to the nuclear infrastructure, the industrial base had to be maintained for further production of D-5 Trident II SLBMs and for possible further production of re-entry vehicles. The Department of Energy had to be capable of producing new warheads, but there would be no newly-designed nuclear warhead production.

When the NPR was presented by Deputy Secretary of Defence John Deutch, Under Secretary of Defence for Policy Walter Slocombe and Assistant Secretary of Defence for International Security Policy Ashton Carter to the House Foreign Affairs Committee in open session on 5 October 1994, the following remarkable conversation took place with regard to the question about nuclear deterrence vis-à-vis chemical and biological weapons. Representative Hamilton asked: 'Why do we need nuclear weapons today ?' Deutch answered: 'We need nuclear weapons to deter other nations that possess nuclear weapons and to deter – well, to deter other nations who possess nuclear weapons from their use against us or our allies'[73]. Representative Berman came back to Deutch' hesitation: 'Is there any other purpose for our nuclear weapons arsenal other than deterring a nuclear attack ?', he asked. Deutch told him again: 'I would say not. I thought I was clear about that, I mean it'[74]. But a few moments later Deutch contradicted himself by saying: 'Let us assume that there is a Saddam Hussein or a Colonel Gadaffi somewhere who is considering – considering chemical attack [sic] against the US, against one of its cities, and will eventually, unfortunately, perhaps have the ability to deliver that by, let's say, a ballistic missile. The fact that we have nuclear weapons could well deter him from that hostile action. I'm not saying that we would use it. I'm just saying to you that the deterrence in situations like that is important.' Berman thereafter asked for a clarification: 'Then you sort of have to amend your earlier answer to indicate that the existence of our nuclear weapons and making sure that they're reliable is to deter nuclear attack and other kinds of attack ?' To this Deutch replicated: 'I will - I believe that is right', adding that the countries he had mentioned were 'not in good standing of the NPT'[75].

The outcome of the NPR was also briefed to the Russians, first of all by Secretary of Defence Perry and Assistant Secretary of Defence Carter to Russian Defence Minister Grachev in New York. Later on, this was repeated to the military staff in Moscow by Ash Carter and the American military attaché in Moscow Gen. John Reppert. The generals of the Russian Strategic Rocket Forces were apparently not unhappy with the results. A status quo gave them more arguments in their battle with the Russian government. On the other hand, those in favour of further reductions and a serious de-legitimisation of nuclear weapons were clearly disappointed. Think-tank analyst Sergei Rogov for instance reported: 'I talked to Ash. I was trying to warn him. Unfortunately, some of my best friends in this [Clinton] administration turned out to be part of the problem, not part of the solution'[76].

To conclude, despite the appearance of leadership, the NPR finally did not result in a major change, let alone a shift towards minimum deterrence. It did not even result in considerable minor changes. The result of the NPR that was made public in September 1994 is generally regarded as a status quo.

CHAPTER 10

LACK OF POLITICAL LEADERSHIP

The NPR in 1993-1994 can be regarded as a classic example of a missed opportunity. The US National Academy of Sciences (CISAC) stated that 'in the end [the NPR] did not go very far toward addressing the most fundamental issues about appropriate numbers, roles, and postures of US nuclear forces in light of the changes brought by the end of the Cold War'[1]. Bruce Blair commented that the NPR 'failed miserably', while preserving 'the Cold War culture of obsessive targeting'[2]. Former Secretary of Defence Robert McNamara called the NPR 'an absolute disgrace'[3].

The purpose of this chapter is to analyse the NPR from the perspective of leadership. One could have predicted that pushing through fundamental changes in US nuclear policy after the Cold War would have been very difficult from a domestic politics point of view (see Chapter 8). The magnitude of interests and beliefs – genuine or ideational – built up during the forty previous years was gigantic. The perceived power of the political opponents of minimum deterrence was extremely strong. Michael Brown explains: 'The NPR [also] demonstrated that radical changes in US nuclear doctrine are unlikely to be suggested by the nuclear establishment. Rather, they will have to be imposed by the political leadership, probably in the form of new Presidential Guidance on the employment of nuclear weapons'[4]. Gen.Charles Horner asserted: 'But don't ask the Pentagon to change the Pentagon. I think it has to come from outside. The Pentagon won't recognize the truth. The executive branch has to provide leadership'[5].

Following the theoretical model that was worked out in Chapter 7, I will split up the analysis in two parts: first, did the political decision-makers who were involved in the NPR behave like *strategic* leaders ? In other words: did they understand the issue ? If so, did they personally believe that the strategic cost-benefit analysis was in favour of change ? And if so, did they have the courage to push these changes through, knowing that they would have to take a lot of heat ? And secondly, in the case they behaved like strategic leaders, did they show *tactical* leadership ? Did they have the personal capacities of pushing through their ideas ?

Key decision-makers

In theory, it is the president, as constitutional Commander-in-Chief, who sets the nuclear guidance that in turn determines the force structure and the operational requirements. In practice, this is not the case. On the other hand, in case nuclear weapons have to be used, it will be the president's decision. The famous black box with the secret codes to launch US nuclear weapons always accompanies the president, wherever he goes.

The nature of the proposed policy changes and the sensitivity of the subject are such that the president has to take the lead. Assuming that fundamental change will quasi-automatically be rejected by the (Chairman of the) JCS, only the president is able to tell the military, and their powerful collaborators in Congress, what the national policy is or should be. Ideally, proposals for fundamental policy change should already be part of the presidential campaign. In that case, the president would have a clear mandate from the electorate to change policy radically.

In the case of the initiative for policy change does not come from the president, then the Secretary of Defence and the National Security Advisor are in the best position to propose such fundamental changes to the president. If other individuals than the Secretary of Defence, the National Security Advisor or the President want to change nuclear policy, they have first to convince one of them. Positively framed, if either the Secretary of Defence or the National Security Advisor is really willing to change US nuclear weapons policy, that individual would have a reasonable chance to succeed on the condition that he plays the political game well. If either the Secretary of Defence or the National Security Advisor behaves like a strategic and tactical leader, he may succeed. In addition, the president has at least to take the heat in case of difficulties. Lastly, the Secretary of Defence and the National Security Advisor should not make each other's life difficult. If the Secretary of Defence takes the initiative, the National Security Advisor has at least to be a passive supporter, and vice versa.

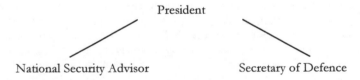

President

National Security Advisor   Secretary of Defence

Figure 2: Key decision-makers for US nuclear weapons policy: the inner circle

As these three high-level decision-makers do not act in a political vacuum and as nuclear policy-making is subject to an interagency process, a broader group of decision-makers is involved. I will start my analysis by looking to the two political appointees who announced the NPR on 29 October 1993: Secretary of Defence Les Aspin and Assistant Secretary of Defence Ashton Carter. Their statements during the press briefing as well as earlier statements, also before they entered the government, were mainly responsible for the high expectations concerning the outcome of the NPR.

Les Aspin and Ash Carter: strategic leadership

Les Aspin
Les Aspin studied history in Yale, earned a master's degree at Oxford University as a Rhodes Scholar, and obtained a Ph.D. in economics at the Massachusetts Institute of Technology (MIT). He was one of the "whiz kids" of McNamara, doing economic analysis in Vietnam. At the age of 32, in 1970, he was elected as a member of the House of Representatives for the Democrats in Wisconsin. He became a defence expert in Congress and in 1985 Chairman of the House Armed Service Committee. Except of his first and last years in Congress when he was quite liberal, Aspin was rather centrist on defence issues linking arms control with force modernization. He was in favour of nuclear disarmament, but he also supported for instance the MX programme[6].

Since the disappearance of the Soviet threat, Aspin again became a fervent defender of arms control without force modernization. When JCS Chairman Colin Powell asked for continued force modernizations at a Congressional hearing in 1990, Les Aspin replied: 'You stand logic on its head when you use arms control as an argument for a larger defence budget'[7]. In September 1991, Aspin was the first who drafted a paper about the nuclear dangers resulting from the *coup d'état* in the USSR[8]. He fully supported the Nunn-Lugar initiative set up two months later. In a speech in January 1992, Aspin also made it clear he believed that most of the new proliferators were undeterrable[9].

Most interesting of all was his paper *From deterrence to de-nuking: a new nuclear policy for the 1990s*, which was part of a whole series of White Papers that were written in 1991-1992 to adapt US military forces to the end of the Cold War[10]. In a draft of January 1992, Aspin recommended for instance a fundamental change in US nuclear declaratory policy, including a no first use policy, on condition that the allies agreed. He was also in favour of introducing PALs in all nuclear weapons systems and he spoke out in favour of a cut-off and a Comprehensive Test Ban Treaty. This was at that time far from evident. President Bush halted testing only in October 1992 for instance. Aspin also toyed with the idea of eliminating ICBMs. He even added: 'if we now had the opportunity to ban *all* nuclear weapons, we would'[11]. To make the latter absolutely clear and linking disarmament to the future of the nonproliferation regime, he maintained: 'it would be in our interest to get rid of nuclear weapons'[12]. However, he did not believe that this would be possible in the short or medium-term. He planned to keep nuclear weapons for at least another 20 years. But he was against force modernizations and more in particular against the modernization of the Minuteman III ICBMs, because the existing missiles would remain reliable until 2010[13].

In a speech at the Johns Hopkins University in February 1992, Aspin repeated his call for a Comprehensive Test Ban Treaty and a cut-off treaty. He also proposed to remove all US nuclear weapons out of Europe[14]. In his commencement speech at the Massachusetts Institute of Technology (MIT) at the beginning of June 1992, only months before becoming Secretary of Defence, he used for the first time the image he would use again while in office: 'But now the Soviet Union has collapsed. The United States is the biggest conventional power in the world. There is no longer any need for the US to have nuclear weapons as an equalizer against other powers. If we were to get another crack at the magic wand, we'd wave it in a nanosecond. *A world without nuclear weapons* would not be disadvantageous to the US. In fact, a world without nuclear weapons *would actually be better.* Nuclear weapons are still the big equalizer but now the US is not the equalizer but the equalize'[15].

As Aspin was one of Clinton's principal defence advisors, it is not surprising that he was asked to become Secretary of Defence in January 1993.

Once in government, Aspin had clearly the idea of making his mark. He did not hide his ambitions in this regard[16]. He had always wanted to become Secretary of Defence. With an annual budget of $260 billion (at that time) and an employer for three million people, the position of Secretary of Defence is one of the most powerful jobs in the US. Now he had the chance to implement the ideas he had gradually built over time.

He did not want to lose time. In his nomination hearing on 7 January 1993, Aspin was clear with regard to the changed circumstances: 'We come together in an extraordinary time. For a parallel, we really have to reach back to the late 1940s…The Cold War that emerged from the global conflict is no more…The world that will replace it is being re-created and it will be recreated by all of us here in this room'[17]. As he later recalled in an interview: 'I still think my strategy was clear and fairly sound: I wanted to get rid of all the tough, divisive issues early in my term as defence secretary. Like a shrewd mayor or governor, I'd get the hard stuff done early and then build for the future'. Tough questions were social issues like the role of women in combat and the gay issue, but also the defence budget, and the bottom-up-review[18]. It is therefore not surprising that Aspin made a lot of enemies right from the beginning. He tried for instance to restructure the Pentagon and to introduce complete new issues in the Defence Department, such as democratisation and human rights.

He scaled back missile defence to a mid-course ground-based system, a decision the Ballistic Missile Defence Organization and US Space Command did not like at all. Aspin also introduced a new round of base closures in March 1993 that led to a lot of grief, especially in Congress. One month later, he ordered – against the military advice and apparently to the surprise of Clinton – the end of restrictions on women flying combat missions and serving on most Navy warships[19]. In May 1993, Aspin supported a zero-yield Comprehensive Test Ban Treaty, in contrast to what the majority of his subordinates in the Department of Defence had recommended, as well as in contrast to mainstream thinking inside the State Department (except the Arms Control and Disarmament Agency) and the National Security Council.

Although the outcome of the Bottom-Up-Review in the summer of 1993 did not totally correspond with his personal view, especially with regard to the conventional weapons force structure[20], Aspin succeeded in pushing through his own threat analysis.

It was no surprise that Aspin himself announced the NPR in October 1993. He also became personally involved in the NPR[21]. According to our definition, Aspin behaved like a strategic leader, at least with regard to nuclear weapons policy.

Ashton Carter
Ashton Carter studied physics and medieval history at Yale University, and obtained a Ph.D. in theoretical physics from Oxford University as a Rhodes

Scholar. He was recruited by Aspin when he was (and again is) a professor at the Kennedy School of Government at Harvard University.

Carter was probably best known for his Office of Technology Assessment (OTA) study in the 1980s, in which he had criticized Reagan's SDI proposal on technological grounds[22]. In the period 1991-1992, Carter wrote or co-authored at least five publications in which he recommended drastic changes with regard to US nuclear weapons policy. 'At hand with the ending of East-West confrontation is the prospect of *radical de-emphasis of nuclear weapons* in the security conceptions of the major powers', he wrote[23].

With regard to the force structure, Carter favoured 'more *dramatic* adjustments in [the] nuclear posture with the objective of promoting desirable nuclear outcomes in the former Soviet Union...steps...such as *elimination of land-based ballistic missiles*, de-MIRVing, and *prompt movement toward deeper cuts* merit careful consideration'[24]. As an academic, he repeated these ideas in testimony before Congress[25]. Furthermore, he did not regard the triad as something that had to be kept indefinitely[26]. Carter was strongly opposed to a prompt launch capability on safety grounds. Finally, he did not regard sub-strategic nuclear weapons as very useful[27].

On declaratory policy Carter was less outspoken. But he seemed to agree with the idea of a no first use and a declaratory ride-out policy. 'Doctrines covering the residual nuclear forces – themselves much shrunk and simplified – would foresee retaliation only and that *only in response to first nuclear use and without any automatic response*', Carter wrote before he entered the government[28]. He is quoted as having said as Assistant Secretary of Defence that: 'Our intention is to have a military that doesn't need to use [nuclear, biological, and chemical] weapons...We can use conventional forces to prevail anywhere in the world'[29]. After he left the Clinton administration, Carter wrote a book with his mentor, former Secretary of Defence William Perry, in which they argued: 'The US cannot and should not depend on the reliability of [the lingering presence of a dangerously casual reliance on non-strategic nuclear weapons to deter an enemy's use of weapons of mass destruction in regional conflict] when dealing with desperate and "rogue" states or with non-state, terrorist attackers. More importantly, *the US has not confronted the wisdom of supposing that it would or should ever be the first nation since 1945 to detonate nuclear weapons in anger*...Non-nuclear counters to weapons of mass destruction, especially chemical and biological weapons, are in fact feasible'[30].

During the NPR, according to Hans Kristensen, 'unlike the military officials, Carter correctly suspected that a stated nuclear deterrence role for weapons of mass destruction scenarios could have a negative impact on the NPT regime, regardless of whether the US was legally bound by its negative security assurances. He therefore instructed the drafting groups to suggest possible political, economical and conventional deterrence options that could complement the US nuclear posture'[31].

Carter's main interest though, before he entered government, seemed to be operational policy[32]. He was for instance in favour of taking nuclear weapons off alert (like de-activating ICBMs) as well as introducing Permissive Action Links (PALs) in nuclear submarines. 'Hasty retaliatory timelines (including provision for retaliation to begin before the provoking attack was even over, and accepting force and command and control configurations that could not accomplish retaliation if orders were delayed too long), dependence on strategic or tactical warning of attack, and subtle interdependencies among legs of the strategic "triad" (as with the supposed dependence of bombers and ICBM on each other for launch on tactical warning...) were accepted in the pursuit of ever more weighty and assured retaliation...The goal should be not only the capability for weighty and assured retaliation but also *freedom from dependence on alerting and warning, and above all, reliance on prompt response*[33]. Three years earlier he had already asked for 'a deterrent that could calmly sit out a crisis without taking any actions that might aggravate it, and that could *ride out a first strike* until the enemy had done his worst and then patiently wait for the president or his successors to deliberate'[34]. 'Weeks of preparations' for a retaliatory attack were needed[35]. Even in the context of START II levels, he argued that 'an inadvertent triggering of the strategic attack plans that are being continued as the basis for deterrence would still be the largest man-made catastrophe in history'[36]. With regard to targeting policy, he explicitly disliked counterforce options[37]. Once out of government, he even seemed to suggest doing away with the Single Integrated Operational Plan (SIOP) – the nuclear war plan – as a whole[38].

Carter warned that rogue states were deterrable, but in other ways than the US was used to. Like Aspin, Carter was in favour of a limited defence shield and conventional pre-emptive attacks against weapons of mass destruction programmes of rogue states. But he argued against developing earth-penetrating nuclear weapons[39] or any new types of nuclear weapons[40].

Before he entered into the government, Ash Carter had admitted that what the US did with regard to its posture had an influence on other countries, not only on Russia[41]. 'It is possible, and highly desirable, that this *dramatic denuclearisation pending among the great powers* will have a salutary effect on thinking about nuclear weapons in other parts of the world and thus on proliferation', he wrote[42].

All these statements point to the fact that Ash Carter was in favour of drastic changes in US nuclear weapons policy. Carter warned: '[the] price of failure to induce a graceful and controlled process of denuclearisation would not just be a historic opportunity lost, but possibly a disaster'[43].

Carter's three main duties in office were threat reduction in Russia (Nunn-Lugar), counterproliferation and nuclear weapons strategy. With respect to the latter, it is useful to quote Carter's written answer to questions by members of Congress during his nomination hearing in May 1993: 'This area [of nuclear weapons strategy] should not be mistaken for old news. *The nature of our [nuclear] forces will change dramatically* as the overall numbers come down, and as the challenge of deterrence changes. This area needs not simply to be managed, but *to be reshaped* and altered *in light of the fundamental changes in the strategic environment*'[44].

The *Washington Post* wrote: 'Because Carter was young, dynamic and smart, outsiders to the US government – especially those who favoured rapid reduction or elimination of nuclear weapons – tended to invest their hopes in him. Indeed, he was becoming a minor cult figure in Washington's small but intense community of nuclear weapons specialists'[45]. Participants in the NPR claim that Carter was enthusiastic at the beginning. 'His statements to colleagues at the time emphasized his determination to implement changes in the nuclear establishment in a way that would fundamentally transform its Cold War preoccupations and force a recognition of the inherent risks in the existing nuclear posture', according to Nolan[46]. Eric Mlyn points out that Ash Carter 'seems to have been the one in the

NPR *most forcefully* pushing significant change'[47]. Like Aspin, Carter can in this regard be regarded as a strategic leader.

Nowadays, Ash Carter admits that he pushed the bureaucracy to think these issues through. But he denies that he personally favoured more changes than those that resulted from the NPR[48]. There is, however, every reason to believe that Carter favoured more changes at that time because he believed, according to his writings, that that was in the US interest.

Beyond Aspin and Carter: bureaucratic opposition and lack of strategic leadership

Except for Secretary of Defence Les Aspin, Assistant Secretary of Defence Ashton Carter and a few assistants, there was a lack of strategic leadership with regard to nuclear policy at each level and in each department that was directly or indirectly involved in the NPR. There was a lack of interest and above all a lack of political will and courage to push through the necessary changes. We will make a distinction between the mid-level appointees, the deputy, principals, and presidential level.

All *civilians* involved at the mid-level – Deputy Assistant Secretary of Defence for International Security Policy Frank Miller, Principal Deputy Under Secretary of Defence Jan Lodal, Under Secretary of Defence Walter Slocombe, Assistant Secretary of Defence for International Security Policy Ash Carter, Special Assistant to the President for Arms Control Bob Bell and Under Secretary of State for Arms Control and International Security Affairs Lynn Davis – had been dealing extensively with nuclear weapons issues before. Miller, Lodal, Davis and Slocombe had already studied the intricate details of operational and force structure policy as government officials in the 1970s. It was at that time that the nuclear posture of the 1980s and 1990s was invented and that the weapons systems that were deployed in the 1990s (like Trident, the MX, the B-1 and B-2) were developed. As one participant of the NPR said, 'they grew up during the Kissinger era'[49]. In the 1990s, they still believed that maximum deterrence was much better – read "more stabilizing" – than minimum deterrence. All of them were political appointees, except Frank Miller who was a career official. In the words of Eric Mlyn: 'Whether administrations were Democratic or Republican, the same people have shaped US nuclear weapons policy over the years...Officials such as Andrew Marshall, Leon Sloss, Walter Slocombe, William Perry, and John Deutch have influenced nuclear weapons policy for decades, and many continue to do so within the Clinton administration despite the end of the Cold War'[50]. Mlyn could easily have added Jan Lodal, Lynn Davis and Frank Miller.

They did not like to see "their" doctrine replaced. In their eyes, changing to a minimum deterrence posture would implicitly have meant admitting that their policy was wrong. As a result, Nolan states, 'two distinct conceptual frameworks were represented [during the NPR] – and were bound to collide: a vision of nuclear security that de-emphasized a reliance on targeting and prompt operations in favour of "mutual assured safety" and co-operative denuclearisation; and the contrasting view that the uncertain character of changes in Russia (and in the international system) compelled adherence to classic deterrence as well as the adoption of new nuclear options for emerging threats'[51]. Les Aspin and Ash Carter together with Steve Fetter and Leo Mackay stood for the first vision; Frank Miller, Bob Bell, Lynn Davis, Jan Lodal, Walter Slocombe, John Deutch and the military stood for the second. One of them asserted in 1998: 'To simply say let's go to a 1,000 and declare no first use means that you have a policy that bears no relation to the world in which we live'. He added: 'That is reality'[52].

Frank Miller, for instance, helped develop PD-59 in the Carter administration and became the civilian nuclear 'tsar' in the Pentagon in 1981. In the 1980s, he fought SDI for the same reasons that he fought minimum deterrence in the 1990s, namely that it would make the posture he helped to develop – maximum deterrence – obsolete. According to Nolan, 'Miller had one basic metric for nuclear deterrence, the familiar axiom that US nuclear forces were needed in quantities sufficient to hold at risk and destroy enemy nuclear launch sites'[53]. This corresponds to the classic deterrence requirements. According to Arkin, Frank Miller 'believes that there are only a small group of experts like him that really understand the finely tuned nuclear system – one that he thinks works well'[54]. Moreover, Miller had also run a large part of the targeting reviews in the Reagan and George W.H.Bush administrations. In 1993, he believed that enough changes were made. 'Not least among the factors driving his judgment was the degree to which he had earned a place at the table in the inner sanctum of the nuclear planning community, a hard-won victory that depended on enduring working relationships', Nolan adds[55].

Frank Miller became Principal Deputy Assistant Secretary of Defence under Ash Carter. While Carter was formally leading the NPR on a daily basis, Miller was *de facto* in charge. 'As he saw it, he would help educate and protect his bosses, tempering their more brash tendencies while interpreting tasking orders in terms that the bureaucracy could understand', in the words of Nolan[56]. After having started up the NPR, Carter got stuck in other policy issues like the denuclearisation of the former Soviet republics. Carter delegated many issues to Miller, who was also formally in charge of coordinating the NPR working groups. Frank Miller personally headed the working group dealing with the future role of US nuclear weapons. Taking into account Miller's position and beliefs mentioned before, it is not surprising that he tried to block changes. As Frank Miller was also in charge of preparing the official briefings to the Steering Committee of the NPR, he had a lot of leverage. It was also Miller who was involved in writing the chapters about nuclear weapons of the Annual Report of the Secretary of Defence to the President and Congress in January 1994. That document contained the first signals of a status quo policy. It was also Miller who announced in June 1993 that the triad would certainly be kept, which was a very clear signal that Carter had lost the game. When Ash Carter left office in 1996, Frank Miller became Acting Assistant Secretary of Defence. In the George W.Bush administration, he became staff member of the NSC.

There is a second fundamental difference between Aspin and Carter on the one hand and these mid-level political appointees on the other. The latter regarded the combination of old instruments (prevention and deterrence) and new instruments (pre-emption and defence) as a solution to the threat of proliferation. They agreed that the proliferation of nuclear weapons was difficult to stop, but they apparently believed that nuclear proliferation was *not* a real security risk for the US. Proliferation could be "managed". The risks depended on the country in particular and its political regime[57]. Similar ideas circulated in academic circles. Stephen Walt for instance argued that proliferation is not too worrying: 'This means that the US will have to learn to live with more nuclear weapon states in the future. *Fortunately, I don't think we will find this too uncomfortable or dangerous*[58]. Paul Bracken, another US academic, likes to call it "an agreed nuclear world"[59]. George Perkovich, in contrast, does not agree with these ideas. He agrees however that Walt's logic applies to the political appointees of the George W.Bush administration (like Robert Joseph, John Bolton, Douglas Feith and Stephen Cambone): 'Rejecting the fundamental premise of the NPT, these officials seek not to create an equitable global regime that actively devalues nuclear weapons and creates conditions for their eventual elimination, but rather to eradicate the bad guys or their weapons while leaving the "good guys" free of nuclear constraints'[60].

This kind of thinking has major consequences. For these appointees, and contrary to US foreign policy rhetoric, nonproliferation is not a priority. As a result, the nonproliferation regime and the Nuclear Nonproliferation Treaty are not crucial instruments either. Some proliferation optimists for instance recommended not fighting for the indefinite extension of the Nuclear Nonproliferation Treaty in 1995[61].

Similarly, many of them do not believe (or at least say so) that there is a link between the spread of nuclear weapons on the one hand and US nuclear policy on the other. For instance, Linton Brooks, the head of the National Nuclear Security Administration, argued as follows in 2004: 'Over the past decade, we have seen very significant reductions in the numbers of US (and Russian) nuclear weapons, reductions in the alert levels of nuclear forces, and the abandonment of US nuclear testing...There is absolutely no evidence that these developments have caused North Korea or Iran to slow down covert programmes to acquire capabilities to produce nuclear weapons'[62]. Regardless of possible changes in US nuclear policy, they argue, rogue states like to have nuclear weapons and will succeed in the end. US nuclear weapons policy therefore should not be made hostage to the political will of others.

While this logic is of course hard to fight, it ignores the benefits of the existing nonproliferation regime. To put it crudely, if there had been no nuclear weapon states in 1998, the chance would have been extremely small that India and Pakistan had tested nuclear weapons. The latter makes clear that there *is* a link between US nuclear policy and proliferation. Cognitive processes like denial may prohibit some people from thinking along these lines. Parochial interests may be another. Graham Allison, a former Assistant Secretary of Defence in the Clinton administration, seems to suggest the latter in 2004: 'Well, the American posture currently says we need to develop a few more additional nuclear weapons, but everyone else needs zero...I remember in government trying to explain that position without smiling, and I could never manage to do it'[63]. At the 2004 Carnegie International Non-Proliferation Conference, Ash Carter pointed to the subtle link between the American need for help of the allies in the fight against terrorism and proliferation on the one hand and the lack of support of the allies for the existing American nuclear posture on the other[64].

The same cognitive processes may prohibit them from thinking about elimination. According to their logic, the elimination of nuclear weapons may be a desirable goal in the long-term (with the emphasis on "long"), but it is something that is simply not feasible. It is therefore even "politically incorrect" to talk about it.

What kind of future scenario do these civilian experts favour ? Most of them do not speak out about the long term, even when they are out of office. They probably have no endgame scenario at hand. And if they have, it probably cannot be squared with article 6 of the Nuclear Nonproliferation Treaty. Take for instance Walter Slocombe. After having been Principal Deputy Under SOD for Policy, he became Under SOD for Policy from September 1994 until the end of 2000. The end of the Cold War did not make a big difference in Slocombe's mind: 'The nuclear era and the Cold War were born at about the same time, but the end of the Cold War will not mean the end of nuclear weapons'[65]. While this is true, it becomes a statement when it is the opening sentence of an article in *Survival* in 1990. In the same article, Slocombe criticized the concept of minimum deterrence, defended the triad and talked already about hedging against political instability in the USSR. In another article one year later, he added a more "realist" twist to his reasoning: 'As instruments of international power, nuclear weapons are in this perspective like other fundamental facts of international power, such as economic strength, societal cohesion, and alliance solidarity – hard to use in the short run, but vital in the long term. They will remain so for a long time'[66].

They are also convinced that nuclear weapons accidents cannot happen in Western industrialized states or that the risk is infinitesimally small. They also believe that the US can improve its defence by building theatre or even "national" missile defence systems, and that the US can and should use military force pre-emptively in the case a rogue state goes nuclear[67].

These last two recommendations belong to the concept of counterproliferation that was introduced by Aspin and Carter. The difference between Aspin and Carter on the one hand and the others, however, is twofold: 1) Aspin and Carter regard missile defence and pre-emptive strikes only as temporary instruments and openly speak about nuclear elimination in term; 2) Aspin and Carter at the same time – and contrary to the others – propose changing the existing maximum deterrence posture to a minimum deterrence posture in the short term.

To conclude, a significant number of highly influential government appointees in the Clinton administration, in contrast to most non-governmental experts, believed that the cost-benefit analysis of nuclear weapons was still very positive and would remain so in the foreseeable future.

Beside beliefs, most of these mid-level officials had also no interest in advocating change. "Where you stand depends on where you sit". Frank Miller as a career bureaucrat had probably most to lose. To introduce a change of thinking in the existing nuclear weapons establishment would have meant the investment of an enormous amount of time and energy.

The *military* are not supposed to set out the broad lines of defence policy. However, as mentioned above they have an extremely important advisory role. As career bureaucrats, they have no personal interest in making too much noise or going against the interests of the organization they represent. The nuclear planning community of the JCS and the Strategic Command (STRATCOM) had most to lose. As Hans Kristensen noted: 'STRATCOM anticipated [the NPR] and headed off any idea of true reductions and thwarted any attempts by the NPR to eliminate the triad of forces'[68]. STRATCOM's Sun City study of 1993 and its extended version of 1994 were determining[69]. The head of STRATCOM Adm.Chiles warned

Congress in April 1994 – *before* the end of the NPR – that he did not like the elimination of ICBMs, a ride-out policy or any other major changes. The nuclear establishment wanted to keep a maximum deterrence posture. According to Arkin and Kristensen: 'It is not surprising that STRATCOM's "preferred" force structure was eventually recommended by the NPR'[70]. This explanation is similar to that of Chairman of the JCS Colin Powell, who said that the main reason for not going to lower levels than 3,500 at the time of START II was that this would have endangered the existence of the triad. The initial US goal for the START II levels was 4,500 against 2,500 for Russia[71]. Colin Powell admitted after he retired that these high levels did not do 'any damage to our modernizing programmes'[72]. The Navy was in the middle of refitting the Trident submarines with D-5 and higher-yield warheads in 1992. Lee Butler explained after he retired that when you are going to the 2,000-level, 'you start trading off systems. That always triggers inter-service rivalry. We're talking tens of billions of dollars. You're talking about the future, the pride, the standing of the ballistic missile submarine force'[73].

Chiles' predecessor Lee Butler – despite his activities before and after the NPR – did not behave much differently during the NPR. In the beginning of 1993, as mentioned before, Lee Butler invited the press to Omaha and explained STRATCOM's "new" thinking. This included the targeting of third world states that possessed chemical and biological weapons, in contrast to official US declaratory policy.

The Directors of the J-5 – McCaffrey and later on Clark – were both Army generals at the time of the NPR. As the Army had no organizational interests anymore in nuclear weapons, one could have expected more willingness on their part to change nuclear policy. This was, however, not the case. First, since the 1960s, interservice co-operation is much more rewarding for the military than interservice rivalry. Interservice rivalry would have meant a smaller defence budget. Secondly, the J-5 is supposed to stand above the services, as it belongs to the *Joint* Staff that served the JCS directly instead of the Army. Thirdly, the JCS and its staff had been strengthened by the 1986 Goldwater-Nichols Act that further diminished the power of the individual services. Fourthly, since the transformation of SAC into STRATCOM in 1992, the J-5 also represented the nuclear planning community. As a result, there were substantial organizational interests involved. Fifth and maybe most fundamentally, the military as a whole took a very defensive attitude right after the Cold War. Taking statements of President Clinton to squeeze the defence budget in order to boost the economy into account, the military wanted to restrict defence savings to a minimum. It was J-5 Director Gen.Lee Butler who in 1990 had helped JCS Chairman Colin Powell thinking through a strategy that kept most of the existing nuclear and conventional force structure. They argued for cautionary reductions and for a capability-based instead of a threat-based planning.

The military and Clinton

The working relationship between the military and civilians at the beginning of the Clinton administration was far from optimal, to say the least. The reasons were partly idiosyncratic, partly political and partly cultural.

Right from the beginning, the military neither liked President Clinton or Secretary of Defence Aspin. Firstly, Clinton was a Democrat. Since the McNamara years, the military are known to favour Republican candidates[74]. Secondly, Clinton did not go to Vietnam[75], in contrast to all senior military officers in the 1990s. They had not forgotten how Secretary of Defence McNamara had dealt with the military during the war, and how American society had treated them thereafter. Or as Vietnam veteran John Wheeler generalized: 'The Clinton administration is largely a networked clique of people who were anti-military and anti-war during the 1960s and carry their biases with them still'[76]. Thirdly, during his electoral campaign, Clinton had focused on the economy. To reduce the deficit, Clinton had called for a reduction of the defence budget. Although his proposal was not very radical in comparison with proposals of defence experts like Robert McNamara, John Steinbruner, or Lawrence Korb who all recommended cutting the defence budget by 50 %, the military were very much afraid of large savings[77]. Lastly, during his campaign Clinton had spoken out in favour of gays in the military, which was a very sensitive issue for the US military. At Clinton's first news conference after having been elected, the president-elect concluded his remarks with: 'I'm not going to change my position on it'[78]. As a result, the military headed by their outspoken Chairman of the JCS and Bush leftover Colin Powell were very suspicious of the Clinton administration right from the start.

The gay issue that already popped up in the first week of the Clinton administration did not improve that relationship either. Despite recommendations by Powell and others for not pushing the gay issue to the forefront of the political agenda from the very beginning, President Clinton tried to keep his campaign promise to give more rights to the gays in the military. This provoked enormous opposition within the military, supported by large sections of American society. Retired Army officer David Hackworth stated that 'in almost a half-century of soldiering or writing about it, I've never seen a president attacked so openly by the nation's fighting forces'[79]. It damaged President Clinton's image considerably right from the beginning.

The military did not like Aspin either because of his criticism vis-à-vis the Pentagon as a former member of Congress. Because of Aspin's initiatives – like scaling back missile defence, base closures, reforming the Pentagon – and his whiz-kid style, this relationship did not improve during the first months either (see below).

To conclude, all these extra sensitivities – although not always rooted on objective grounds – on top of the aforementioned parochial interests made it even more difficult to discuss changes in nuclear policy.

An indication that some of the senior military officials defended the nuclear status quo, not because they believed in maximum deterrence, but because they had to save their organizations, is the fact that many of them spoke out in favour of minimum deterrence or even elimination once they retired. Once retired, the head of STRATCOM Gen.Lee Butler for instance became one of the most eloquent individuals speaking out in favour of abolition.

General Lee Butler graduated from the Air Force Academy in 1961, flew with F-4's in Vietnam and with nuclear-capable F-16s and B-52, was a commander at a nuclear bomber base, obtained a Masters degree in International Politics in Paris, was a professor at the Air Force College teaching nuclear weapons policy, became J-5 Director under Colin Powell when the Cold War came to a halt, and ended his career as head of the US Strategic Air Command. Gen.Lee Butler was one of the most knowledgeable nuclear weapons experts in the US[80].

Lee Butler's efforts to change US nuclear policy as a career bureaucrat were more remarkable than most of his predecessors and successors. From his very first day as head of the US Strategic Air Command, for instance, he personally made a considerable effort in going through the whole target list. He can be personally credited of having reduced the number of targets from 10,000 in 1991 to 2,500 at the beginning of 1994[81]. Once retired, he called the Single Integrated Operational Plan, with the possible exception of the Soviet nuclear war plan, 'the single most absurd and irresponsible document that I had ever reviewed in my life'[82]. Despite his position, Lee Butler agreed with the unilateral/reciprocal measures announced by Bush in the period 1990-1992. When Colin Powell asked him to imagine another step, Lee Butler recommended taking the bombers off-alert in 1991, which became the official policy shortly thereafter. According to his own account later on, he personally agreed with START II levels of 2,000 (instead of 3,500). He apparently also had a list of thirty other recommendations for changing US nuclear policy.

The change for which he probably will be mostly remembered is the transformation of SAC into STRATCOM. Lee Butler proposed it to the Air Force Chief of Staff on 9 July 1991 and three days later to all four-star generals of the Air Force. He convinced them to melt Strategic Air Command (SAC) with Tactical Air Command. Both were huge organizations with a colourful history. During the summer of 1991, his plans were worked out and STRATCOM was established on 1 June 1992[83].

On the other hand, Lee Butler could have done much more. As Director of the J-5, Lee Butler had written the Base Force together with Colin Powell[84]. In a hearing before Congress at the beginning of April 1992, Lee Butler did not give the impression of wanting drastic force reductions: 'I would urge that there [be]…no precipitous drawdown in [US] forces until we have some better understanding of how hard realities of economic collapse play into [the Russian] long-range plans for force modernization'[85]. He had a similar attitude with respect to the nuclear force structure. 'A US nuclear deterrent force is a key element in the pervasive international role we must continue to play well into the future', he said in the same hearing[86]. A year later, in 1993, Lee Butler warned: 'The crucial point here is to avoid eroding the deterrent value of the strategic forces by budget driven decisions that ignore vital planning considerations, or depreciate the carefully conceived rationale that underpinned our objectives in the START negotiations'[87].

In addition, Lee Butler did not advocate a change in declaratory policy. On the contrary, Gen.Lee Butler told the press in February 1993 that STRATCOM would also start targeting third world states, although the latter would contradict US policy of offering the same states negative security guarantees. Furthermore, Lee Butler did not abolish the Single Integrated Operational Plan. He wanted to make it more flexible and adaptive. In short, Lee Butler was not an advocate of major changes during the NPR. One reason he kept quiet at that time may have been that he hoped to become the successor of Colin Powell as Chairman of the JCS in September 1993, which did not happen in the end[88].

Once retired Lee Butler took a completely different view and spoke out in favour of nuclear elimination[89]. Lee Butler was one of the most active members of the Canberra Commission in 1996 and the CISAC study one year later (see appendix). Lee Butler is not a unique case. More than sixty former generals and admirals from around the world spoke out in favour of elimination in December 1996. In theory, it may be that some of them changed their mind the day they retired. But it is too much of a coincidence that nearly all these generals and admirals kept quiet while in office and spoke out against nuclear weapons once they retired. A more credible explanation is that thanks to their experience, they thought the issue through and changed their mind at a certain point in time *during* their career. Lee Butler explains: 'Up to [the point I became CINCSAC] I had developed a series of reservations and doubts that progressively deepened. I had no basis for understanding whether these concerns were based on lack of information and insight or whether they were rooted in the reality of bureaucratic processes run amuck by the intrusion of the self-serving profit interests of the military-industrial complex, by the collision of cultures and turf in the Pentagon for budget dollars, or simply by the towering forces of alienation and isolation that grew out of the mutual demonisation between the US and the Soviet Union over a period of forty-five years. I just didn't know. Beginning in early 1991, I went through the process that very quickly accelerated and confirmed my worst fears and my worst concerns. What we have done in this country,…, is this: the creation of gargantuan agencies with mammoth appetites and a sense of infallibility that consume infinite resources in pursuit of a messianic vision of a demonisation'[90].

During their career, these generals had to keep quiet. Too much controversy or criticism is not liked inside the government, or for that matter in any organization. Those who do not follow this basic rule risk punishment by being excluded from meetings, by not getting promoted, or even worse, by having to resign. They would never have become general in the first place if they had spoken out earlier.

Frank von Hippel is an example of a *civilian* appointee who did speak out while in government. As a scientist at Princeton University, von Hippel had followed the nuclear weapons debate for over twenty years. In September 1993, he arrived in the Clinton administration as Assistant Director for National Security in the Office of Science and Technology Policy (OSTP) in the White House. As he had written extensively about nuclear weapons, von Hippel was known for his liberal views. He also played a major role in convincing Secretary of Energy O'Leary to support the extension of the test moratorium in May 1993. When von Hippel later on entered the government, officials said: 'But he has an agenda !' In December 1994 – seven months earlier than planned – von Hippel decided to quit his job due to what he describes as 'a continual barrage of urgent phone calls, faxes and interagency meetings'[91]. He concluded: *'There is little opportunity inside the government to achieve fundamental changes in policy.* This is especially true in the areas of arms control and nonproliferation policy, where many agencies have to sign off, and officials therefore only have the freedom to innovate at the margins of the current policy consensus. Any new ideas face a brutal obstacle course. Testimony and speeches have to be "cleared" with other agencies; proposed new initiatives must be agreed at interagency meetings; cables communicating proposals to foreign governments must be circulated for interagency clearance; and frequent turf battles, reorganizations, and transfers of personnel militate against the development of effective interagency collaborations on policy development'[92].

To conclude, all mid-level officials and appointees involved in the NPR – except Ash Carter – resisted major changes. Not one of them can be qualified as a strategic leader with regard to nuclear policy at that time. The problem was certainly not a lack of knowledge. All of them had a very good understanding of what US nuclear policy was about. Contrary to the Deputy and Principal level, the mid-level appointees spent much of their time during the NPR dealing with nuclear weapons. They judged that a change in US nuclear policy was not desirable at that time. Some of them probably believed that maximum deterrence was more credible and stabilizing than minimum deterrence. Most of them had elaborated the concept of maximum deterrence earlier in their career. Prestige, social pressure as well as a lack of courage withheld others to change the doctrine in the 1990s.

Deputies level

The mid-level actors, however, could have easily been overridden by the deputy's level. The Deputies Committee established, reviewed and monitored the interagency working groups[93]. Four times a week, Deputy National Security Advisor Sandy Berger, who was the Chairman of the Committee, met with his counterparts in the White House trying to resolve the difficulties in the field of international security that were not resolved by lower levels.

Contrary to the mid-level group, nuclear weapons policy was only a small part of their portfolio. But it was the Deputy Committee that agreed with halting the National Security Council-led interagency working group on arms control in the spring of 1993 and that delegated it to the Defence Department.

Those who were regarded as being the major players with regard to nuclear weapons policy were John Deutch (DOD), William Perry (DOD)[94], William Owens (DOD), and Leon Fuerth (NSC).

John Deutch, who was born in Belgium and who emigrated to the US before the Second World War, was known for his conservative views on nuclear weapons, comparable to those of Frank Miller, Walter Slocombe and Jan Lodal. As a reaction to Aspin's draft *From Deterrence to De-nuking* at the beginning of 1992, Deutch (out of office) made clear that he was against a Comprehensive Test Ban Treaty and against a no-first use, that he did not see a link between disarmament and proliferation, and that he was in favour of 'lower yield more accurate nuclear weapons, neutron devices, or earth-penetrators that may have more deterrent value in a new world of multiple threats'[95].

Deutch had considerable experience in the field. He had been Assistant Secretary for Technology and later on Under Secretary of Energy in the Carter administration. He was one of the few Democrats who participated in blue ribbon panels such as the Scowcroft Commission and the Reed-Wheeler committee, in respectively the Reagan and George W.H.Bush administration. Deutch was also a professor in chemistry at the Massachusetts Institute of Technology (MIT), where he later became Provost. Thanks to his academic and government experience, he also had very good relations with the defence industry. He is therefore described as 'a quintessential member of the military-industrial-academic complex'[96] and a 'card-carrying member of the defence and nuclear establishments'[97]. Before he went to the Defence Department, he was for instance on the advisory board of Martin Marietta, United Technology Corporations, and TRW[98].

John Deutch is also known for his dominating character – he apparently treated some Assistant Secretaries as children[99] – and, maybe related, for his efficient decision-making capacity. He became Under Secretary of Defence for Acquisition and Technology in the Clinton administration and was regarded as "action officer" to tackle the toughest issues in the Defence Department[100]. For instance it was Deutch who dealt with the test moratorium, the Bottom-Up-Review, the NPR, Haiti in 1994, and the acquisition reform. Deutch was also in charge of a report on counterproliferation, which finally recommended spending yearly $400 million on counterproliferation[101].

John Deutch became Deputy Secretary of Defence in January 1994. But he had already been involved in the NPR before. As Frank von Hippel points out with regard to the NPR: 'There was a lack of interest and knowledge about arms control on the part of the president, the National Security Advisor, the Secretary of Defence, the Secretary of State. It all got passed down to the second and third level...And there you had this big gorilla, Deutch'[102]. Since January 1994, he also formally became co-chair of the Steering Committee of the NPR. Secretary of Defence Perry had delegated the NPR to Deutch. When Carter's office briefed Deutch and Owens at the end of April 1994, the Steering Committee was not "a priori" against changes in the US nuclear posture. Deutch and Owens were especially interested in savings, for instance by eliminating ICBMs. Strong opposition from the military and the Republicans as well as the mid-level officials against such a move apparently outweighed any financial and strategic benefits. Assistant Secretary of Defence Ash Carter could not convince Deutch either.

Taking Deutch' beliefs and interests mentioned above into account, it is not surprising to discover that he was not the most active advocate for change. In the same vein, he accepted a fight with Secretary of Energy Hazel O'Leary by writing her a letter in July 1994, asking whether she had allocated enough money for the nuclear weapons programme[103]. Deutch was also against co-operation with Minatom, the Russian counterpart of the Department of Energy[104]. Before, he had also opposed a deal with North Korea[105].

It was Deutch who presented most of the public briefings of the NPR at the end. During one of these briefings, he admitted that there was a role for nuclear weapons in deterring chemical and biological weapons attack (see chapter 9). In March 1995, John Deutch became Director of the CIA. Ten years later, in an article in *Foreign Affairs*, he asked for further reductions of the deployed weapons, but at the same time stuck to many of the ideas he had always defended: a triad of SLBMs, ICBMs and bombers; no CTBT; nuclear deterrence vis-à-vis chemical and biological weapons attacks; no no-first use; and no elimination[106].

Adm.William Owens – Vice-Chairman of the JCS and formally in charge of the Steering Committee of the NPR (together with Perry and later on Deutch) – was personally in favour of drastic changes in US nuclear weapons policy, like the elimination of ICBMs, the elimination of tactical nuclear weapons and consequently the withdrawal of American nuclear weapons from Europe, mainly for budgetary reasons[107]. Once retired, he stated in a hearing of the Senate Foreign Relations Committee on Bush's Nuclear Posture Review on 16 May 2002: 'to see the Russians more like England and France than like the old Soviet enemy, then we should have very much on the table this issue of tactical nuclear weapons...and really get to the core of getting rid of them if we can. A part of this is our own problem (...because) many policymakers in our country believe the NATO nuclear force is critical to holding NATO together and to having a genuine capability against what I'm not sure, unless it's the Russians (...) So (...) it just seems to me that we should find a way to come to grips with the fact that NATO does not need a nuclear force...and that should be step one in leading us to a decision to get to zero on tactical nuclear weapons and dramatically affect the business of proliferation'[108]. But while in office, Owens did not want to push too much, taking into account the level of opposition within the military. Ultimately, he probably believed that the battle was not worth fighting.

Leon Fuerth, the assistant for National Security Affairs to Vice-President Al Gore, studied at New York University, worked in the State Department dealing with intelligence and Soviet weapons of mass destruction in the 1970s, and became staff member in the House Permanent Select Committee on Intelligence. It is there that he met Gore in 1981[109]. Fuerth became Gore's legislative assistant in 1984. It is difficult to distinguish Fuerth's ideas from Gore's with regard to nuclear weapons. From Fuerth's letter to Aspin dated 13 February 1992, it becomes clear that he is rather conservative, probably a bit more than Gore. Contrary to Aspin, at that time, Fuerth was extremely cautious about the future of Russia and stressed the concept of force structure stability. 'Deep reductions require extra attention to stability', Fuerth wrote. 'A distinction has to be made between levels we may be forced to keep for want of practical means to go lower, and levels we rationalize as being indispensable. The much lower totals proposed in [Aspin's] paper are closer to my idea of what we should aim at and of what should be the basis for discussions with the Russians, if only for the longer-term'[110]. In other words, Fuerth did not only admit that the force levels were partly set for bargaining purposes, he also seemed to rule out reciprocal reductions (contrary to Aspin) and saw the 2,000 level as a long-term objective (contrary to Aspin). In the same letter, he also discarded the option of eliminating ICBMs (contrary to Aspin).

During the NPR, Fuerth was occasionally briefed by Ash Carter's office. Taking into account both Fuerth's own ideas and Clinton's overall political calculation, it can be assumed that Fuerth did not care very much when Ash Carter ran into difficulties.

Although not widely known, Fuerth was a key player in the Clinton administration with regard to foreign and defence policy including nuclear arms control. Richard Holbrooke for instance described Fuerth as 'one of those powerful but rarely seen people who play major roles behind the scene in Washington'[111]. National Security Advisor Anthony Lake consulted Fuerth on different occasions[112]. Fuerth was also a sitting member of the Principals Committee[113].

To conclude, with hard-liners like Deutch and Fuerth and pragmatists like Owens, Berger and Perry, it is not surprising to find that support for Ash Carter's and Aspin's actions was limited at the Deputy level. The Deputies' inertia, however, could have been overrun by the Principals...

Principals level

The Principals Committee met twice a week under chairmanship of National Security Advisor Anthony Lake. Participants were Secretary of Defence Aspin who was succeeded by William Perry in February 1994, Chairman of the JCS Colin Powell who was replaced by John Shalikashvili, Secretary of State Warren Christopher, CIA Director James Woolsey, US Ambassador at the UN Madeline Albright, and occasionally Secretary of Energy O'Leary. I also include Vice-President Al Gore at this level. William Perry was the key figure with respect to the NPR.

William Perry, who studied mathematics at Stanford University and who obtained his Ph.D. from Penn State University, is – like Deutch – somebody with very good relations in the academic world (as professor at Stanford), the defence industry – running his own defence company – and the government. Perry had already been Under Secretary of Defence for Research and Engineering in the Carter administration. In that capacity, he became known for having pushed through "stealth" technology. Perry, like Deutch, also served on different "blue ribbon panels" about nuclear weapons policy.

Contrary to Deutch, however, Perry could imagine changes in US nuclear weapons policy after the Cold War. Perry for instance published *A New Concept of Cooperative Security* together with Ash Carter and John Steinbruner in 1992. In that study, he called for instance for nuclear weapons for 'background deterrent functions only' in order to 'ensure high standards of safety for the security and control of these weapons'[114]. In practice, this meant a ride-out policy and no reliance on LOW or LUA. A no first use was also implied in a CISAC report of the US National Academy of Sciences in 1991, in which he and Ash Carter had been involved in the beginning. Referring to this study and to the consequences of the Gulf War, Perry wrote in 1992: 'A panel of the National Academy of Sciences has recommended that the US limit the role of its nuclear weapons to being a deterrent against a nuclear attack only. The demonstration of [this] powerful new conventional military capability adds important new support for that recommendation…Therefore, the US would no longer need to extend its nuclear forces to deter non-nuclear attacks'[115]. In *A New Concept of Cooperative Security* he also made a link between disarmament and proliferation. When he left the Clinton administration, Perry wrote a book together with Ash Carter titled *Preventive Defence*, in which they proposed to eliminate ICBMs and to restrict the role of nuclear weapons to deter nuclear weapon attacks.

As Deputy Secretary of Defence, Perry formally participated in the NPR as co-chairman of the Steering Committee. In practice, Perry was not actively involved in the NPR[116]. He certainly did not succeed in pushing through his (more liberal) ideas[117]. Besides, the NPR was Aspin's and not Perry's brainchild. In February 1994, he became Secretary of Defence. Despite his personal ideas, Perry did not push for drastic changes during the NPR[118]. Perry set out his own priorities right from the beginning. That he stuck to his priorities was an indication of his managerial capabilities, which were generally applauded. His priorities consisted in managing the existing crises in the world (like Bosnia) as well as the Pentagon itself, including a reform of the Defence Department's acquisition policy. He also focused on military-to-military relations with Russia and China, and the Cooperative Threat Reduction Programme (the former Nunn-Lugar programme).

He also took over many issues from the State Department as there was a perceived lack of leadership[119].

Concerning the NPR, Perry made a different political cost-benefit calculation than Aspin. Although he probably shared many of Aspin's strategic views, Perry concluded that the battle was not worth fighting. During Perry's nomination hearing on 2 February 1994, he already made clear that he was cautious in the field of strategic policy: 'Until the forces in the former Soviet Union come significantly closer to START I levels, I would not favour actions that would take US forces much below these levels'[120]. He also referred to the fact that President Clinton had twice made clear to Congress that the president supported the continued production of Trident II missiles.

On 17 March 1994, Perry gave a speech at the George Washington University in which he further elaborated US relations with Russia and US nuclear policy. He was cautious about Russia's future. In addition, for the first time in the Clinton administration somebody of his level talked publicly about a role for nuclear deterrence against chemical and biological weapons attacks. For this, Perry was criticized in an editorial of the *New York Times*: 'The new policy reeks of a desperate effort to find any possible justification to maintain the Pentagon's huge but obsolescent nuclear arsenal. It would encourage would-be proliferators to follow Mr Perry's leadership backward'[121]. A day later Perry wrote a letter back to the *New York Times*, in which he defended his policy: 'You imply I am searching for ways to justify a large nuclear arsenal. Not so. I strongly support deep reductions in our nuclear arsenal...We are committed to a nuclear posture based on the [sic] minimum number of nuclear weapons to meet our security needs'[122].

The NPR however was a failure. Perry announced the results of the NPR as a "lead and hedge" strategy. William Perry took a huge responsibility in not supporting major changes during the 1993-1994 NPR. When the outcome of the NPR became clear, *The Washington Post* observed: 'Four US officials said that after Aspin was replaced by William Perry in January, the scope of the nuclear review was scaled back and key work turned over to military officers and Bush administration holdovers'[123].

To conclude, the NPR was Aspin's idea. The other principals were much more cautious. They probably did not believe that Aspin could win the battle inside the Defence Department, but they did not obstruct setting up the NPR either. However, once Aspin was gone, no other principal was willing to fight for it.

Presidential level
In the end, the president is in charge, especially concerning changes in one of the most sensitive domains of public policy. The highest political decision-maker – in this case the American president – has to take the initiative, or at least actively and publicly support a fundamental policy change if it is initiated by others, such as the Secretary of Defence or the National Security Advisor. This is especially true if public opinion and most political decision-makers are not interested in the proposed policy change. This rule applies even more to policy domains that are regarded as sensitive, like national security. The president has to take the heat. He has to articulate very clearly and publicly why a policy change is in the interest of the nation. If the military know that the president, the Commander-in-Chief, stands firmly behind a certain policy change, they are substantially handicapped in

their opposition. The president of the US is therefore a very powerful man. Some even regard him as the most powerful man in the world. He is especially influential with regard to foreign and defence policy. Following this logic, John Steinbruner (Maryland University) accurately predicted already in 1992: 'The commitment to traditional programmes is so deeply entrenched that one cannot expect the Defence Department to initiate a fundamental redesign. The next *President* will have to issue fresh instructions to military planners for the unavoidable transition to occur effectively and coherently'[124]. He continued: 'The distinction between co-operation and confrontation cannot be settled by means of any bureaucratic exercise or even by an authoritative declaration of policy from the newly elected President. Within the US political system, fundamental policy results from the accumulation of specific actions. It must be validated through congressional votes on the defence budget as well as sustained by public opinion. Because the next administration will not command an established consensus on these central questions, it will face an unusually demanding problem of policy leadership. To initiate the process of adjustment, the new President must formulate the issues directly and explicitly in a fundamental review of security policy'[125].

This image of a very powerful president gives the impression that the American president can push through more or less every decision he likes. In practice, however, this is not the case. His knowledge is limited. He cannot focus on every issue and he has to set priorities. His time is more limited than anybody else, at least in relative terms. The result is, as Halperin and Kanter point out, that 'in general, Presidents do not address an issue unless one participant or a coalition makes a sustained effort to get him to do so'[126].

If the president behaves like a strategic and tactical leader, it is extremely difficult for others to prevent him reaching his goals. But 'persuasive power... amounts to more than charm or reasoned argument', warns Neustadt[127]. As George Elsley, adviser of Truman, pointed out: 'The president's job is *to lead public opinion*, not to be a blind follower. You can't sit around and wait for public opinion to tell you what to do...You must decide what you're going to do and do it, and attempt to educate the public to the reasons for your action'[128]. Steve Miller (Harvard University) applies this to arms control: 'the strong and direct commitment of the President and his close associates in the White House seems to be a decisive element in determining whether and how much arms control can succeed'[129].

In practice, presidents have not always taken up their responsibilities with regard to nuclear policy. Former CIA Director Stansfield Turner remarks: 'Surprisingly... presidents have not played decisive roles in deciding numbers of nuclear weapons or plans for targeting them...We can surmise a number of reasons for their reluctance to grapple directly with these wasteful and risky practices. One is that mastering nuclear terminology and technology is time consuming. It also requires perseverance, because military officers are always reluctant to involve civilians in war plans...One reason this process took so long is that is has been neither necessary nor advantageous for a president to stir up the issue of reducing the numbers of nuclear weapons. It was not necessary because all had confidence that they could control any release of nuclear weapons, no matter how many we had. Also, there was no political advantage to taking on the issue, only the risk of being painted as soft on communism and of challenging the proclivities of the military and the military-industrial complex for more and more weapons'[130]. Janne Nolan adds: 'It is clear that those who have ultimate authority for determining the structure of nuclear forces, beginning with the president, have neglected their constitutional responsibilities. The blatant contradiction between the abstract political beliefs of leaders about nuclear weapons, on the one hand, and the pragmatic realities of war planning, on the other, has created a fundamental lack of political accountability in the formulation of the nation's nuclear posture – in short, a failure of democracy in this vital area'[131].

Some presidents succeeded in the field of nuclear arms control, at least partially. President Kennedy for instance chose the Single Integrated Operational Plan proposed by his civilian advisors (like McNamara) instead of the one of Chairman of the JCS Lemnitzer[132]. If President Nixon had been a strong opponent of nuclear arms control, the SALT and ABM Treaties would never have been signed. President George W.H.Bush also displayed leadership by signing two arms control treaties and initiating unilateralist/reciprocal actions.

As soon as President Clinton, for instance, had spoken out in favour of NATO expansion, the bureaucracy – in this case the State Department and the Defence Department – halted their opposition against NATO expansion[133]. The crucial question therefore becomes why Clinton did not speak out in favour of a fundamental change in US nuclear policy.

President Clinton
Although Clinton publicly had said that he would spend most of his time on domestic issues, Aspin felt not constrained by the White House. It is reasonable to assume that – as Nolan writes – it was the "Aspin-Clinton show" whereby Clinton delegated most of the defence issues, including the NPR, to Aspin. Aspin was at least implicitly supported by the president[134].

But crucial is of course that President Clinton did not speak out when the NPR ran into difficulties. It can be argued that at that point none of the other principals actively supported the NPR anymore and that Clinton therefore was not going to push something through against the advice of his principal advisers. The fact that at the beginning of 1994 no other principal actively supported the NPR, however, is not an independent variable. Clinton did not speak out on nuclear issues during the period Aspin was in power, except with regard to the nuclear testing moratorium in July 1993, and nonproliferation in his speech at the UN General Assembly two months later. In his first year in office, he even made clear to Congress that he supported the continued production of Trident II missiles. Janne Nolan concludes: 'Most important, [Clinton] and his close White House and cabinet advisers never indicated clearly that they had a stake in the outcome [of the NPR]'[135]. This lack of interest also applied to issues like North Korea and Iraq. 'Nuclear diplomacy was the subject of only three Principals' committee meetings in all of 1993: "We had a gaping void at the top of the bureaucracy", says a State Department official...With no one at the top in charge, American diplomatic strategy was one of drift punctuated by spasms of zigzagging', according to Leon Sigal[136].

With a president who did not speak out, the opponents of the NPR felt no constraints whatsoever. They could test the willingness of the advocates of change through bureaucratic battles. Once Aspin was gone, it became more or less impossible for Ash Carter to push through any radical changes without public support from his superiors, including the president. It is interesting to speculate what the result of the NPR might have been if Clinton had explicitly supported the effort to change US nuclear policy fundamentally right from the beginning *and* if Aspin had stayed in power. With a determined Secretary of Defence and Assistant Secretary of Defence, who were explicitly supported by the president, and with a National Security Advisor and Secretary of State who were not categorically opposed, it is difficult to see how the military and civilian bureaucrats in the Defence Department could have obstructed efforts to adapt US nuclear policy to the changed international circumstances. Stansfield Turner's optimism about the future says as much about the opportunity missed in the past: 'In my view, the forces of resistance are sufficiently in retreat that a firm commitment from a president could move us forward aggressively'[137].

What has to be explained is why Clinton did not speak out on these issues. Why did Clinton not behave as a strategic leader in this field ? A definite answer cannot be given. But by looking to statements and decisions in other domains, we may find some indications. A first answer may be that he simply had too many other issues to deal with. Although this is certainly true, it only displaces the question to another one: why did Clinton not regard nuclear weapons policy as one of his priorities ?

As president, he is the only individual who has to look to the whole picture. A distinction has to be made between his strategic calculation and his political cost-benefit analysis (see chapter 7).

Strategic calculation

Before being elected, Clinton was in favour of further nuclear weapons reductions. In his December 1991 campaign speech, Clinton was more outspoken with regard to nuclear than conventional reductions: 'We can *dramatically reduce* our nuclear arsenals through negotiations *and other reciprocal actions*. But as an irreducible minimum, we must retain a survivable nuclear force to deter any conceivable threat...now that the nuclear arms race has finally reversed its course, it is time for a prudent slowdown in strategic modernization. We should stop the production of the B-2 Bomber. That alone could save US$15 to US$20 billion by 1997'[138]. He was also against further testing. When he was asked during his first news conference after having been elected in November 1992 what his top priorities with regard to foreign and defence policy would be, Clinton stated: 'My top priorities will be [1] settling on a multi-year plan for a defence budget that I think keeps the defence of this country the strongest in the world and deals with the necessity to downscale; [2] pursuing our *continued efforts to reduce nuclear weapons* with Russia *and with other nuclear powers*; [3] working hard *to stop the proliferation of weapons of mass destruction* – nuclear, biological and chemical; [4] keeping the Middle East peace process on track; [5] and doing what I can to strengthen global economic growth'[139]. His first three priorities had all – directly or indirectly – to do with nuclear weapons, and they can be interpreted as quite liberal. Aspin had similar ideas. As Secretary of Defence, he indicated in one of his first congressional hearings: 'Not since the early 1960s have we had a president determined to cooperate with the Congress on a *progressive* agenda for America. We have one now'[140].

According to Michael Krepon, '[Clinton's] heart seems to be in the right place on nuclear disarmament matters'[141]. Taking into account his liberal views on domestic and foreign policy issues, there was a reasonable chance that if somebody would have asked him, he would at least privately have come out in favour of Aspin's proposals. This counterfactual is supported by his liberal views on nuclear testing before his election, his decision to stop nuclear testing in July 1993, and his successful pushing for a Comprehensive Test Ban Treaty; his campaign promise and policy to keep the ABM Treaty intact or change it only marginally with the consent of Russia; the continued importance of nuclear nonproliferation both during his campaign and in office; his fight with the military about gays; his foreign policy vis-à-vis Russia, Haiti, Bosnia and Kosovo; and his personal views about NATO expansion[142]. With regard to the latter, the rumour goes that the speeches of Vaclav Havel and Lech Walechsa at the opening of the Holocaust Museum in Washington DC had a very strong emotional impact on Clinton[143]. The hypothesis that Clinton had liberal ideas is also supported by looking to the political appointees he had appointed, in particular Les Aspin[144]. On a more psychological level, his liberal views might be related to his optimist nature. As Rockman argues, Clinton 'is not a man of hardened heart or enemies lists, or depressive moods. In fact, by all accounts he is an extraordinarily ebullient man with an overriding sense of optimism'[145].

The odds are, however, that Clinton never took the time to invite somebody to explain American nuclear policy in detail, and that he never thought this relative complex issue through. The question then becomes why. First of all, unlike Jimmy Carter who was a nuclear engineer or unlike John F.Kennedy, Clinton had never been much interested in nuclear weapons. As the first American president born after the Second World War, he saw Russia and defence issues in a different perspective.

Secondly, before becoming president, Clinton had never dealt with foreign and defence policy. Contrary to George W.H.Bush and most of his predecessors, Clinton had therefore no strong vision on foreign and defence policy, and he never exposed such a vision during his two terms either. After two years in office, his performance in the field of foreign policy was qualified by American political scientists as 'vacillation, indecision, and the lack of a guiding principle or compass that might provide bearing for leaders and a direction for followers on a set of policies or a Clinton doctrine...cast adrift, buffeted by political calculations with only minimal evidence of coherence and consistency...lack of innovating thinking'[146]. They continued: 'many of Clinton's foreign policy decisions have not flowed from a strategic outlook but have been ad hoc responses to developments at home and abroad and attempts to satisfy domestic constituencies'[147]. US policy vis-à-vis Russia, but especially vis-à-vis China and Bosnia are examples.

US nuclear weapons policy struggled with similar problems. Robert Manning, a major Democratic party ideologist, does not hide his disappointment with Clinton's nuclear policy at the beginning of 1995: 'Our nonproliferation policy has been largely ad hoc and driven by events. It should instead be typified by dogged top-level engagement and inspired by a larger strategic vision: using the momentum of an US-Russian nuclear build-down to move forward a world without nuclear weapons'[148]. Five years later, Manning's assessment was identical: 'In a strategy-free White House, bureaucratic inertia often guides national security policy…We need [nuclear weapons] because we need'em. Nobody at the top on nuclear decision-making will pose the fundamental questions: Where do nuclear weapons fit into our defence policy, and how many do we need ?'[149]

This lack of foreign policy vision, however, is not totally surprising. Clinton had not announced a major shift in foreign and defence policy during his campaign. On the contrary, he had been very quiet on these issues. One of the reasons was that he was not very knowledgeable in this regard, especially in comparison with the incumbent Republican candidate George W.H.Bush. Neither did he have government experience in this field. More fundamentally, Clinton had deliberately focused on domestic issues during his campaign. He had criticized President Bush of having spent too much time on foreign policy, like the Gulf War. One of Clinton's famous campaign slogans was: 'It's the economy, stupid'. Clinton had also promised to 'focus like a laser beam' on the economy. The economy, social security, a balanced budget, and education were Clinton's policy priorities.

Thirdly, in the field of foreign policy, Clinton was mostly interested in short-term issues where the human touch was visible like Bosnia, Haiti, Somalia, and Kosovo. A long-term foreign policy, let alone a defence strategy, was not his piece of cake. As a senior aide remarked: '[Clinton] does not think in geo-strategic terms. It may be that a guy who is not a geo-strategist type has less of an intuitive sense of how you re-jigger NATO or refine the START treaty. He might look right past you. But ask him to look at people walking down the streets or to deal with social unrest, and he'll react. That's something he has an intuitive feel for'[150]. Richard Haass called it his 'preference for symbolism over substance and short-term crisis management over long-term strategizing'[151]. Contrary to what the electoral campaign would have suggested, President Clinton nevertheless spent a reasonable amount of time on foreign policy issues, although probably less than his predecessors[152].

Fourthly, a president relies on his principals and especially on his National Security Council staff. If they not inform him, they can be blamed as well. This, however, is a two-edged sword. It is the president's responsibility to appoint the right people in the first place and to create an efficient working relationship, so that he will be fully informed. The Clinton foreign policy team was from the beginning seen as rather weak, except maybe for Aspin and his team in the Defence Department[153]. In addition, some of Clinton's subordinates felt intimidated by the way Clinton put his ideas forward[154]. Lastly, principals like Aspin and Woolsey had difficulties in getting the attention of the president or even the National Security Advisor[155]. All this does not enhance the prospects of getting the best advice from his political appointees.

Fifthly, some argue that Clinton changed his ideas on foreign policy while in office. He became more of a "realist" and more pragmatic over time, they argue[156]. This change of thinking or at least his policy of 'not-rocking-the-boat-with-the-military-and-the-Republicans' was caused by the political difficulties he had experienced during his first year(s) such as the gay issue, low opinion ratings, problems with pushing through domestic issues like healthcare, his inability to convince the Europeans to take up their responsibility in Bosnia in the spring of 1993, the debacle in Somalia and Haiti in the fall of 1993, and the electoral disaster in November 1994. From then on, Clinton would only occasionally take a soft position on defence issues because he feared that the Republicans would exploit it.

Clinton's defence policy became more and more dominated by political calculations (see below). The defence budget is a first example. Already in December 1993, in his first year in office, Clinton offered DOD $11 bn more. One year later, he added another $25 bn spread over a period of six years[157]. In January 1999, President Clinton announced the largest increase in the defence budget since the Reagan administration: another $112 billion spread over a period of six years. President Clinton who was facing impeachment charges because of the Lewinsky affair, was, according to William Hartung, 'an easy target' for the military in the autumn of 1998. Hartung stated: 'It has not escaped notice in the Pentagon that the accusations against Mr Clinton – having a sexual relationship with a subordinate and lying about it – would end the career of any officer'[158]. Clinton stood in an extremely weak position vis-à-vis the military.

Another example of a policy change as a result of domestic politics is Clinton's shift with regard to NMD. Before he was elected, Clinton had stated he 'would only consider modest changes in [the ABM Treaty] that clearly enhanced US security interests and were negotiated in good faith with Russia'. He had also said that the bulk of his proposed defence cuts would originate in reorienting SDI[159]. In his second term, however, the Clinton administration agreed that the ABM Treaty may have to be adapted, even if the Russians would not agree. 'To avoid of being accused of softness on defence', Clinton even decided that NMD would be deployed as soon as technological feasible[160].

A third indication was his choice for his second Secretary of Defence. To replace Aspin, he nominated Bobby Inman, somebody who was not regarded as liberal. Inman finally did not take the job. Nor was Perry seen as a visionary. In his second term, Clinton even appointed William Cohen, a Republican.

Gregory Foster, professor at the National Defence University, already pointed out in 1994 that Clinton 'lacks moral authority less because of his perceived character flaws than because he has failed to demonstrate the courage, the decisiveness, integrity, and vision necessary to counteract such flaws. This has left him largely unable either to galvanize the popular will in common cause or to exercise effective civilian control over the military'[161]. In the field of nuclear weapons policy, Clinton had no sophisticated knowledge – let alone a vision – either. He probably never made a personal judgment with regard to the future of US nuclear weapons policy. And in the unlikely case he did, it was certainly pushed aside by political considerations.

Political calculation

Regardless of his personal beliefs on foreign and defence policy, Clinton did not push the nuclear weapons issue because he did not see the political benefits. It would have yielded strong opposition and minor political gains. First and foremost, a lot of opposition could have been expected in the case of a fundamental change in nuclear weapons policy (see Chapter 8). There were bureaucratic organizations whose interests would have been seriously hurt by switching from a maximum to a minimum deterrence posture: STRATCOM and the nuclear planning community, the Air Force and to a lesser extent the Navy. The nuclear establishment succeeded in convincing the JCS to support its interests. Going against the JCS is always extremely risky. That applies especially to the Democrats.

Clinton knew that the Republicans could exploit radical changes in the nuclear posture. Some Republicans lawmakers were for instance against the elimination of ICBMs because it would hurt the local economy in their districts[162]. Others, like Jesse Helms, probably genuinely believed in maximum deterrence[163]. All of them had a tendency to exploit "soft" defence policy decisions. In addition, the Republicans were very angry because Clinton's domestic policy was so middle-of-the-road that it was hardly distinguishable from the Republican programme. As Stephen Schwartz clarified in the context of the non-ratification of the Comprehensive Test Ban Treaty: 'Clinton's ability to "spin" events to his advantage, his remarkable ability to connect – or appear to connect – with the concerns of individual voters, and his ability to outmaneuver Republicans in the political arena have all infuriated the increasingly conservative Republican members of Congress, some of whom no longer hide their contempt for the president'[164].

Furthermore, because of his Vietnam-past – or better the lack of it – Clinton was personally extremely vulnerable to attacks from the military and the Republicans. During his campaign, Clinton had neither convinced the military that he was "their" man.

Clinton knew very well that he was vulnerable. Anticipating criticism from the military, candidate Clinton had asked and got the support of more than thirty foreign policy experts and retired generals like Paul Nitze, Samuel Huntington and Gen.William Odom. In an advertisement published in major newspapers a few weeks before the presidential election, they admitted that 'in recent times, the national leadership of the Democratic Party [has] too often lacked clear understanding and firm purpose in world affairs'. At the same time, they made clear that Bill Clinton had other intentions. Clinton had 'resisted those at home – and in his own party – who propose reckless cuts in our national defence capabilities, rather than careful reductions that will maintain strength still needed to meet potential threats'[165].

Clinton's speech at Georgetown University in December 1991, that was basically written by Anthony Lake, gave an indication of his ambiguous defence policy. 'We can and must *substantially reduce our military forces and spending* because the Soviet threat is decreasing and our allies are able to and should shoulder more of the defence spending based on what we need to protect our interests'. At the same time, he continued: '*First* we should provide for *a strong defence*, then we can talk about defence savings'[166]. A few months later, the second part of that message came also across when he endorsed the continuation of the $13 billion Seawolf submarine programme based in Connecticut that the George W.H.Bush administration was trying to cancel. Winning the primaries was Clinton's first priority[167]. The same message was heard in a presidential debate on TV a few weeks before the presidential election: 'We do have to maintain the world's strongest defence'[168]. But despite all these moderate statements, the military were not convinced.

Once elected, Clinton's reputation in the eyes of the military did not improve. Clinton appointed Les Aspin as Secretary of Defence, who had criticized the Pentagon before. But above all, there was the gay issue. Although it is difficult to explain why Clinton made an issue out of it during his first week in office, some arguments have been put forward. Firstly, the gay community had actively supported Clinton during his campaign. He wanted to compensate the gays. Secondly, his electoral victory may have made him slightly immune to warnings from some of his advisors (like Powell and Aspin), who recommended not rocking the boat with the military on the gay issue right from the beginning. Thirdly, Clinton had already withdrawn some of his foreign policy promises. More particularly, Clinton had criticized Bush because Haitian refugees were sent back on the high seas. After the elections, partly as a result of Clinton's declarations, a massive emigration gulf arose, something Clinton could not accept either. Clinton therefore had to change his mind on Haiti. Clinton and some of his political advisors might have felt that he had to show that he also kept some campaign promises, like the gays in the military. Fourthly, Clinton may have wanted to make clear vis-à-vis the military who was in power.

If the latter hypothesis is true, Clinton did not succeed. Due to immense pressure from the military, supported by a large part of public opinion, Clinton had to back down on the gay issue. This move was not only bad for his relationship with the military (and the gay community), but was also disastrous for his overall image. As Neustadt points out: 'in political warfare, the outcome for a President depends as much or more on the *first* battles. These are the battles that decide his public image and create a pattern for his Washington reputation'[169]. Indeed, the opinion polls were not promising during his first months in office.

Once on the defensive, Clinton had the tendency to move to the political centre instead of defending his own policy choices. Clinton stole ideas from his opponents (in the field of welfare reform, crime policy and government spending) and was afraid of pushing his own through. Once he felt he was not doing well in the opinion polls, his strategy consisted in denying the Republican opponents any major issue[170]. He tried to please everyone[171]. Columnist of the *New York Times* William Safire criticized him as follows: '[But] centrism is vapid when it is the suffocator of interests, seeking to please rather than trying to move. Clinton's approach, in most cases, has been to follow the primrose path of polling down the middle'[172]. It was not by chance that Clinton had been actively engaged in the Democratic Leadership Council in the second half of the 1980s. The major goal of the DLC was to move the Democratic party back on the right track – literally and figuratively – after having lost the elections in 1980 and thereafter[173]. Clinton became the chairman of DLC in May 1990.

Right after the gay issue, Clinton may have made clear to Aspin that he did not want to have other defence issues reaching his desk. In other words, Clinton delegated everything to Aspin, and the latter was supposed to manage it in an appropriate way. Aspin would meet Clinton personally only twice in 1993[174].

By backing down on the gay issue, Clinton had shown to the military that he was beatable. As Richard Kohn noted: 'Nothing did more to harm the launching of the Clinton administration than "gays in the military" for it announced to Washington and the world that the President could be rolled'[175]. JCS Chairman Colin Powell, a hero from the 1991 Gulf War, was certainly not to forget that. The restructuring of the defence procurement (or better the lack of it), the Bottom-Up-Review and later on the NPR are all examples of bureaucratic battles won by the military and their civilian colleagues in the Defence Department. President Clinton never felt in a position to go against the wishes of the military. The weaknesses of the Clinton administration led to serious questions about civilian control over the military (see further).

Beside the opposition that could have been expected, Clinton also knew that it would only bring minor political gains that would compensate for the enormous political costs. Clinton liked to see tangible results. Potential benefits in the area of nuclear weapons policy however – like preventing nuclear accidents and proliferation – are by definition not visible and therefore cannot be exploited for political reasons. In addition, potential strategic benefits would probably show up only in the medium and long term, which is not very relevant politically speaking. The Clinton administration also knew that the short-term costs of the existing nuclear policy were not regarded as problematic by public opinion. On the other hand, it is easily forgotten that public opinion is malleable. After the American and Russian nuclear weapons were de-targeted in 1994 for instance, Clinton spoke on many occasions about the fact that there were no Russian missiles anymore pointed at American's children at sleep[176]. As a result, Clinton gave at least the impression that all (or most) nuclear weapons were gone and that the Cold War nuclear dangers had passed away. It is therefore not surprising to find out that public opinion was no longer worried about nuclear weapons. Furthermore, changing decades old policy for which there existed a bipartisan consensus would have been perceived as implicitly admitting that the former policy was wrong. Clinton felt he did not have that credibility. Clinton apparently felt neither self-secure enough to convince opponents that US nuclear policy changes would make a positive difference in other countries as well. A shift towards minimum deterrence was only supported by non-governmental experts and a badly organized peace movement. The booming US economy in the second half of the 1990s did not help either. The US could easily afford a huge defence budget and a corresponding force structure. Lastly, there were more than enough justifications available for Clinton for keeping the existing policy.

Clinton's political calculation turned out to be correct. When his Secretary of Defence Les Aspin and Assistant Secretary of Defence Ash Carter tried to adapt nuclear policy to the new circumstances, the military and some influential Republicans strongly opposed any changes (see Chapter 9). They used all the means at their disposal to test the political courage and particularly that of Ash Carter, once Aspin was gone.

But again, this calculation is not only a dependent variable. Clinton could have influenced the outcome substantially if he had put his presidential weight behind Aspin's proposals. Clinton never did so. He did not want to spend political capital on this issue. The military found this out very soon, and exploited it.

To conclude, President Clinton did not behave like a strategic leader during the NPR. As Janne Nolan emphasized: 'Absent any clear directives originating from the president about the critical importance of adapting nuclear policies to new circumstances, the outcome [of the NPR] was virtually guaranteed...The president, in other words, has to stake his prestige on the success of the undertaking'[177]. That was clearly not the case.

Lastly, Clinton did not change gears *after* the NPR either (see chapter 11). In 1999, Senator Alan Cranston implicitly attacked Bill Clinton when he pointed out obstacles to nuclear abolition: 'Leaders today are under-creative, over-cautious, distracted by day-to-day demands. Their destinations are determined by polls'[178].

Joseph Cirincione (Carnegie Endowment for International Peace) also stated that Clinton was 'unwilling or unable to lead the defence establishment. He follows the most cautious of his advisors, reluctant to propose any initiative that does not already enjoy a consensus. It is the politics of status quo in a time of radical change. A minimalist agenda that unintentionally courts maximum risk'[179]. The period 1993-2000, except for the signing of the Comprehensive Test Ban Treaty, was characterized by a complete paralysis in the field of nuclear arms control and disarmament.

A posteriori, one can ask whether any president could have pushed through such a package, taking into account decades of Cold War thinking and corresponding interests. It is, however, sufficient to look to the accomplishments of the George W.H.Bush administration to see the difference.

Lack of tactical leadership by Aspin and Carter ?
To push through fundamental policy changes, it is not sufficient to be a strategic leader. To succeed, tactical leadership is needed as well. I will limit the subjects of my analysis to those who had shown strategic leadership during the NPR: Les Aspin and Ash Carter.

Les Aspin
Les Aspin was a visionary man, a strategic thinker. The danger of visionaries, however, is that they do not always have a clue on how to implement their ideas. The reason Aspin was fired was, as it is generally understood, that he was not managing the Pentagon very well. Ironically, it was Aspin who as a member of Congress had criticized the military of not having been able to run the Pentagon. The military were of course suspicious of Les Aspin. In his memoirs, Colin Powell for instance remembered Aspin as a member of Congress during the George W.H.Bush period as follows: '[But], except for his support of Desert Storm, Aspin had been beating my brains out almost since I had become chairman. He had tried to scuttle the Base Force'[180]. As already mentioned above, this negative attitude from the military vis-à-vis Aspin did not improve in the first months. Aspin tried to make his mark by pushing through changes that the bureaucracy did not like. Aspin knew very well that he was not popular inside the Pentagon. Sometimes, he signalled negative feelings about this bureaucratic conservatism to a few observers[181].

But there was more. The Pentagon bureaucracy, especially the military, did not like Aspin's personal style. The military regarded Aspin as a whiz kid, and compared him with McNamara. Aspin had his own ideas about a lot of things and most of the time he believed that these views were not bad, to say the least. Worse, Aspin apparently sometimes gave the impression that it did not matter what the military thought because *his* ideas would be pushed through, as he was formally in charge. Some regarded him as abrasive and rude towards his subordinates, especially in informal encounters[182]. The military also felt a lack of access, something which did not improve their working relationship[183].

In addition, Aspin's personal style was difficult to reconcile with the culture inside the Pentagon. The way Aspin was dressed, for instance, was completely the opposite as that of most people in the Pentagon. As Elizabeth Drew mentions: 'Aspin's shambling style, his thin greying hair often awry, his posture – Aspin's head was often tilted, seeming nearly even with his shoulders, giving the impression that this large man was constantly looking up at people and had no neck – didn't offer the picture of a crisp Defence Secretary'[184].

The way Aspin led meetings was neither what the military were used to. Aspin had the capacity to listen very well and to ask a lot of questions. But he did not always convey his own thoughts and, consequently, decisions were not always taken. The same topics were debated over and over again[185]. Meetings seemed more like academic seminars instead of punctual-and-to-the-point, something that was needed for running "the largest company in the world" with a budget of over $250 billion a year and over 3 million people on its pay-roll. Powell called Aspin in private 'The Professor'[186]. Aspin showed the same kind of indecision at the principals meetings. As Fred Barnes reported: '[he] drove others crazy by refusing to take a firm position'[187]. One example was the way he dealt with the North Korean crisis[188].

This indecisive attitude can be partly explained by his experience as a member of Congress. Aspin said in an interview just before his death in 1995: '[In Congress] you can keep a low profile on things you want to avoid. In the executive branch, you can't pick and choose. The agenda comes at you like a train. A legislative leader shouldn't get out front on a key issue. A leader in Congress must find the middle. Wait to announce your position until you've gauged the mood and pinpointed the centre of gravity. Otherwise, those on the other side won't talk to you. Keep open all lines of communication by holding your position to yourself until the end. An executive branch leader must do the opposite. You must get your position out early because you're trying to marshal support from the outset. It's a tougher way to work'[189].

Lastly, the Secretary of Defence is supposed to be the key spokesman of the Defence Department, and the crucial link between public opinion and the Pentagon. When Aspin presented his own thoughts in public meetings, he sometimes stumbled over his words. He was not a very good speaker. One example was his performance in Congress after the Somalia disaster in October 1993. The disaster itself and Aspin's reaction in Congress led 25 Republican Congressmen to write a letter to President Clinton, in which they strongly recommended to replace Aspin. David Gergen, a Reagan appointee who was hired by President Clinton to restore public confidence in the failing administration in the summer of 1993, had attended that meeting as well and also wrote a negative report about Aspin[190].

In short, despite his formal position, Aspin did not have the "earned authority" to push radical changes through. His position further weakened when he started to compromise. The Bottom-Up-Review, for instance, did not end up with major changes. Even his already watered-down "win-hold-win" proposal did not get the final approval by the military. As Marc Millot contended: 'The threat and policy-oriented sections [of the Bottom-Up-Review] are consistent with Secretary Aspin's perspective, but the force-sizing and force structure implications are more in line with the view of Chairman Powell'[191]. Most of the savings did not come from weapons modernization cuts but from a reduction in armed personnel (from 1.6 to 1.4 million) and from expected inflation benefits. According to Colin McInnes, the Bottom-Up-Review was, contrary to what Aspin had announced, more budget-driven than threat-driven. 'It offered no guidance for when force should be used, what interests should be defended, and why two MRCs should form the basis for planning'[192]. In contrast to McNamara in the 1960s, Aspin failed as a manager of the Defence Department. Colin Powell made that already privately clear to President Clinton when Powell retired at the end of August 1993[193].

A couple of weeks later, on 3 October 1993, eighteen Americans were shot dead in Somalia. CNN showed pictures of dead bodies of American soldiers dragged behind Somali vehicles in the streets of Mogadishu. The American people and the president felt humiliated. Clinton immediately decided to withdraw US troops from Somalia. He probably also decided at that time to get rid of his Secretary of Defence. Aspin was blamed for the disaster in the media as he had refused to send heavier equipment. Les Aspin himself thought about leaving his job after Somalia, but finally decided to stay on. Aspin even 'went on the offensive, making some public appearances and continued with his various Pentagon initiatives',[194] like the NPR.

A few days after Mogadishu, Haiti became a trouble spot. Contrary to Aspin's advice, President Clinton decided to send a gunboat with 200 US "civic assistance" troops to Haiti. Arriving at Port-au-Prince, the US ship did not dare to enter the harbour as Haitian rioters were shooting in the air. It was a second humiliation for the US in a couple of weeks time. This time Aspin had been right, but he had not been able to press his views through[195].

Clinton, who was not doing well in the polls, felt that somebody in his foreign and defence team had to go. Aspin was not a personal friend of Clinton and as he had not helped Clinton during the election campaign as much as Anthony Lake or Sandy Berger, Aspin was the easiest to sack. Nor did Aspin have the same standing in the foreign policy community as Warren Christopher.

Lastly, Clinton had not forgotten how Aspin had refused to support the president publicly with regard to the gay issue. Loyalty to the president has to come first or that is at least what could be expected from the Secretary of Defence. But that was not what happened. A few days after Clinton's inauguration, Aspin told interviewers about the gay issue: 'If we can't work it out, we'll disagree, and the thing won't happen'. As Powell commented later on: Aspin 'had publicly predicted the failure of Clinton's first presidential initiative'[196]. To conclude, Clinton was disappointed by the overall performance of Aspin. Aspin was becoming more of a liability than an asset. On 15 December 1993, Aspin was told that he had to resign.

Post facto, it is interesting to speculate whether Aspin would have succeeded in pushing through the NPR if he had stayed in power. Eric Mlyn is optimistic: 'One might imagine that Les Aspin, had he continued in the position of secretary of defence (and had he survived), might have been able to implement more substantial changes to overall US strategic policy'[197]. On the other hand, Aspin made several tactical mistakes during the NPR. According to the terms of references, working groups would run the NPR. Right from the beginning, however, it became clear that few new ideas would come out of these working groups. Looking to the composition of the working groups, inertia could have been predicted. 'Participants maneuver to involve those they think will favour their position and to exclude those they think will oppose it', Halperin and Kanter explain[198]. If this is true, Aspin manoeuvred badly. Three arguments, however, can be made to defend Aspin's decision to set up working groups. Firstly, nobody expected that the degree of inertia in the working groups would be that considerable. Secondly, refusing to set up working groups would also have led to criticism, namely that the political appointees did not interact with the bureaucracy. A radical reform has to involve the bureaucratic system. Thirdly, Aspin and Carter may have speculated that whatever the outcome of these low-level working groups would have been, the two of them were finally in charge. They could always have pressured the working groups to come up with new options. In case they kept refusing, Aspin and Carter could have ordered a new study until they got what they wanted.

A second tactical mistake by Aspin was that he had failed to follow up what Carter was doing. In the first months, Ashton Carter had not much time for the working groups. Thirdly, the anecdote mentioned above about Aspin's attendance of Carter's briefing indicates that Aspin was not the master of his time.

It is not clear whether Aspin could have pushed through the NPR if he had stayed in power. He certainly had underestimated the resistance from the bureaucracy, and he had not convinced enough political appointees in the Defence Department to change US nuclear policy. 'There was little interest [in the NPR] everywhere else, and Aspin probably should have thought this through', according to Steve Fetter[199]. His weak management skills made it all the more difficult.

After having resigned as Secretary of Defence in December 1993, Aspin nevertheless agreed to become chairman of the president's Foreign Intelligence Advisory Board. He died in May 1995 at the age of 56.

Ashton Carter

Carter was well aware from the beginning that pushing through the necessary changes would be difficult. In a foreword of a study in 1991, he already indicated that: 'Organizations as large and complex as those that grew up over half a century of Cold War to build and operate nuclear weapons do not change all by themselves when the times change: *a deliberate effort must be made* to reshape them so that they come to embody the new attitudes that have emerged in political relations'[200]. A year after, he stated in another report: 'Redirecting the thoughts and emotions of large numbers of people usually requires substantial time and often a crystallizing crisis'[201].

Ashton Carter clearly showed strategic leadership behaviour. However he did not succeed. The major explanation for his failure is that, once Aspin was gone, there was no senior "champion" left to support him. Another element of the explanation of Carter's failure is his lack of tactical leadership. Carter did not follow up the working groups very well. He intervened quite late in the process. Carter had delegated supervision to Frank Miller[202]. The reason for doing so was that he had other priorities, like the denuclearisation of Belarus, Kazakhstan and Ukraine, and counterproliferation. Like Aspin, he probably thought that he would have been able to intervene in the end and overrule the conclusions of the working groups. Some observers point to his "Harvard arrogance" in this regard[203].

In addition, his personal style – like Aspin's – did not invite others to compromise. His attitude towards subordinates was called 'rude and abrasive'[204]. His behaviour is compared with McNamara's whiz kids that came from "ivy league" universities and acted as if they knew more about technical-military issues than those dealing with it on a daily basis[205]. The point is not that Carter did not know what he was talking about – he probably knew it better than anybody else –

the problem was the *way* he talked about it. On a regular basis, he started or ended his interventions by shouting: 'Hey, you guys are all wrong'[206].

Furthermore, Carter also made some questionable decisions. For instance he offended the career officials and Frank Miller in particular by not informing them of the appointment of Steve Fetter and Leo Mackay. Later on he offended the career officials and particularly the military again by presenting quasi-official briefings to Deutch and Owens with options that were not supported by the working groups. This was completely against the terms of reference, at least in the eyes of the bureaucracy[207]. As one observer remarked: 'the military thought Carter was playing games with them'[208]. On the other hand, Carter's decision can be justified starting from the assumption that the goal of the NPR was to come up with new options. The only way to do so was bypassing the working groups[209].

In the same vein, Carter tried to bypass the heavy bureaucratic procedures with regard to the implementation of the Nunn-Lugar programme. The latter led to clashes with the State Department and the Department of Energy[210].

Lack of tactical leadership and the bureaucracy
This lack of tactical leadership on behalf of Aspin and Carter should, however, put into perspective. The lack of strategic leadership on behalf of the other political appointees and especially the president is a much more determining factor in explaining the status quo. In addition, the power and influence of the nuclear bureaucracy and the US military in general cannot be underestimated either. It is easy to criticize Aspin – as Colin Powell did – for having ruined Clinton's gay proposal right at the beginning. But was it Colin Powell's role as Chairman of the JCS to speak out vigorously and publicly against gays in the military during the presidential campaign in 1992 ? And it is of course much easier to be categorized as a "good manager" (like Perry), by not rocking the boat with the bureaucracy.

All the generals involved in the NPR were of outstanding quality, partly due to structural reforms inside the military after the debacle in Vietnam. Together with Frank Miller, they managed to control the bureaucratic process during the NPR. According to Nolan: 'The core leadership group, including Generals McCaffrey and Clark in particular, were adept at deflecting attention from proposals with which they disagreed and, according to one participant, "hopelessly outmatched Carter in the art of the bureaucracy"'[211]. When the military heard that Ash Carter did not follow the terms of reference, they played the game hard: firstly, by writing a letter to the Vice-Chairman of the JCS, and secondly, by leaking the story to Congress. They put pressure on Ash Carter to stop pushing for more changes. When all this did not succeed, the bureaucratic bomb exploded. Ash Carter was – in the words of Nolan – "called on the carpet"[212] (see chapter 9).

One Pentagon official, who had argued for more cuts, suggested afterwards: 'These civilian guys [like Ash Carter] were fearful of pressing the military too far'[213]. If this is true and most indications point in this direction, the following questions have to be asked: who is finally in charge of US defence policy ? The civilian leaders appointed by the president and approved by the Senate, or military and civilian bureaucrats ?

The way Assistant Secretary of Defence Ash Carter was summoned during the NPR and the way the military always got what they wanted from the Clinton administration calls into question whether there is not something structurally biased with regard to civilian control of the US military[214]. The obstruction of the Pentagon bureaucracy during the NPR can, indeed, be characterized as 'unusual' and 'unprecedented'[215].

The NPR points to the broader question to what extent political appointees have real power and to what extent the bureaucracy supported by conservatives in Congress, especially in the field of defence, forms a major and structural obstacle for policy change.

Without making references to the NPR, Edward Luttwak wrote in the same period: 'The scandal in question is nothing less than the collapse of civilian control over the military policies and military strategy of the US...The power of decision that our civilian President is supposed to exercise through his appointed civilian officials has been seized by an all-military outfit that most Americans have never even heard of: the mixed Army-Navy-Marine-Air Force "Joint Staff"...The Great Pentagon Reform has since shown us that the only thing worse than interservice rivalry is interservice harmony...Whether the issue was military service for homosexuals, post-Soviet budget levels, or military action in ex-Yugoslavia, Powell overruled the newly inaugurated Clinton with contemptuous ease...How the Joint Staff exercises that franchise can be seen from the way it conditioned the much publicized "Bottom-up-review"...resisting any genuine reappraisal of the mix of US forces...In short, in a world bereft of the Soviet threat, the Joint Staff planners had ingeniously succeeded in justifying the array of forces they had wanted all along'[216]. Luttwak may have easily added the NPR if he had written his article six months later.

In the end, it remains remarkable how a small number of people in the Defence Department – the nuclear priesthood – were able to unite the whole Pentagon behind their struggle. As retired admiral and former Director of the CIA Stansfield Turner adds: 'A small club of zealous military experts has dominated the military's input on nuclear weapons policy... As recently as 1994, they successfully twisted the NPR into a meaningless effort'[217]. In 2005, a similar analysis is made by John Hamre, president of CSIS and a former Deputy Secretary of Defence: 'A shrinking community of nuclear experts holds on to a massive and aging inventory as a security blanket for a future they cannot define'[218]. This explanation is not unique for the US. Looking to the inertia in nuclear weapons policy in both the US and Russia, Alexei Arbatov also points to 'the incapability of the political leaders to assert their control over the military establishments and lobbyists of the defense industry'[219].

The lack of political leadership by Clinton and his appointees kept maximum deterrence alive in the first decade after the Cold War. As Lee Butler wrote in 2000: 'But with the change in administrations [in 1993], momentum was lost. I am dumbfounded by the state of today's US leadership'[220]. John Isaacs agrees: 'The Clinton years should be judged on opportunity costs; that is, seven years in which there was scant progress toward reducing or eliminating weapons of mass destruction'[221]. Robert Manning – a Democrat – concludes: 'The US failure to fundamentally rethink the role of nuclear weapons is one of Clinton's grand strategic failures'[222]. At the end of Clinton's term, *The Washington Post* looked at the bigger picture: 'the American link with Russia in geopolitics and arms control, Mr Clinton will not be forgiven if all he ends up doing is playing to the gallery and muddling along'[223].

CHAPTER 11

NUCLEAR POLITICS BEYOND THE 1993-1994 NUCLEAR POSTURE REVIEW

Having already been paralysed during his first two years in office, the political circumstances for bold policy initiatives on the part of President Clinton did not improve thereafter. Clinton lost the congressional elections in the autumn of 1994, and after 1996, much of his time and energy was taken up by the Lewinsky affair.

In this final chapter, we will have a look to two other major issues in the field of nuclear weapons policy after the Cold War: 1) Comprehensive Test Ban Treaty; and 2) the debate about nuclear deterrence against chemical and biological weapons. While we have touched upon these policy issues in part One, the internal political debate was not considered. Here, more insight is given to the question which departments and which individuals played a key role in the final outcome and why. The conclusions only confirm the analysis of the 1993-1994 NPR.

Comprehensive Test Ban Treaty
At first glance, President Clinton behaved like a strategic leader in negotiating and signing the Comprehensive Test Ban Treaty (CTBT) in September 1996. Indeed, if there was one nuclear weapons issue he had promised to tackle during his campaign, it was nuclear testing. On 18 September 1992, one month before Bush announced a test moratorium, candidate Clinton told the audience at Sandia Laboratory that he was in favour of a CTBT: 'I know there is a big dispute about [a ban], but let me say that France has stopped testing; Russia has stopped testing. And I perceive the biggest threat in the future to be, as I've said earlier, the proliferation of nuclear technology…and I think to contain that, we ought to get out there and join the parade on working toward a comprehensive test ban, and then focus our energies on this proliferation issue'[1].

The significance of the signing of the CTBT, however, should be put in perspective. First of all, the Clinton administration inherited the nuclear test moratorium from the Bush administration. After having initiated a test moratorium in August 1985 and again in October 1989, Gorbachev introduced a new unilateral test moratorium in October 1991. France followed in April 1992. President Bush decided, although not wholeheartedly, to stop testing in October 1992. He announced a nine-month moratorium and agreed in principle with a CTBT. Pressure from the Democrats in Congress and more in particular from Hatfield and Exon was crucial. Both of them had pushed through a resolution in 1992 asking for a CTBT to be realized by 30 September 1996, allowing maximum 15 safety and reliability tests in the period from mid-1994 to 1996, 12 by the US and 3 by the UK (as the UK hold its tests in the US). President Bush agreed, partially because it was linked to the construction of a Superconducting Supercollider in Texas, his home base. He also believed that the Chinese would continue to test (which they did), which in turn would allow the US to continue testing as well. One day before leaving office, President Bush called for the resumption of testing in a classified report to Congress[2].

Secondly, to push through the extension of the moratorium and the CTBT, the Clinton administration had to make a deal with the nuclear laboratories of the Department of Energy. In his 3 July 1993 radio talk, President Clinton spoke not only about the extension of the test moratorium and a CTBT, but also about a safety and reliability programme that had to be set up by and for the laboratories. Clinton disregarded a Chinese test in October. In November 1993, Clinton signed a PDD that formally established the so-called Stockpile and Stewardship Programme (SSP). The labs would receive $4.1 billion per year. Under pressure from the Republicans, Bob Bell (NSC) brokered a deal in the autumn of 1995 that increased this amount to $4.5 billion per year, which was, as already said, on average more than what the labs got during the Cold War. The George W.Bush administration further increased this amount to $6.4 billion for fiscal year 2004.

Thirdly, despite the fact that Clinton had spoken out in favour of a CTBT during his campaign, once in government it took a considerable amount of time and a lot of bureaucratic infighting to put forward a proposal with a zero-yield CTBT. One of the first decisions the Clinton administration had to tackle was the extension of the test moratorium. National Security Advisor Anthony Lake set up a National Security Council-led interagency review right at the beginning. At the assistant secretary level, only the Arms Control and Disarmament Agency favoured an extension of the test moratorium[3]. Under Secretary of Defence Deutch who was not in favour of an extension played a crucial role at this stage. However, at the Vancouver Summit on 4 April 1993, President Clinton and President Yeltsin agreed that multilateral negotiations for a CTBT would start at an early date.

At the principals meeting of 14 May 1993, Secretary of State Christopher, National Security Advisor Lake, Secretary of Defence Aspin[4], and Chairman of the JCS Powell were in favour of further testing in the short-term and were only in favour of a 1-KT test ban treaty. Only Thomas Graham (ACDA) and Jack Gibbons (OSTP) were against further testing and in favour of a zero-yield CTBT. Secretary of Energy Hazel O'Leary asked for a two-week extension of the decision. The Democrats in Congress – especially Dellums – found out about the interagency review and wrote a letter to Anthony Lake, indicating that a CTBT in their eyes corresponded to a true zero-yield[5]. Lake and Bell (NSC) discovered that most people on Capitol Hill were against the proposal of the administration to conduct a last series of nine tests. They also understood that the Democrats were against a 1-KT proposal[6].

In the meantime, O'Leary consulted with experts like Frank von Hippel who was introduced by Daniel Ellsberg, and she finally decided *against* further testing. Ultimately, Aspin also switched to his former view, against further testing. Even JCS Chairman Colin Powell agreed in the end because the military did not want to spend money on safety tests. Because of a vague promise to the labs for more money for a new safety and reliability programme, Clinton finally decided to extend the test moratorium despite a lot of opposition from lower-levels in the Defence Department, the State Department and the National Security Council.

President Clinton publicly announced on 3 July 1993 that no further testing would be held, at least until September 1994. He also announced that formal negotiations for a CTBT would start. Under Secretary of State Lynn Davis travelled around the world to talk to the major players. On 10 August 1993, the UN Conference on Disarmament in Geneva mandated the Ad Hoc Committee on a Nuclear Test Ban to work out the specifics of the negotiations. Multilateral negotiations finally started in Geneva in January 1994. After a last battle with the Defence Department after the Chinese and the French had resumed testing right after the NPT 1995 conference, President Clinton with the support of scientists like Sidney Drell (Stanford University) and 24 senators and 113 representatives announced a true zero-yield ban on 11 August 1995, one day after France. Germany had played a significant role in convincing both the US and France[7].

Fourthly, the signing of the CTBT was also the result of a compromise between the nuclear weapon states and the non-nuclear weapon states at the 1995 NPT extension conference. It was part of the so-called "programme of action" of the "principles and objectives for nuclear nonproliferation and disarmament". A CTBT was the only concrete policy issue for which a deadline was agreed at that time, namely 1996. Without this promise, the NPT would probably not have been extended indefinitely.

Fifthly, the entry into force procedure of the CTBT was, practically speaking, rather demanding, requiring the ratification of all states having nuclear reactors. This makes that the CTBT is still not in force in 2005.

Nevertheless, the signing of the CTBT by Clinton in September 1996 can be regarded as an example of presidential leadership. It shows that fundamental change is possible in the case the president speaks out. Unfortunately, this was one of the few cases about which Clinton had spoken out.

While the signing of the CTBT was Clinton's major accomplishment in the field of nuclear arms control, the best example of *lack of leadership* was his failure to convince the Senate to ratify it[8]. Republican Senator Jesse Helms had asked the administration to submit the Kyoto Climate Treaty and the TMD demarcation agreements *before* submitting the CTBT. Clinton, however, refused because he knew that the Republicans would never ratify both treaties. It was also Senator Helms that had taken the lead in abolishing not only the bipartisan Arms Control Caucus in Congress, but also the more than 30-year old Arms Control and Disarmament Agency (ACDA), established as an independent entity by President Kennedy. Helms only agreed with the ratification of the Chemical Weapons Convention in 1997 on the condition that the Arms Control and Disarmament Agency would be abolished. Although Clinton had explicitly stated in his radio talk on 3 July 1993 that ACDA would remain in existence as an independent agency, the Arms Control and Disarmament Agency ceased to exist and was integrated into the State Department on 1 April 1999[9]. This example also shows that presidents can lose fights after having spoken out publicly.

Chairman of the Foreign Relations Committee Jesse Helms refused to hold hearings on the CTBT ratification, even after all 45 Democratic senators sent him a public letter on 20 July 1999. Under heavy Democratic pressure and with the go-ahead of National Security Advisor Samuel Berger on 22 September 1999, the Republican majority finally agreed on 30 September to hold a vote. But the Democrats were not aware that the Republicans, led by Senator Jon Kyl (Arizona), had worked very hard and secretly to solidify enough opposition against ratification since the spring of 1999. 'Staffers prepared elaborate briefing books for this inside game, and meetings were scheduled with (and letters and phone calls generated from) experts known to be against the treaty, including former secretaries of defence and weapons scientists'[10]. As Schwartz put it: 'By late September, 44 Republicans were firmly against the treaty, although the Democrats didn't know it'[11].

In the end, the Republicans played it extremely hard procedurally by providing only ten hours for Senate debate. After finding out that they would not obtain enough votes, the Democrats tried to uphold the voting at the end, but failed. On 13 October 1999, the Senate voted Republican versus Democrat *against* the CTBT ratification: only 48 voted in favour, 19 short of the required 67 votes. The last time that that had happened was in 1919 when the Republicans led by Henry Cabot Lodge vetoed Woodrow Wilson's Versailles Treaty.

The arguments of the opponents of ratification were twofold: the CTBT verification system was unsatisfactory, and the CTBT precluded the option of holding future tests to maintain a reliable nuclear arsenal. Both arguments were decisively rejected by 32 Nobel Prize Winners for physics, the American Geophysical Union and the Seismological Society of America. And why had 52 countries in the world (including 26 of the necessary 44 countries including France and the UK) already ratified the CTBT at that time, if the verification system was unsatisfactory[12] ? The criticism against the treaty had also been rejected by the major bureaucratic stakeholders and more particularly the JCS and the directors of national labs, at least in 1996[13].

The vote is a classic example of how foreign policy and national interests can be undermined by domestic politics. François Heisbourg – a French defence expert - pointed afterwards to the 'deeply autistic political establishment' in the US[14]. Daryl Kimball is also clear: 'Most Republicans so distrust and despise President Clinton that they were willing to inflict damage to Bill Clinton even if it meant harming US national security…Distracted by domestic policy issues, scandal, and the war in Kosovo, President Clinton failed to heed repeated appeals to designate a group inside his government focused solely on the task of CTBT ratification'[15]. Terry Deibel agrees: 'the CTBT train wreck seems less the stuff of history than an accident of politics, an executive-legislative stalemate that resulted from clashing institutional interests, partisan struggle, intra-party factionalism, and personal vindictiveness'. He also pointed to a lack of presidential leadership. 'Clinton had not mounted a public campaign on the treaty's behalf, he had not appointed a high-level official within the administration to lobby for its passage, and he had not recruited a senior Republican senator to work for the CTBT in the Republican caucus'[16]. *The Economist* afterwards warned: 'If America refuses multilateral entanglements, it may be blissfully free; but it will also be alone. It will be a leader with no one to lead, in a world made unstable by its very isolation. This is sovereignty, all right. But a superpower should be bigger, and wiser, than that'[17]. The vote had also negative spill-over effects for other aspects of the nonproliferation regime. International Atomic Energy Agency Director Mohamed ElBaradei for instance said: 'The Senate vote against the ban on nuclear tests was a devastating blow to our efforts to gain acceptance of more intrusive inspections of nuclear facilities around the world'[18].

In January 2000, President Clinton asked former Chairman of the JCS John Shalikashvili to head an effort to make the CTBT more acceptable to the Senate. Shalikashvili accepted, but he immediately made clear that he had no hope for CTBT ratification during the remainder of the Clinton administration[19].

The Russian Duma – in contrast to the US Senate – ratified the CTBT in April 2000 after it had ratified START II and right before the start of the 2000 NPT Review Conference. Five years later, 175 states have signed and 121 have ratified the CTBT.

Nuclear deterrence against chemical and biological weapons

Probably the worst decision the Clinton administration made from a nonproliferation and disarmament point of view, was emphasizing that nuclear weapons also had a role to play in deterring chemical and biological weapons attacks. This undermined the negative security guarantees and excluded a no first use. It re-legitimised nuclear weapons after the Cold War, based on a shaky strategic rationale. It is therefore worth looking at how this decision had been made and where it originated. The origins of this policy shift go back to the search for a new threat after the Cold War. Chairman of the JCS Colin Powell at that time predicted that the political relationship with the USSR would drastically improve, with serious implications for the US defence budget. He therefore started to pinpoint "rogue states" possessing "weapons of mass destruction" as the new threat to the US. The military already changed their planning in October 1989[20]. After a short internal battle with Secretary of Defence Cheney, the latter agreed with Powell's Base Force in mid-1990. President Bush announced the new strategy on 2 August 1990. This shift in military planning had significant consequences for nuclear weapons policy, especially with regard to the question how to deter chemical and biological weapons attacks.

Declaratory policy

The first references to nuclear deterrence vis-à-vis 'increasingly capable Third World threats' can be traced back to the JCS Military Net Assessment of March 1990[21]. Secretary of Defence Cheney mentioned this new emphasis in a hearing before Congress in June 1990 and repeated it in his report *Defence Strategy for the 1990s: the regional defence strategy* in the autumn of 1992. Cheney suggested: 'In the decade ahead, we must adopt the right combination of deterrent forces, tactical and strategic…to mitigate risks from weapons of mass destruction and their means of delivery, whatever the source. For now, this requires retaining ready forces for a survivable nuclear deterrent, including tactical forces'[22]. In the meantime, the Reed-

Wheeler report of October 1991 had plainly recommended getting rid of the negative security assurances. As Thomas Reed testified in Congress in January 1992: 'We are not comfortable with the…suggestion that a nation can engage in any level of chemical or biological aggression and still be shielded by an American non-nuclear pledge'[23]. US official policy, however, kept the negative security guarantees.

The Clinton administration basically made the same threat assessment, although it was a bit more optimistic vis-à-vis the future of Russia. The spread of weapons of mass destruction was regarded as the biggest threat. There was, however, a significant difference in emphasis and in ways of coping with this threat among the different departments and agencies. The JCS Doctrine for Joint Nuclear Operations of April 1993 stated for instance that 'the fundamental purpose of US nuclear forces is *to deter the use of weapons of mass destruction*, particularly nuclear weapons' thanks to 'low-yield weapons'[24]. When this document became public and was criticized, the Pentagon immediately downplayed its importance[25].

The State Department – already anxious about Secretary of Defence Aspin's emphasis on traditional State Department issues like human rights, democratisation and especially nonproliferation[26] – as well as the Arms Control and Disarmament Agency were quite upset, because it undermined the negative security guarantees. The non-nuclear weapon states cared about these guarantees, and the State Department had helped push them through in the past. The Defence Department, in contrast, had never regarded the negative security guarantees as very important because they were not legally binding, and therefore, according to the Defence Department, irrelevant in times of war.

The overall relationship of the State Department and the Arms Control and Disarmament Agency on the one hand and the Defence Department on the other did not improve when the Defence Department started its Counterproliferation Initiative in June 1993. Many Pentagon officials assumed that the spread of weapons of mass destruction was more or less inevitable, and that there were limits to the existing nonproliferation approach. There was a growing fear in the State Department that counterproliferation would replace nonproliferation. The latter would of course have meant a substantial bureaucratic shift from the State Department to the Defence Department[27].

The Department of Defence, however, made clear that nonproliferation and counterproliferation were complementary. The Bottom-Up-Review of September 1993, for instance, pointed out that: 'our strategy for addressing the new dangers from nuclear weapons and other weapons of mass destruction and seizing opportunities to prevent their use must involve a multi-pronged approach. *First*, it includes *nonproliferation* efforts…DOD must *also* focus on *counterproliferation* efforts to deter, prevent, or defend against the use of weapons of mass destruction if our nonproliferation endeavours fail'[28]. The Bottom-Up-Review was in turn a compromise within the Defence Department. While Aspin and probably also Carter saw counterproliferation as a means to de-legitimise nuclear weapons, others in the Defence Department saw it as the perfect vehicle to give nuclear weapons a new mission[29]. The second group succeeded in including the following passage in the Bottom-Up-Review: 'the US will need to retain the capacity for nuclear retaliation against those who might contemplate the use of weapons of mass destruction'. And '[the] maintenance of flexible and robust nuclear and conventional forces to deter weapons of mass destruction attacks through the credible threat of devastating retaliation' was emphasized[30].

President Clinton personally emphasized *nonproliferation* in his speech at the UN General Assembly in September 1993. By the same philosophy, the Counterproliferation Initiative was publicly announced by Secretary of Defence Les Aspin in a speech - one of his last - at the National Academy of Sciences on 7 December 1993. Aspin explicitly mentioned that the Defence Department was 'looking at improving *non*-nuclear penetrating munitions to deal with underground installations'[31].

Tensions between the Defence Department and the State Department increased further after Aspin resigned[32]. Statements from Pentagon officials about North Korea in December 1993 were incompatible with declarations of the State Department[33]. Assistant Secretary of State Robert Galluci was not allowed to promise negative security guarantees to North Korea, although Assistant Secretary of Defence Ash Carter offered them to Ukraine in December 1994[34].

The *New York Times* painted a grim picture of the cohesion inside Clinton's foreign policy team at the end of the first year: 'Nobody on this national security team was ready to take a bullet for the other guy, said a congressional staff member in close contact with all the main players. For months now they have been rattled. When you talk to the White House guys, they dump on the State Department. State dumps on the White House and the Pentagon. The Pentagon dumps back on them. There was just no sense of team anymore. When people are confident, you don't have that'[35].

At the January 1994 NATO Summit, the US did not succeed in convincing its allies of the importance of the concept of counterproliferation. Despite the negative reactions of the allies and despite the ongoing NPR, the January 1994 Report of the Secretary of Defence to the President and Congress repeated that a role for nuclear weapons had to be considered with regard to the threat of chemical and biological weapons.

One month later, a compromise between the State Department and the Defence Department was worked out by the White House (NSC): counterproliferation would be defined as nonproliferation performed by the Defence Department[36]. According to Sokolski, the State Department had won the battle[37]. In practice, the differences of opinion remained.

Secretary of Defence William Perry, after only one month in charge, emphasized the role of nuclear weapons to deter chemical and biological weapons attacks in a speech at George Washington University in March 1994. As already mentioned, it was the first time in the Clinton administration that somebody of his level did so.

In June 1994, the Strategic Advisory Group of STRATCOM warned: 'Those who argue that biological and chemical threats can always be safely deterred without requiring the last resort of US nuclear forces must bear the burden of proof for their argument. Until they make a compelling case that nuclear force is not necessary for successful deterrence, it is not in the nation's interest to forswear the uncertainty as to how we would respond to clear and dangerous threats of other weapons of mass destruction. "Measured ambiguity" is still a powerful tool for the President trying to deter an intransigent despot'[38].

The NPR - in September 1994 - did not speak out on this issue (at least publicly), taking into account the demand of the National Security Council and more in particular Bob Bell to keep quiet until the NPT 1995 Conference was over[39]. However, Deputy Secretary of Defence Deutch did not deny a role for nuclear weapons in deterring chemical and biological weapons attacks when he presented the outcome of the NPR (see chapter 9).

Right before the start of the 1995 NPT Conference in April 1995, Secretary of State Warren Christopher repeated the negative security guarantees, adding explicitly that the goal was to convince as many states as possible of the desirability of an indefinite extension of the NPT.

Once the indefinite extension had been obtained, it could have been expected that the differences between the State Department and the Arms Control and Disarmament Agency on the one hand, and the Defence Department on the other would have erupted again. That is also exactly what happened. As Scott Sagan describes: 'The resulting bureaucratic battles produced incidents that demonstrate how difficult it is for the US government to maintain the ambiguity desired in this [sic] official nuclear policy'[40].

The immediate cause of the conflict was the signing of the protocols of the African Nuclear Weapon Free Zone Treaty in Pelindaba (South Africa) in April 1996. Vice-President Al Gore had planned a trip to South Africa and he had made clear that he wanted to sign the protocols of the Treaty. The State Department and the Arms Control and Disarmament Agency supported him. The Department of Defence, however, because of the new emphasis on nuclear deterrence against chemical and biological weapons, was strongly against. Secretary of Defence Perry, for instance, had publicly repeated the emphasis on nuclear deterrence against chemical and biological weapons attacks in March 1996. The clash became visible both in interagency meetings and in public statements[41].

The threat by the JCS that they would oppose the ratification process of the African Nuclear Weapon Free Zone Treaty led to a compromise that was favourable to the Defence Department[42]. The US would sign the relevant protocols without a formal reservation. However, at the same time the US would make clear that it could still use nuclear weapons in Africa in cases of chemical or biological weapons use. This was of course completely against the spirit and the letter of the Pelindaba Treaty.

Vice-President Al Gore signed the relevant protocols of the treaty on 11 April 1996. The same day, staff member of the National Security Council Bob Bell – apparently with approval from the highest levels - immediately announced at a White House briefing that signing these protocols did not preclude the use of nuclear weapons by the US in Africa, especially in the case of an attack with weapons of mass destruction (see chapter 4).

Probably not coincidentally, ten days later Assistant Secretary of Defence for Atomic Energy Harold Smith gave one of the most provoking statements in the entire nuclear history of the US. In a breakfast meeting with the press on 23 April 1996, Smith not only stated that the US might use nuclear weapons in a preventive strike against the Libyan chemical weapons programme. Smith linked a specific nuclear weapons type – the B61-11 - to a specific target in Libya. Not by chance, it was Smith who had introduced the B61-11 programme in October 1993 (see further)[43]. This statement provoked a lot of reaction in the arms control community.

One week later, the Defence Department published a report that was the successor of *Soviet Military Power,* the Defence Department's secret "bible" during the Cold War. The 1996 edition was titled *Proliferation: threat and response.* Secretary of Defence Perry further explained the document in May 1996 by distinguishing three key concepts: prevention, defence and deterrence.

In April 1997, Congress ratified the Chemical Weapons Convention on the condition that US policy would, with regard to the negative security guarantees, be reviewed within six months. Not by chance, a small interagency group led by Frank Miller (DOD) and Bob Bell (NSC) was already writing new presidential nuclear guidance[44]. In November 1997, President Clinton changed presidential guidance by signing PDD-60. According to leaks in the press, it emphasized deterrence in general and nuclear deterrence against chemical and biological weapons attacks in particular. The Defence Department, especially the nuclear establishment, had won the battle again. At the same time, the negative security guarantees remained in place. As a result, ambiguity reigned.

It is therefore not by chance that the US had major difficulties in convincing its European allies to adopt a similar policy in NATO[45]. At the Washington Summit in 1999, the NATO Allies prevented the publication of the *Weapons of Mass Destruction initiative* as a separate document. Instead, it was confined to a couple of paragraphs in the Summit Communiqué that was accompanied by a fact sheet[46].

Targeting policy

It could have been expected that a change in declaratory policy would have had consequences for targeting policy. In November 1989, Secretary of Defence Cheney had already asked for a targeting review. Taking into account the military shift in thinking about threats, the review at the beginning of 1991 - led by Vice-Chairman of the JCS Robert Herres - recommended a further reduction in the target base as well as the acceptance of the principle of targeting rogue states with weapons of mass destruction[47].

Dick Cheney, who had already spoken publicly about this new mission in June 1990, asked the head of the US Strategic Command Gen.Lee Butler, to set up another targeting study right after the Gulf War in the spring of 1991. This report of the STRATCOM Deterrence Study Group – the so-called Reed-Wheeler Report – reiterated what former studies had already proposed, namely, a new operational and force structure policy and, more in particular, a nuclear expeditionary force with 'a handful of weapons, on alert, day to day' to be used against China and other Third World states[48]. It also asked for new command and control capabilities, capable of updating the Single Integrated Operational Plan (SIOP) – the nuclear war plans - in a short period of time. The Reed-Wheeler report was finalized in October 1991 and was briefed to Congress in January 1992. A few months before, a General Accounting Office (GAO) report had already mentioned the new direction in targeting policy[49].

Cheney's Annual Report to the President and Congress in February 1992 stated that US nuclear strategy 'must now encompass potential instabilities that could arise when states or leaders perceive they have little to lose from employing weapons of mass destruction'. It also talked about 'adjustments' in the nuclear guidance. These adjustments referred to the Joint Strategic Capabilities Plan of the JCS that would result from Cheney's NUWEP. The changes consisted in re-targeting US nuclear weapons 'beyond Russia and China to other countries developing weapons of mass destruction'[50]. One of the goals of the newly established STRATCOM in June 1992 was precisely to co-ordinate targeting planning and to take planning away from the regional CINCs.

At the end of 1992, the head of the US Strategic Command Gen.Lee Butler set up another internal STRATCOM Strategic Planning Group for adapting the Single Integrated Operational Plan to the new circumstances and to the new strategy. The goal was to make a much more 'adaptive', 'flexible', 'real-time' nuclear plan, in Butler's words a 'living SIOP'. The Single Integrated Operational Plan also had to be revisable in a period of less than six months instead of more than a year. Lee Butler talked publicly about these new operational plans in February 1993[51], when the Clinton administration had just kicked off. In that interview, Lee Butler admitted that he had not yet spoken with Secretary of Defence Les Aspin. In April 1993, he testified in Congress that JCS Chairman Colin Powell had asked him to centralize nuclear planning and targeting of non-strategic nuclear weapons[52]. One month later he publicly introduced the concept of 'generic targets' (instead of specific targets) in an interview in *Jane's Defence Weekly*[53]. In July 1993, Butler formally approved the "living SIOP" and in 1994 the living Single Integrated Operational Plan was born[54].

Also the concept of "a stable nucleus" was introduced. The latter is 'a core set of targets and special attacks that do not change substantially over time, thereby eliminating the need, and the time involved, in making major changes'. As Arkin and Kristensen conclude: 'Reductions [in the force structure] could now be accommodated as long as the stable nucleus was not threatened'[55].

The number of targets in Russia was also reduced further. The remaining targets included 'interlinked capabilities of communications, electrical power, and other networks, rather than [to] their individual elements. It was a reform specifically intended to reduce the gross number of targets without a change in national guidance'[56].

Force structure policy
During the Cold War, targeting policy shaped and was shaped by force structure policy. This is what happened after the Cold War as well. The new targets in the Third World needed new types of nuclear warheads, at least in the eyes of the nuclear establishment. Formally, it is up to the Defence Department to ask for new warheads, weapons or weapons systems. The Nuclear Weapons Council, in which both the Department of Energy and the Defence Department are represented, then has to agree. The Nuclear Weapons Council had already approved the development of new low-yield nuclear penetration warheads in 1990[57]. At the same time, scientists at the Department of Energy labs were talking openly about so-called mini-nukes and tiny-nukes. More specifically, they were proposing 10-ton "micronukes" against bunkers, 100-ton "mini-nukes" against ballistic missiles, and 1000-ton (or 1 KT) "tiny-nukes" for battlefield attacks, as well as other exotic warheads[58]. The Reed-Wheeler report of October 1991 also recommended developing new nuclear warheads: 'The technology is now at hand to develop power projection weapons and very low yield nuclear weapons in earth-penetrators with precision guidance'[59].

However, the regional military commanders were not overly interested in new nuclear weapons. As a result the Air Force took the lead in establishing a new nuclear weapons programme in December 1991. As Arkin explained: 'If the commands couldn't think up the new requirements on their own, the air force and the laboratories would suggest the nuclear weapons they needed'[60]. The Navy followed a bit later. Its STRATPLAN 2010 asked for a nuclear reserve force with low yield weapons 'providing a wider range of targeting options for maintaining a credible nuclear deterrence in the new world order'[61]. Ultimately, the nuclear establishment got what it wanted when Central Command asked for the development of a new nuclear-armed Air-Launched stand-off missile in July 1992[62].

As a result, and also because of Cheney's above mentioned report of November 1992, the Department of Energy asked for money in its fiscal year 1994 budget for developing new nuclear weapons and, more specifically, for a precision low-yield nuclear warhead[63]. The Clinton administration, despite its apparent reluctance vis-à-vis a new role for nuclear weapons, continued what the George W.H.Bush administration had started. Around the time the NPR was started in October 1993, Assistant Secretary of Defence for Atomic Energy Harold Smith asked for research and development money for the B61-11 earth-penetrator[64].

However, Congress, at that time still dominated by the Democrats, explicitly prohibited research and development of new low-yield nuclear weapons programmes on 10 November 1993. Consequently, both the head of the US Strategic Command Adm.Chiles, testifying in a hearing in April 1994, and John Deutch, presenting the results of the NPR in September 1994, denied that new warheads were under development. 'I want to stress that at the present time we do not see the need for a new nuclear warhead to be added to our arsenal. No new-designed nuclear warhead is required as a result of this review', Deutch stated[65].

But everything depends on how "a new nuclear warhead" is defined. According to Hans Kristensen, the Clinton NPR secretly agreed with the replacement of the 9 MT B53 bomb by the smaller and safer B61-11 earth-penetrator bomb. Officially, it was only a "modification" of the existing B61-7 bomb. The physics package was the same, but the fusing and firing parts were completely different in order to modify it into an earth-penetrator. On 29 November 1994, two months after the results of the NPR had been released, the Nuclear Weapons Council endorsed the development of the B61-11. According to Kristensen, Frank Miller waited to ask for such an approval until the Congressional elections, won by the Republicans, were over[66]. Deputy Secretary of Defence John Deutch endorsed the decision in February 1995, after which briefings were held in Congress. On 18 April 1995 – a week before the start of the NPT 1995 review and extension conference – the Department of Energy submitted a secret request to Congress asking for $3.3 million for the B61-11[67]. Congress agreed in the summer of 1995. A few months later, Assistant Secretary of Defence for Atomic Energy Harold Smith demanded an acceleration of the B61-11 programme, which was also approved. In March 1997, six years after the Cold war, a new nuclear warhead - the B61-11 - was introduced into the US nuclear arsenal.

A similar story happened a couple of years later. In 1999, the Defence Department asked the Department of Energy to develop conventional and nuclear weapons that could be used against hardened and deeply buried targets. But the Department of Energy felt constrained by the fiscal year 1994 law – the so-called

Spratt-Furse Amendment - that prohibited research and development. As a result, two high-ranking Republicans sponsored a bill in 2000 to overcome this obstacle. In the summer of the same year, 26 Democrats wrote a letter to the ranking Democrat on the House Armed Services Committee objecting to this provision.

The outcome of the Congressionally mandated 2001 Bush Nuclear Posture Review was revealed in January 2002. A classified briefing was organized for Congress on 8 January 2002. An unclassified version was briefed to the press one day later. Parts of the classified report were leaked in March 2002[68]. The Bush NPR was co-chaired by Assistant Secretary of Defence for International Security Policy David Crouch and John Gordon, head of the National Nuclear Security Administration, a newly established department in DOE that had to manage the nuclear weapons complex. There was also an outside informal committee involved, namely the Deterrence Concept Advisory Group headed by Keith Payne.

The 2001 NPR recommended mini-nukes. John Gordon stated in Congress in February 2002 that studies 'would proceed beyond the "paper" stage and include a combination of component and sub-assembly tests and simulations'[69]. But Republicans in Congress had not (yet) succeeded in getting rid of the legislative ban on research and development of mini-nukes. Thanks to the result of the 2002 Congressional elections, the advocates of mini-nukes finally smelled victory. In November 2002, $15 million were earmarked for research on bunker-busters for a period of three years. In February 2003, the Republicans in the House of Representatives released a paper titled *Differentiation and Defence: An Agenda for the Nuclear Weapons Programme* in favour of mini-nukes. One month later, the Defence Department fiscal year 2004 budget requested for the first time money for mini-nukes. The US Senate Armed Services Committee voted to lift the ban on research and development of mini-nukes on 9 May 2003. Its Chairman, Sen. JohnWarner, stated: 'Without committing to deployment, research on low-yield nuclear warheads is a prudent step to safeguard America from emerging threats and enemies who go deeper and deeper underground'[70]. Five days later, in the House Armed Service Committee, Carl Levin, the Committee top's Democrat, argued: 'Instead of being a leader in the effort to prevent the proliferation of nuclear weapons, we are recklessly driving down the same road'[71]. A compromise was reached only to spend money on basic design. This immediately led to negative reactions by Linton Brooks, the new head of the National Nuclear Security Administration, and by Secretary of Defence Donald Rumsfeld. As a result, the full Senate approved the original text, allowing research and development in a 51-43 partisan vote on 20 May 2003. For the engineering development phase, the government needed an additional approval by Congress. Around the same period, the Air Force began studying modifications to convert the B61 and B83 bombs into an earth penetrator.

But the legislative battle was not over yet. The House Appropriations Subcommittee, responsible for the budget, did not free the whole amount of money that was asked for. It only allowed $5 million (instead of $15 million) for the nuclear bunker-busters, and cancelled the $6 million for the mini-nukes programme altogether as well as the $25 million for shortening the period needed to restart nuclear tests. Even some Republicans disagreed with the administration. David Hobson, Republican and chairman of the Energy and Water Development

Appropriations subcommittee stated: 'Unfortunately, the Department of Energy continues to ask Congress to fund a Cold War arsenal, and the nuclear weapons complex necessary to maintain that arsenal, even though we no longer face a Cold War adversary…The Cold War ended over a decade ago, but the stockpile has changed very little since then'[72]. Secretary of Energy Spencer Abraham reacted strongly in an op-ed in *The Washington Post* one week later. He called those who slashed the nuclear weapons budget "hysterics"[73]. In September 2003, the Senate re-introduced all the money the administration had asked for. Two months later, a House-Senate conference committee worked out a compromise that was signed by President Bush in November 2003 in the form of the National Defence Authorization Act. Only $7.5 million (instead of $15 million) was earmarked for the nuclear bunker-busters; $6 million for mini-nukes, of which $4 million would only be released if the administration handed in a document that spelled out which nuclear weapons would be withdrawn and which would be introduced in the future; and $25 million for the testing programme, although the period for preparing new tests would not be shortened from 24-36 months to 18 months.

In a hearing on 23 March 2004, David Hobson repeated: 'Until we receive a revised stockpile plan from [the Department of Defence] that shows that real change in the size and the composition of the stockpile…I do not believe that we should spend our limited budget resources on expansion of NNSA's nuclear weapons activities'[74]. Linton Brooks did not understand why it was such a contentious issue. He replied a couple of weeks later: 'What we are doing is almost identical to what the last Administration did (they adapted the B61-11 to penetrate a few meters into soil; we want to do the same thing into rock)'[75].

The opponents of the new nuclear weapons - led by David Hobson - prevailed in November 2004, when the House and Senate Energy Appropriations Conference Committee agreed to eliminate all the funds required for mini-nukes ($9 mn) and bunker-busters ($27 mn) for fiscal year 2005, although some money was directed to study ways to improve the reliability and lifespan of existing warheads.

In January 2005, Rumsfeld fought again back by writing a memo to Energy Secretary Abraham in which he asked to include $4 million for an earth-penetrating nuclear weapon in FY 06 and $14 million in FY 07 budgets.

CONCLUSION

The bipolar system of the Cold War prevented the radical build-down of the irrational nuclear overkill-capacity. In 1989, nothing less than a revolution took place in international politics. The 45-year long Cold War, which dominated foreign and domestic policy in more or less every state around the world, died a smooth and non-violent death. The significance of the fall of the Berlin Wall cannot be underestimated. In the 20th century, this event is comparable only with 1918 and 1945. One of the two superpowers ceased to exist in December 1991. This quiet revolution made a *tabula rasa* of the defence priorities in the US. Russia - the major successor state of the former USSR - became a Partner of Peace in the framework of the Atlantic Alliance. It also cooperated with the Allies to keep the peace in the former Yugoslavia.

From a strategic point of view, one could have expected that the changes in the nuclear postures of the nuclear weapon states, and more specifically of the US and Russia, would have been accelerated. There were at least four major reasons to radically alter the nuclear postures. First, most experts were already in agreement during the Cold War that the force structures of both superpowers were excessive, that the declaratory policies were far from satisfying, and that the operational policies were far too dangerous. In their view, minimum deterrence could have kept the peace as well. Because of lower alert-levels the fear of a first-strike during a crisis is much smaller under a minimum deterrence posture. The tendency towards an arms race is also smaller. More relevant today, minimum deterrence is a much safer posture in peacetime, with considerably fewer chances of accidents and unauthorized use. One can question its credibility, but that of maximum deterrence can be questioned as much, if not more. China had already demonstrated during the Cold War that a credible deterrent does not automatically mean maximum deterrence. Last but not least, the financial costs attached to minimum deterrence are much smaller.

It is not by chance that France and the UK embarked on a minimum deterrence course in the aftermath of the Cold War. In the same vein, the US could have moved to such a minimum deterrent, keeping only a minimum number of nuclear weapons and a corresponding declaratory and operational policy. A few dozens of strategic warheads - say 50 to 100 - based on a few invulnerable submarines not on hair-trigger alert would have been sufficient. A no first use doctrine coupled with legally binding negative security guarantees for the non-nuclear weapon states could have accompanied this limited force and operational structure.

Secondly, the Cold War nuclear posture was always explicitly legitimised by pointing to the conventional and nuclear weapons threat from the East. The end of the Cold War meant the disappearance of the "red" enemy. Cooperating with, rather than containing, Russia became one of the key US foreign policy objectives. Keeping a huge nuclear deterrent at the same time, justified as a hedge against a resurgent Russia, was not consistent with this overall foreign policy goal of cooperation. To keep nuclear weapons for deterring the so-called rogue states was also hard to justify. Even the US administration admitted that these states could not always be deterred. In short, there were no consistent strategic political or military arguments to keep a Cold War-style maximum deterrence posture.

Thirdly, considering the existence of nuclear weapons and the corresponding security dilemma, states felt the need to imitate the existing nuclear weapons states. As a result five states had openly tested nuclear weapons before 1968: the US, the former USSR, the UK, France and China. They were recognized as "Nuclear Weapon States" by the Nuclear Non-Proliferation Treaty (NPT) that was concluded in 1968. Other states acquired nuclear weapons as well. Israel (although not openly), India and Pakistan never signed the NPT but nowadays also possess nuclear weapons. Although the basic reasons for acquiring nuclear weapons are regional security concerns, it cannot be denied that the existence of nuclear weapons in other states is not an irrelevant factor either. In the extreme, it is very unlikely that states like Iran or North Korea, or even India and Pakistan, would have tried to acquire nuclear weapons had nuclear weapons never been invented. It was the acquisition of nuclear weapons by the US that forced the former USSR to produce nuclear weapons. The latter was a major incentive or at least a major justification for France and the UK to build nuclear weapons, although prestige was not an insignificant factor either. India reacted partly to the Chinese threat, and Pakistan to the Indian one.

This does not mean that the elimination of nuclear weapons by one state would automatically mean the elimination of the other nuclear weapons arsenals. The point is that the longer the nuclear weapon states do not fulfil their obligation to eliminate nuclear weapons as agreed upon in the NPT and as clarified in the NPT Review Conferences later on, the more non-nuclear weapon states will get nervous and may start acquiring nuclear weapons as well (contrary to their NPT obligations).

A fourth reason why one could have expected that the US would have changed its nuclear posture drastically was the risk associated with the Russian nuclear legacy. Although these problems may not have been immediately clear in 1989, the nuclear reactor incident in Chernobyl in 1986, the military coup against Gorbachev in August 1991 and the existence of non-Russian nuclear successor states were major indications. From 1993 onwards, it became clear that Russia's enormous political and economic transition problems could have serious consequences regarding the control of its huge nuclear weapons infrastructure. The risks of nuclear accidents, unauthorized use, brain drain, incidents with unpaid soldiers, illegal export of fissile material or whole weapons or weapons systems were - and still are - not negligibly small. The environmental, safety and proliferation dangers connected with the remaining Russian nuclear infrastructure are nowadays one of the most daunting international security concerns. It would have been in the interest of the US to have stimulated the de-alerting or deactivating – ideally dismantling - of most of the Russian (and therefore also American) nuclear weapons as soon as possible.

In short, the end of the Cold War opened a gigantic "window of opportunity" for nuclear arms control and disarmament. On the basis of the four strategic reasons mentioned above, one could have expected that the US would have changed its posture from a Cold War-style maximum deterrence policy to a minimum deterrent right after the Cold War. These expectations were shared by a lot of knowledgeable scientists, (former) diplomats and policy-makers, especially in the US. The 1990s experienced a proliferation of studies arguing in favour of elimination, or at least a minimum deterrence posture as soon as possible.

While the US took significant steps to contain and to reduce the Russian nuclear weapons legacy in the form of the Nunn-Lugar (later called Cooperative Threat Reduction) Programme, and while it convinced the non-Russian successor states to dismantle their nuclear weapons, the US was much less willing to drastically change its own nuclear posture. No major effort took place to transform the existing Cold War nuclear posture fundamentally. *Nuclear inertia* reigned.

A distinction is made between force structure, declaratory and operational policy. Of course US nuclear force structure did undergo significant changes after the Cold War. Substantial reductions in absolute numbers were pushed through by the George W.H.Bush administration, especially with regard to sub-strategic nuclear weapons and deployed strategic nuclear weapons thanks to the START I Treaty (1991) and the so-called Presidential Initiatives. However, deep cuts in absolute and relative numbers did not take place with regard to the overall number of warheads. It took the Clinton administration three years to get START II (1993) ratified. Despite the Russian ratification in the spring of 2000, START II will never be implemented. Instead, Bush succeeded in signing and ratifying the SORT Treaty in 2002.

The overall result is that the total number of US nuclear warheads gradually diminished from 21,000 in 1990 to 10,500 in 2000. Five years later, that number is still the same. Seventy percent of these weapons are still deployed: 5,886 strategic warheads based on a triad of ICBMs, SLBMs, and strategic bombers, and 1,120 sub-strategic nuclear weapons. The principle of "rough parity", or balancing, with Russia still applies.

The US stopped nuclear testing in 1992 and signed the Comprehensive Test Ban Treaty in September 1996. Despite this general positive trend, the US nuclear force structure had not made a fundamental shift from maximum to minimum deterrence. What was the military and/or political justification for keeping thousands of nuclear weapons ? What is the relative weight of building down after first having built up an irrational overkill-capacity, especially if the build-down does not affect this overkill-capacity ? Even Secretary of State Madeline Albright agreed in June 1998 that there was a gap between the political and nuclear reality: 'For until we bring our nuclear arsenals and postures into line with post-Cold War realities, each of us will be forced to maintain *larger arsenals* at higher states of alert than would be ideal'.

Due to pressure from the non-nuclear weapon states at the 2000 NPT Review Conference, US declaratory nuclear policy became more explicit with regard to the end goal, *in casu* elimination. President Clinton also cancelled the doctrine that stated that a protracted nuclear war was winnable. On the other hand, the overall nuclear mission still starts from the assumption that nuclear weapons are vital to protect US national interests. In the same vein, US nuclear policy still does not exclude threatening and using nuclear weapons against conventional, chemical and biological weapons attacks. It still refuses to declare a no first use policy. The negative security guarantees repeated in the framework of the 1995 NPT Review and Extension Conference are still not legally binding. For reasons of deterrence, ambiguity reigns.

With regard to operational policy, a distinction is made between safety and targeting policy. Safety became at least rhetorically a major theme in US nuclear weapons policy. In practice, the major accomplishments in this regard are the de-alerting of the strategic bombers by President Bush in 1991 and the introduction of Permissive Action Links (PALs) in SLBMs as a result of the Nuclear Posture Review in the Clinton administration. Except for the merely symbolic de-targeting gesture in 1994, targeting policy did not change significantly. Although adaptive targeting options may have become available, the Cold War-style SIOP options - including massive attack options against counterforce targets - remained in place.

To conclude, US nuclear weapons policy did change. Surprising from a strategic point of view, however, was that the posture did not transform itself into a minimum deterrent. The extent of the changes was much smaller and the pace of change was much slower than one could have expected taking into account the geo-strategic revolution in 1989. It would have been naïve to have expected that the US would have eliminated its nuclear arsenal right away after the Cold War. On the other hand, substantial and concrete steps in the direction of elimination - as the NNWS expected - did not occur either, or only to a very limited extent.

More realistically, one could have expected that US nuclear weapons policy would have been transformed from a maximum to a minimum deterrence posture, or at least would have moved substantially in that direction. But strangely enough, even that evolution did not take place. The character of the nuclear arsenal and the nature of the doctrine and operational policy in the beginning of the twenty-first century are very similar to the average US Cold War nuclear policy. US nuclear weapons policy *anno* 2005 can only be categorized as maximum deterrence.

To find out that US nuclear policy did not change fundamentally after the Cold War, was remarkable as such. From a political scientist's point of view, the fascinating question becomes *why* that was the case.

The roots of inertia in US nuclear weapons policy, according to my analysis, lay not in external factors (like Russia or China), but predominantly in domestic politics. To put it crudely, if the US had wanted to shift its policy from maximum to minimum deterrence, it could have easily done so regardless of whether Russia would have followed or not.

Why did the US not take the initiative ? Here, I plunge into the field of US political decision-making. Because of the sensitivity of the subject and the nature of the changes, the decision to radically alter policy could only have been taken at the highest levels. That means that the American president had to be convinced of the necessity of these changes. Once convinced, the president had to take the lead in pushing the decision through.

Pushing through radical policy changes is never easy. Beside the strategic implications of a decision, politicians also have more opportunistic - call it domestic politics - considerations to take into account. The key factor affecting this analysis is the power distribution of the major (domestic) actors, both advocates and opponents of change, involved.

In the case of US nuclear weapons policy after the Cold War, the political variables pointed in the direction of a status-quo. Political decision-makers could have expected a lot of opposition against radical change by at least two major constituencies in US society: the nuclear bureaucracy and the Republicans. The former had strong parochial interests to defend in terms of budget, personnel, prestige and autonomy. STRATCOM and the nuclear planning community, the three national laboratories Livermore, Los Alamos and Sandia, and civilian Pentagon experts in the field of nuclear weapons policy were the strongest opponents of any major change. The Republicans are in general more conservative. In contrast, the power of the advocates of fundamental policy change - the arms control community and a couple of former politicians, diplomats and generals, as well as the peace movement - was not very big, to say the least.

The final decision is of course based on both a strategic and political analysis, and lies in the hands of the politicians. Only political leadership can overcome these obstacles. Political leadership means to have the willingness and courage to push through radical changes based on a thorough understanding of the issues at stake and based on statesmanship that lets national interests prevail over parochial interests (strategic leadership). At the same time, political leadership requires having the capacity to push this decision through inside the government (tactical leadership).

Unfortunately, political leadership did not exist with regard to US nuclear weapons policy after the Cold War, especially in the Clinton and George W.Bush administrations. President George W.H.Bush succeeded – over four years – in negotiating and concluding the START I and START II Treaties, in getting START I ratified, and in proposing and implementing substantial unilateral/reciprocal reductions, especially with regard to the number of sub-strategic nuclear weapons and the alert-levels for the strategic bombers. The Clinton administration - having twice as much time available - only succeeded in getting START II ratified and the CTBT signed. The ratification of the latter was submitted to the Senate, but failed to get the necessary votes for ratification.

However, the Clinton administration did make a promising start by announcing the Nuclear Posture Review in September 1993. In the words of Secretary of Defence Les Aspin, the NPR would be the first major nuclear policy review in fifteen years time looking "beyond START II". Aspin put Ashton Carter, one of his key Assistant Secretaries, in charge of the NPR. Both Aspin and Carter personally aspired to major changes in US nuclear policy. They firmly believed that it would be in the national interest of the US to adapt the US Cold War nuclear posture to the changed international political circumstances.

But major bureaucratic resistance against radical changes - supported by the Republicans in Congress - resulted in nothing less than a status-quo in 1994. Both the lower-level military and civilian Pentagon officials rejected any fundamental change. In the meantime, Secretary of Defence Les Aspin had to resign two months after the start of the NPR. His successor - former Deputy Secretary of Defence William Perry - had other priorities. Assistant Secretary of Defence Ash Carter was the only political appointee left pushing for changes. As Carter was not explicitly backed (anymore) by his superiors - Slocombe, Deutch and Perry - in the Defence Department, and as the bureaucracy was well aware of that, the latter played the game hard. In addition, there was a major lack of interest in the White House and the State Department. President Clinton also lacked the earned authority to push through radical changes in defence policy as a result of his past as well as the gay issue in the beginning of his term.

What are the major policy implications deriving from this analysis ? The inconsistencies in US nuclear policy mentioned above are likely to attract more and more criticism from the rest of the international community: from Russia and China because they are both treated as a partner and a nuclear target at the same time, and because their nuclear deterrents will be undermined (especially in the case of China) in case of deployment of NMD; from the non-nuclear weapon states (including the allies) because they do not feel respected in the framework of the NPT and particularly because of the lack of high-level commitment to the goal of elimination on the part of the NWS and especially the US.

The likelihood of a nuclear weapon exploding in the future is small but according to many experts on the rise. Accidents in Russia are waiting to happen. It can also be expected that the number of nuclear weapon states will gradually increase further. Taking into account the nature of the political regimes of some of these proliferating states and taking into account their geographical closeness to each other, a nuclear war is not beyond imagination. Knowing that some of these political regimes export these sensitive materials, the threat of nuclear terrorism becomes more real as well.

All these dangers can be mitigated if the nuclear weapon states radically alter their postures and policies. In a world without nuclear weapons the risks mentioned above do not exist. In a world with minimum deterrence postures in anticipation of a nuclear weapons free world, the likelihood of accidents and proliferation will be minimized.

How likely is it that US nuclear weapons policy will change fundamentally in the near future ? What are the basic requirements for such a policy change ? What is needed is political leadership at the highest levels, read a personal commitment by the American president. That means that the president has to be interested, gets the necessary information, makes up his mind, takes the decision to radically alter the US posture, and lays out a strategy to do this effectively.

In practice, the American president has to state his objectives right from the beginning (for instance during his Inaugural Address or in one of his State of the Union speeches), or even during his campaign. The president has personally to take the lead in educating public opinion as to why such a radical policy change is in the national interest of the US, as the American citizens have been told for decades that a maximum deterrence posture would be best. The president has to create a bipartisan consensus in order to avoid difficulties with the Congress. He also needs a Secretary of Defence who is also determined to radically change US nuclear policy, and who is gifted with the earned authority to push these changes through inside the Defence Department.

Ideally, a major societal debate would also take place[2]. A new occasion may be the proposed appointment of a 12-member Congressional commission to assess US nuclear weapons policy that is supposed to report back in 2008[3]. But if, for one reason or another, this societal debate is not held, it is up to the political leaders to take their responsibilities and to push through the necessary changes in the interest of the nation.

The odds are that in reality the US will continue dismantling its nuclear arsenal and in changing its policy towards minimum deterrence, but not in a drastic way.

The only variable that may turn everything around is a major nuclear accident (for instance in Russia) and/or a new proliferating country (say Iran, Saudi-Arabia, and/or Brazil). The same applies to a deliberate nuclear exchange between, for instance, India and Pakistan. Another worst-case scenario remains the detonation of a "dirty bomb" or a crude nuclear explosive by Al Qhaeda.

It is up to the American political decision-makers to take their responsibility and to push through the changes that are known to be in the national interest. As the US is by far the most powerful state, the only superpower left, the number one with regard to modern conventional weapons, and the leader in the fight against proliferation in the past, it is also "bound to lead" and bring to an end the existing overkill-capacity and the dangers of nuclear proliferation.

APPENDIX: MINIMUM DETERRENCE ADVOCATES AFTER THE COLD WAR

The following list is not exhaustive, although the main reports, statements, books and volumes (edited or special monographs) published after the Cold War are included. The list only mentions those studies focusing on changes in the overall nuclear policy (in contrast to changes of just one specific aspect of nuclear policy).

The studies in favour of minimum deterrence (or at least going substantially in the direction of minimum deterrence) are in chronological order:

- The SIPRI book titled *Security without nuclear weapons ? Different perspectives on non-nuclear security* with pro and anti-nuclear views edited by Regina Cowen Karp in 1992.

- The Pugwash book *A nuclear-weapon-free-world: Desirable ? Feasible ?* edited by Joseph Rotblat, Jack Steinberger and Bhalchandra Udgaonkar, published in 1993.

- The volume *Reducing nuclear danger* by McGeorge Bundy, who was National Security Advisor to President Kennedy and President Johnson; former Chairman of the Joint Chiefs of Staff Admiral William Crowe; and Stanford physicist Sidney Drell. It was published by the Council on Foreign Relations in 1993.

- The Nuclear Strategic Study Group of the Centre for Strategic and International Studies (CSIS) published the volume *A nuclear peace: the future of nuclear weapons in US foreign and defence policy* in June 1993, and a second book *Toward nuclear peace* in 1994.

- The Steering Committee Project on Eliminating Weapons of Mass Destruction of the Henry Stimson Centre under the chairmanship of General Andrew Goodpaster published three reports: *Beyond the nuclear peril: the year in review and the years ahead* in January 1995, *An Evolving US Nuclear Posture Review* in December 1995, and *An American Legacy. Building a Nuclear-Weapons-Free-World* in March 1997.

- The April 1995 volume *Beyond the NPT: A nuclear-weapon-free world* by the International Network of Engineers and Scientists Against Proliferation (INESAP) that was prepared for the Nuclear Nonproliferation Treaty Review and Extension Conference.

- The "Abolition 2000" NGO statement that was written during the April 1995 NPT Extension and Review Conference and supported later by more than 1,000 peace, environmental, human rights and religious organizations in the world.

- Statement of Principles of the "Coalition to Reduce Nuclear Dangers" issued in February 1996.

- *Report of the Canberra Commission on the Elimination of Nuclear Weapons* in August 1996, presented to the UN General Assembly one month later. The Canberra Commission was set up by a government, namely Australia, asking a group of international experts to propose concrete steps towards elimination. Prime Minister Paul Keating established the Canberra Commission in November 1995 as a result of the resumption of the French nuclear tests in the Pacific and the consequent global protests.

- *Statement on Nuclear Weapons by International Generals and Admirals* on 4 December 1996 initiated by Gen.Andrew Goodpaster and Gen.Lee Butler, and signed by 60 other retired generals and admirals from 17 countries.

- A *Model Nuclear Weapons Convention* was issued in April 1997 coordinated by the Lawyers' Committee on Nuclear Policy with the technical guidance of the International Network of Engineers and Scientists against Proliferation (INESAP). It was presented by Costa Rica to the UN General Assembly in November 1997.

- *The future of US Nuclear Weapons Policy*, a study by the Committee on International Security and Arms Control (CISAC) of the US National Academy of Sciences in June 1997 chaired by Gen.William Burns.

- The monograph *Caging the nuclear genie: an American challenge for global security* by former Admiral and CIA Director Stansfield Turner in 1997.

- Carnegie Commission on Preventing Deadly Conflict co-chaired by Cyrus Vance and David Hamburg of December 1997.

- In January 1998, the Council on Foreign Relations published the report of the John McCloy Roundtable on the Elimination of Nuclear Weapons chaired by General Larry Welch.

- *Statement on Nuclear Weapons by International Civilian leaders* on 2 February 1998, organized by the State of the World Forum and led by the late Senator Alan Cranston. It was signed by 52 (former) prime ministers or heads of state, including Jimmy Carter, Michael Gorbachev, Ruud Lubbers, Helmut Schmidt, and Michel Rocard.

- The monograph *The Gift of Time* in 1998 by Jonathan Schell. Excerpts of it have been published in 'The Nation' in February 1998.

- The "Middle Powers Initiative" founded in March 1998 by the following NGOs: International Association of Lawyers Against Nuclear Arms, International Peace Bureau, International Network of Engineers and Scientists for Global Responsibility, International Physicians for Prevention of Nuclear War, Nuclear Peace Age Foundation, Parliamentarians for Global Action, State of the World Forum.

- *The morality of nuclear deterrence: an evaluation* by *Pax Christi Bishops in the US* issued 10 June 1998 on the 15ᵗʰ anniversary of their famous pastoral letter *Challenge of peace* of 1983. The report was signed by 75 US Catholic bishops.

- The Pugwash volume *Nuclear weapons. The road to zero* in 1998 edited by Joseph Rotblat.

- The report *Jump-START: retaking the initiative to reduce post-Cold War nuclear dangers* by the "Committee on Nuclear Policy" on 25 February 1999.

- The 402-page edited volume *The nuclear turning-point: a blueprint for deep cuts and de-alerting of nuclear weapons*, published in 1999 by the Brookings Institution. Authors include Bruce Blair, Steve Fetter, Jonathan Dean, James Goodby, George Lewis, Janne Nolan, Theodore Postol, Frank von Hippel, and Harold Feiveson.

- *The Report of the Tokyo Forum for Nuclear Nonproliferation and Disarmament.* The Forum was set up by the Japanese government in August 1998 after the Indian and Pakistani nuclear tests and had 23 experts from 17 countries co-chaired by former Under Secretary-General of the UN Yasushi Akashi and Nobuo Matsunaga (Japanese Institute of International Affairs). Its report was released on 25 July 1999.

- The establishment of an International Commission on Weapons of Mass Destruction, set up by the UN and led by former International Atomic Energy Agency director Hans Blix, in 2003.

- *The Road to Nuclear Security* written by Lawrence Korb with Peter Ogden and published by the Center for American Progress in December 2004.

- *The Atlanta Consultation II on the Future of the NPT*, The Carter Center, January 2005.

- Sidney Drell and James Goodby, *What are nuclear weapons for ? Recommendations for restructuring US strategic nuclear forces*, Arms Control Association, April 2005.

Notes

Introduction

[1] Stephen Rademaker, 'US fully complies with all aspects of key NPT clause', 3d of February 2005.
[2] John Hamre, 'Toward a nuclear strategy', in: *The Washington Post*, 2d of May 2005, p.A17.

Chapter 1

[1] Lawrence Freedman, *The evolution of nuclear strategy*, 1989, 66.
[2] The five states that had exploded a nuclear device before 1967 were called 'nuclear weapon states' according to the Nuclear Nonproliferation Treaty (1968). These are: US, USSR (now Russia), UK, France, and China. India and Pakistan are "de facto" nuclear weapon states since 1998. Israel is a nuclear weapon state since the late 1960s, but it does not admit that it possesses nuclear weapons. North Korea announced in the beginning of 2005 that it also possesses nuclear weapons. Some experts however doubt whether the latter is true.
[3] Lawrence Freedman, *ibid.*, 430.
[4] Similar concepts are used by other authors, although the exact content may differ: "minimum and maximum deterrence" by Barry Buzan, *An introduction to Strategic Studies*, 1987; "deterrence by punishment and deterrence by denial" by Glenn Snyder, *Deterrence and defense*, 1961; "existential deterrence and counterforce/countervailing" by Robert Jervis, *The illogic of American nuclear strategy*, 1984.
[5] The same number had been used by Morton Halperin in an *Arms Control Association* briefing in January 2002. Http://www.armscontrol.org/aca/panel.asp?print.
[6] We will use the term "sub-strategic" instead of "tactical" nuclear weapons.
[7] Tactical warning corresponds to warning by satellites and/or radar signalling that an attack is underway.
[8] There is some confusion in the literature about the term launch-under-attack. For a similar view, see Michael Brower, 'The future of US nuclear strategy', in: Michèle Flournoy (ed), *Nuclear weapons after the Cold War. Guidelines for US policy*, HarperCollins, 1993, p.100; Bruce Blair, *Global zero alert for nuclear forces*, Brookings, 1995, p.45. For the view that LUA is more or less identical to LOW, see Bruce Blair, *Strategic command and control*, Brookings, 1985.
[9] John Holdren, 'Getting to zero', in: Maxwell Bruce and Tom Milne (eds), *The force of reason*, 1998.
[10] Charles Glaser, 'Nuclear policy without adversary', in: *International Security*, Spring 1992. For advocates of non-nuclear counterforce targeting, see Michael Mazarr, 'Nuclear weapons after the cold war', in: *Washington Quarterly*, Spring 1992; US National Academy of Sciences, CISAC, *The Future of US Nuclear Weapons Policy*, 1997, 6, 64.
[11] Bruce Blair, *Strategic Command and Control: redefining the nuclear threat*, 1985, 4-5; Cindy Williams, 'The future of US strategic command, control, communications, and intelligence', in: Michèle Flournoy (ed), *Nuclear weapons after the Cold War*, 1993, 243.
[12] John Steinbruner, 'National security and the concept of strategic stability', in: *Journal of Conflict Resolution*, September 1978, 421, quoted by Bruce Blair, *Strategic Command and Control*, 44.
[13] Patrick Morgan, *Deterrence: a conceptual analysis*, 1983, 86.

[14] For instance Richard Ned Lebow and Janice Stein, *We all lost the Cold War*, 1994, 367-8; Robert Jervis, 'Strategic theory: what's new and what's true', in: Roman Kolkowicz (ed), *The logic of nuclear terror*, 1987, 50; Barry Buzan, *An Introduction to Strategic Studies: Military Technology and International Relations*, 1987, 196; John Steinbruner, 'The effect of strategic force reductions on nuclear strategy', in: *Arms Control Today*, May 1988, 4-5; Desmond Ball, 'Can nuclear war be controlled ?' in: *Adelphi Papers*, 1981.

Chapter 2

[1] The first comprehensive study on this subject is: Kurt Campbell, Ashton Carter, Steven Miller and Charles Zraket, *Soviet Nuclear Fission. Control of the Nuclear Arsenal in a Disintegrating Soviet Union*, CSIA Studies in International Security, no.1, November 1991. Others are: Graham Allison, Owen Coté, Richard Falkenrath, and Steven Miller, *Cooperative denuclearization*, 1993; Graham Allison, Ashton Carter, Steven Miller and Philip Zelikow, *Avoiding nuclear anarchy*, 1996; Matthew Bunn, *The next wave; urgently needed new steps to control warheads and nuclear material*, 2000; Matthew Bunn and Anthony Wier, *Controlling nuclear warheads and materials: a report card and action plan*, Harvard University, March 2003; Matthew Bunn and Anthony Wier, *Securing the bomb 2005: the new global imperatives*, Harvard University, May 2005.

[2] John Lepingwell, 'START II and the politics of arms control in Russia', in: *International Security*, Fall 1995, 69.

[3] Alexei Arbatov, 'Military reform in Russia: dilemmas, obstacles, and prospects', in: *BCSIA Discussion Paper*, September 1997, 59; Jeff Ehrlich, 'US general applauds security of Russia nukes', in: *Defense News*, 10-16 November 1997.

[4] Bruce Blair, 'Command, control, and warning for virtual arsenals', in: Michael Mazarr (ed), *Nuclear weapons in a transformed world*, 1997, 60; Bruce Blair, *Global zero alert for nuclear forces*, 1995, 18.

[5] *Arms Control Today*, January/February 1999, 16.

[6] Vladimir Orlov, 'NPT architecture under attack', in: *Arms Control and Security Letters*, # 1 (135), February 2003.

[7] Bruce Blair, Harold Feiveson and Frank von Hippel, 'Taking nuclear weapons off hair-trigger alert', in: *Scientific American*, November 1997, 85.

[8] Lachlan Forrow (and others), 'Accidental nuclear war – a post-cold war assessment', in: *New England Journal of Medicine*, April 1998, 1326.

[9] Steve Fetter, 'Future directions in nuclear arms control and verification', in: *INESAP Info Bulletin*, April 1998, 52.

[10] Vladimir Belous, 'Key aspects of the Russian nuclear strategy', in: *Security Dialogue*, vol 28 (2), 1997, 168; Bruce Blair, *ibid.*, 1995, 43.

[11] Bruce Blair, *ibid.*, 1995, 46.

[12] Bruce Blair, *ibid*, 1995, 47.

[13] 'Report Jump-START of the Committee on Nuclear Policy', in: *Arms Control Today*, January/February 1999, 15.

[14] David Mosher and Lowell Schwartz, *Beyond the nuclear shadow*, RAND, May 2003. See also: Jonathan Landay, 'Russia's missile surveillance is in decay', in: *The Philadelphia Inquirer*, 10th of January 2000.

[15] Matthew Bunn, 'Plutonium at the Summit', in: *Christian Science Monitor*, 26th of April 2000.

[16] To produce a nuclear weapon, only a few kilograms of highly-enriched uranium are needed. To acquire the necessary amount of fissile material is the most difficult hurdle in producing nuclear weapons.

[17] Both claims come from the so-called Baker-Cutler report of January 2001. Howard Baker and Lloyd Cutler (co-chairs), *A report card on the DOE Nonproliferation programs with Russia*, DOE, Washington DC, 10 January 2001.

[18] Graham Allison, 'How to stop nuclear terror', in: *Foreign Affairs*, vol.83, no.1, January/February 2004, p.66.

[19] Bruce Blair, Harold Feiveson, and Frank von Hippel, *ibid.*, 82-89; William Odom, 'Military lessons and US forces', in: Graham Allison and Gregory Treverton (eds), *Rethinking American security*, 1992, 340; George Perkovich, 'A nuclear third way in South Asia', in: *Foreign Policy*, Summer 1993; Jonathan Dean, 'The final stage of nuclear arms control', in: *The Washington Quarterly*, August 1994, 43; Kurt Campbell, Ashton Carter, Steven Miller and Charles Zraket, *Soviet Nuclear Fission*, 1991, 129; Sam Nunn and Bruce Blair, 'From nuclear deterrence to mutual safety', in: *The Washington Post*, 22d of June 1997, C1; US National Academy of Sciences, CISAC, *The future of US nuclear weapons policy*, 1997, 40-41, 62-63.

[20] For a short overview of different non-proliferation instruments, see Tom Sauer, 'The "Americanization" of EU Nuclear Non-Proliferation Policy, in: *Defense and Security Analysis*, vol.20, no.2 (June 2004), pp.113-131.

[21] Strobe Talbott, 'Dealing with the bomb in South Asia', in: *Foreign Affairs*, March/April 1999, 112. My emphasis.

[22] UN, NPT/CONF.2000/28 (vol.I, part I and II), 22d of May 2000. My emphasis. At the 2003 NPT Prepcom and at the 2005 NPT Review Conference, the US made clear that it no longer supported all 13 steps. My emphasis.

[23] NPT/Conf.1995/L.5. My emphasis.

[24] International Court of Justice, Legality of the threat or use of nuclear weapons, 8th of July 1996. My emphasis.

[25] Ibid.

[26] Some Allied observers 'were reminded of Soviet practices in the Warsaw Pact'. Harald Müller, 'Nuclear weapons and German interests: an attempt at redefinition', in: *PRIF Report*, 55, 2000, 19.

[27] Felicity Hill, NGO report from GA First Committee, Week 1, 15 October 2001, at: www.reachingcriticalwill.org.

[28] Mohamed El Baradei, 'Towards a safer world', in: *The Economist*, 17th of October 2003.

[29] Mohamed El Baradei, 'Saving ourselves from self-destruction', in: *International Herald Tribune*, 13d of February 2004. See also Mohamed El Baradei, 'Preemption is not the model', in: *The Washington Post*, 23d of April 2003, p.A35.

[30] Mohamed El Baradei, 'Curbing nuclear proliferation', in: *Arms Control Today*, November 2003. My emphasis.

[31] Drake Bennett, 'Critical mess', in: *The American Prospect*, vol.14, issue 7, 3 July 2003.

[32] 'Brazil's move to enrich uranium is raising eyebrows', in: *Taipei Times*, 8 October 2003.

[33] NPT/Conf.2005/PC.II/WP.17, 6th of May 2003.

[34] The First Committee Monitor, no.1, October 6-10, 2003, at: www.reachingcriticalwill.org.

[35] Laila Frevalds, George Papandreou and Erkki Tuomioja, 'Toughen the treaties', in: *International Herald Tribune*, 27 January 2004.

[36] Colum Lynch, 'US effort on arms opposed', in: *The Washington Post*, 20th of April 2004. See also Tom Sauer, 'A new nuclear order: the need for introspection in US Nonproliferation Policy, in: *Strategic Insights*, vol.3, issue 5 (May 2004), http://www.ccc.nps.navy.mil/si/2004/may/sauerMay04.asp.

[37] Reuters, 'Brazil's envoy criticizes Bush nuclear policy', 14th of May 2004.

[38] Wade Boese, 'NPT meeting marked by discord', in: *Arms Control Today*, June 2004.

[39] Guy Dinmore, 'US allies fret at hard line of "nuclear hawks"', in: *Financial Times*, 4th of February 2005.

[40] Richard Russell, 'A Saudi nuclear option ?', in: *Survival*, vol.43, no.2, Summer 2001; Richard Russell, 'Saudi nukes', in: *The Washington Times*, 5 January 2004.

[41] President Clinton's speech at the Richard Nixon Centre on the 1st of March 1995, in: USIS, 3d of March 1995, 5.

[42] Madeline Albright, speech at the Henry Stimson Centre, 10th of June 1998.

[43] Madeline Albright, 'A call for American consensus', in: *Time Magazine*, 22d of November 1999.

[44] USNATO, The Washington File 198, 17th of October 1996, 17. However, on other occasions Perry legitimised the US nuclear arsenal by pointing to the risks of the spread of nuclear weapons (see further).

[45] John Holum's testimony before the Senate Governmental Affairs Subcommittee on International Relations, Proliferation and Federal Services on the 18th of March 1998, in: *Disarmament Diplomacy*, no.24, March 1998, 38. For a similar reasoning by a non-American expert, see Alexei Arbatov, 'Superseding US-Russian nuclear deterrence', in: *Arms Control Today*, January/February 2005. For the opposite reasoning, see chapter 10.

[46] Paul Nitze, 'Replace the nuclear umbrella', in: *International Herald Tribune*, 19th of January 1994; William Perry, 'Desert Storm and deterrence', in: *Foreign Affairs*, vol.70, no.4, Fall 1991, 66; Seth Cropsey, 'The only credible deterrent', in: *Foreign Affairs*, March/April 1994; Michael MccGwire, 'Is there a future for nuclear weapons ?', in: *International Affairs*, 70 (2), 1994, 213; Paul Warnke, 'Strategic nuclear policy and nonproliferation', in: *Arms Control Today*, May 1994, 5; Lt Col Gary Lane, *New conventional weapons*, Maxwell Air Force Base, Air University, 2001. Others, like nuclear scientists working at the nuclear weapons labs, do not agree. See for instance: Kathleen Bailey, 'Why we have to keep the bomb', in: *The Bulletin of the Atomic Scientists*, January/February 1995, 34; Thomas Dowler and Joseph Howard, 'Stability in a proliferated world', in: *Strategic Review*, Spring 1995, 26-37; Keith Payne, 'The case against nuclear abolition and for nuclear deterrence', in: *Comparative Strategy*, 17: 30-33, 98; Stephen Younger, *Nuclear weapons in the 21st Century*, June 2000.

[47] Andrew Goodpaster, 'An evolving US nuclear posture', Henry Stimson Centre, December 1995, 10; US National Academy of Sciences, CISAC, *The future of US nuclear weapons policy*, 1997, 27.

[48] Strategic Survey, 'Nuclear weapons: the abolitionist upsurge', IISS, 1997/98, 45.

Chapter 3

[1] 'Presidential election forum: the candidates on arms control', in: *Arms Control Today*, September 2000. My emphasis.

[2] http://www.georgebush.com/speeches/92399_htm. My emphasis.

[3] Jonathan Landay, 'Rumsfeld reportedly resists firm limits on nuclear arms', in: *Mercury News*, 27th of April 2002.

[4] Robert McNamara, 'Apocalypse soon', in: *Foreign Policy*, May/June 2005.

[5] 'A small step to arms reduction', in: *Financial Times*, 14th of May 2002.

[6] Lee Butler, 'Zero tolerance', in: *The Bulletin of the Atomic Scientists*, January/February 2000, 75.

[7] *Disarmament Diplomacy*, April 1998, 43. My emphasis.

[8] Christine Kucia, 'Congress approves research on new nuclear weapons', in: *Arms Control Today*, June 2003.

[9] X, 'US Senate committee agrees to lift ban on development of small-scale nukes', in: *AFP*, 10th of May 2003; Helen Dewar, 'GOP blocks Democrats' effort to halt nuclear arms studies', in: *The Washington Post*, 21st of May 2003, pA04.

[10] Walter Pincus, '$27 Million sought for nuclear arms study', in: *The Washington Post*, 20th of March 2004.

[11] Sidney Drell (and others), 'A strategic choice: new bunker busters versus nonproliferation', in: *Arms Control Today*, March 2003.

[12] John Kerry on New Strategies to Meet New Threats, 1 June 2004.

[13] http://www.uspolicy.be/Issues/Defense/rumsfeld.072502.htm.

[14] Interview with John Bolton by the Arms Control Association, 'A new strategic framework ?' In: *Arms Control Today*, March 2002, vol.32, no.2.

[15] Bruce Blair, 'Removing the hair trigger on nuclear forces', remarks at the 7th Carnegie International Nonproliferation conference, 11-12th of January 1999, Washington DC.

[16] Bob Bell's speech at the Carnegie Endowment for International Peace Conference, 11-12 January 1999. My emphasis.

[17] Dean Wilkening, 'The future of Russian strategic nuclear force', in: *Survival*, Autumn 1998, 105.

[18] US Senate Appropriations Committee, Defence Appropriations Subcommittee Fiscal Year 1996, 14th of March 1995, 97, quoted by Daniel Plesch, 'Western nuclear doctrine: changes and influences', in: Joseph Rotblat (ed), *Nuclear weapons: The road to zero*, 1998, 245. My emphasis.

[19] US General Eugene Habiger interviewed by the Defence Writer's Group, 31st of March 1998.

[20] William Arkin, Robert Norris and Joshua Handler, *Taking stock*, 1998, 12.

[21] However, rumours stated that this program was (also) halted in 2000 because of financial and technical problems. See, X, 'Russia's strategic forces stumble', in: *Jane's Intelligence Review*, 2d of October 2000.

[22] Ed Warner in Congressional Hearing on the 31st of March 1998, in: *Disarmament Diplomacy*, April 1998, 42.

[23] Bruce Blair and Frank Von Hippel, at the MIT SSP Conference, *The future of Russian-US arms reductions*, 2-6 February 1998, 40.

[24] Dean Wilkening, 'The future of Russia's strategic nuclear force', in: *Survival*, Autumn 1998, 105, 111.

[25] William Arkin and Hans Kristensen, 'Dangerous directions', in: *The Bulletin of the Atomic Scientists*, March/April 1998, 29.

[26] *Disarmament Diplomacy*, April 1998, 42.

[27] William Arkin, 'What's new ?' in: *The Bulletin of the Atomic Scientists*, November-December 1997, 25.

[28] William Cohen, SOD Annual Report to the President and Congress, 2000, chapter 6.

[29] William Arkin, 'No nukes, or new nukes ?', in: *The Bulletin of the Atomic Scientists*, November/December 2000, 84.

[30] Robert Norris and Hans Kristensen, 'US nuclear forces in 2003', in: *The Bulletin of the Atomic Scientists*, May/June 2003.

[31] Robert Norris and William Arkin, 'US Nuclear Forces 2001, NRDC Nuclear Notebook', in: *The Bulletin of the Atomic Scientist*, March/April 2001, 77-79.

[32] Hans Kristensen and Joshua Handler, 'The USA and counterproliferation', in: *Security Dialogue*, 1996, vol.27 (4), 392.

[33] Wesley Clark in Senate Armed Service Committee hearing about the ratification of START, 17th of May 1995. My emphasis.

[34] Quoted by Joseph Cirincione in his Congressional testimony before the Senate Foreign Relations Committee on the 16th of May 2002. My emphasis.

[35] David Hafermeister, 'Reflections on the GAO report on the nuclear triad', in: *Science and Global security*, 1997, 387. See also Aspin paper, in: Congressional report, House Committee on Armed Services, 102d Congress, *Shaping nuclear policy for the 1990s: a compendium of views*, 17th of December 1992, 20.

[36] Harold Feiveson talks about START IV without ICBMs and in a further stage '100 on bombers and 96 on SLBMs – 200 warheads, of which 24, on the SLBMs, are survivable'. In: MIT SSP Conference, *ibid.*, 19-20; Leo Mackay, *Post-Cold War frameworks for US nuclear policy*, 1993, 340; Charles Glaser, *Analyzing strategic nuclear policy*, 257-284; Glenn Buchan, *US nuclear strategy for the post-cold war era*, RAND, 1994, xiv-xv. A critic of elimnating ICBMs is for instance Baker Spring, 'What the Pentagon's nuclear doctrine review should say', in: *The Heritage Backgrounder*, 26th of May 1994, 6.

[37] General Eugene Habiger, 'Strategic forces for deterrence', in: *Joint Forces Quarterly*, Winter 1996-1997, 68.

[38] Walter Pincus, 'Commander seeks alternate uses for ICBMs', in: *The Washington Post*, 21 April 2005.

[39] IISS, Strategic Survey 1989-1990; Robert Norris and William Arkin, 'Estimated nuclear stockpiles 1945-1993', in: *The Bulletin of the Atomic Scientists*, December 1993, 57.

[40] Robert Norris and Hans Kristensen, 'NRDC Nuclear Notebook: US Nuclear Forces 2004', in: *The Bulletin of the Atomics Scientists*, May/June 2004.

[41] One more submarine will be converted to a non-nuclear mission.

[42] The two strategic nuclear submarine bases are King's Bay Submarine Base (Georgia) and the Naval Submarine Base in Bangor (Washington).

[43] William Arkin, Robert Norris and Hans Kristensen, 'NRDC Nuclear Notebook: Russian Nuclear Forces 2002', in: *The Bulletin of the Atomic Scientists*, July/August 2002. The numbers offered by John Deutch when he presented the NPR on the 22d of September 1994 were much higher: 6,000 – 13,000.

[44] Robert Norris and Hans Kristensen, ibid.

[45] Robert Norris and Hans Kristensen, 'NRDC Nuclear Notebook: Dismantling US nuclear warheads', in: *The Bulletin of the Atomic Scientists*, vol.60., no.1, January/February 2004, p.73.

[46] Wade Boese, 'Bush plans to cut atomic arsenal', in: *Arms Control Today*, July/August 2004.

[47] The Russian numbers do not include a number of intact nuclear warheads of indeterminate status – possibly as many as 10,000. For the numbers until 2002, see: Robert Norris and Hans Kristensen, 'NRDC Nuclear Notebook: Global Nuclear Stockpiles 1945-2002', in: *The Bulletin of the Atomic Scientists*, November/December 2002.

[48] The pits are surrounded by chemical explosives. When the weapon is detonated, the explosives compress the pit into a supercritical mass, and a fission chain reaction is triggered. For more information, see: Steve Fetter and Frank von Hippel, 'Does the US need a new plutonium-pit facility ?', in: *Arms Control Today*, May 2004.

[49] Bruce Hall, newsletter by e-mail, 21st of July 1999.

[50] David Albright, Frans Berkhout and William Walker, *Plutonium and HEU 1996*, 1997.

[51] For a critical analysis from the US Air Force, see Brian Polser, 'Theater Nuclear Weapons in Europe: the contemporary debate', in: *Strategic Insights*, vol.III, issue 9, September 2004.

[52] Robert Norris and William Arkin, 'US Nuclear Forces 2001, NRDC Nuclear Notebook', in: *The Bulletin of the Atomic Scientist*, March/April 2001, 77-79.

[53] PR/CP (2005) 075, Ministerial meeting of the DPC and NPG, Brussels, 9th of June 2005.

[54] Maarten Rabaey, '"Kernwapens in basis Kleine Brogel kunnen pasmunt zijn voor Navo-uitbreiding"', in: *De Morgen*, 11th of March 2004.

[55] Robert Norris and Hans Kristensen, 'US nuclear weapons in Europe', in: *The Bulletin of the Atomic Scientists*, vol.60, no.6, November/December 2004, pp 76-77.

[56] Quoted by Dirk Van Der Maelen, a Belgian member of parliament, in a written question to the Minister of Foreign Affairs on the 22d of February 2005. Belgische Kamer van Volksvertegenwoordigers, Schriftelijke vragen en antwoorden, 18 april 2005, QRVA 51 074.

[57] *Disarmament Diplomacy*, November 1999, 59.

[58] Walter Slocombe, 'Is there still a role for nuclear deterrence ?' in: *NATO Review*, November-December 1997. My emphasis.

[59] Nuclear Posture Review, submitted to Congress on 31st of December 2001. Http://www.globalsecurity.org/wmd/library/policy/dod/npr.htm.

[60] David Yost, 'Europe and nuclear deterrence', in: *Survival*, Autumn 1993, 98.

[61] Keith Payne, 'The Nuclear Posture Review: setting the record straight', in: *The Washington Quarterly*, 28 (3), Summer 2005, p.145-146.

[62] Harald Müller, 'Transparency in nuclear arms: toward a nuclear weapons register', in: *Arms Control Today*, October 1994, 3-7.

[63] Harald Müller, 'Nuclear weapons and German interests: an attempt at redefinition', in: *PRIF Report*, no.55, 2000, 10.

[64] Robert Norris and Hans Kristensen, 'NRDC Nuclear Notebook: US nuclear forces, 2004', in: *The Bulletin of the Atomic Scientists*, May/June 2004, p.70.

Chapter 4

[1] NATO Strategic Concept, November 1991, 10, 13. My emphasis.
[2] Jeffrey Smith, 'Clinton directive changes strategy on nuclear arms', in: *The Washington Post*, 7th of December 1997, A1.
[3] Bob Bell interviewed by Jim Lehrer on Newshour on the 8th of January 1998. My emphasis.
[4] Les Aspin, *Annual Report of SOD to the President and the Congress*, 1997, Chapter 20, Strategic Nuclear Forces.
[5] *Disarmament Diplomacy*, February 1998, 36. My emphasis.
[6] Nuclear Posture Review, submitted to Congress on 31st of December 2001. Http://www.globalsecurity.org/wmd/library/policy/dod/npr.htm. My emphasis.
[7] Clinton NPR slide 2.
[8] *Disarmament Diplomacy*, April 1998, 44.
[9] Richard Sokolsky, 'Demystifying the US Nuclear Posture Review', in: *Survival*, vol.44, no.3, Autumn 2002, 137.
[10] Congressional hearings, Senate Appropriations Committee, 12th of June 1990, 304.
[11] DOD briefing of the Nuclear Posture Review, 22d of September 1994.
[12] USNATO Wireless File 40, 5th of March 1996, 22.
[13] USNATO Wireless File 77, 25th of April 1996, 35. My emphasis.
[14] Janne Nolan, *An elusive consensus*, 1999, 78. My emphasis.
[15] Jonathan Wright, 'US adopts Clinton policy on use of nuclear weapons', in: *Reuters*, 22d of February 2002.
[16] US National Academy of Sciences, CISAC, *The future of US Nuclear Weapons Policy*, 1997, 54.
[17] Interview with military official; BBC documentary on VRT (Flemish public television), Panorama, 'Oorlog, leugens en videotape' ('War, Lies, and Videotape'), 17th of December 1998.
[18] Brad Roberts, 'Chemical disarmament and international security', in: *Adelphi Papers*, 267, Spring 1992, 20-1; Kathleen Bailey, 'Problems with a chemical weapons ban', in: *Orbis*, Spring 1992, 248.
[19] Harold Feiveson (ed), *The nuclear turning-point*, 1999, 39.
[20] Hans Kristensen and Joshua Handler, 'The USA and counterproliferation', in: *Security Dialogue*, vol.27 (4), 1996, 394-5.
[21] A letter from George Bush to Saddam Hussein on the 9th of January 1991 stated: 'The US will not tolerate the use of chemical and biological weapons or the destruction of Kuwait oil fields and installations'...'You and your country will pay a terrible price if you order unconscionable actions of this sort'. In: *Weekly Compilation of Presidential Documents*, 12th of January 1991, vol.21, no.3, 44, quoted by Scott Sagan, 'The commitment trap', in: *International Security*, Spring 2000, 93.
[22] James Baker and Thomas de Frank, *The politics of diplomacy*, 1995.
[23] Michèle Flournoy (ed), *Nuclear weapons after the Cold War*, 1993, 45.
[24] Scott Sagan, 'The commitment trap', in: *International Security*, Spring 2000.
[25] Marc Millot, Roger Molander, and Peter Wilson, *'The day after...' study*, 1993.
[26] Michael Quinlan, 'It is crucial to enhance deterrence', in: *Financial Times*, 16th of March 2005.
[27] Gregory Schulte, 'Responding to proliferation – NATO's role', in: *NATO Review*, July 1995, 18.
[28] William Perry, 'US security policy stresses prevention, deterrence', in: USNATO Wireless File 40, 5th of March 1996, 18. My emphasis.

[29] William Perry, speech at the Kennedy School of Government (Harvard University), 13th of May 1996; in: USIS, 14th of May 1996, 27. My emphasis.

[30] This fact is admitted by both minimum deterrence adepts like George Bunn, 'Expanding nuclear options: is the US negating its non-use pledges ?' In: *Arms Control Today*, May/June 1996, 7-10; and maximum deterrence advocates like David Gompert and others, 'Nuclear first use revisited', in: *Survival*, Autumn 1995, 29. The latter recommended "a no first use policy against weapons of mass destruction" (instead of a general no first use policy).

[31] Michael Quinlan, 'It is crucial to enhance deterrence', in: *Financial Times*, 16th of March 2005.

[32] Daniel Plesch, 'Western nuclear doctrine', in: Joseph Rotblat (ed), *The road to zero*, 1998, 250. My emphasis.

[33] George Bunn and Roland Timerbaev, 'Security assurances to NNWS: possible options for change', in: *PPNN Issue review*, no.7, September 1996, 5.

[34] Robert Joseph, 'Regional implications of NBC proliferation', in: *Joint Force Quarterly*, Autumn 1995, 69.

[35] Michael May and Roger Speed, *The role of US nuclear weapons in regional conflicts*, 1994.

[36] UN, NPT/CONF.1995/32/DEC.2. My emphasis.

[37] Lynn Davis at a press conference in Beijing on the 5th of November 1996, in: USNATO Wireless File 211, 5th of November 1996, 14.

[38] Remarks by Harald Muller at the 7th Carnegie International Nonproliferation Conference, January 11-12, 1999.

[39] Steven Pearlstein, 'Canadian seeks shift in NATO nuclear policy', in: *The Washington Post*, 24th of October 1998, A26.

[40] William Drozdiak, 'Bonn proposes that NATO pledges no-first-use of nuclear weapons', in: *Washington Post*, 23d of November 1998; Ian Traynor, 'Bonn wants NATO pledge on no-first use', in: *The Guardian*, 19th of November 1998.

[41] *Disarmament Diplomacy*, December 1998/January 1999, 55.

[42] Randall Palmer, 'Canada deviates from NATO policy on nukes', in: *Reuters*, 19th of April 1999.

[43] Dana Priest and Walter Pincus, 'US rejects "no first use" atomic policy', in: *The Washington Post*, 24th of November 1998, A24.

[44] Nicola Butler, 'NATO in 1999: a concept in search of a strategy', in: *Disarmament Diplomacy*, no.35, March 1999, 6.

[45] USNATO Wireless File 66, 6th of April 1995, 8.

[46] USNATO Wireless File 66, 6th of April 1995, 4.

[47] William Cohen, *SOD Annual Report to the President and Congress*, 1998. My emphasis.

[48] Jeffrey Smith, 'Clinton directive changes strategy on nuclear arms', in: *The Washington Post*, 7th of December 1997, A1; see also the editorial 'Back from a nuclear brink', in: *The Washington Post*, 11th of December 1997, A26.

[49] Bob Bell interviewed by Jim Lehrer on Newshour (PBS), 6th of January 1998. My emphasis. See also Bob Bell, 'Strategic agreements and the CTB Treaty', in: *Arms Control Today*, January/February 1998, 3-10.

[50] Craig Cerniello, 'Clinton issues new guidelines on US nuclear weapons doctrine', In: *Arms Control Today*, November/December 1997, 23.

[51] Bruce Blair, *Global zero alert for nuclear forces*, 1995, 74.

Chapter 5

[1] Bruce Blair, *The logic of accidental nuclear war*, 1993, 272. Government sources talk about "a few days". Lee Butler speaks about 72 hours, Boston speech, 22d of November 1998.

[2] Clinton NPR slide 23.

[3] Hans Kristensen and Stephen Young, 'Taking the pulse of the US nuclear arsenal', in: *BASIC Nuclear Futures*, October 1998. The Atlantic fleet SSBNs patrol most of the time in

the Northeast Atlantic Ocean and sometimes in the Mediterranean Sea; the Pacific fleet normally patrols south of Alaska.

[4] Bruce Blair, Harold Feiveson and Frank von Hippel, 'Taking nuclear weapons off hair-trigger alert', in: *Scientific American*, November 1997, 84.

[5] William Cohen, *SOD Annual Report to the President and the Congress*, 2000, Chapter 6.

[6] Walter Pincus, 'Nunn urges US, Russia to ease hair-trigger nuclear alerts', in: *The Washington Post*, 22 May 2003, A23.

[7] David Ottoway and Steve Coll, 'Unplugging the war machine', in: *The Washington Post*, 12th of April 1995, A28; Harold Feiveson (ed), *The nuclear turning-point*, 1999, 101; Lee Butler interviewed by Jonathan Schell, *The gift of time*, 1998, 191-194.

[8] Bruce Blair, in: *Federation of American Scientists Public Interest Report*, January/February 1998.

[9] Hans Kristensen, 'US strategic nuclear reform in the 1990s', March 2000 paper, website Nautilius Institute.

[10] Ash Carter, in: US, Congressional Report, House Committee on Armed Services, 102d Congress, *Shaping nuclear policy for the 1990s: a compendium of views*, 17th of December 1992, 117.

[11] Dean Wilkening, 'The future of Russia's strategic nuclear force', in: *Survival*, Autumn 1998, 107.

[12] 'Presidential election forum: the candidates on arms control', in: *Arms Control Today*, September 2000.

[13] Nuclear Posture Review, submitted to Congress on 31st of December 2001. Http://www.globalsecurity.org/wmd/library/policy/dod/npr.htm.

[14] DEFCON 5 (for all forces except the strategic nuclear forces) and 4 (for the strategic nuclear forces) are the normal peacetime positions. DEFCON 3 means troops on standby to await further orders. Nuclear submarines are ordered to prepare for departure, for instance. The DEFCON 3 alert was, for example, raised during the crises in 1960, 1962 and 1973. During the Cuban missile crisis in 1962, the alert was raised further to DEFCON 2. See Bruce Blair, 'Alerting in crisis and conventional war', in: Ashton Carter, John Steinbruner, and Charles Zraket, *Managing nuclear operations*, 1987, p.77-78.

[15] John Pike, Bruce Blair, and Stephen Schwartz, 'Defending against the bomb', in: Stephen Schwartz (ed), *Atomic Audit*, 1998, 306.

[16] William Broad, 'US-Russian talks revive old debates on nuclear warnings', in: *The New York Times*, 1st of May 2000; Wade Boese, 'Leaked documents detail US ABM strategy', in: *Arms Control Today*, May 2000; Stephen Schwartz, 'The folly of US nuclear diplomacy', in: *Newsday*, 7th of May 2000, B5.

[17] Bruce Blair, *Global zero alert for nuclear forces*, 1995, 58, 100.

[18] Bruce Blair, *Global zero alert*, 1995, 79-90.

[19] Lachlan Forrow and others, 'Accidental nuclear war – a post-cold war assessment', in: *New England Journal of Medicine*, April 1998, 1326.

[20] Walter Slocombe, 'Is there still a role for nuclear deterrence ?', in: *NATO Review*, November-December 1997, 25.

[21] Michael Gordon, 'US warns of A-alert if computers misread year', in: *The New York Times*, 22d of February 1999, A8; David Buchan, 'US-Russian missile data vision mired in disputes', in: *Financial Times*, 3d of May 2000.

[22] Walter Slocombe, *ibid.*, 25; Christopher Bellamy, 'NATO's megadeaths gets a slimmer look', in: *The Independent*, 14th of December 1996.

[23] Bruce Blair, 'America doesn't need all these nuclear warheads', in: *International Herald Tribune*, 14th of June 2000.

[24] William Cohen, *SOD Annual report*, 1997, Chapter 20 Strategic nuclear forces.

[25] Robert Spulak, 'The case in favor of US nuclear weapons', in: *Parameters*, Spring 1997, 106-118.

[26] US National Academy of Sciences, CISAC, *The future of US nuclear weapons policy*, 1997, 64.

[27] Hans Kristensen and Joshua Handler, 'The USA and counterproliferation', in: *Security Dialogue*, 1996, vol. 27 (4), 390.

[28] William Arkin and Hans Kristensen, 'Dangerous directions', in: *The Bulletin of the Atomic Scientists*, March/April 1998, 28; Jeremy Stone, 'The war plan decoded', in: *Journal of the Federation of American Scientists*, March/April 1999.

[29] Bruce Blair, 'Cold War era assumptions drive US nuclear force levels: why the target list should shrink', in: *Issue Brief of the Coalition to Reduce Nuclear Dangers and the Centre for Defence Information*, vol.4, no.7, 18th of May 2000.

[30] Leon Sloss, 'US strategic forces after the cold war', in: *The Washington Quarterly*, Autumn 1991, 154.

[31] Jeffrey Smith, 'The dissenter', in: *The Washington Post*, 7th of December 1997.

[32] Bruce Blair, *The logic of accidental nuclear war*, 1993, 41.

[33] Bruce Blair, John Pike and Stephen Schwartz, 'Targeting and controlling the bomb', in: Stephen Schwartz (ed), *Atomic Audit*, 1998, 199.

[34] Nuclear Posture Review, submitted to Congress on 31st of December 2001. http://www.globalsecurity.org/wmd/libary/policy/dod/npr.htm. My emphasis.

[35] Press conference by Vice-President Cheney and UK Prime Minister Tony Blair in London on the 11th of March 2002. Http://www.uspolicy.be/Issues/Terrorism/cheney.031102.htm.

[36] Richard Sokolsky, 'Demystifying the US Nuclear Posture Review', in: *Survival*, vol.44, no.3, Autumn 2002, 139.

[37] Bruce Blair, John Pike and Stephen Schwartz, *ibid.*, 203.

[38] Steve Fetter, 'Future directions in nuclear arms control and verification', in: *INESAP Info Bulletin*, April 1998, 53.

[39] William Arkin and Hans Kristensen, 'Dangerous directions', in: *The Bulletin of the Atomic Scientists*, March/April 1998, 30.

[40] Bruce Blair, John Pike and Stephen Schwartz, *ibid.*, 199. At that time, Iraq and Libya were also mentioned.

[41] Eric Schmitt, 'Head of nuclear forces plans for a new world', in: *The New York Times*, 25th of February 1993.

[42] Bruce Blair, *Global zero alert*, 1995, 7.

[43] Hans Kristensen, 'Targets of opportunity', in: *The Bulletin of the Atomic Scientists*, September/October 1997, 26.

[44] Hans Kristensen, 'US strategic nuclear reform in the 1990s', March 2000, website Nautilus Institute. See also: William Arkin, 'Not just a last resort ?', in: *The Washington Post*, 15th of May 2005, p.B01.

[45] Michael Brown, 'The US manned bomber and strategic deterrence in the 1990s', in: *International Security*, Fall 1989, 14.

[46] Marc Millot, 'Facing the emerging reality of regional nuclear adversaries', in: *The Washington Quarterly*, 17, 3, Summer 1994, 54.

[47] Michael Brown, 'Nuclear doctrine and virtual nuclear arsenals', in: Michael Mazarr (ed), *Nuclear weapons in a transformed world*, 1997, 43; Michael Brown, 'The "end" of nuclear arms control', in: *PRAC paper*, no.1, March 1993; US National Academy of Sciences, CISAC, *ibid.*, 2, 64.

[48] Glen Buchan, *US nuclear strategy for the post-cold war era*, 1994, xii, 36-39; for a similar view, see Stansfield Turner, *Caging the nuclear genie*, 1997, 112; Morton Halperin, 'Reducing the threat, Draft Nuclear Policy Review', draft unpublished paper, November 1996; US National Academy of Sciences, CISAC, *ibid.*, 1997, 64.

Chapter 6

[1] Leo van der Mey, 'India tussen kernstopverdrag en bom', in: *Internationale Spectator*, January 1997, 34.

[2] For the politics behind the policy, see chapter 11.

3 George W.Bush, 'A distinctly American internationalism', speech delivered at the Ronald Reagan Presidential Library, Simi Valley, California, 19th of November 1999. Ftp://ftp.nautilus.org/nnnnet/references/bush111999.txt.

4 Statement by Eric Javits, US Ambassador at the 2002 NPT Prepcom, 11th of April 2002, quoted by Rebecca Johnson, 'The 2002 Prepcom: papering over the cracks ?', in: *Disarmament Diplomacy*, no.64, May/June 2002, p.9.

5 Christine Kucia, 'Pentagon memo raises possibility of nuclear testing', in: *Arms Control Today*, December 2002.

6 The names of these systems change on a regular basis. I stick to the names provided by the Clinton administration.

7 Lisbeth Gronlund, 'ABM: just kicking the can', in: *The Bulletin of the Atomic Scientists*, January/February 1998, 15-16.

8 George Lewis and Theodore Postol, 'Portrait of a bad idea', in: *The Bulletin of the Atomic Scientists*, July/August 1997, 18-25.

9 Harold Feiveson (ed), *The nuclear turning-point*, 1999, 89.

10 Bruno Tertrais, 'Nuclear disarmament: how to make progress', in: Darryl Howlett & John Simpson, Harald Müller and Bruno Tertrais, 'Effective non-proliferation', in: *Chaillot Paper*, no.77, April 2005, p.37 (footnote 24).

11 Tom Sauer, 'Back to arms control: limiting US National Missile Defence', in: *Contemporary Security Studies*, vol.25, no.1 (April 2004), pp.93-130.

12 Michael Klare, *Rogue states and nuclear outlaws*, 1995, 27.

13 Secretary of State Warren Christopher, in: US Information Service (USIS), 23d of January 1995, 5.

14 Janne Nolan, *An elusive consensus*, 1999, 2.

15 Secretary of Defence William Cohen, *Proliferation: Threat and responses*, November 1997, quoted by Gilles Andréani, 'The disarray of nonproliferation policy', in: *Survival*, Winter 1999/2000. My emphasis.

16 USIS, 18th of January 1995.

17 USNATO Wireless File Security Issues Digest, 11th of April 1995, 20.

18 USNATO Wireless File Security Issues Digest, 5th of March 1996, 20.

19 Lee Butler interviewed by Jonathan Schell, 'The gift of time', in: *The Nation*, 2d of February 1998, 204.

20 Marc Millot, 'Facing the emerging reality of regional nuclear adversaries', in: *The Washington Quarterly*, 17, 3, 1994, 45.

21 For the politics behind the policy, see chapter 11.

22 Bill Clinton, 28th of May 1998.

23 Bill Clinton, video-taped remarks to Carnegie Nonproliferation Conference, 16th of March 2000.

24 Rebecca Johnson, 'NPT Interim report 3 May 2003', http://www.acronym.org.uk/npt/03inter1.htm.

25 Rebecca Johnson, 'NPT Interim report 3 May 2003', http://www.acronym.org.uk/npt/03inter1.htm.

26 Quoted by John Wolfstahl, 'US nuclear policy and the future of arms control', in: *Yaderni Kontrol*, vol.8, no.1-2, Winter-Spring 2003, 4.

27 White House, Office of the Press Secretary, 'President announces new measures to counter the threat of WMD. Remarks by the President on WMD proliferation at the National Defence University', 11 February 2004.

28 The US Senate only ratified the Additional Protocol of the IAEA at the end of March 2004, and did so with many exemptions.

29 Joseph Cirincione, 'President Bush's new plan to stop proliferation', in: *YaleGlobal online*, 13th of February 2004

30 Lynn Davis, 'Proliferation', in: Frank Carlucci (ed), *Taking charge: a bipartisan report to the President Elect on foreign policy and national security*, 2000, RAND, 170.

[31] James Caroll, 'Washington shares the blame', in: *Boston Globe*, 19th of May 1998, A15.

[32] Quoted by Janne Nolan, 'The next Nuclear Posture Review ?' in: Harold Feiveson (ed), *The nuclear turning-point*, 1999, 245. My emphasis.

[33] USNATO, Wireless File 87, 5th of May 1995.

[34] Madeline Albright, speech at Henry Stimson Centre, 10th of June 1998.

[35] Quoted by Holum when he gave a speech at the Carnegie Endowment on the 12th of February 1996. In: USIS, 14th of February 1996, 2.

[36] ACDA website.

[37] Bryan Taylor, *Breaking the disarmament deadlock*, 1998, cover.

[38] Walter Slocombe, 'Is there still a role for nuclear deterrence ?', in: *NATO Review*, November-December 1997, 26. My emphasis.

[39] General Habiger interviewed by the Defence Writers Group, 31st of March 1998.

[40] USNATO Wireless File 94, 15th of May 1997.

[41] USNATO Washington File 280, 4th of December 1996, 29. My emphasis.

[42] Alberto Carnesale and others, *Living with nuclear weapons*, Harvard University Press, 1983.

[43] Stephen Schwartz, 'Introduction', in: Stephen Schwartz (ed), *Atomic Audit*, 1998, 28. My emphasis.

[44] Les Aspin, *SOD Annual Report to the President and Congress*, 1994, 57.

[45] Jeffrey Smith, 'Clinton directive changes strategy on nuclear arms', in: *The Washington Post*, 7th of December 1997, A8.

[46] Keith Payne (ed), *Rationale and Requirements for US Nuclear Forces and Arms Control*, January 2001.

[47] Janne Nolan, in Arms Control Association Panel Briefing, 22d of January 2002.

Conclusion Part I

[1] Remarks prepared by Secretary of Defence William Perry to the Henry Stimson Center on the 20th of September 1994. My emphasis.

[2] DOD briefing on NPR, 22d of September 1994. My emphasis.

[3] Walter Slocombe, 'Is there still a role for nuclear deterrence ?', in: *NATO Review*, November-December 1997, 23. My emphasis.

[4] Congressional Hearing, Senate Governmental Affairs, Subcommittee on International Security, Proliferation and Federal Services, 12th of February 1997. My emphasis.

[5] *Disarmament Diplomacy*, April 1998, 41. My emphasis.

[6] DOD briefing on NPR, 22 September 1994.

[7] Congressional hearing of the House Foreign Affairs Committee, 5th of October 1994.

[8] Andrew Goodpaster, *An American legacy*, Final Report of the Henry Stimson Centre, 1997, 7.

[9] Lee Butler interviewed by Jonathan Schell, 'The gift of time', in: *The Nation*, 2d of February 2000.

[10] Keith Payne, 'Post-cold war requirements for US nuclear deterrence policy', in: *Comparative Strategy*, 1998, 253.

[11] Robert McNamara, 'Apocalypse soon', in: *Foreign Policy*, May/June 2005.

Chapter 7

[1] Charles Lindblom, *The policy-making process*, 1968.

[2] Daniel Kahnemann and Amos Tversky, *Judgment under uncertainty*, 1982.

[3] Alexander George speaks about the trade-off between the search for high-quality decisions and the need for acceptability, consensus, or support. In: Alexander George, *Presidential decision-making in foreign policy*, 1980, intro.

[4] Peter Haas, 'Introduction', in: *International Organization*, Winter 1992, 2; see also Ernst Haas, *When knowledge is power*, 1990.

[5] For a similar distinction between interests and beliefs, see Judith Goldstein and Robert Keohane, *Ideas and foreign policy*, 1993, 3-4.

[6] Alexander George, *Presidential decision-making in foreign policy*, 1980, 57.

[7] Richard Little and Steve Smith (ed), *Belief systems and international relations*, 1988, 47-48.

[8] Freeman Dyson, *Weapons and hope*, 1983, 231.

[9] Steve Smith, 'Belief systems and the study of international relations', in: Richard Little and Steve Smith, *Belief systems and international relations*, 1988, 12.

[10] David Barash, *The arms race and nuclear war*, 1987, 320.

[11] John Steinbruner, *The cybernetic theory of decision*, 1974, 117.

[12] Morton Halperin, *Bureaucratic politics and foreign policy*, 1974, 99.

[13] Yacoov Vertzberger, *The world in their minds*, 1990, 122.

[14] Richard Neustadt, *Presidential power*, 1980, 115.

[15] Ken Booth and Nicholas Wheeler, 'Beyond nuclearism', in: Regina Cowen Karp (ed), *Security without nuclear weapons ?*, 1992, 24.

[16] The use of the word 'strategic' in the context of leadership has nothing to do with the use of the same word in the context of 'strategic' cost-benefit calculations, let alone with 'strategic' nuclear weapons.

[17] Morton Halperin and Arnold Kanter, *Readings in American Foreign Policy*, 1973, 18.

[18] Alexander George, *Presidential decision-making and foreign policy*, 1980, 32.

[19] Yacoov Vertzberger, *ibid.*, 358.

[20] Bruce Russett, *Controlling the sword*, 1990, 52.

[21] Morton Halperin and Arnold Kanter, *ibid.*, 18-19. My emphasis.

Chapter 8

[1] Michael Mazarr, 'Introduction', in: *The Washington Quarterly*, Summer 1997, 82.

[2] James Fallows, *National Defense*, 1981, 62. My emphasis.

[3] USIA Washington File, 22d of March 2000. My emphasis.

[4] Stephen Schwartz (ed), *Atomic Audit*, 1998.

[5] Stephen Schwarz, 'Four trillion dollars and counting', in: *The Bulletin of the Atomic Scientists*, November/December 1995, 35.

[6] For instance, when presenting the results of the NPR, John Deutch stated that 'there's been a 70 percent reduction in the amount of money we're spending on nuclear weapons'. In: DOD briefing NPR, 22d of September 1994, 5. It is, however, unclear which number Deutch is talking about. According to the same viewgraph, the US nuclear weapons budget was nearly 14 billion $ in 1994, which does not correspond with the numbers used by Stephen Schwartz.

[7] Carla Robbins, 'US nuclear arsenal is poised for war: is it the right one ?' In: *Wall Street Journal*, 20th of October 1999.

[8] James Canan, 'The new order in Omaha', in: *Air Force Magazine*, March 1994.

[9] Stephen Schwarz (ed), *Atomic Audit*, 1998.

[10] Sergei Rogov, 'Nuclear weapons in the multipolar world', Centre for Naval Analyses, quoted in: *Journal of Federation of American Scientists*, March/April 1999; US Congressional Budget Office, *Estimated budgetary impacts of alternative levels of strategic forces*, 1998.

[11] Michael Brown, 'Phased nuclear disarmament and US defense policy', in: *Occasional paper of the H. Stimson Centre*, October 1996, 19.

[12] Donald Cotter, 'Peacetime operations', in: Ash Carter, John Steinbruner, and Charles Zraket (ed), *Managing nuclear operations*, 1987, 18. In Russia, the Strategic Rocket Forces still had 150,000 troops on its payroll in 2000. See: Igor Khripunov, 'Last leg of the triad', in: *The Bulletin of the Atomic Scientists*, July/August 2000, 58.

[13] Tom Zamora, 'New jobs for old labs ?', in: *The Bulletin of the Atomic Scientists*, November 1992, 15.

[14] John Deutch, DOD Briefing NPR, 22d of September 1994, 5.

[15] Holly Idelson, 'What's left of the nuclear plants ?' in: *Air Force Magazine*, August 1992, 69; Peter Gray, 'Nuclear weapons: build down/clean up', in: Mark Green (ed), *Changing America: blueprints for the new administration*, 1992, 273; Donald Cotter, 'Peacetime operations', in: Ash Carter, John Steinbruner, and Charles Zraket (ed), *Managing nuclear operations*, 1987, 20.

[16] Harald Müller and Makarim Wibisono, 'Approaches to nuclear disarmament', in: *PPNN Issue Review*, no 12, April 1998, 2.

[17] James Fellows, *National Defense*, 1981, 64.

[18] Scott Sagan, 'SIOP-62: the nuclear war plan briefing to President Kennedy', in: *International Security*, Summer 1987, 23; Terry Terriff, *The Nixon administration and the making of US nuclear strategy*, 1995, 61, 109; Ashton Carter, John Steinbruner, and Charles Zraket (ed), *Managing Nuclear Operations*, 1987, 2.

[19] Adm.Mitchell in Congressional Hearing before the Senate Armed Services Committee on the 11th of May 1993, in: Congressional Hearings, DOD Authorization for Appropriations for FY 1994 and the future years defence program, 1994, 23.

[20] Mike Brown, 'Nuclear doctrine and virtual nuclear arsenals', in: Michael Mazarr, *Nuclear weapons in a transformed world*, 1997, 36.

[21] Scott Sagan, 'Why do states build nuclear weapons ?', in: *International Security*, Winter 1996/97, 64.

[22] Coit Blacker and Gloria Duffy (ed), *International Arms Control*, 1984, 34-35, quoted in: Lynn Eden, 'The end of superpower nuclear arms control ?', in: Regina Cowen-Karp (ed), *Security without nuclear weapons ?*, 1992, 170.

[23] Steve Miller, 'Politics over promise', in: *International Security*, Spring 1984, 81.

[24] Alan Cranston, 'The role of civilian society', remarks at the Nuclear Age Peace Foundation on 30th of April 1999, in: *Waging Peace Worldwide*, Special Report, Summer 1999, vi.

[25] See for instance Lt. Col. Gary Lane, *New conventional weapons: reducing the reliance on a nuclear response toward aggressors*, 2001.

[26] Owen Coté, *The politics of innovative military doctrine*, 1996, 81.

[27] Michael Nacht, 'Does arms control has a future ?', seminar at the SSP of MIT on the 9th of April 1998.

[28] Richard Kohn, 'Out of control: the crisis in civil-military relations', in: *National Interest*, Spring 1994, 4, 10.

[29] Daniel Ford, *The Button*, 1985, 105. In the meantime, SAC became STRATCOM.

[30] Steve Miller, 'Politics over promise', in: *International Security*, Spring 1984, 83.

[31] William Hartung and Michelle Ciarocca, 'Tangled web', May 2000, website worldpolicy.org.

[32] Sean Lynn-Jones, 'Lulling and stimulating effects of arms', in: Albert Carnesale and Richard Haass (eds), *Superpower arms control*, 1987, 229.

[33] Paul Stockton, 'The new game on the Hill', in: *International Security*, Fall 1991, 153.

[34] *Ibid.*, 154.

[35] *Ibid.*, 146-147; James Fellows, *National Defense*, 1981, 169.

[36] *Ibid.*, 154.

[37] Janne Nolan, *Guardians of the arsenal*, 1989, 274.

[38] Harold Lasswell, *National Security and individual freedom*, 1950. For a critical review, see Aaron Friedberg, 'Why didn't the US become a garrison state ?', in: *International Security*, Spring 1992.

[39] Richard Kohn, 'Out of control: the crisis in civil-military relations', in: *National Interest*, Spring 1994, 4.

[40] Andrew Bacevich, 'Civilian control: a useful fiction ?' in: *Joint Forces Quarterly*, Autumn/Winter 1994/1995, 79.

[41] Janne Nolan, *The guardians of the arsenal*, 1989, 46.

[42] Janne Nolan, *ibid.*, 59.

[43] A former Navy official interviewed by Janne Nolan, in: Janne Nolan, *Guardians of the arsenal*, 1989, 257.

[44] Bruce Blair, *The logic of accidental nuclear war*, 1993, 54.

[45] Brian Hall, 'Overkill is not dead', in: *New York Times Magazine*, 15th of March 1998.

[46] Stansfield Turner, *Caging the nuclear genie*, 1997, 38.

[47] Janne Nolan, *ibid.*, 33.

[48] Glenn Buchan, *US military strategy for the post-cold war era*, 1994, xiii.

[49] Owen Coté, *The politics of innovative military doctrine: the US Navy and the Fleet Ballistic Missiles*, 1996, 85.

[50] David Rosenberg, 'Origins of overkill', in: Steven Miller (ed), *Strategy and nuclear deterrence*, 1984, 166-167.

[51] Janne Nolan, *An elusive consensus*, 1999, 21.

[52] Jack Snyder, *The ideology of the offensive*, 1984, 25.

[53] Fred Kaplan, *The wizards of armageddon*, 1983, 237.

[54] Daniel Ford, *The button*, 1985, 42.

[55] Robert Dahl, *Controlling nuclear weapons*, 1985, 7.

[56] Henry Kissinger, *The White House Years*, 1979, 217, quoted in: Scott Sagan, *Moving targets*, 1989, 196.

[57] Terry Terriff, *The Nixon administration and the making of US nuclear strategy*, 1995, 61.

[58] Lee Butler, 'The risks of nuclear deterrence', speech at the National Press Club, 2d of February 1998.

[59] Paul Bracken, *The command and control of nuclear forces*, 1983, 239.

[60] Glenn Buchan, *US nuclear strategy for the post-cold war era*, 1994, 46. My emphasis.

[61] Quoted by: Hugh Gusterson, *Nuclear rites. A weapons laboratory at the end of the cold war*, 1996, 1.

[62] Colin Powell, *My American journey*, 1995, 452, 486.

[63] Stansfield Turner interviewed by Jonathan Schell, 'The gift of time', in: *The Nation*, 2d of February 1998, 40.

[64] Charles Horner in a hearing before the Senate Armed Services Committee on the 22d of April 1993, DOD Authorization for Appropriations for FY 1994 and the future years defence program, 487-488. In line with his bureaucratic position, Horner favoured the development and deployment of a ballistic missile defence system instead.

[65] Janne Nolan, *Guardians of the arsenal*, 1989, 260.

[66] Charles Horner interviewed by Jonathan Schell, 'The gift of time', in: *The Nation*, 2d of February 1998, 24.

[67] Barry Posen, *The sources of military doctrine*, 1984.

[68] Lawrence Freedman, *The evolution of nuclear strategy*, 1989, 24; Desmond Ball, *The politics of force levels*, 1980, 68.

[69] Graham Spinardi, 'Why the US Navy went for hard-target counterforce in Trident II', in: *International Security*, Fall 1990, 150; Desmond Ball, *ibid.*, 60-66.

[70] Owen Coté, *The politics of innovative military doctrine*, 56.

[71] Owen Coté, *ibid.*, 45-46.

[72] Robert Levine, 'The evolution of US policy toward arms control', in: George Breslauer and Philip Tetlock, *Learning in US and Soviet foreign policy*, 1991, chapter 5.

[73] Lee Butler, speech at the John F.Kennedy Library in Boston, 22d of November 1998, quoted in: *Disarmament Diplomacy*, no.32, November 1998, 39.

[74] Janne Nolan, *Guardians of the arsenal*, 1989, 258; see also Lee Butler interviewed by Jonathan Schell, 'The gift of time', in: *The Nation*, 2d of February 1998, 194.

[75] Bruce Blair, *Global zero alert for nuclear forces*, 1995, 11.

[76] Glenn Buchan, *US nuclear strategy for the post-cold war era*, 1994, 39.

[77] Interview with Steve Fetter in Washington DC on the 24th of June 1998.

[78] Hugh Gusterson, *Nuclear rites*, 1996, 2; Hugh Miall, *Nuclear weapons: who's in charge*, 1987, 91.

[79] Peter Feaver, *Guarding the guardians*, 1992, 59.

[80] Lee Butler, speech at National Press Club, on the 2d of February 1998. My emphasis.

[81] Michael MccGwire, 'Anatomy of the argument', in: Joseph Rotblat (ed), *Nuclear weapons. The road to zero*, 1998, 26.

[82] Robert Saundby, 'Morality and war: a British view', in: *Air University Quarterly Review*, Summer 1954, 3-4, quoted by: Bret Cillessen, 'Embracing the bomb: morality, and nuclear deterrence in the US Air Force, 1945-1955', in: *Journal of Strategic Studies*, March 1998, 114.

[83] McGeorge Bundy, William Crowe and Sidney Drell, *Reducing nuclear danger*, 1993, 35-36. My emphasis.

[84] William Crowe, *The line of fire*, 1993, 257-258.

[85] 'JFK on Nuclear Weapons and Non-Proliferation', in: Carnegie Endowment Proliferation News and Resources, 17th of November 2003.

[86] Janne Nolan, *Guardians of the arsenal*, 1989, 45. My emphasis.

[87] Harald Müller, 'Arms control and disarmament at a watershed', in: *Disarmament Diplomacy*, no.29, August/September 1998, 4.

[88] Andrew Mack, 'Nuclear weapons: a powerful case for getting rid of them', in: *The New York Times*, 19th of August 1996.

[89] Morton Halperin, *Bureaucratic politics and foreign policy*, 1974, 77.

[90] See for instance UK Ambassador Soutar, in: *Disarmament Diplomacy*, May 1998, 34.

[91] DOD briefing of the Nuclear Posture Review on the 22d of September 1994, 4.

[92] Website NGO Committee on Disarmament.

[93] David Barash, *The arms race and nuclear war*, 1987, 320.

[94] Terry Deibel, 'The death of a Treaty', in: *Foreign Affairs*, September/October 2002, 145.

Chapter 9

[1] Congressional hearing of the Senate Armed Services Committee, Briefing on the Results of the Nuclear Posture Review, 1994, 31. My emphasis.

[2] Michael Wines, 'US revises its nuclear strategy', in: *International Herald Tribune*, 30-31st of October 1993, 3.

[3] Les Aspin, *Report of the Bottom-Up Review*, October 1993, 6. My emphasis.

[4] Lee Butler in a congressional hearing before the Senate Armed Services Committee on the 22d of April 1993, DOD Authorization for Appropriations for FY 1994 and the future years defense program, 1995, 484. My emphasis.

[5] News release, 'Secretary of Defence Aspin announces Nuclear Posture Review', Office of the Assistant SOD for Public Affairs, 29th of October 1993. My emphasis.

[6] Les Aspin, 'From deterrence to de-nuking', in: US Congress report, *Shaping the nuclear policy for the 1990's*, 102d Congress, December 1992, 16.

[7] Eric Mlyn, 'US nuclear policy and the end of the cold war', in: T.V. Paul, *The absolute weapon*, 1998; Dunbar Lockwood, 'Pentagon begins policy review of post-cold war nuclear strategy', in: *Arms Control Today*, December 1993, 23. My emphasis.

[8] Michael Wines, 'US revises its nuclear strategy', in: *International Herald Tribune*, 30-31st of October 1993, 3; News release, SOD Aspin announces Nuclear Posture Review, Office of the Assistant SOD for Public Affairs, 29th of October.

[9] David Ottaway and Steve Coll, 'Unplugging the war machine', in: *The Washington Post*, 12th of April 1995, A28.

[10] Dunbar Lockwood, 'Pentagon begins policy review of post-cold war nuclear strategy', in: *Arms Control Today*, December 1993, 27. My emphasis.

[11] Dunbar Lockwood, *ibid.*

[12] Jeffrey Smith, 'Nuclear arms doctrine to be reviewed. Comprehensive evaluation will be first since end of cold war', in: *The Washington Post*, 19th of October 1993, 17.

[13] US National Academy of Sciences, *The future of US nuclear weapons policy*, 1997, 19.

[14] Dunbar Lockwood, 'Pentagon begins policy review of post-cold war nuclear strategy', in: *Arms Control Today*, December 1993, 27.

15 *Ibid.*

16 Janne Nolan, *An elusive consensus*, 1999, 38.

17 Steve Miller, 'Dismantling the edifice: strategic nuclear forces in the post-Soviet era', in: Charles Hermann (ed), *American Defense Manual 1994*, Lexington Books, 1994, 83; Robert Manning, 'Ending the nuclear century', in: *The New Democrat*, January/February 1995, 55.

18 Interview with Steve Fetter on 24th of June 1998 in Washington DC.

19 Interview with former DOD official.

20 Les Aspin, 'From deterrence to de-nuking', in: US Congress Report, *Shaping the nuclear policy for the 1990's*, 102d Congress, December 1992, 16.

21 Eric Schmitt, 'Head of nuclear forces plans for a new world', in: *The New York Times*, 25th of February 1993; William Arkin and Hans Kristensen, 'Dangerous directions', in: *The Bulletin of the Atomic Scientists*, March/April 1998, 30.

22 Janne Nolan, *An elusive consensus*, 1999, 120. My emphasis.

23 Lynn Davis, 'Limited nuclear options', in: *Adelphi Paper*, 1975, no.121, 4; Terry Terriff, *The Nixon administration and the making of nuclear strategy*, 1995, 159-160.

24 Another hypothesis is that conservative individuals in these departments and agencies might have thought that Aspin would not succeed in pushing through the changes he had in mind and therefore were less concerned. In: Janne Nolan, *ibid.*, 39-40.

25 Morton Halperin, 'Reducing the nuclear threat: Nuclear policy review' (draft of unpublished paper), November 1996.

26 *Ibid.*

27 News release, 'Secretary of Defence Aspin announces Nuclear Posture Review', Office of the Assistant Secretary of Defence for Public Affairs, 29th of October 1993.

28 Janne Nolan, *Guardians of the arsenal*, 1989, 248.

29 David Ottaway and Steve Coll, 'Unplugging the war machine', in: *The Washington Post*, 12th of April 1995, A28.

30 Glenn Buchan, *US nuclear strategy for the post-cold war era*, 1994, 1.

31 Janne Nolan, *An elusive consensus*, 1999, 46.

32 Interview with Leo Mackay (by telephone) on the 10th of February 1999.

33 Http://www.fas.org/irp/offdocs/pdd18.htm.

34 Final Communiqué of the DPC and NPG, 26th of May 1993; 9th of December 1993; 24th of May 1993.

35 Denied by NATO sources, interview.

36 Les Aspin, *Annual Report of the Secretary of Defence to the President and the Congress*, January 1994, 57.

37 Les Aspin, *Annual Report of the Secretary of Defence to the President and the Congress*, January 1994, 62.

38 Les Aspin, *ibid.*, 57. My emphasis.

39 Les Aspin, *ibid.*, 61.

40 Les Aspin, *ibid.*, 59.

41 Les Aspin, *ibid.*, 147.

42 Les Aspin, *ibid.*, 147. My emphasis.

43 William Arkin, 'Bad posture', in: *The Bulletin of the Atomic Scientists*, July/August 1994, 64.

44 Janne Nolan, *An elusive consensus*, 1999, 51-52.

45 Michael Gordon, 'Defense Chief calls caution toward Russia vital', in: *The New York Times*, 15th of March 1994.

46 Janne Nolan, 'Preparing for the 2001 Nuclear Posture Review', in: *Arms Control Today*, November 2000.

47 Glenn Buchan, *ibid.*, xii, 34-35.

48 For another proposal to work out options, see Morton Halperin, 'Reducing nuclear threat: Nuclear Policy Review' (draft unpublished paper), November 1996.

49 Elaine Grossman, 'Four services sign letter to block Carter's nuclear posture briefing', in: *Inside the Air Force*, 29th of April 1994, 1; David Ottaway and Steve Coll, 'Unplugging the war

machine', in: *The Washington Post*, 12ᵗʰ of April 1995, A28; Michael Boldrick, 'The Nuclear Posture Review: liabilities and risks', in: *Parameters*, Winter 1995-1996, 83-84.

[50] Congressional hearing before the Senate Armed Services Committee on the 20th of April 1994, 103d Congress, S.2182, Part 1, 977.

[51] Elaine Grossman, 'Four services sign letter to block Carter's nuclear posture briefing', in: *Inside the Air Force*, 29ᵗʰ of April 1994, 9.

[52] Elaine Grossman, *ibid.*, 1; William Arkin, 'Bad posture', in: *The Bulletin of the Atomic Scientists*, July/August 1994, 64.

[53] Elaine Grossman, 'Carter presents option to put all nukes on subs, creating "monad"', in: *Inside the Air Force*, 6ᵗʰ of May 1994, 1; Elaine Grossman, 'DOD eyes reducing to 1,500 nuclear weapons under alternative force posture', in: *Inside the Air Force*, 20ᵗʰ of May 1994, 1.

[54] Janne Nolan, *An elusive consensus*, 1999, 53.

[55] Elaine Grossman, 'Carter presents option to put all nukes on subs, creating "monad"', in: *Inside the Air Force*, 6ᵗʰ of May 1994, 1.

[56] Janne Nolan, *ibid.*, 1999, 55.

[57] Interview with Steve Fetter (by telephone) on the 8ᵗʰ of February 1999.

[58] Janne Nolan, *ibid.*, 1999, 55-56.

[59] NATO DPC/NPG, Final Communiqué, 24th of May 1994.

[60] Elaine Grossman, 'Nuclear review to back 500 ICBMs, but DOD lacks funds for bombers, subs', in: *Inside the Air Force*, 3d of June 1994, 1.

[61] President William Clinton, *National Security Strategy*, July 1994.

[62] Interviews.

[63] X, 'Air Force, J-5 protest aspects of Carter's Nuclear Posture proposals', in: *Inside the Air Force*, 12ᵗʰ of August 1994, 1.

[64] Elaine Grossman, 'At last minute, nuclear posture review backs 450-500 ICBMs – for now', in: *Inside the Air Force*, 23d of September 1994, 11-12.

[65] Elaine Grossman, *ibid.*, 1.

[66] Jeffrey Smith, 'Clinton decides to retain Bush nuclear arms policy', in: *The Washington Post*, 22d of September 1994, A1, A26.

[67] In the Senate, Chairman of the JCS John Shalikashvili was replaced by Vice-Chairman of the JCS William Owens. SOD Perry was also absent. Congressional hearing before the Senate Armed Services Committee, 22d of September 1994, Briefing on results of the NPR, 103d Congress, 1994.

[68] NPR, slide 15.

[69] Hans Kristensen, 'The unruly hedge', in: *Arms Control Today*, December 2001.

[70] NPR Briefing, 22d of September 1994, 6. My emphasis.

[71] Bruce Blair, *Global zero alert for nuclear forces*, 1995, 73.

[72] NPR Briefing, 22d of September 1994, 15.

[73] Congressional hearing of the House Foreign Affairs Committee, US Nuclear Policy, 5ᵗʰ of October 1994.

[74] *Ibid.*

[75] *Ibid.*

[76] David Ottaway and Steve Coll, 'Unplugging the war machine', in: *The Washington Post*, 12ᵗʰ of April 1995, A28.

Chapter 10

[1] US National Academy of Sciences, CISAC, *The future of US nuclear weapons policy*, 1997, 19.

[2] Bruce Blair, *Global zero alert for nuclear forces*, 1995, 76.

[3] Robert McNamara interviewed by Jonathan Schell, 'The gift of time', in: *The Nation*, 2d of February 1998, 26.

[4] Michael Brown, 'Phased nuclear disarmament and US defense policy', in: *Occasional Paper of the Henry Stimson Centre*, October 1996, 19.

[5] Charles Horner interviewed by Jonathan Schell, *ibid.*, 24.

[6] James Lindsay, *Congress and nuclear weapons*, 1991, 118.

[7] Paul Stockton, 'The new game on the Hill', in: *International Security*, Fall 1991, 164.

[8] Steve Miller, 'Western diplomacy and the Soviet nuclear legacy', in: *Survival*, Autumn 1992, 25.

[9] Les Aspin, 'National security in the 1990's: defining a new basis for US military forces', comments before the Atlantic Council of the US, 6th of January 1992, quoted by: Michèle Flournoy, 'Implications for US military strategy', in: Robert Blackwill and Albert Carnesale (ed), *New Nuclear Nations*, 1993, 143.

[10] Les Aspin, 'From deterrence to de-nuking: a new nuclear policy for the 1990s', 21st of January 1992, in: US Congress, House of Representatives Committee on Armed Services, Defence Policy Panel, 'Shaping nuclear policy for the 1990's: a compendium of views', 102d Congress, 2nd session, Washington DC, US Government Printing Office, December 1992, 1-24.

[11] *Ibid.*, 10. My emphasis.

[12] *Ibid.*, 18. My emphasis.

[13] *Ibid.*, 21.

[14] AP, 18th of February 1992 (website Lexis-Nexus).

[15] Les Aspin, 'Three propositions for a new era nuclear policy', MIT Commencement speech, 3d of June 1992. My emphasis.

[16] *The Economist*, 18th of December 1993.

[17] Congressional Hearings, Nominations before the Senate Armed Services Committee, first session, 103d Congress, Senate, 1994, 11-12.

[18] Ken Adelman, 'Summing up', in: *The Washingtonian*, July 1995, 26. Remember that the Bottom-Up-Review was supposed to deal with nuclear weapons as well.

[19] Fred Barnes, 'You're fired', in: *The New Republic*, 10-17 January 1994; R. Apple, 'Aspin resigns from Cabinet', *The New York Times*, 16th of December 1993.

[20] John Isaacs, 'Bottoms up', in: *The Bulletin of the Atomic Scientists*, November 1993, 12-13.

[21] Robert Manning, 'Drop the big one', in: *The New Democrat*, January/February 1997; Janne Nolan, *An elusive consensus*, 1999; interviews.

[22] OTA, *Ballistic Missile Defense Technologies*, 1985.

[23] Ashton Carter and Steven Miller, 'Cooperative security and the former Soviet Union: near-term challenges', in: Janne Nolan (ed), *Global engagement*, 1994, 546. My emphasis.

[24] Kurt Campbell, Ashton Carter, Steven Miller, and Charles Zraket, *Soviet Nuclear Fission*, November 1991, 128. My emphasis.

[25] Ashton Carter, 'Reducing the nuclear dangers from the former Soviet Union', in: *Arms Control Today*, January/February 1992, 14.

[26] See also Ashton Carter and William Perry, *Preventive Defense*, 1999, 90.

[27] Ashton Carter, 'Emerging themes in nuclear arms', in: *Daedalus*, Winter 1991, 245.

[28] Ashton Carter and Steven Miller, *ibid.*, 546. My emphasis.

[29] Jim Mann, 'New US nuclear policy to focus on "rogue" regimes', in: *Los Angeles Times*, 9th of May 1994, A8.

[30] Ashton Carter and William Perry, *ibid.*, 1999, 136. My emphasis.

[31] Hans Kristensen, 'US strategic nuclear reform in the 1990s', website Nautilus Institute, March 2000; see also implicitly, Janne Nolan, *An elusive consensus*, 1999, 46.

[32] Ashton Carter, John Steinbruner and Charles Zraket (eds), *Managing Nuclear Operations*, 1987.

[33] Ashton Carter and Steven Miller, *ibid.*, 551. My emphasis.

[34] Ashton Carter, 'Emerging themes in nuclear arms', in: *Daedalus*, Winter 1991, 235. My emphasis.

[35] Ashton Carter, William Perry, and John Steinbruner, *A new concept of cooperative security*, 1992, 47.

[36] *Ibid.*, 47.

[37] Ashton Carter, 'Emerging themes in nuclear arms', in: *Daedalus*, Winter 1991, 241; Ashton Carter's letter to Les Aspin on the 5th of February 1992, in: US Congress, House of Representatives Committee on Armed Services, Defence Policy Panel, 'Shaping nuclear policy for the 1990's: a compendium of views', 102d Congress, 2nd session, Washington DC, US Government Printing Office, December 1992, 118.

[38] Ash Carter and John Deutch, 'No nukes ? Not yet' in: *Wall Street Journal*, 4th of March 1997.

[39] Ashton Carter, 'Emerging themes in nuclear arms', in: *Daedalus*, Winter 1991, 238.

[40] Ashton Carter, William Perry, and John Steinbruner, *A new concept of cooperative security*, 1992, 8; Ashton Carter, 'Overhauling counterproliferation', in: *Technology in Society*, vol.26, nos.2 &3, April/July 2004.

[41] Ashton Carter, 'Reducing the nuclear dangers from the former Soviet Union', in: *Arms Control Today*, January/February 1992, 14.

[42] Ashton Carter and Steven Miller, *ibid.*, 552. My emphasis.

[43] Ashton Carter, William Perry, and John Steinbruner, *A new concept of cooperative security*, 1992, 19.

[44] Congressional hearings, Nominations before the Senate Armed Services Committee, first session, 103d Congress, 1994, 777. My emphasis.

[45] David Ottaway and Steve Coll, 'Unplugging the war machine', in: *The Washington Post*, 12th of April 1995, 1.

[46] Janne Nolan, *An elusive consensus*, 1999, 41; interviews.

[47] Eric Mlyn, 'US nuclear policy and the end of the Cold War', in: T.V.Paul, *The absolute weapon*, 1998, 206. My emphasis.

[48] Interviews with Ash Carter in Cambridge (Mass.) on the 6th of February 1998 and the 30th of November 1998.

[49] Interview with Leo Mackay (by telephone) on the 29th of January 1998.

[50] Eric Mlyn, *ibid.*, 206.

[51] Janne Nolan, *ibid.*, 1999, 45-46.

[52] Interview DOD official.

[53] Janne Nolan, *ibid.*, 43.

[54] William Arkin, 'A tale of two Franks', in: *The Bulletin of the Atomic Scientists*, March/April 1995, 80.

[55] Janne Nolan, *An elusive consensus*, 1999, 44.

[56] *Ibid.*, 43.

[57] For similar views in the academic world, see: Kenneth Waltz, 'More may be better', in: Scott Sagan and Kenneth Waltz (1995), *ibid.*, 44; John Mearshimer, 'Back to the future', in: *International Security*, Summer 1990; John Mearshimer, 'The case for a Ukrainian nuclear deterrent', in: *Foreign Affairs*, Summer 1993; William Martel and William Pendley, *Nuclear coexistence*, April 1994; Borut Grgic, 'There are worse things than a nuclear Iran', in: *International Herald Tribune*, 2 December 2004.

[58] Letter by Stephen Walt to Les Aspin, 10th of February 1992, in: US Congress, House of Representatives Committee on Armed Services, Defence Policy Panel, 'Shaping nuclear policy for the 1990's: a compendium of views', 102d Congress, 2nd session, Washington DC, US Government Printing Office, December 1992, 608. My emphasis. For a similar view, see Alberto Carnesale (ed), *Living with nuclear weapons*, 1983.

[59] Paul Bracken, 'Thinking (again) about arms control', in: *Orbis*, vol.48, no.1, Winter 2004, 155.

[60] George Perkovich, 'Bush's nuclear revolution', in: *Foreign Affairs*, March/April 2003.

[61] Marc Millot, 'Facing the emerging reality of regional nuclear adversaries', in: *The Washington Quarterly*, Summer 1994.

[62] Linton Brooks, 'US nuclear weapons policies and programs', speech at the Heritage Foundation Conference "US Strategic Command: beyond the war on terrorism", 12th of May 2004. For a similar reasoning by a French observer with close connections to the

French defence ministry, see Bruno Tertrais, 'Nuclear disarmament: how to make progress', in: *Chaillot Paper*, no.77, April 2005, p.30-31.

63 Council on Foreign Relations, 'The challenges facing nonproliferation', transcript of the interview by Graham Allison with Mohamed El-Baradei, 14th of May 2004.

64 2004 Carnegie International Non-Proliferation Conference in June 2004, US nuclear posture panel summary, www.ceip.org/files/projects/npp/resources/2004conference. See also: Ashton Carter, 'How to counter WMD', in: *Foreign Affairs*, vol.83, no.5, September/Ocotber 2004, p.81-82.

65 Walter Slocombe, 'Strategic stability in a restructured world', in: *Survival*, July/August 1990, 299.

66 Walter Slocombe, 'The continued need for extended deterrence', in: *The Washington Quarterly*, 1991, 161.

67 Walter Slocombe, 'Force, Pre-emption and legitimacy', in: *Survival*, vol.45, no.1, Spring 2003, pp.117-130.

68 Hans Kristensen, 'US strategic nuclear reform in the 1990's', Nautilus Institute website, March 2000.

69 Hans Kristensen, 'The matrix of deterrence', May 2001, www.nautilus.org/nukestrat/USA/force/index.html.

70 William Arkin and Hans Kristensen, 'Dangerous directions', in: *The Bulletin of the Atomic Scientists*, March/April 1998, 30. See also Hans Kristensen, 'The matrix of deterrence', May 2001, www.nautilus.org/nukestrat/USA/force/index.html.

71 Michael MccGwire, 'The anatomy of the argument', in: Joseph Rotblat (ed), *Nuclear Weapons. The road to zero*, 1998, 26; CISAC even speaks of a 2,000 START II level proposed by Yeltsin, in: US National Academy of Sciences, CISAC, *The future of US nuclear weapons policy*, 1997, 60.

72 Brian Hall, 'Overkill is not dead', in: *The New York Times Magazine*, 15th of March 1998.

73 *Ibid.*

74 Ole Holsti, 'A widening gap between the US military and civilian society ? Some evidences: 1976-1996', in: *International Security*, Winter 1998/1999, 8.

75 The fact that three leading Republicans – House Speaker Newt Gingrich, Senate Majority leader Trent Lott, and Dich Cheney – did not go to Vietnam neither, was apparently not noticed.

76 Col.Charles Dunlop, 'Welcome to the junta: the erosion of civilian control of the US military', in: *Wake Forest Law Review*, 1994, vol.29, 366-367. It is not by chance that Presidential candidate Al Gore mentioned the fact that he *did* go to Vietnam in his speeches. See for instance his foreign policy speech at the International Press Institute in Boston on the 30th of April 2000.

77 David Rosenbaum, 'Pentagon spending could be cut in half', in: *The New York Times*, 13th of December 1989.

78 X, 'Excerpts from President-elect's News Conference in Arkansas', in: *The New York Times*, 13th of November 1992.

79 David Hackworth, 'Rancour in the ranks: the troops versus the President', in: *Newsweek*, 28th of June 1993, quoted by Charles Dunlap, 'Welcome to the junta: the erosion of civilian control of the US military', in: *Wake Forest Law Review*, 1994, vol.29, no.2.

80 For an overview of his life and career, see Jeffrey Smith, 'The dissenter', in: *The Washington Post*, 7th of December 1997, W18.

81 David Ottaway and Steve Coll, 'Unplugging the war machine', in: *The Washington Post*, 12th of April 1995, A28.

82 Lee Butler, speech to the Canadian Network for Abolition of nuclear weapons, 11th of March 1999.

83 Lee Butler, 'Disestablishing SAC', in: *Air Power History*, Fall 1993, 4-6.

84 Michael Klare, *Rogue states and nuclear outlaws*, 1995, 10.

85 William Arkin, 'Unindicted co-conspirators', in: *The Bulletin of the Atomic Scientists*, July/August 1992, 12.

86 Ivo Daalder, 'What vision for the nuclear future ?' In: *The Washington Quarterly*, Spring 1995, 132.

87 Congressional hearing before the Senate Armed Services Committee on the 22d of April 1993, DOD Authorization for Appropriations for FY 1994 and the future years defence program, 1994, 407.

88 David Ottaway and Steve Coll, *ibid.*.

89 A cynical explanation would be that Lee Butler de-legitimised nuclear weapons in order to level the playing field for what has been described by some as an alternative for nuclear deterrence, namely missile defence. Lee Butler was part of the Rumsfeld Commission in 1998 that gave a boost to NMD, and the agency he led, STRATCOM, nowadays has missile defence in its portfolio. In the same vein, this may explain why the head of SPACECOM Gen.Charles Horner was in favour of elimination during his active career (see Chapter 8).

90 Lee Butler, 'The responsibility to end the nuclear madness', speech at the Nuclear Age Peace Foundation, 30th of April 1999, in: *Waging Peace Worldwide*, Summer 1999, Special report, iii.

91 Frank von Hippel, 'Working in the White House on nonproliferation and arms control', in: *Federation of American Scientists Public Interest Report*, March/April 1995.

92 Frank von Hippel, *ibid.* My emphasis.

93 Stephen Cambone, *A new structure for national security policy planning*, 1998, 225-226.

94 See principals level.

95 Letter from John Deutch to Les Aspin, in: US Congress, House of Representatives Committee on Armed Services, Defence Policy Panel, 'Shaping nuclear policy for the 1990's: a compendium of views', 102d Congress, 2nd session, Washington DC, US Government Printing Office, December 1992, 205-206.

96 Nick Kotz, 'Mission impossible; John Deutch is quick, smart, and tough', in: *The Washingtonian*, December 1995, 45.

97 Thomas Lippman and Jeffrey Smith, 'Arms wrestling with the Pentagon', in: *The Washington Post*, 4th of August 1994, A29.

98 For instance, Deutch received 42,500 $ in consulting fees in 1992. See: Patrick Sloyan, 'Pentagon's sweet deal: top-brass gave breaks to ex-employer', in: *Newsday*, 30th of June 1994, A3, quoted by Sanford Gottlieb, *Defense addiction*, 1997, 25.

99 Interviews.

100 Nick Kotz, *ibid.*, 53.

101 DOD press briefing on the NPR on the 22d of September 1994; NPR slide 32.

102 Nick Kotz, 'Mission impossible', in: *The Washingtonian*, December 1995, 45.

103 Thomas Lippman and Jeffrey Smith, 'Arms wrestling with the Pentagon', in: *The Washington Post*, 4th of August 1994, A29; Peter Gray, 'O'Leary versus Deutch', in: *The Bulletin of the Atomic Scientists*, November/December 1994, 10-11.

104 Andrew and Leslie Cockburn, *One point safe*, 1997, 191.

105 Leon Sigal, *Disarming strangers*, 1998, 189-190.

106 John Deutch, 'A nuclear posture for today', in: *Foreign Affairs*, vol.84, no.1, January/February 2005.

107 Michael Boldrick, 'The Nuclear posture review: liabilities and risks', in: *Parameters*, Winter 1995-1996, 82; Janne Nolan, *An elusive consensus*, 1999, 43, 51.

108 Otfried Nassauer, 'Retired Senior US Commander recommends "zero tacnukes"', in: *PENN Newsletter*, no.16, July 2002, 6.

109 Sean O'Neill, 'Leon Fuerth. Tutoring "Prince Albert"', in: *World Policy Journal*, Winter 1999/2000, 57.

110 Letter of Leon Fuerth to Les Aspin, 13th of February 1992, in: US Congress, House of Representatives Committee on Armed Services, Defence Policy Panel, 'Shaping nuclear

policy for the 1990's: a compendium of views', 102d Congress, 2nd session, Washington DC, US Government Printing Office, December 1992, 231.

[111] Sean O'Neill, 'Leon Fuerth. Tutoring "Prince Albert"', in: *World Policy Journal*, Winter 1999/2000, 55.

[112] *Ibid.*, 55.

[113] *Ibid.*, 56.

[114] Ashton Carter, William Perry and John Steinbruner, *A new concept of cooperative security*, 1992, 8.

[115] William Perry, 'Desert Storm and deterrence in the future', in: Joseph Nye and Roger Smith (eds), *After the Storm: lessons from the Gulf War*, 1992, 260.

[116] Interview with Leo Mackay (by telephone) on the 10th of February 1999.

[117] Sanford Gotlieb, *Defense addiction*, 1997, 260.

[118] Interview with Steve Fetter in Washington DC on the 24th of June 1998.

[119] Interview with Leo Mackay (by telephone) on the 10th of February 1999.

[120] Congressional hearings before the Senate Armed Services Committee, William Perry's nomination hearing on the 3d of February 1994, 62.

[121] X, 'Mr Perry's backward nuclear policy', in: *New York Times*, 24th of March 1994, A22.

[122] William Perry, 'Small nuclear arsenal is defense dept. goal', in: *The New York Times*, 31st of March 1994.

[123] Jeffrey Smith, 'Clinton decides to retain Bush nuclear arms policy', in: *The Washington Post*, 22d of September 1994, A26.

[124] John Steinbruner, 'Conventional and nuclear defense', in: Mark Green, *Changing America: Blueprints for a new administration*, 1992, 233. My emphasis.

[125] John Steinbruner, 'Conventional and nuclear defense', in: Mark Green (ed), *Changing America: blueprints for the new administration*, 1992, 239.

[126] Morton Halperin and Arnold Kanter, *Readings in American Foreign Policy*, 1973, 16.

[127] Richard Neustadt, *Presidential power*, 27.

[128] Charles Kegley and Eugene Wittkopf, *American Foreign Policy*, 1987, 306. My emphasis.

[129] Steve Miller, 'Politics over promise', in: *International Security*, Spring 1984, 89, referring to McGeorge Bundy, 'To cap the volcano', in: *Foreign Affairs*, October 1969.

[130] Stansfield Turner, *Caging the nuclear genie*, 1997, 109-110; see also John Newhouse, *De wapenwedloop*, 1990, 456.

[131] Janne Nolan, *Guardians of the arsenal*, 1989, 284.

[132] Janne Nolan, *Guardians of the arsenal*, 1989, 74. For leadership examples of McNamara, see also Steven Weber, 'Interactive learning in US-Soviet arms control', in: George Breslauer and Philip Tetlock (ed), *Learning in US and Soviet foreign policy*, 1991, 794-797.

[133] James Goldgeier, 'NATO expansion: the anatomy of a decision', in: *The Washington Quarterly*, Winter 1998, 98.

[134] Janne Nolan, *An elusive consensus*, 1999, 40.

[135] Janne Nolan, *ibid.*, 51.

[136] Leon Sigal, *Disarming strangers*, 1998, 53.

[137] Stansfield Turner, *Caging the nuclear genie*, 1997, 108.

[138] Bill Clinton, 'A new covenant for American security', speech delivered on the 12th of December 1991 at Georgetown University, published in: *Harvard International Review*, Summer 1992, 28. My emphasis.

[139] X, 'Excerpts from President's elect's New Conference in Arkansas', in: *The New York Times*, 13th of November 1992. My emphasis.

[140] Aspin's nomination hearing on the 7th of January 1993, Nominations before the Senate Armed Services Committee, first session, 103d Congress, 1994, 12. My emphasis.

[141] Michael Krepon, 'Do it better and smarter', in: *The Bulletin of the Atomic Scientists*, vol.51, no.6, November/December 1995, p.13.

[142] On his liberal arms control policy, see Janne Nolan, *An elusive consensus*, 1999, 38; on his liberal defence policy, see Janne Nolan , 'Cooperative security in the US', in: Janne Nolan,

Global Engagement, 1994, 512-513; on the CTBT, see Clinton's speech at Sandia Lab in September 1992, quoted by Frank von Hippel and Tom Collina, 'Testing, testing, 1,2,3 forever', in: *The Bulletin of the Atomic Scientists*, July/August 1993, 30; on his liberal foreign policy ideas, see Thomas Friedman, 'Clinton and foreign issues: spasms of attention', in: *The New York Times*, 22d of March 1993, A3.

[143] Bert Wayne, *The reluctant superpower*, 1997, 198.

[144] Janne Nolan, *An elusive consensus*, 1999, 38; Stephen Cambone and Patrick Garrity, 'The future of US nuclear policy', in: *Survival*, Winter 1994/1995, 73.

[145] Bert Rockman, 'Leadership style and the Clinton presidency', in: Colin Campbell and Bert Rockman, *The Clinton presidency*, 1996, 349.

[146] Larry Berman and Emily Goldman, 'Clinton's foreign policy at midterm', in: Colin Campbell and Bert Rockman, *The Clinton presidency: first appraisals*, 1996, 291, 294, 296.

[147] Larry Berman and Emily Goldman, *ibid.*, 297-8.

[148] Robert Manning, 'Ending the nuclear century', in: *The New Democrat*, January/February 1995, 54.

[149] Robert Manning, 'Abbot and Costello. Nuclear policy', in: *Intellectual Capital.com*, 17th of February 2000.

[150] Thomas Friedman, 'Clinton and foreign issues: spasms of attention', in: *The New York Times*, 22d of March 1993.

[151] Richard Haass, 'The squandered presidency', in: *Foreign Affairs*, May/June 2000, 136-137.

[152] Leslie Gelb, 'Where's Bill ?' In: *The New York Times*, 11th of March 1993.

[153] Colin Campbell, 'Managing the sandbox: why the Clinton White House failed to cope with gridlock', in: Colin Campbell and Bert Rockman (ed), *The Clinton presidency: first appraisals*, 1996, 67; David Halberstam, *War in a time of peace*, 2002, 241-242.

[154] Leslie Gelb, 'Where's Bil ?' In: *The New York Times*, 11th of March 1993.

[155] David Halberstam, *ibid.*, 2002. For Woolsey, see p.244; for Aspin, see p.244, 256-257, 259.

[156] See also Stephen Walt, 'Two cheers for Clinton's foreign policy', in: *Foreign Affairs*, March/April 2000, 78.

[157] Lawrence Korb, 'Our overstuffed armed forces', in: *Foreign Affairs*, November/December 1995, 28.

[158] William Hartung, 'Ready for what ? The new politics of Pentagon spending', in: *World Policy Journal*, Spring 1999, 19-20.

[159] Dunbar Lockwood, 'On Clinton's calendar', in: *The Bulletin of the Atomic Scientists*, January/February 1993, 7.

[160] Stephen Walt, 'Two cheers for Clinton's foreign policy', in: *Foreign Affairs*, March/April 2000, 73. Finally, Clinton did not give the go-ahead for the deployment of NMD. But he did not halt the development neither.

[161] Gregory Foster, 'Clinton's choice', in: *The Bulletin of the Atomic Scientists*, January/February 1995, 19.

[162] Stephen Cambone and Patrick Garrity, 'The future of US nuclear policy', in: *Survival*, Winter 1994-1995, 79.

[163] John Parachini, 'US Senate ratification of the CWC', in: *Nonproliferation Review*, Fall 1997, 64.

[164] Stephen Schwartz, 'Outmaneuvered, outgunned, and out of view', in: *The Bulletin of the Atomic Scientists*, January/February 2000.

[165] 'Bill Clinton: a leader for America in the post-cold war era', advertisement in: *The New York Times*, 17th of August 1992.

[166] Bill Clinton, 'A new covenant for American security', speech delivered on the 12th of December 1991 at Georgetown University, published in: *Harvard International Review*, Summer 1992, 27. My emphasis.

[167] Lawrence Korb, 'Our overstuffed armed forces', in: *Foreign Affairs*, November/December 1995, 30.

[168] X, 'Campaign '92', in: *The Washington Post*, 16th of October 1992.

[169] Richard Neustadt, *Presidential power*, 1980, 125. My emphasis.

[170] Fred Greenstein, 'The presidential leadership style of Bill Clinton: an early appraisal', in: *Political Science Quarterly*, vol.108, no.4, 1993-1994, 596.

[171] Scott Webster, 'Bill Clinton, political centrism and presidential leadership', paper prepared for APSA, Boston, 1998.

[172] William Safire, 'The Demo-Labor Party', in: *The New York Times*, 12th of November 1997.

[173] John Hale, 'The making of the New Democrats', in: *Political Science Quarterly*, volume 110, no.2, 1995.

[174] David Halberstam, *War in a time of peace*, 2002, 244.

[175] Richard Kohn, 'Out of Control', in: *National Interest*, Spring 1994, 13; see also Lawrence Korb, 'Our overstuffed armed forces', in: *Foreign Affairs*, November/December 1995, 28.

[176] For instance Clinton's remarks to the Community in Des Moines, 21st of February 1996; his remarks at a fundraising diner in New York City, 15th of February 1996; his remarks to the community in Rochester, New York, 17th of February 1996 [all on ACDA website]; Clinton's speech in Los Alamos on the 3d of February 1998, in: *Disarmament Diplomacy*, February 1998, 36.

[177] Janne Nolan, *An elusive consensus*, 1999, 103-104, 107.

[178] Alan Cranston, 'The role of civil society', remarks at the Nuclear Age Peace Foundation, on the 30th of April 1999, in: *Waging Peace Worldwide*, Special report, Summer 1999, vi.

[179] Joseph Cirincione, 'Nonproliferation paralysis: the decline and stall of US policy', in: *Disarmament Diplomacy*, September 1998, no.30, 5.

[180] Colin Powell, *My American Journey*, 1995, 563.

[181] John Isaacs, 'Pentagon clings to costly lifestyle', in: *The Bulletin of the Atomic Scientists*, April 1993, 4.

[182] Interviews.

[183] Colin Powell, *ibid.*, 578.

[184] Elizabeth Drew, *On the edge*, 1994, 357; Colin Powell, *ibid.*, 578.

[185] Eric Schmitt, 'A stormy tenure', in: *The New York Times*, 16th of December 1993, A1; David Evans, 'His indecision was final', in: *The Washington Post*, 19th of December 1993, C3.

[186] David Halberstam, *War in a time of peace*, 2002, 246.

[187] Fred Barnes, 'You are fired', in: *The New Republic*, 10 & 17 January 1994, 13; see also Colin Powell, *ibid.*, 575.

[188] Barton Gellman and Jeffrey Smith, 'Hesitant by design', in: *The Washington Post*, 14th of November 1993.

[189] Ken Adelman, 'Summing up', in: *The Washingtonian*, July 1995, 28.

[190] Elizabeth Drew, *ibid.*, 358.

[191] Marc Millot, 'Facing the emerging reality of regional nuclear adversaries', in: *The Washington Quarterly*, Summer 1994, 54.

[192] Colin McInnes, 'From the bottom-up ?' in: *Contemporary Security Policy*, December 1994, 160-161, 164.

[193] Elizabeth Drew, *ibid.*, 356-357.

[194] Thomas Friedman, 'Others tottered earlier, but Aspin fell'' in: *The New York Times*, 17th of December 1993, B13.

[195] Barton Gellman and Jeffrey Smith, 'Hesitant by design', in: *The Washington Post*, 14th of November 1993, A1.

[196] Colin Powell, *ibid.*, 570; see also Craig Rimmerman, 'Promise Unfulfilled', in: Craig Rimmerman, *Gay rights, military wrongs*, 1996, 111-126.

[197] Eric Mlyn, 'US nuclear policy and the end of the Cold War', in: T.V. Paul, *The absolute weapon*, 1998, 206.

[198] Morton Halperin and Arnold Kanter (ed), *Readings in American Foreign Policy*, 1973, 20.

[199] Interview with Steve Fetter in Washington DC on the 24th of June 1998.

[200] Ashton Carter, 'Foreword', in: Michèle Flournoy, *Nuclear weapons after the Cold War*, xiii. My emphasis.

[201] Ashton Carter, William Perry, and John Steinbruner, *A new concept of cooperative security*, 1992, 6.

[202] Janne Nolan, *An elusive consensus*, 1999, 51.

[203] Interviews.

[204] William Arkin, 'Bad posture', in: *The Bulletin of the Atomic Scientists*, July-August 1994, 64.

[205] William Arkin, *ibid.*, 64; interviews; Janne Nolan, 'Preparing for the 2001 Nuclear Posture Review', in: *Arms Control Today*, November 2000.

[206] Interviews. See for instance Carter's reaction vis-à-vis the State Department concerning North Korea, in: Leon Sigal, *Disarming strangers*, 1998, 60.

[207] Michael Boldrick, 'The Nuclear Posture Review: liabilities and risks', in: *Parameters*, Winter 1995-1996, 83.

[208] Interview Clinton appointee.

[209] Janne Nolan, *An elusive consensus*, 1999, 56.

[210] Interview.

[211] Janne Nolan, *An elusive consensus*, 1999, 51.

[212] *Ibid.*, 1999, 55.

[213] Jeffrey Smith, 'Clinton decides to retain Bush nuclear arms policy', in: *The Washington Post*, 22d of September 1994.

[214] Andrew Bacevich, 'Clinton's military problems – and ours', in: *National Review*, 13th of December 1993; Richard Kohn, 'Out of control: the crisis in civil-military relations', in: *National Interest*, Spring 1994, in which he typifies Clinton as the 'president with less experience, interest, understanding, and credibility in military affairs than any since the 1920s', 4; Edward Luttwak, 'Washington's biggest scandal', in: *Commentary*, May 1994; Thomas Ricks, 'The widening gap between the military and society', in: *Atlantic Monthly*, July 1997; Ole Holsti, 'A widening gap between the US military and civilian society ? Some evidence, 1976-96', in: *International Security*, Winter 1998/1999. For a critique of the latter, see Joseph Collins, in: 'Correspondence', *International Security*, Fall 1999.

[215] Jeffrey Smith, 'Clinton decides to retain Bush nuclear arms policy', in: *The Washington Post*, 22d of September 1994; Michael Boldrick, 'The nuclear posture review', in: *Parameters*, Winter 1995-1996, 83.

[216] Edward Luttwak, 'Washington's biggest scandal', in: *Commentary*, May 1994, 29-31.

[217] Stansfield Turner, *Caging the nuclear genie*, 1997, 118-119.

[218] John Hamre, 'Toward a nuclear strategy', in: *Washington Post*, 2 May 2005, p.A17.

[219] Alexei Arbatov, 'Superseding US-Russian nuclear deterrence', in: *Arms Control Today*, Jnauary/February 2005.

[220] Lee Butler, 'Zero tolerance', in: *The Bulletin of the Atomic Scientists*, January/February 2000, 73.

[221] John Isaacs, 'Test ban fizzles', in: *The Bulletin of the Atomic Scientists*, November/December 1999, 22.

[222] Robert Manning, 'Abbot and Costello Nuclear policy', in: *Intellectual Capital.com*, 17 February 2000.

[223] Stephen Rosenfeld, 'Drift on the slope to a minimum nuclear deterrent', in: *International Herald Tribune*, 7th of March 2000.

Chapter 11

[1] Frank von Hippel and Tom Collina, 'Nuclear junkies: testing, testing, 1,2,3 – forever', in: *The Bulletin of the Atomic Scientists*, July/August 1993, 30.

[2] Walter Pincus, 'Nuclear arms plans: saving, not scrapping', in: *The Washington Post*, 9th of January 2002, A04.

[3] Frank von Hippel and Tom Collina, 'Nuclear junkies: testing, testing, 1,2,3 – forever', in: *The Bulletin of the Atomic Scientists*, July/August 1993, 28.

[4] Frank von Hippel and Tom Collina do not seem to agree with regard to the attitude of Les Aspin. They state: 'By mid-May, Les Aspin was leading the charge. The SOD, according to Defence Daily (May 14, 1993), had "flatly turned down the urgings of two top advisers, the Joint Chiefs of Staff, the Energy Department and the directors of the three US nuclear weapons laboratories to defy a substantial majority in Congress and continue to test nuclear warheads through the 1990's"'. Frank von Hippel and Tom Collina, 'Nuclear junkies', in: *The Bulletin of the Atomic Scientists*, July/August 1993, 31.

[5] Jeffrey Smith and Ann Devroy, 'US drops nuclear test plans', in: *The Washington Post*, 30th of June 1993.

[6] Spurgeon Keeny and others, 'The administration, Congress and testing', in: *Arms Control Today*, August 1993, 6.

[7] Harald Müller, 'Nuclear weapons and German interests: an attempt at redefinition', in: *PRIF Report*, no.55, 2000, 7.

[8] Christopher Ogden, 'Call this leadership ?', in: *Time Magazine*, 18th of October 1999; Tony Judt, 'An errant superpower flaunts its ignorance', in: *International Herald Tribune*, 18th of October 1999; Daryl Kimball, 'How the US Senate rejected CTBT ratification', in: *Disarmament Diplomacy*, no.40, September/October 1999, 8; Stephen Schwartz, 'Outmaneuvered, outgunned, and out of view. Test Ban debacle', in: *The Bulletin of the Atomic Scientists*, January/February 2000, 24-31.

[9] In 2005, the State Department also merged the arms control and nonproliferation bureaus. See: Nicholas Kralev, 'Powell OKs merging arms-focused bureaus', in: *The Washington Times*, 12 January 2005.

[10] Terry Deibel, 'The death of a treaty', in: *Foreign Affairs*, September/October 2002, 146-147.

[11] Stephen Schwartz, 'Outmaneuvered, outgunned, and out of view', in: *The Bulletin of the Atomic Scientists*, January/February 2000, 27.

[12] Jacques Chirac, Tony Blair and Gerhard Schröder, 'A treaty we all need', in: *The New York Times*, 8th of October 1999.

[13] The lab directors did not support CTBT ratification anymore in 1999. Eliot Marshall, 'Scientific groups endorse test ban', in: *Science*, 15th of October 1999, vol.286, 388; Kurt Gottfried, 'Sowing nuclear misconceptions', in: *Nature*, 13th of January 2000, 131-133.

[14] François Heisbourg, 'A shotgun note that could reverberate around the world', in: *International Herald Tribune*, 18th of October 1999.

[15] Daryl Kimball, 'How the US Senate rejected CTBT ratification', in: *Disarmament Diplomacy*, no.40, September/October 1999, 11-12.

[16] Terry Deibel, 'The death of a treaty', in: *Foreign Affairs*, September/October 2002, 143, 151.

[17] X, 'America's world', in: *The Economist*, 23d of October 1999.

[18] William Drozdiak, 'Allies ask: does US really want arms control ?', in: *International Herald Tribune*, 16th of June 2000.

[19] Bradley Graham, 'Shaliskashvili will head effort to revive nuclear test ban treaty', in: *The Washington Post*, 28th of January 2000, A14; US Department of State, Washington File, 13th of March 2000.

[20] Hans Kristensen, 'Targets of opportunity', in: *The Bulletin of the Atomic Scientists*, September/October 1997, 22.

[21] Hans Kristensen, 'Targets of opportunity', in: *The Bulletin of the Atomic Scientists*, September/October 1997, 22.

[22] William Arkin, 'Nuclear junkies', in: *The Bulletin of the Atomic Scientists*, July/August 1993, 27.

[23] William Arkin, 'Agnosticism when real values are needed', in: *Federation of American Scientists Public Interest Report*, September/October 1994, 8; Jeffrey Smith, 'US urged to cut 50 % of A-arms', in: *The Washington Post*, 6th of January 1992, A1.

[24] William Arkin 'Agnosticism when real values are needed', in: *Federation of American Scientists Public Interest Report*, September/October 1994, 9; David Ottaway and Steve Coll, 'US debates to halt nuclear spread', in: *Washington Post*, 10th of April 1995.

[25] Hans Kristensen, 'Targets of opportunity', in: *The Bulletin of the Atomic Scientists*, October/November 1997.

[26] Elizabeth Drew, *On the edge,* 1994, 356.

[27] Heather Wilson, 'Missed opportunities', in: Peter Hays (ed), *American Defense Policy*, 1997, 451.

[28] Les Aspin, *The report of the Bottom-up-Review*, October 1993, 6. My emphasis.

[29] Interview with Matthew Bunn in Cambridge (Mass.) on the 26th of July 1999.

[30] Les Aspin, *The report of the Bottom-up-Review*, October 1993, 6.

[31] Http://www.fas.org/irp/offdocs/pdd18.htm. My emphasis.

[32] Jim Mann, 'New US nuclear policy to focus on rogue regimes', in: *Los Angeles Times*, 9th of May 1994.

[33] Leonard Spector, 'Neo-nonproliferation', in: *Survival*, Spring 1995; Matthias Dembinski (and others), 'NATO and nonproliferation', in: *PRIF Report*, 1994, 42-45.

[34] Leon Sigal, *Disarming strangers*, 1998, 112.

[35] Thomas Friedman, 'Others tottered earlier, but Aspin fell', in: *The New York Times*, 17th of December 1993.

[36] Harald Müller and Mitchell Reiss, 'Counterproliferation', in: *The Washington Quarterly*, Spring 1995, 144.

[37] Henry Sokolski, 'Mission impossible', in: *The Bulletin of the Atomic Scientists*, March/April 2001, p.67.

[38] Hans Kristensen, 'Targets of opportunity', in: *The Bulletin of the Atomic Scientists*, September/October 1997, 25.

[39] Janne Nolan, *An elusive consensus*, 1999, 75.

[40] Scott Sagan, 'The commitment trap', in: *International Security*, Spring 2000, vol.24, no.4, 102.

[41] Janne Nolan, *An elusive consensus*, 1999, 79.

[42] Janne Nolan, 'The next Nuclear Posture Review ?', in: Harold Feiveson (ed), *The nuclear turning-point*, 1999, 273.

[43] Greg Mello, 'New bomb, no mission', in: *The Bulletin of the Atomic Scientists*, May/June 1997.

[44] Janne Nolan, 'The next Nuclear Posture Review ?' in: Harold Feiveson (ed), *The nuclear turning-point*, 1999, 267.

[45] Gilles Andréani, 'The disarray of US nonproliferation policy', in: *Survival*, Winter 1999-2000, 56-57.

[46] Nicola Butler, 'NATO at 50: papering over the cracks', in: *Disarmament Diplomacy*, June 1999, 5.

[47] Janne Nolan, *An elusive consensus*, 1999, 65; Janne Nolan, 'Preparing for the 2001 Nuclear Posture Review', in: *Arms Control Today*, November 2000.

[48] Janne Nolan, *An elusive consensus*, 1999, 67.

[49] GAO, *Strategic weapons. Nuclear weapons targeting process*, September 1991.

[50] Hans Kristensen and Joshua Handler, 'The USA and counterproliferation', in: *Security Dialogue*, vol.27, 1996, 389.

[51] Eric Schmitt, 'Head of nuclear forces plans for a new world', in: *The New York Times*, 25th of February 1993, B7.

[52] William Arkin, 'Nuclear junkies', in: *The Bulletin of the Atomic Scientists*, July/August 1993, 27.

[53] Hans Kristensen, 'Targets of opportunity', in: *The Bulletin of the Atomic Scientists*, September/October 1997, 24.

[54] Hans Kristensen, *ibid.,* 24; Hans Kristensen, 'US strategic nuclear reform in the 1990's', website Nautilus Institute, March 2000.

55 William Arkin and Hans Kristensen, 'Dangerous directions', in: *The Bulletin of the Atomic Scientist*, March/April 1998, 30.

56 Ibid., 28.

57 William Arkin, 'Nuclear junkies', in: *The Bulletin of the Atomic Scientists*, July/August 1993, 24.

58 Thomas Dowler and Joseph Howard III, 'Countering the threat of the well-armed tyrant: a modest proposal for small nuclear weapons', in: *Strategic Review*, Fall 1991; Thomas Ramos, 'The future of theater nuclear weapons', in: *Strategic Review*, Fall 1991.

59 William Arkin, 'Agnosticism when real values are needed', in: *Federation of American Scientists Public Interest Report*, September/October 1994, 8-9.

60 William Arkin, 'Nuclear junkies', in: *The Bulletin of the Atomic Scientists*, July/August 1993, 24.

61 Janne Nolan, *An elusive consensus*, 1999, 67.

62 William Arkin, *ibid.*, 24.

63 William Arkin, *ibid.*, 23, 27; Tom Zamora, 'New jobs for old labs ?' In: *The Bulletin of the Atomic Scientists*, November 1992, 15.

64 Hans Kristensen, 'Targets of opportunity', in: *The Bulletin of the Atomic Scientists*, September/October 1997, 26.

65 DOD Briefing, NPR, 22 September 1994.

66 Hans Kristensen, 'Targets of opportunity', in: *The Bulletin of the Atomic Scientists*, September/October 1997, 27.

67 Greg Mello, 'New bomb, no mission', in: *The Bulletin of the Atomic Scientists*, May/June 1997.

68 Michael Gordon, 'US nuclear plan sees new weapons and new targets', in: *The New York Times*, 10th of March 2002.

69 Walter Pincus, 'Nuclear plans go beyond cuts', in: *The Washington Post*, 19th of February 2002.

70 AFP, 'US Senate committee agrees to lift ban on development of small-scale nukes', 11th of May 2003.

71 Ken Guggenheim, 'Democrats push to retain nuclear ban', in: AP, 19th of May 2003.

72 James Sterngold, 'Battle brewing over Bush's plan for new nuclear arms', in: *San Francisco Gate.com*, 15 July 2003.

73 Spencer Abraham, 'Facing a new nuclear reality', in: *The Washington Post*, 21st of July 2003.

74 Karen Roston, 'Congress critical of Bush nuclear weapons budget', in: *Arms Control Today*, April 2004.

75 Linton Brooks, 'US nuclear weapons policies and programs, speech at the Heritage Foundation Conference "US Strategic Command: beyond the war on terrorism', 12th of May 2004.

Conclusion

1 Madeline Albright, speech at the Henry Stimson Center, 10th of June 1998. My emphasis.

2 Jonathan Schell, 'The folly of arms control', in: *Foreign Affairs*, September/October 2000, 46; John Steinbruner, interview.

3 Walter Pincus, 'House proposed Commission to assess nuclear forces', in: *The Washington Post*, 29th of May 2005, p.09.

BIBLIOGRAPHY

1. Books

Albright, David, Frans Berkhout, and William Walker, *Plutonium and highly enriched uranium 1996: World inventories, capabilities, and policies.* SIPRI and Oxford University Press, Oxford, 1997.

Allison, Graham and Gregory Treverton, *Rethinking America's security*, W.W.Norton & Company, New York, 1992.

Allison, Graham, and William Ury (ed), *Windows of opportunity. From cold war to peaceful competition in US-Soviet relations*, Ballinger Publishing Company, 1989.

Allison, Graham, Ashton Carter, Steven Miller and Philip Zelikow, *Cooperative denuclearization. From pledges to deeds*, Center for Science and International Affairs, Harvard University, Cambridge, January 1993.

Allison, Graham, *Essence of decision*, HarperCollins, New York, 1971.

Allison, Graham, Owen Cote, Richard Falkenrath, and Steven Miller, *Avoiding nuclear anarchy. Containing the threat of loose Russian nuclear weapons and fissile material*, MIT Press, Cambridge, 1996.

Arkin, William, Robert Norris, and Joshua Handler, *Taking stock. Worldwide nuclear deployments 1998*, NRDC, March 1998.

Baker, James, and Thomas de Frank, *The politics of diplomacy*, G.P.Putnam & Sons, 1995.

Ball, Desmond, *Politics and force levels. The strategic missile program of the Kennedy administration*, University of California Press, 1980.

Barash, David, *The arms race and nuclear war*, Wadsworth Publishing Company, Belmont, 1987.

Binnendijk, Hans and James Goodby, *Transforming nuclear deterrence*, National Defense University Press, July 1997.

Blackwill, Robert, and Albert Carnesale (ed), *New nuclear nations. Consequences for US policy*, Council on Foreign Relations Press, New York, 1993.

Blair, Bruce, *Strategic Command and Control: redefining the nuclear threat.* Brookings Institution, Washington DC, 1985.

Blair, Bruce, *The logic of accidental nuclear war.* The Brookings Institution, Washington DC, 1993.

Blair, Bruce, *Global zero alert for nuclear forces*, The Brookings Institution, Washington DC, 1995.

Booth, Ken, and Steve Smith, *International Relations Theory today*, Pennsylvania State University Press, 1995.

Bracken, Paul, *The command and control of nuclear forces*, Yale University Press, New Haven, 1983.

Breslauer, George, and Philip Tetlock (ed), *Learning in US and Soviet Foreign Policy*, Westview Press, Boulder, 1991.

Brodie, Bernard, *The absolute weapon.* Harcourt Brace, New York, 1946.

Bruce, Maxwell, and Tom Milne (ed), *The force of reason*, Macmillan, Basingstoke, 1998.

Buchan, Glenn, *US Nuclear strategy for the post-cold war era*, RAND, 1994.

Bundy, McGeorge, William Crowe, Sidney Drell, *Reducing nuclear danger*, Council on Foreign Relations Press, New York, 1993.

Bunn, Matthew, *The next wave. Urgently needed new steps to control warheads and nuclear material*, Harvard University, 2000.

Bunn, Matthew and Anthony Wier, *Controlling nuclear warheads and materials: a report card and action plan*, Harvard University, March 2003.

Bunn, Matthew and Anthony Wier, *Securing the bomb 2005: the new global imperatives*, Harvard University, May 2005.

Bush, George, and Brent Scowcroft, *A world transformed*, Alfred Knopf, New York, 1998.

Buzan, Bary, *An introduction to strategic studies: military technology and international relations*. Macmillan, London, 1987.

Cambone, Stephen, *A new structure for national security policy planning*, CSIS press, Washington DC, 1998.

Campbell, Colin, and Bert Rockman, *The Clinton presidency. First appraisals*, Chatham House Publishers, Chatham, 1996.

Campbell, Kurt, Ashton Carter, Steven Miller and Charles Zraket, *Soviet Nuclear Fission. Control of the nuclear arsenal in a disintegrating Soviet Union*, Center for Science and International Affairs, Harvard University Press, Cambridge, November 1991.

Canberra Commission Report on the elimination of nuclear weapons, August 1996.

Carlucci, Frank (ed), *Taking charge*, RAND, 2000.

Carnesale, Alberto (ed), *Living with nuclear weapons*. Harvard University Press, Cambridge (Mass.), 1983.

Carnesale, Alberto and Richard Haass (ed), *Superpower arms control*, Harper & Row, Cambridge, 1987.

Carter, Ashton and William Perry, *Preventive Defense. A new security strategy for America*, Brookings Institute, 1999.

Carter, Ashton, John Steinbruner and Charles Zraket (ed), *Managing Nuclear Operations*, Brookings Institution, 1987.

Carter, Ashton, William Perry, and John Steinbruner: *A new concept of cooperative security*, Brookings Institute, 1992.

Cockburn, Andrew, and Leslie Cockburn, *One point safe*, Anchor books, 1997.

Coté, Owen, *The Politics of innovative military doctrine: the US Navy and Fleet Ballistic missiles*, PhD dissertation MIT, 1996.

Cowen Karp, Regina (ed), *Security without nuclear weapons ? Different perspecives on non-nuclear security*. Oxford University Press/SIPRI, 1992.

Crowe, William, *The line of fire*, Simon and Schuster, 1993.

Dahl, Robert, *Controlling nuclear weapons: democracy versus guardianship*, Syracuse University Press, 1985.

Davis, Zachary, and Benjamin Frankel (eds), *The proliferation puzzle. Why nuclear weapons spread and what results ?* Frank Cass, London, 1993.

Deutsch, Karl, *The nerves of government. Models of political communication and control*, Macmillan, 1963.

Downs, Anthony, *Inside bureaucracy*, Little, Brown, Boston, 1967.

Drew, Elisabeth, *On the edge: the Clinton presidency*, Simon & Schuster, 1994.

Dyson, Freeman, *Weapons and Hope*. Harper and Row, New York, 1983.

Erikson, Erik, *Childhood and society*, WW Norton and Company, 1963 (2 ed).

Feaver Peter, *Guarding the guardians*. Cornell University Press, Ithaca, 1992.

Feiveson, Harold (ed), *The nuclear turning-point. A blue print for deep cuts and de-alerting of nuclear weapons*, Brookings Institution, Washington DC, 1999.

Feldman, Shai, *Israeli nuclear deterrence*, Columbia University Press, 1982.

Fellows, James, *National defense*, Random House, 1981.

Festinger, Leon, *A theory of cognitive dissonance*, Row, Evanston, 1957.

Fischer, David, *Towards 1995: the prospects for ending the proliferation of nuclear weapons*. Darthmouth/UNIDIR, 1993.

Flournoy, Michèle (ed), *Nuclear weapons after the cold war. Guidelines for US policy*, HarperCollins, 1993.

Ford, Daniel, *The button. The Pentagon's command and control system – does it work ?* Simon & Schuster, New York, 1985.

Freedman, Lawrence, *The evolution of nuclear strategy*. Macmillan, London, 1989.

Gardner, Howard, *Leading minds. An anatomy of leadership*, BasicBooks, New York, 1995.

Garrity, Patrick, and Steven Maaranen, *Nuclear weapons in the changing world*, Plenum Press, New York, 1992.

George, Alexander, *Presidential decision-making in foreign policy: the effective use of information and advice*, Westview Press, 1980.

Glaser, Charles, *Analyzing strategic nuclear policy*, Princeton University Press, Princeton, 1990.

Goldstein, Judith, and Robert Keohane (ed), *Ideas and foreign policy. Beliefs, institutions, and political change*, Cornell University Press, 1993.

Goodpaster, Andrew (chair), *An American Legacy. Building a nuclear-weapon-free world*. The final report of the Steering Committee, Project on eliminating weapons of mass destruction, Henry Stimson Center, March 1997.

Goodpaster, Andrew (chair), *An evolving US nuclear posture*. Second report of the Steering Committee, Project on eliminating weapons of mass destruction, Henry Stimson Center, December 1995.

Goodpaster, Andrew (chair), *Beyond the nuclear peril: the year in review and the years ahead*. Report of the Steering Committee, Project on eliminating weapons of mass destruction, Henry Stimson Center, January 1995.

Gottlieb, Sanford, *Defense addiction. Can America kick the habit ?* Westview Press, 1997.

Gray, Colin, *House of Cards: why arms control must fail*. Cornell University Press, Ithance, 1992.

Green, Mark, *Changing America: blueprints for the new administration*, Newmarket Press, 1992.

Greenstein, Fred, *Personality and politics*, Princeton University Press, Princeton, 1987.

Gusterson, Hugh, *Nuclear rites. A weapons laboratory at the end of the cold war*, University of California Press, 1996.

Haas, Ernst, *When knowledge is power*, University of California Press, Berkeley, 1990.

Halberstam, David, *War in a time of peace*, 2002.

Halperin, Morton, and Arnold Kanter, *Readings in American Foreign Policy; a bureaucratic perspective*, Little Brown, Boston, 1973.

Halperin, Morton, *Bureaucratic politics and foreign policy*, Brookings Institute, 1974.

Hays, Peter (ed), *American Defense Policy*, John Hopkins University Press, Baltimore, 1997.

Hermann, Charles (ed), American Defense Manual 1994, Lexington Books, 1994

Heywood, Andrew, Politics, Macmillan, 1997.

Hilsman, Roger, *The politics of policy-making in defense and foreign affairs*, Prentice-Hall, 1993.

IISS, *Strategic Survey 1997/1998.*

IISS, *Strategic Survey, 1989/1990.*

IISS, *Strategic Survey*, 2001/2002.

Iklé, Fred, and Sergei Karaganov (co-chairman), *Harmonizing the evolution of US and Russian defense policies*, CSIS, 1993.

INESAP, *Beyond the NPT: a nuclear-weapons free world*, 1995.

Jervis, Robert, *Perception and misperception in international politics*, Princeton University Press, Princeton, 1976.

Jervis, Robert, *The illogic of American nuclear strategy*, Cornell University Press, Ithaca, 1984.

Kaplan, Fred, *The wizards of armageddon*, Simon & Schuster, New York, 1983.

Kennan, George, *Memoirs 1925-1950*, Little, Brown, Boston, 1967.

Klare, Michael, *Rogue states and nuclear outlaws. America's search for a new foreign policy*, Hill and Wang, New York, 1995.

Kolkowics, Roman (ed), *The logic of nuclear terror*. Allen and Unwin, Boston, 1987.

Korb, Lawrence, *The road to nuclear security*, December 2004, 20 p.

Kull, Steven, *Minds at war; Nuclear reality and the inner conflicts of defense policymakers*, Basic Books, New York, 1988.

Lane, Gary, *New conventional weapons: reducing the reliance on a nuclear response toward aggressors*, US Air University, 2001.

Lasswell, Harold, *National security and individual freedom*, McGraw Hill, New York, 1950.

Lifton, Robert, and Richard Falk, *Indefensible weapons. The political and psychological case against nuclearism*. Basic Books, New York, 1982.

Lindblom, Charles, *The policy-making process*, Prentice-Hall, Englewood Cliffs, 1968.

Lindsay, James, *Congress and Nuclear Weapons*, The Johns Hopkins University Press, 1991.

Little, Richard, and Steve Smith (ed), *Belief systems and international relations*, Basil Blackwell, 1988.

Mackay, Leo, *Post-Cold War frameworks for US nuclear policy*, PhD thesis, Harvard University, Cambridge, March 1993.

Martel, William, and William Pendley, *Nuclear coexistence. Rethinking US policy to promote stability in an era of proliferation*. Air War College, Alabama, 1994.

May, Michael, and Roger Speed, *The role of US nuclear weapons in regional conflicts*, CISAC, Stanford University, 1994.

Mazarr, Michael, *Nuclear weapons in a transformed world*, St.Martin's Press, 1997.

Miall, Hugh, *Nuclear Weapons: who's in charge ?* Macmillan, Basingstoke, 1987.

Miller, Steven (ed), *Strategy and nuclear deterrence*, Princeton University Press, Princeton, 1984.

Millot, Marc, Roger Molander, and Peter Wilson, *"The day after..." study: nuclear proliferation in the post-cold war period*, RAND, 1993.

MIT Security Studies Program Conference Summary, *The future of Russian-US arms reductions*, 2-6 February 1998.

Mlyn, Eric, *The state, society, and limited nuclear war*, State University of New York Press, 1995.

Morgan, Patrick, *Deterrence. A conceptual analysis*. Sage, London, 1977.

Morgenthau, Hans, *Politics among nations*, fifth edition, Knopf, New York, 1973.

Mosher, David, and Lowell Schwartz, *Beyond the nuclear shadow*, RAND, 2003.

Neustadt, Richard, *Presidential power. The politics of leadership from FDR to Carter*, John Wiley & Sons, (1960), 1980.

Newhouse, John, *De wapenwedloop. Oorlog en vrede in het nucleaire tijdperk* (War and peace in the nuclear age), De Haan, 1990.

Nolan, Janne, *An elusive consensus. Nuclear weapons and American security after the Cold War*, Brookings Institution, Washington DC, 1999.

Nolan, Janne, *Global engagement*, Brookings Institute, Washington DC, 1994.

Nolan, Janne, *Guardians of the arsenal. The politics of nuclear strategy*, Basic Books, New York, 1989.

Nye, Joseph, and Roger Smith, *After the storm, Lessons from the Gulf War*, Madison Books, 1992.

O'Hanlon, Michael, *Defense planning for the late 1990s. Beyond the Desert Storm framework*, Brookings Institution, Washington DC, June 1995.

Olson, Mancur, *The logic of collective action*, Harvard University Press, Cambridge, 1971, (1965).

Olson, Mancur, *The rise and decline of nations*, Yale University Press, New Haven, 1982.

Our global neighbourhood, The Report of the Commission on Global Governance, Oxford University Press, 1995.

Paul, T.V., *The absolute weapon*, University of Michigan Press, 1998.

Posen, Barry, *The sources of military doctrines: France, Britain, and Germany between the two world wars*, Cornell University Press, Ithaca, 1984.

Powell, Colin, *My American journey*, Random House, New York, 1995.

Reychler, Luc, *Patterns of diplomatic thinking: a cross-national study of structural and social-psychological determinants*, Praeger Publishers, New York, 1979.

Rimmerman, Craig (ed), *Gay rights, military wrongs*, Garland, 1996.

Rokeach, Milton, *The open and closed mind*, Basic Books, New York, 1960.

Rotblat, Joseph, Jack Steinberger, and Bhalchandra Udgaonkar (eds), *A nuclear weapons free world. Desirable ? Feasible ?* Westview Press/Praeger, Boulder, 1993.

Rotblat, Joseph (ed), *Nuclear weapons. The road to zero*, Westview Press, 1998.

Russett, Bruce, *Controlling the sword: the democratic governance*, Harvard University Press, Cambridge, 1990.

Sagan, Scott, *The limits of safety. Organizations, accidents and nuclear weapons*. Princeton University Press, Princeton, 1993.

Sagan, Scott, *Moving targets. Nuclear strategy and national security*, Princeton

University Press, Princeton, 1989.

Saga, Scott, and Kenneth Waltz, *The spread of nuclear weapons*. W.W.Norton and Company, New York/London, 1995.

Sauer, Tom, *Nuclear arms control. Nuclear deterrence in the post-cold war period*, Macmillan/St.Martin's Press, Basingstoke, 1998.

Schelling, Thomas, *The strategy of conflict*. Oxford University Press, Oxford, 1966 (1960).

Schwartz, Stephen (ed), *Atomic Audit*, The Brookings Institute, Washington DC, 1998.

Sigal, Leon, *Disarming strangers. Nuclear diplomacy with North-Korea*, Princeton University Press, Princeton, 1998.

SIPRI Yearbook 2002.

Smith, Gerard, *Doubletalk. The story of the first Strategic Arms Limitation Talks*, Doubleday & Company, New York, 1980.

Snyder, Glenn, *Deterrence and defense*. Princeton University Press, Princeton, 1961.

Snyder, Jack, *The ideology of the offensive. Military decision making and the disasters of 1914*, Cornell University Press, Ithaca, 1984.

Steinbruner, John, *The cybernetic theory of decision. New dimensions of political analysis*, Princeton University Press, Princeton, 1974.

Taylor, Brian, *Breaking the disarmament deadlock*, Council for a Livable World Education Fund, June 1998.

Terriff, Terry, *The Nixon administration and the making of US nuclear strategy*, Cornell University Press, Ithaca, 1995.

The Commission of Global Governance, *The report of the Commission on Global Governance. Our Global Neighbourhood*. Oxford University Press, Oxford, 1995.

Turner, Stansfield, *Caging the nuclear genie. An American Challenge for Global Security*, Westview Press, Boulder, 1997.

US National Academy of Sciences, Committee on International Security and Arms Control, *The future of US Nuclear Weapons Policy*, National Academy Press, Washington DC, 1997, 110 p.

Van Evera, Stephen, *Guide to methods for students of political science*, Cornell University Press, Ithaca, 1997.

Vertzberger, Yaacov, *The world in their minds. Information, cognition, and perception in foreign policy decisionmaking*, Stanford University Press, 1990.

Viotti, Paul, and Mark Kauppi, *International relations theory: realism, pluralism, globalism*, Macmillan, New York, 1987, 613 p.

Wayne, Bert, *The reluctant superpower: US' policy in Bosnia, 1991-95*, StMartin's Press, 1997.

Younger, Stephen, *Nuclear weapons in the 21st century*, June 2000.

Zelnick, Bob, *Gore. A political life*, Regnery Publications, 1999.

2. Articles in magazines

Adelman, Ken, Summing up (interview with Les Aspin), in: *Washingtonian*, July 1995, 25-28.

Adler, Emanuel, The emergence of cooperation. National epistemic communities and the international evolution of the idea of nuclear arms control, in: *International Organization*, 46, 1, Winter 1992.

Albright, Madeline, A call for American consensus, in: *Time Magazine*, 22 November 1999.

Allison, Graham, How to stop nuclear terror, in: *Foreign Affairs*, vol.81, no.1, January/February 2004, 64-74.

Andréani, Gilles, The disarray of US non-proliferation policy, in: *Survival*, Winter 1999/2000, 42-61.

Andreasen, Steve, Reagan was right: Lest's ban ballistic missiles, in: *Survival*, vol.46, no.1, Spring 2004.

Arbatov, Alexei, Military reform in Russia: dilemmas, obstacles, and prospects, in: *BCSIA Discussion Papers*, Harvard University, September 1997.

Arbatov, Alexei, Superseding US-Russian nuclear deterrence, in: *Arms Control Today*, January/February 2005.

Arkin, William, A tale of two Franks, in: *The Bulletin of the Atomic Scientists*, March/April 1995, 80.

Arkin, William, Agnosticism when real values are needed: nuclear policy in the Clinton administration, in: *Federation of American Scientists Public Interest Report*, vol 47, no.5, September/October 1994.

Arkin, William, and Hans Kristensen, Dangerous directions, in: *The Bulletin of the Atomic Scientists*, March/April 1998, 26-31.

Arkin, William, Bad posture, in: *The Bulletin of the Atomic Scientists*, July/August 1994, 64.

Arkin, William, No nukes, or new nukes ?, in: *The Bulletin of the Atomic Scientists*, November/December 2000, 84.

Arkin, William, Nuclear Junkies: those lovalbe little bombs. In: *The Bulletin of the Atomic Scientists*, July/August 1993, 22-26.

Arkin, William, Robert Norris, and Hans Kristensen, Russian nuclear forces 2002, in: *The Bulletin of the Atomic Scientists*, July/August 2002.

Arkin, William, Unindicted co-conspirators, in: *The Bulletin of the Atomic Scientists*, July/August 1992, 12-13.

Arkin, William, What's "new" ?, in: *The Bulletin of the Atomic Scientists*, November/December 1997, 22-27.

Aspin, Les, Three propositions for a new era nuclear policy, Commencement address at MIT, 1 June 1992.

Bacevich, A.J., Civilian control: a useful fiction ? in: *Joint Forces Quarterly*, Winter 1994-1995, 76-79.

Bacevich, A.J., Clinton's military problem – and ours, in: *National Review*, 13 December 1993, 36-40.

Bailey, Kathleen, <u>Problems with a chemical weapons ban</u>. In: *Orbis*, Spring 1992.

Bailey, Kathleen, <u>Why we have to keep the bomb</u>. In: *The Bulletin of the Atomic Scientists*, January/February 1995, 30-37.

Ball, Desmond, <u>Can nuclear war be controlled ?</u> in: *Adelphi papers*, 169, 1981.

Barnes, Fred, <u>You're fired</u>, in: *The New Republic*, 10 & 17 January 1994, 12-14.

Bell, Bob, remarks at the 7th Carnegie International Non-proliferation Conference, 11-12 January 1999.

Bell, Robert, <u>Strategic agreements and the CTB Treaty: striking the right balance</u>, in: *Arms Control Today*, January/February 1998, 3-10.

Belous, Vladimir, <u>Key aspects of the Russian nuclear strategy</u>, in: *Security Dialogue*, vol.28 (2), 1997, 159-171.

Blair, Bruce, <u>Cold war era assumptions drive US nuclear force levels: why the target list should shrink</u>, in: *Coalition to reduce nuclear dangers & CDI Issue Brief*, vol.4, no.7, 18 May 2000.

Blair, Bruce, Harold Feiveson, and Frank Von Hippel, <u>Taking Nuclear Weapons off Hair-Trigger Alert</u>, in: *Scientific American*, November 1997, 82-89.

Blair, Bruce, in: *Federation of American Scientists Public Interest Report*, January/February 1998.

Blair, Bruce, <u>Loose cannon</u>, in: *National Interest*, Summer 1998, 87-92.

Blair, Bruce, <u>Removing the hair trigger on nuclear forces</u>, remarks prepared for 7th Carnegie International Non-proliferation Conference, 11-12 January 1999.

Blechman, Barry, and Cathleen Fischer, <u>Phase out the bomb</u>, in: *Foreign Policy*, Winter 1994-1995, 79-95.

Boese, Wade, <u>Leaked documents detail US ABM strategy</u>, in: *Arms Control Today*, May 2000.

Boese, Wade, <u>NPT meeting marked by discord</u>, in: *Arms Control Today*, June 2004.

Boese, Wade, <u>Bush plans to cut atomic arsenal</u>, in: *Arms Control Today*, July/August 2004.

Boldrick, Michael, <u>The nuclear posture review: liabilities and risks</u>, in: *Parameters*, Winter 1995-1996, 80-91.

Bracken, Paul, <u>The second nuclear age</u>, in: *Foreign Affairs*, vol.79, no.1, January/February 2000, 146-156.

Bracken Paul, <u>Thinking (again) about arms control</u>, in: *Orbis*, vol.48, no.1, Winter 2004, pp.149-160.

Brown, Michael, <u>Phased nuclear disarmament and US defense policy</u>, in: *Occasional Paper, Henry Stimson Center*, no.30, October 1996.

Brown, Michael, <u>The "end" of the nuclear arms control</u>. In: *Project on rethinking arms control paper* no.1, University of Maryland, March 1993.

Brown, Michael, <u>The US manned bomber and strategic deterrence in the 1990s</u>, in: *International Security*, vol.14, no.2, Fall 19895-46.

Bundy, McGeorge, William Crowe and Sidney Drell, <u>Reducing nuclear danger</u>, in: *Foregin Affairs*, Spring 1993, 140-155.

Bunn, George, and John Rhinelander, Viewpoint: The Duma-Senate logjam on arms control: what can be done ? In: *Nonproliferation Review*, Fall 199773-87.

Bunn, George, and Roland Timerbaev, Security assurances to NNWS: possible options for change, in: *PPNN Issue Review*, no.7, September 1996.

Bunn, George, Expanding nuclear options: is the US negating its non-use pledges ? in: *Arms Control Today*, May/June 1996, 7-10.

Bunn, George, The legal status of US negative security assurances to non-nuclear weapon states, in: *Nonproliferation Review*, Spring-Summer 1997, 1-17.

Bush, George, A distinctly American internationalism, speech delivered at the Ronald Reagan Library, Semi Valley, California, 19th of November 1999.

Bush, George, jr, A distinctly American internationalism, speech at the Ronald Reagan Presidential Library, 19 November 1999.

Bush, George, jr, A period of consequences, speech at The Citadel, 23 September 1999.

Butler, Lee, Disestablishing SAC, in: *Air Power History*, Fall 1993, 4-11.

Butler, Lee, Integrity is up to you, in: *Proceedings*, April 1994, 42-43.

Butler, Lee, remarks at the National Press Club, 4th of December 1996.

Butler, Lee, remarks at the Stimson Center Award, 8th of January 1997.

Butler, Lee, speech at the JFK Library, Boston, 22d of November 1998, in: *Disarmament Diplomacy*, no.32, November 1998, 38-41.

Butler, Lee, speech to the Canadian Network for Abolition of nuclear weapons, 11th of March 1999.

Butler, Lee, The responsibility to end the nuclear madness, speech at the Abolition Strategy Meeting, 30th of April 1999, in: *Waging Peace Worldwide*, special report, Summer 1999, iii-v.

Butler, Lee, The risks of nuclear deterrence: from superpowers to rogue leaders, speech at the National Press Club, 2d of February 1998.

Butler, Lee, Zero tolerance, in: *The Bulletin of the Atomic Scientists*, January/February 2000, 20-21, 72-75.

Butler, Nicola, NATO at 50: papering over the cracks, in: *Disarmament Diplomacy*, no.38, June 1999, 2-8.

Butler, Nicola, NATO in 1999: a concept in search of a strategy, in: *Disarmament Diplomacy*, no.35, March 1999, 4-10.

Cambone, Stephen, An inherent lesson in arms control, in: *The Washington Quarterly*, Spring 2000, 207-218.

Cambone, Stephan, and Patrick Garrity, The future of US nuclear policy. In: *Survival*, Winter 1994-1995, 73-95.

Canan, James, The new order in Omaha, in: *Air Force Magazine*, March 1994, 26-29.

Carpenter, Ted, Closing the nuclear umbrella, in: *Foreign Affairs*, March/April 1994, 8-13.

Carter, Ashton, Emerging themes in nuclear arms control, in: *Daedalus*, Winter 1991.

Carter, Ashton, John Deutch, and Philip Zelikow, Catastrophic terrorism. Tackling the new danger, in: *Foreign Affairs*, Winter 1998/1999, 78-94.

Carter, Ashton, Reducing the nuclear dangers from the former Soviet Union, in: *Arms Control Today*, January/February 1992, 10-14.

Carter, Ashton, Overhauling counterproliferation, in: *Technology in Society*, vol.26, Nos.2&3, April/July 2004.

Carter, Ashton, How to counter WMD, in: *Foreign Affairs*, vol.83, no.5, September/October 2004, pp.72-85.

Cerniello, Craig, Clinton issues new guidelines on US nuclear weapons doctrine, in: *Arms Control Today*, November/December 1997, 23.

Cillessen, Brat, Embracing the bomb: ethics, morality, and nuclear deterrence in the US Air Force, 1945-1955, in: *Journal of Strategic Studies*, vol.21, no.1, March 1998, 96-134.

Cirincione, Joseph, Non-proliferation paralysis, in: *Disarmament Diplomacy*, September 1998.

Cirincione, Joseph, The assault on arms control, in: *The Bulletin of the Atomic Scientists*, January/February 2000, 32-36.

Clinton, Bill, A democrat lays out his plan. A new Covenant for American security, in: *Harvard International Review*, Summer 1992, 26-28, 62-64.

Clinton, Bill, remarks prepared for delivery by Governor Bill Clinton at the Foreign Policy Association, 1 April 1992.

Collins, Joseph, and Ole Holsti, Correspondence. Civil-military relations: how wide is the gap ? In: *International Security*, Fall 1999, vol.24, no.2, 199-207.

Coté, Owen, The Trident and the Triad. Collecting the D-5 dividend. In: *International Security*, vol.16, no.2, Fall 1991, 117-145.

Cranston, Alan, The role of civil society, speech at the Abolition Strategy Meeting, 30th of April 1999, in: *Waging Peace Worldwide*, special report, Summer 1999, vi-vii.

Cropsey, Seth, The only credible deterrent. In: *Foreign Affairs*, March/April 1994, 14-20.

Daalder, Ivo, Nuclear weapons in Europe: why zero is better, in: *Arms Control Today*, January/February 1993.

Daalder, Ivo, What vision for the nuclear future ? In: *The Washington Quarterly*, Spring 1995, 127-142.

Davis, Lynn, Limited nuclear options. Deterrence and the New American Doctrine. In: *Adelphi Papers*, no.121, 1975.

Dean, Jonathan, The final stage of nuclear arms control, in: *The Washington Quarterly*, Autumn 1994, 31-52.

Deibel, Terry, The death of a treaty, in: *Foreign Affairs*, September/October 2002.

Dembinski, Matthias, Alexander Kelle and Harald Müller, NATO and nonproliferation: a critical appraisal. In: *PRIF Report*, no.33, April 1994.

Dering, Scott, The politics of military base closures, 1988-1995. Bureaucratic control of distributive politics, paper prepared for delivery at 1998 APSA Meeting, 3-6 September 1998.

Deutch, John, A nuclear posture for today. In: *Foreign Affairs*, vol.84, no.1, January/February 2005.

Dowler, Thomas, and Joseph Howard II, Countering the threat of the well-armed tyrant: a modest proposal for small nuclear weapons. In: *Strategic Review*, Fall 1991, 34-40.

Dowler, Thomas, and Joseph Howard II, Stability in a proliferated world. In: *Strategic Review*, Spring 1995, 26-37.

Dunlap, Charles, Welcome to the junta: the erosion of civilian control of the US military, in: *Wake Forest Law Review*, vol.29, no.2, 1994, 341-392.

Dunn, Lewis, Continuing nuclear proliferation. In: *Adelphi Paper*, no.263, Winter 1991.

Ehrlich, Jeff, US general applauds secruity of Russia nukes, in: *Defense News*, 10-16 November 1997.

Fetter, Steve, Future directions in nuclear arms control and verification, in: *INESAP Information Bulletin*, no.15, April 1998, 50-54.

Fetter, Steve, Does the US need a new plutonium-pit facility ? In: *Arms Control Today*, May 2004.

Fetter, Steve, Verifying nuclear disarmament, in: *Occasional Paper, Henry Stimson Center*, no.29, October 1996.

Forrow, Lachlan, and others, Accidental nuclear war – a post-cold war assessment, in: *New England Journal of Medicine*, vol 338, no.18, 30 April 1998, 1326-1331.

Foster, Gregory, Clinton's choice, in: *The Bulletin of the Atomic Scientists*, January/February 1995, 18-19.

Freedman, Lawrence, Does deterrence have a future ?, in: *Arms Control Today*, October 2000.

Freedman, Lawrence, Great powers, vital interests and nuclear weapons. In: *Survival*, Winter 1994-1995, 35-52.

Friedberg, Aaron, Why didn't the US become a garrison state ? In: *International Security*, vol.16, no.4, Spring 1992, 109-142.

Funabashi, Yoichi, Clinton's foreign policy: a victim of globalization ? A view from Asia, in: *Foreign Policy*, Winter 1997-1998, 51-54.

Gabel, Josiane, The role of US nuclear weapons after September 11, in: *The Washington Quarterly*, 28 (1), Winter 2005-2005, pp.181-195.

Gaidar, Yegor, Clinton's foreign policy: a victim of globalization ? A view from Russia, in: *Foreign Policy*, Winter 1997-1998, 64-66.

Glaser, Charles, Nuclear policy without an adversary. US planning for the Post-Soviet Era, in: *International Security*, vol.16, no.4, Spring 1992, 34-78.

Glaser, Charles, The flawed case for nuclear disarmament, in: *Survival*, vol.40, no.1, Spring 1998, 112-128.

Goldgeier, James, NATO expansion, in: *The Washington Quarterly*, Winter 1998.

Gompert, David, Kenneth Watman, and Dean Wilkening, Nuclear first use revisited. In: *Survival*, Autumn 1995, 27-44.

Gottfried, Kurt, Sowing nuclear misconceptions, in: *Nature*, vol.403, 13 January 2000, 131-133.

Grand, Camille, The European Union and the non-proliferation of nuclear weapons, in: *Chaillot Paper* 37, January 2000.

Gray, Peter, O'Leary v. Deutch, in: *The Bulletin of the Atomic Scientists*, November/December 1994, 10-12.

Greenstein, Fred, The presidential leadership style of Bill Clinton: an early appraisal, in: *Political Science Quarterly*, vol.108, no.4, 1993-1994, 589-601.

Gronlund, Lisbeth, ABM: just kicking the can, in: *The Bulletin of the Atomic Scientists*, January/February 1998, 15-16.

Grossman, Elaine, At last minute, nuclear posture review backs 450-500

ICBMs – for now, in: *Inside the Air Force*, vol.5, no.38, 23 September 1994, 1, 10-13.

Grossman, Elaine, Carter presents option to put all nukes on subs, creatin "monad", in: *Inside the Air Force*, vol.5, no.18, 6 May 1994, 1, 4-5.

Grossman, Elaine, Despite Chiles' testimony, Stratcom states need for new nuclear weapon, in: *Inside the Air Force*, vol.5, no.17, 29 April 1994, 1, 8.

Grossman, Elaine, DOD eyes reducing to 1,500 nuclear weapons under alternative force posture, in: *Inside the Air Force*, vol.5, no.20, 20 May 1994, 1, 14-15.

Grossman, Elaine, DOD has "significant" ability to alter nuclear weapons targeting on short notice, in: *Inside the Air Force*, 7th of August 1994, 1.

Grossman, Elaine, DOD, DOE officials to discuss new nuclear weapon at Los Alamos in mid-June, in: *Inside the Air Force*, vol.5, no.22, 3 June 1994, 1, 11.

Grossman, Elaine, Four services sign letter to block Carter's nuclear posture briefing, in: *Inside the Air Force*, vol.5, no.17, 29 April 1994, 1, 8-11.

Grossman, Elaine, Nuclear posture review move to set minimum of 350 ICBMs, 66 B-52Hs, in: *Inside the Air Force*, vol.5, no.33, 19 August 1994, 1, 9.

Grossman, Elaine, Nuclear review to back 500 ICBMs, but DOD lacks funds for bombers, subs, in: *Inside the Air Force*, vol.5, no.22, 3 June 1994, 1, 10-11.

Grossman, Elaine, Posture review gives thumbs-up to re-motor ICBMs, fund industrial base, in: *Inside the Air Force*, vol.5, no.35, 2 September 1994, 1, 4.

Grossman, Elaine, With Chiles refusing to back 350 ICBMs, nuclear review briefed to White House, in: *Inside the Air Force*, vol.5, no.37, 16 September 1994, 1, 4.

Haas, Peter, Do regimes matter ? Epistemic communities and Mediterranean pollution control, in: *International Organization*, 43, 3, Summer 1989, 377-403.

Haas, Peter, Introduction, in: *International Organization*, Winter 1992.

Haass, Richard, The squandered presidency, in: *Foreign Affairs*, May/June 2000, 136-140.

Habiger, Eugene, Strategic forces for deterrence, in: *Joint Forces Quarterly*, Winter 1996-1997, 64-69.

Hafemeister, David, Reflections on the GAO report on the nuclear triad, in: *Science and Global Security*, 1997, vol.6, 383-393.

Hale, John, The making of the New Democrats, in: *Political Science Quarterly*, vol.110, no.2, 1995, 207-232.

Halperin, Morton, Reducing the nuclear threat. Draft Nuclear Policy Review, November 1996.

Hansen, Chuck, The end of openness ? In: *The Bulletin of the Atomic Scientists*, May/June 1999, 3-4.

Hartung, William, and Michelle Ciarocca, Tangled web: The marketing of missile defense 1994-2000, May 2000, website worldpolicy.org.

Hartung, William, Ready for what ? The new politics of Pentagon spending, in: *World Policy Journal*, Spring 1999, 19-24.

Hermann, Charles, Changing course: when governments choose to redirect foreign policy, in: *International Studies Quarterly*, 34, 1990, 3-21.

Hertsgaard, Mark, DOE's real nuclear scandal, in: *The Nation*, 9-16 August 1999.

Hitchens, Theresa, Clinton review challenges triad, in: *Defense News*, 6 March 1994, 3.

Hitchens, Theresa, Uncertainty over Russia clouds US nuclear strategy, in: *Defense News*, 20-26 June 1994, 38.

Hitchens, Theresa, US to review nuke policy, in: *Defense News*, 25-31 October 1993, 3, 28.

Holsti, Ole, A widening gap between the US military and civilian society ? Some evidence, 1976-96, in: *International Security*, Winter 1998/99, vol.23, no.3, 5-42.

Idelson, Holly, What's left of the nuclear plants ? In: *Air Force Magazine*, August 1992, 68-71.

Isaacs, John, A raging moderate, in: *The Bulletin of the Atomic Scientists*, September 1992, 3-4.

Isaacs, John, Bottoms up, in: *The Bulletin of the Atomic Scientists*, November 1993, 12-13.

Isaacs, John, Pentagon clings to costly lifestyle, in: *The Bulletin of the Atomic Scientists*, April 1993, 3-5.

Isaacs, John, Test ban fizzles, in: *The Bulletin of the Atomic Scientists*, November/December 1999, 21-22.

Johnson, Alastair, Thinking about strategic culture, in: *International Security*, vol.19, no.4, Spring 1995, 32-64.

Josepth, Robert, Regional implications of NBC proliferation. In: *Joint Forces Quarterly*, Autumn 1995, 64-69.

Joseph, Robert, and John Reichart, The case for nuclear deterrence today, in: *Orbis*, Winter 1998, 7-19.

Jospeth, Robert and Ronald Lehman, US nuclear policy in the 21st Century, in: *National Defense University Strategic Forum*, no.145, August 1998.

Jump-START: retaking the initiative to reduce post-cold war nuclear dangers, in: *Arms Control Today*, January/February 1999, 15-19.

Keating, Paul, Eliminating nuclear weapons, speech at University of New South Wales, 25th of November 1998, in: *Disarmament Diplomacy*, no.32, November 1998, 34-38.

Keeny, Spurgeon, Frank von Hippel, James Leonard, and John Isaacs, The administration, Congress and nuclear testing, in: *Arms Control Today*, July/August 1993, 3-7.

Khripunov, Igor, Last leg of the triad, in: *The Bulletin of the Atomic Scientists*, July/August 2000, 58-64.

Kimball, Daryl, How the US Senate rejected CTBT ratification ? In: *Disarmament Diplomacy*, no.40, September/October 1999, 8-15.

Kohn, Richard, Out of control. The crisis in civil-military relations, in: *The National Interest*, Spring 1994, 3-17.

Korb, Lawrence, Our overstuffed armed forces, in: *Foreign Affairs*, vol.74, no.6, November/December 1995, 22-34.

Kotz, Nick, Mission impossible: John Deutch is quick, smart, and tough, in: *Washingtonian*, December 1995.

Kozyrev, Andrei, The lagging partnership, in: *Foreign Affairs*, May/June 1994, 59-71.

Krasner, Stephen, Structural causes and regime consequences: regime as intervening variables, in: *International Organization*, vol.36, no.2, 1982, 185-205.

Kreiger, Dale, Defensively off-target, in: *Johns Hopkins Magazine*, June 1994.

Krepon, Michael, Do it better and smarter, in: *The Bulletin of the Atomic Scientists*, vol.51, no.6, November/December 1995, p.13-14.

Kristensen, Hans, and Joshua Handler, The USA and counterproliferation. A new and dubious role for nuclear weapons. In: *Security Dialogue*, vol.27 (4), 1996, 387-399.

Kristensen, Hans, and Stephen Young, Taking the pulse of the US nuclear arsenal, in: *BASIC Nuclear futures*, October 1998.

Kristensen, Hans, Targets of opportunity. How nuclear planners found new targets for old weapons, in: *The Bulletin of the Atomic Scientists*, September/October 1997, vol.53, no.5.

Kristensen, Hans, The matrix of deterrence, May 2001, www.nautilus.org/nukestrat/USA/force/index.html.

Kristensen, Hans, The unruly hedge, in: *Arms Control Today*, December 2001.

Kristensen, Hans, US strategic nuclear reform in the 1990s, March 2000, on web-site of Nautilus Institute.

Kuchins, Andrew, Summit with substance, in: *Carnegie Endowment for International Peace Policy Brief*, 16th of May 2002.

Kucia, Christine, Pentagon memo raises possibility of nuclear testing, in: *Arms Control Today*, Decmeber 2002.

Kucia, Christine, Congress approves research on new nuclear weapons, in: *Arms Control Today*, June 2003.

Lehrer, Jim, Newshour with Charles Krause, Bob Bell and Bruce Blair, 6 January 1998.

Lepingwell, John, START II and the politics of arms control in Russia, in: *International Security*, vol.20, no.2, Fall 1995, 63-91.

Lewis, George, and Theodore Postol, Portrait of a bad idea, in: *The Bulletin of the Atomic Scientists*, July/August 1997, 18-25.

Lockwood, Dunbar, On Clinton's calendar, in: *The Bulletin of the Atomic Scientists*, January/February 1993, 6-8.

Lockwood, Dunbar, Pentagon begins policy review of post-cold war nuclear strategy, in: *Arms Control Today*, December 1993, p.23, 27.

Luttwak, Edward, Washington's biggest scandal, in: *Commentary*, May 1994, 29-33.

Mack, Andrew, Missile proliferation in the Asian Pacific. In: *Peace Research Centre of the National University of Canberra Working Paper*, no.82, 1990.

Manning, Robert, Abbot and Costello nuclear policy, in: *IntellectualCapital.com*, 17 February 2000.

Manning, Robert, Drop the big one, in: *The New Democrat*, January/February 1997.

Manning, Robert, Ending the nuclear century, in: *The New Democrat*, January/February 1995, 54-56.

Manning, Robert, The nuclear age: the next chapter, in: *Foreign Policy*, Winter 1997/1998, 70-84.

Marshall, Eliot, Scientific groups endorse test ban, in: *Science*, vol.286, 15 October 1999, 387-388.

Mazarr, Michael, Introduction to Special Issue: Nuclear Arms Control, in:

The Washington Quarterly, vol.20, no3, Summer 1997, 77-86.

Mazarr, Michael, Nuclear weapons after the Cold War, in: *The Washington Quarterly*, Spring 1992

Mazarr, Michael, Virtual nuclear arsenals. In: *Survival*, Autumn 1995, 7-26.

MccGwire, Michael, Is there a future for nuclear weapons ? In: *International Affairs*, 70 (2), 1994, 211-228.

McInnes, Colin, From the Bottom Up ? Conventional forces and defence policy after the Cold War, in: *Contemporary Security Policy*, vol.15, no.3, December 1994, 147-169.

McNamara, Robert, Apocalypse soon, in: *Foreign Policy*, May/June 2005.

McNaugher, Thomas, Ballistic missiles and chemical weapons. In: *International Security*, Fall 1990, vol.15, no.2

Mearshimer, John, Back to the future. In: *International Security*, Summer 1990.

Mearshimer, John, The case for a Ukrainian nuclear deterrent. In: *Foreign Affairs*, Summer 1993, 50-66.

Mearshimer, John, The false promise of international institutions, in: *International Security*, vol.19, no.3, Winter 1994/1995, 5-49.

Mello, Greg, New bomb, no mission, in: *The Bulletin of the Atomic Scientists*, May/June 1997, 28-32.

Mello, Greg, That old designing fever, in: *The Bulletin of the Atomic Scientists*, January/February 2000, 51-57.

Miller, Steven, Politics over promise. Domestic impediments to arms control, in: *International Security*, vol.8, no.4, Spring 1984, 67-90.

Miller, Steven, The case against a Ukrainian nuclear deterrent. In: *Foreign Affairs*, Summer 1993, 67-80.

Miller, Steven, Western diplomacy and the Soviet nuclear legacy, in: *Survival*, vol.34, no.3, Autumn 1992, 3-27.

Millot, Marc, Facing the emerging reality of regional nuclear adversaries, in: *The Washington Quarterly*, 17, 3, Summer 1994, 41-71.

Mitchell, Gordon, US National Missile Defence: technical challenges, political pitfalls and disarmament opportunities, in: *ISIS Briefing Paper*, no.23, May 2000.

Müller, Harald, Transparancy in nuclear arms: toward a nuclear weapons register. In: *Arms Control Today*, October 1994, 3-7.

Müller, Harald, and Makarim Wibisono, Approaches to nuclear disarmament: two views, in: *PPNN Issue Review*, no.12, April 1998.

Müller, Harald, and Mitchell Reiss, Counterproliferation: putting new wine in old bottles, in: *The Washington Quarterly*, Spring 1995, 143-154.

Müller, Harald, Arms control and disarmament at a watershed, in: *Disarmament Diplomacy*, no.29, August/September 1998, 2-5.

Müller, Harald, Nuclear weapons and German interests: an attempt at redefinition, in: *PRIF Report*, no.55, 2000, 25 p

Müller, Harald, Remarks at the 7th Carnegie International Non-Proliferation Conference, 11-12th of January 1999.

Müller, Harald, Farewell to arms. What's blocking nuclear disarmament ? In: *IAEA Bulletin*, 46 (2), March 2005, pp.12-15.

Naim, Moises, Clinton's foreign policy: a victim of globalization ? In: *Foreign Policy*, Winter 1997-1998, 34-45.

Nolan, Janne, Preparing for the 2001 Nuclear Posture Review, in: *Arms Control Today*, November 2000.

Norris, Robert and William Arkin, US Nuclear Forces 2001, NRDC Notebook, in: *The Bulletin of the Atomic Scientists*, March/April 2001, 77-79.

Norris, Robert, and William Arkin, Estimated nuclear stockpiles 1945-1993, in: The *Bulletin of the Atomic Scientists*, December 1993.

Norris, Robert, and Hans Kristensen, Global nuclear stockpiles, 1945-2002, in: *The Bulletin of the Atomic Scientists*, November/December 2002.

Norris, Robert, and William Arkin, US nuclear stockpile, July 1998, in: *The Bulletin of the Atomic Scientists*, July/August 1998, 69-71.

Norris, Robert, and William Arkin, US Nuclear Forces, 2001; NRDC Nuclear Notebook, in: *The Bulletin of the Atomic Scientists*, March/April 2001, 77-79.

Norris, Robert, and Hans Kristensen, US nuclear forces 2003, in: *The Bulletin of the Atomic Scientists*, May/June 2003.

Norris, Robert, and Hans Kristensen, US nuclear forces 2004, in: *The Bulletin of the Atomic Scientists*, May/June 2004.

Norris, Robert, and Hans Kristensen, Dismantling US nuclear warheads, in: *The Bulletin of the Atomic Scientists*, vol.60, no.1, January/February 2004.

Norris, Robert, and Hans Kristensen, US nuclear weapons in Europe, in: *The Bulletin of the Atomic Scientists*, vol.60, no.6, November/December 2004, pp76-77.

Nye, Joseph, Nuclear learning and US-Soviet relations, in: *International Organization*, 1988.

O'Neill, Sean, Leon Fuerth: tutoring "Prince Albert", in: *World Policy Journal*, Winter 1999/2000, 55-62.

Ochmanek, David, and Richard Sokolsky, Employ nuclear deterrence, in: *Defense News*, 12-18th of January 1998.

Ogden, Christopher, Call this leadership ? In: *Time Magazine*, 18 October 1999.

Panofsky, Wolgang, and George Bunn, The doctrine of the NWS and the future of non-proliferation. In: *Arms Control Today*, July/August 1994, 3-9.

Panofsky, Wolfgang, Dismantling the concept of "weapons of mass destruction", in: *Arms Control Today*, April 1998, 3-8.

Panofsky, Wolfgang, The future of non-proliferation in relation to the nuclear doctrines of the NWS. Paper deliverd at the VII Amaldi Conference, 22-23 September 1994, Warsaw.

Parachini, John, US Senate ratification of the CWC: lessons for the CTBT, in: *Nonproliferation Review*, Fall 1997, 62-72.

Payne, Keith, Post-Cold war requirements for US nuclear deterrence policy, in: *Comparative Strategy*, 17, 1998, 227-277.

Payne, Keith, The case against nuclear abolition and for nuclear deterrence, in: *Comparative Strategy*, 17, 1998, 3-43.

Payne, Keith, The Nuclear Posture Review: setting the record straight, in: *The Washington Quarterly*, 28 (3), Summer 2005, pp.135-151.

Perkovich, George, A nuclear third way in South Asia. In: *Foreign Policy*, Summer 1993.

Perkovich, George, Bush's nuclear revolution: a regime change in nonproliferation, in: *Foreign Affairs*, March/April 2003.

Perry, William, Desert Storm and Deterrence. In: *Foreign Affairs*, Fall 1991, vol.20, no.4.

Polser, Brian, Theater Nuclear Weapons in Europe: the contemporary debate, in: *Strategic Insights*, vol.III, issue 9, September 2004.

Postol, Theodore, The nuclear danger from shortfalls in the capabilities of Russian early warning satellites: a cooperative Russian-US remedy, paper presented at Technology Working Group, MIT Security Studies Program, March 1998.

Putnam, Robert, Diplomacy and domestic politics: the logic of two-level game, in: *International Organization*, vol.42, no.3, Summer 1988.

Quester, George, and Victor Utgoff, No first use and nonproliferation: redefining extended deterrence. In: *The Washington Quarterly*, Spring 1994, 17:2, 103-114.

Ramos, Thomas, The future of theater nuclear forces. In: *Strategic Review*, Fall 1991, 41-47.

Ricks, Thomas, The widening gap between the military and society, in: *The Atlantic Monthly*, July 1997.

Roberts, Brad, Chemical disarmament and International Security. In: *Adelphi Papers*, Spring 1992, 75p.

Robinson, Paul and Kathleen Bailey, To zero or not to zero: a US perspective on nuclear disarmament, in: *Security Dialogue*, vol 28(2), 1997, 149-158.

Rosenberg, David, Origins of overkill, in: *International Security*, Spring 1983.

Roston, Karen, Congress critical of Bush nuclear weapons budget, in: *Arms Control Today*, April 2004.

Rotblat, Joseph, Remember your humanity. In: *The Bulletin of the Atomic Scientists*, March/April 1996, 26-28.

Sagan, Scott, SIOP-62: The nuclear war plan briefing to President Kennedy, in: *International Security*, vol.12, no.1, Summer 1987, 22-51.

Sagan, Scott, The commitment trap. Why the United States should not use nuclear threats to deter biological and chemical weapons attacks, in: *International Security*, vol.24, no.4, Spring 2000, 85-115.

Sagan, Scott, Why do states build nuclear weapons ? Three models in search of a bomb. In: *International Security*, Winter 1996/1997, vol.21, no.3, 54-86.

Sapolsky, Harvey, Eugene Gholz, and Allen Kaufman, Security lessons from the Cold War, in: *Foreign Affairs*, vol.78, no.4, July/August 1999, 77-89.

Sapolsky, Harvey, Restructuring US defense industry, in: *International Security*, Winter 1999/2000, 5-51.

Sauer, Tom, A new nuclear order: the need for introspection in US nonproliferation policy, in: *Strategic Insights*, vol.3, issue 5 (May 2004), http://www.ccc.nps.navy.mil/si/2004/may/sauerMay04.asp

Sauer, Tom, Back to arms control: limiting US National Missile Defence, in: *Contemporary Security Policy*, vol.25, no.1 (April 2004), pp.93-130.

Sauer, Tom, The "Americanization" of EU Nuclear Non-Proliferation Policy, in: *Defense and Security Analysis*, vol.20, no.2 (June 2004), pp.113-131.

Schell, Jonathan, The folly of arms control, in: *Foreign Affairs*, September/October 2000, 22-46.

Schell, Jonathan, The gift of time. The case for abolishing nuclear weapons, in: *The Nation, (Special issue)*, 2/9 February 1998.

Schmitt, Burkard (ed), Effective non-proliferation, in: *Chaillot Paper*, no.77, April 2005, 70 p.

Schulte, Gregory, Responding to proliferation – NATO's role. In: *NATO Review*, July 1995, 15-19.

Schulte, Gregory, Dispelling myths about NATO's nuclear posture, in: *Washington File* 34, 20th of February 1997.

Schwartz, Stephen, Four trillion dollars and counting. In: *The Bulletin of the Atomic Scientists*, November/December 1995, p.32-52.

Schwartz, Stephen, Miscalculated ambiguity: US policy on the use and threat of use of nuclear weapons, in: *Disarmament Diplomacy*, no.23, February 1998, 10-15.

Schwartz, Stephen, Missed opportunities, in: *The Bulletin of the Atomic Scientists*, March/April 2000, 71-72.

Schwartz, Stephen, Outmaneuvered, outgunned, and out of view, in: *The Bulletin of the Atomic Scientists*, January/February 2000, 24-31.

Seigle, Grey, DOD boosts THAAD development programme, in: *Jane's Defence Weekly*, 27 January 1999.

Simpson, John, Nuclear non-proliferation in the post-Cold War era. In: *International Affairs*, 1994, 70(1), 17-39.

Sloan, Stanley, NATO nuclear strategy: issues for US policy, in: *CRS report for Congress*, 25 July 1996.

Slocombe, Walter, Is there still a role for nuclear deterrence ? In: *NATO Review*, November-December 1997, 23-26.

Slocombe, Walter, Strategic stability in a restructured world, in: *Survival*, vol.32, no.4, July/August 1990, 299-312.

Slocombe, Walter, The administration's approach, in: *The Washington Quarterly*, Summer 2000, 79-85.

Slocombe, Walter, The continued need for extended deterrence, in: *The Washington Quarterly*, Autumn 1991, 157-172.

Slocombe, Walter, The countervailing strategy, in: *International Security*, Spring 1981.

Sloss, Leon, US strategic forces after the cold war: policies and strategies, in: *The Washington Quarterly*, Autumn 1991, 145-155.

Sokolski, Henry, Mission impossible, in: *The Bulletin of the Atomic Scientists*, March/April 2001.

Sokolsky, Richard, Demystifying the US Nuclear Posture Review, in: *Survival*, vol.44, no.3, Autumn 2002.

Spector, Leonard, Neo-nonproliferation. In: *Survival*, Spring 1995, vol.37, no.1.

Spinardi, Graham, Why the US Navy went for hard-target counterforce in Trident II (and why it didn't get there sooner), in: *International Security*, vol.15, no.2, Fall 1990, 147-190.

Spring, Baker, What the Pentagon's nuclear doctrine review should say, in: *The Heritage Foundation Backgrounder*, 26th of May 1994.

Spulak, Robert, The case in favor of US nuclear weapons, in: *Parameters*, Spring 1997, 106-118.

Steinbruner, John, The effect of strategic force reductions on nuclear strategy, in: *Arms Control Today*, May 1988.

Sterngold, James, Noted scientists reject nuclear quest, in: *San Francisco Chronicle*, 20 May 2003.

Stockton, Paul, The new game on the Hill, in: *International Security*, vol.16, no.2, Fall 1991, 146-170.

Stone, Jeremy, The war plan decoded, in: *Federation of American Scientists Public Interest Report*, vol.52, no.2, March/April 1999.

Talbott, Strobe, Dealing with the bomb in South Asia, in: *Foreign Affairs*, March/April 1999, 110-122.

Thayer, Bradley, Nuclear weapons as a Faustian bargain, in: *Security Studies*, 5, no.1, Autumn 1995, 149-163.

Towell, Pat, Aspin brings activist views to a changed world, in: *Congressional Quarterly*, 9 January 1993, 80-83.

Utgoff, Victor, Nuclear weapons and the deterrence of biological and chemical warfare, in: *Occasional Paper of the The Henry Stimson Center*, no.36, October 1997, 31 p.

van der Mey, Leo, India tussen kernstopverdrag en bom, in: *Internationale Spectator*, January 1997.

Von Hippel, Frank, and Tom Zamora-Collina, Nuclear junkies: testing, testing, testing, 1, 2, 3 – forever, in: *The Bulletin of the Atomic Scientists*, July/August 1993, 28-32.

Von Hippel, Frank, Paring down the arsenal, in: *The Bulletin of the Atomic Scientists*, May/June 1997, 33-40.

Von Hippel, Frank, Working in the White House on nonproliferation and arms control, in: *Federation of American Scientists Public Interest Report*, vol.48, no.2, March/April 1995.

Walt, Stephen, Two cheers for Clinton's foreign policy, in: *Foreign Affairs*, March/April 2000, 63-79.

Warnke, Paul, Strategic nuclear policy and non-proliferation. In: *Arms Control Today*, May 1994, 3-5.

Webster, Scott, Bill Clinton, political centrism & presidential leadership, paper prepared for delivery at 1998 APSA meeting, Boston, 3-6 September 1998.

Wilkening, Dean, The future of Russia's strategic nuclear force, in: *Survival*, vol.40, no.3, Autumn 1998, 89-111.

Wolfstahl, John, US nuclear policy and the future of arms control, in: *Yaderni Kontrol*, vol.8, no.1-2, Winter-Spring 2003.

Worth, Robert, Clinton's Warriors, in: *World Policy Journal*, vol.xv, no.1, Spring 1998.

X, Air Force, J-5 protest aspects of Carter's Nuclear Posture proposals, in: *Inside the Air Force*, vol.5, no.32, 12 August 1994.

X, America's world, in: *The Economist*, 23 October 1999.

X, Don't ban the bom, in: *The Economist*, 4th of January 1997, 13-14.

X, Presidential election forum, in: *Arms Control Today*, September 2000.

X, Russia's strategic forces stumble, in: *Jane's Intelligence Review*, 2d of October 2000.

X, John Bolton interviewed by the Arms Control Association, in: *Arms*

Control Today, March 2002.
Yesson, Eric, <u>Strategic make-believe and strategic reality</u>, in: *International Security*, vol.14, no.3, 1989-1990, 182-193.
Yost, David, <u>Europe and nuclear deterrence</u>. In: *Survival*, Autumn 1993, 97-120.
Zamora, Tom, <u>New jobs for old labs ?</u> in: *The Bulletin of the Atomic Scientists*, November 1992.
Zoellick, Robert, <u>A Republican foreign policy</u>, in: *Foreign Affairs*, vol.79, no.1, January/February 2000, 63-78.

Index